Cervantes

Cervantes

Jean Canavaggio

TRANSLATED FROM THE FRENCH BY

J. R. Jones

W·W·Norton & Company

NEW YORK   LONDON

The text of this book is composed in 12/13.5 Garamond No. 3,

with display type set in Caslon Open Face and Garamond No. 3.

Composition and manufacturing by

the Maple-Vail Book Manufacturing Group.

Book and ornament design by Margaret M. Wagner.

First Edition

Library of Congress Cataloging-in-Publication Data

Canavaggio, Jean.

{Cervantès. English}

Cervantes / by Jean Canavaggio; translated from the French by

J. R. Jones.—1st ed.

p. cm.

Translation of: Cervantès.

1. Cervantes Saavedra, Miguel de, 1547–1616—Biography.

2. Authors, Spanish—17th century—Biography. I. Title.

PQ6337.C2313   1990

863'.3—dc20

{B}   89–9462

ISBN 0-393-02812-7

W. W. Norton & Company, Inc.

500 Fifth Avenue, New York, N. Y.. 10110

W. W. Norton & Company Ltd.

37 Great Russell Street, London WC1B 3NU

1 2 3 4 5 6 7 8 9 0

Prologue

> This, I repeat, is the face of the author of *Galatea* and *Don Quixote de la Mancha* . . . He was a soldier for many years and in captivity for five and a half, where he learned to have patience in adversity. He lost his left hand from a harquebus shot during the naval battle at Lepanto. He considers his wound beautiful, though it is ugly-looking, because he received it on the most memorable and exalted occasion that passing centuries have seen . . .

WITH a few lines slipped into the preface of the *Exemplary Novellas* (Novelas ejemplares)* three years before his death, Cervantes points the way along which it is now our turn to travel, following so many others. In recalling a past from which he retains only two or three high points, Cervantes does not go so far as to sketch an account of his life. He was neither Teresa of Avila, who wrote for her confessor, nor Rousseau, who will invent literary autobiography a hundred and fifty years later. But he captures in bold outline, in the inscription below his self-portrait, the few images which still identify him in the collective memory today: the fighter at Lepanto, the captive in Algiers, the author of *Don Quixote*. Though inseparable, these images are held together by a bond that is problematical for us. It is to the writer that the soldier owes his having been saved from anonymity; but the transition from the sword to the pen, from arms to letters, was not accomplished in a single move. How do we explain it? It is partly the result of circumstances, but it is also an expression of the choices of a man whose inner world inevitably eludes us.

To rediscover the traces of this existence, beyond the images hallowed by posterity, has been for more than two centuries the major

---

* Translator's note: The original title of Cervantes' works appears in parentheses after the first occurrence of the title in English.

goal of all who have come up against this enigma. One permanent concern has guided them: to reconstruct in its successive stages a journey that has long been imperfectly understood. The systematic exploration of public and private archives begun in the eighteenth century by the first biographers, continued to our day by a constellation of scholars, has permitted us gradually to assemble a considerable amount of documentation on the events which are landmarks in the life of Cervantes: his birth, his military campaigns, his captivity, the vicissitudes of his family, his missions in Andalusia, his stay at Valladolid, his career as a writer, his relations with his fellow writers—these are points on which partial light has been shed. Astrana Marín's monumental biography, in spite of its defects and inadequacies, gives us an idea of the extent of the work carried out.

But so many obscure points remain! We know nothing, or almost nothing, about the writer's childhood years and adolescence; we frequently lose track of him for months, indeed for years, between the end of his Andalusian commissions and his final move to Madrid. We are altogether ignorant of the motives which underlie most of his decisions: his departure for Italy, his embarkation in Don Juan de Austria's galleys; his marriage to a woman nearly twenty years his junior; his desertion of their home after three years of life together; his return to writing after a silence of almost twenty years. We have lost a large number of his works; we doubt the authenticity of some that have been attributed to him after the fact; and with regard to those we still have, which have made him famous, we have only the scantiest information about their genesis. The autographs that have come down to us amount to little more than notarized records, statements of accounts, and two or three letters. Finally, not one of the so-called portraits is trustworthy.

One can understand why innumerable legends have flourished in this shifting soil: Cervantes' love affairs, his repeated jailings at Seville and other places, his dealings with the powerful, his squabbles with his fellow writers, his bitter exchanges with Avellaneda (the mysterious author of the apocryphal *Don Quixote*) are but a few of the episodes in which it is extremely difficult to separate true from false. Fictionalizing them may irritate or amuse, but it is to some extent excusable. It reflects not only the desire to fill—at any cost—the gaps in our information; it also reveals a deeper aspiration: to discover, beyond the chain of events, the personality of the man who experienced them, at the risk of forging a fantasy portrait out of them. That aspiration is also the goal of our own generation. But it inspires us to attempt something more substantial than a framework of unwarranted assumptions, yet more imaginative than a police-style investigation, which pays attention only to concrete facts: it means going back to the Cervantine texts, in order to seek in the work, if not the man himself, anything that can throw light on him.

Legions of interpreters have been conducting this research—the most delicate of all such activities—for more than a century. But the more attentive they become to minutiae, the more their object tends to disappear—for two essential reasons: first, because one must take what the author tells us about himself with caution: the data he gives us obliquely through his fictions, such as "The Captive's Tale" interpolated in *Don Quixote,* are all the more difficult to use since Cervantes repeatedly delegates his powers to pseudo-narrators whom he repudiates at the first opportunity. And as for those texts in which he expresses himself in his own name, assuming his own identity (dedications, prefaces, the *Journey to Parnassus* [Viaje del Parnaso]), it is less their documentary content that makes them valuable than the way in which Cervantes puts himself into the picture; they are, if you will, the scattered fragments of a portrait of the artist, the reliability of which does not need verification.

Above all, the poems, novels, romances, novellas, plays, and interludes constitute a specific universe that, because it expresses the desires and dreams of the man who engendered it, inevitably reveals his personal experience. The Cervantine texts yield unexpected glimpses into their author, as the tools of analysis become sharper and the angles of approach multiply. But this Cervantes is merely the shadow of an elusive being who long ago created himself by an act of writing and whose work, since that time, has been enriched with new meanings. Our way of perceiving it is no longer that of seventeenth-century readers, who laughed at Don Quixote's follies but preferred *Galatea,* the *Exemplary Novellas,* and *Persiles.* We still admire the novellas, if not necessarily those which were the favorites of the seventeenth century. We are amazed by the interludes, which were originally unpretentious farces. Finally, we have discovered, in what was at the outset only a burlesque epic, the first and greatest of modern novels.

Caught in this evolution, which he certainly did not foresee, Cervantes has been remade, over the years, by his admirers, each genera-

tion retouching, correcting, rearranging the portrait entrusted to it.
More cautious than our predecessors, we have doubts about the stereotypes they produced; yet we are only half satisfied with the completely provisional likenesses we have substituted for them: the author
of *Don Quixote* is always just beyond the image we form of him for
ourselves. The sly condemner of established values, he strips all types
of conformity of their pretensions. But what is the source of his reservations and his disapproval? His disappointments as an old soldier
ill-repaid for his services? His supposed commerce with the ideas of
Erasmus? His presumed membership in the minority caste of descendants of converted Jews? And if it is true that, in him, refractory
attitudes go side by side with more orthodox behavior, where does one
seek the principle that governs their contradictions? We have for a
long time confined ourselves to the terrain of controlled, deliberate
activities. We have tried only recently to plunge into the depths of
the irrational in order to decode the symbolic configurations that Cervantine fictions might provide us. Certain scholars have put forth
hypotheses that call into question the exaggerated idealization of the
manco de Lepanto—"the one-handed veteran of Lepanto"—and condemn the saint's-life approach as no longer valid; but the psychobio-
graphical dossier on which their theories are founded remains singularly
thin, without sufficient documentation. Perhaps it does reveal masochistic tendencies or even latent homosexuality, as someone has recently
affirmed. But in its laconic brevity, it also permits a whole array of
possible scenarios. He who sets out in search of obsessive metaphors
must be cautious, unless he is willing to rely on a dreary collection of
fantasies arranged to suit some clinician.

To explain Cervantes is a hazardous undertaking, finding ourselves
as we do between a life which has ceased to exist, to which we have
only indirect access, and the works of the man who lived it four hundred
years ago, a man now dead, whose works have escaped and have a life
of their own. But can one tell Cervantes' story—or at least tell it
better? Such is the risk that we have chosen to run when we set for
ourselves three ambitious objectives.

First: to establish with all the necessary rigor what we know about
Cervantes; to separate the imaginary from the certain and the plausible. Today, one can no longer maintain, even though it is a matter of
commonly held opinion, that Cervantes was a student of the Jesuits at
Seville; that he was captured off the Saintes-Maries-de-la-Mer; that his
poem, the "Epistle to Mateo Vázquez" ("Epístola a Mateo Vázquez")

is a fundamental document; that *Don Quixote* was written in the squalor of a dungeon; that the letter to Cardinal Sandoval—an obvious forgery—reveals the presentiment of death. What is indispensable is a critical account of the episodes and actions that make up Cervantes' life-experience, even if that life-experience is perceived only from the outside.

Next: to put back into his milieu and into his period a writer who in the eyes of the layman is the incarnation and epitome of the Golden Age of Spain, the *Siglo de Oro.* Thanks to first-rate studies, today we have a clearer and more delicately shaded picture of the Spain of the first three Hapsburgs. Cervantes, an obscure actor in a heroic adventure, the clear-eyed witness of a time of doubts and crisis, is the interpreter of a nation that he observed at a turning point in its history and for which he felt solidarity to the end. His testimony, as will doubtless be obvious, is not pure documentary evidence. It comes from an imaginary world in which it would be absurd to see nothing but the stylized reflection of the real world. Don Quixote and Sancho are in one sense the man who invented them; they are also Spain; they are, to an extent, a part of ourselves. But they are above all autonomous characters, even though the analyst's scalpel cuts away the illusion of life and reveals them to be creatures of paper.

Finally: to the extent possible, to make contact with Cervantes: not by trying with all our might to penetrate his mystery, but by following the movement of a being whose destiny, whatever Cervantes' goal may have been while he was alive, we are striving to make intelligible. This course is not without risks: to describe a life is also to construct it; to bring a man back to life is to fix him for eternity. The person we are seeking cannot be reduced to the individual his relatives knew; or to the *raro inventor,* the remarkably imaginative writer, who drew his own self-portrait; or to the series of myths, from superman to reprobate, which he has inspired since his death and which remains to be studied. Beyond these masks, each one of which has its bit of truth, he is the shadowy profile that we attribute to the secret narrator, disguised behind his doubles: that ever-present absentee whose unmistakable voice we always recognize among a thousand others. This conjectural profile that our pencil tirelessly redraws and that others will be able to correct must be, before all else, the profile of a writer. May this account of his life awaken or revive in us the desire to read him!

Cervantes

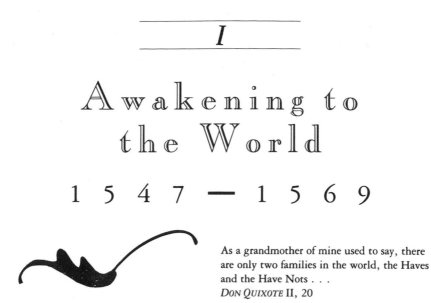

I

Awakening to the World

1 5 4 7 — 1 5 6 9

As a grandmother of mine used to say, there are only two families in the world, the Haves and the Have Nots . . .

Don Quixote II, 20

AT THE TURNING POINT OF A CENTURY

WITHIN the circle of artistically important towns which the environs of Madrid offer to the curiosity of the tourist, Alcalá de Henares has somewhat the appearance of a poor relation. Its patrimony, certainly, hardly bears comparison with that of its rivals; nor does it enjoy, like them, an exceptional site: no loop of the Tagus isolates it on its cliff, like Toledo, calling it to the admiring attention of the visitor; no mountain range looms above it, as at Segovia, accentuating the contrast between the snowy peaks and the tawny expanses of the Castilian plateau. The hurried traveler who heads east in the direction of Zaragoza, passing Barajas and its airport, is not aware that he is reaching the outskirts of a historic city. Along the eighteen miles that separate Alcalá from the Puerta de Sol, the countryside that comes into view was not so long ago still the vineyards and wheat fields of New Castile; today it reveals nothing but the expansion of the capital: its tentacles reach as far as the first buttresses of a *meseta* whose bare ridges define the horizon.

13

Our traveler must consent to leave the highway, which runs at some distance from the Henares, a tributary of the Tagus whose name ("hayfields") recalls the grasslands that embellish its banks, where bulls still graze. In compensation, and without warning, he will discover the face of a sleeping village. There remains no, or almost no, vestige of the ancient Complutum of Pliny and Trajan, and nothing survives from the medieval fortress Al-kalá Nahar, built at the river's edge by Muslim invaders. But the admirable Plateresque façade of the Complutensian University, founded in 1508 by Cardinal Cisneros, still bears witness to the glorious epoch when this center of humanism, consecrated by the publication of the first polyglot Bible, rivaled Salamanca in attracting students. An epoch long past: the silence that envelops palaces and monasteries, all along its placid streets, speaks volumes of the irremediable decline that the rise of Philip II's Madrid meant for the city on the Henares.

Behind the Misericordia Hospital, in the heart of the old Jewish quarter, is a house with a certain elegance and charm, its patio graced by a fig tree, its steep stairway leading to the upper stories, its rooms, with exposed beams, furnished in the Renaissance style. It is there, they say, that the most illustrious of the sons of Alcalá, the author of *Don Quixote,* was born. But this stage set is unfortunately only an illusion. The house where Cervantes was actually born, unknown to historians for a long time, was defaced over the centuries by its successive owners. Identified in 1941 thanks to the research of Luis Astrana Marín, it nevertheless fell to the demolisher's pick, and in its place stands a reconstruction built in perfect conformity with the architectural norms of the sixteenth century but incompatible with the modest origins of the great writer.

We will never actually know under what roof Cervantes first saw the light. But we can at least accept Alcalá as his birthplace, without question. It is past the time when ten villages in Spain claimed the glory of being the new Homer's fatherland. Advances in scholarship have dispelled such legends since the rediscovery, in the mid-eighteenth century, of the young Miguel's baptismal certificate: a providential discovery that allows us to know the date of the ceremony but not the birthday of our hero. Cervantes was baptized on the 9th of October, 1547, in Santa María la Mayor. Was he born on the 29th of September, San Miguel's day? Or was he born a week later, taking his place in the bosom of the Church without delay? We are inclined to believe the latter, in view of the customs of an age when particularly high infant mortality discouraged postponing baptism for the new-born.

The important year 1547 sees the disappearance of two monarchs of the first rank, Francis I in France and Henry VIII in England, redoubtable enemies of the Hapsburgs' empire, whose deaths occur at the very moment when Charles V reaches the zenith of his power. Reigning for thirty years over Castile and Aragon, Naples and Sicily, the Low Countries and the Franche Comté, Bohemia and Austria, Charles of Ghent did not attempt to federate these numerous domains, which had been united under his scepter by the play of interacting successions and alliances. To create Europe by unifying it did not enter into the schemes of a prince who, while proving himself to be one of the founders of the modern state, felt himself in many respects to be the inheritor of an ancient order. Respectful of the peculiarities and traditions of his hereditary possessions, he strove to assume in Western Christendom the charismatic role that the imperial office, obtained by election, conferred upon him; but he never claimed the political supremacy that his title carried in previous ages. Even so, his symbolic preeminence will be sharply contested: in the short run by his immediate neighbors, who are anxious to re-establish the former balance for their own benefit, and who now face an uncertain future because of the deaths of their respective sovereigns; in the long run by the Turk and the Reformation, a double menace that weighs heavy on an empire founded on unanimous adherence to the same values and the same faith.

Of these two menaces, the one embodied by the Turk is undoubtedly the more spectacular. Almost absolute master of the Eastern Mediterranean, the Ottoman Empire turns its gaze toward the other basin, the Spanish lake protected by the padlock of Malta. One of the trump cards the Turk counts on to establish himself there is obviously the support of his North African vassals, who nevertheless prefer the status quo, comforted by the expedition launched against Algiers by Charles V six years earlier. At least they hope to avert the peril: so long as the network of *presidios*—the string of forts held by the Spanish from Orán to La Goleta on the Maghreb coastline—is preserved: and so long as the Barbary corsairs prefer the immediate profits of piracy to the more hazardous gains of war at sea. The other danger, the Reformation, seems more insidious when it dissembles behind the genius of Erasmus, whose ideas had lately had fervent admirers at court; it spreads serious anxiety when it openly assumes the guise of the Lutheran heresy, whose advances the emperor is striving to halt. Spanish public opinion rejoices at the victory won at Muehlburg in April of 1547 over the German Protestant princes. But that is only the prelude to a long-drawn-out spiritual combat waged henceforth by the Catholic Church, obsessed with her own renewal. To that end, she inaugurates at Trent the famous council whose sessions will last more than twenty years.

Why should Alcalá not be proud to be the intellectual capital of a nation that has become in the course of years the preponderant element in the great empire? One might have believed at the beginning of the reign that the dominant role would fall to the Low Countries, the capstone of the Burgundian heritage, which had seen Charles V come into the world and which were the first to engage in the great adventure of capitalism. But after 1530, everything pushes Castile to take the lead over the Northern Provinces: it is a unified territory, gathering the Cantabrian north and the Andalusian south around the central plateau; it has a flourishing population whose impetus will maintain itself until mid-century, and a prosperous economy founded on the resources of a dynamic agriculture and on the expansion of a textile industry with significant exports; it rests on solid institutions forged by the Catholic Rulers which had survived the ordeal of the Revolt of the Communes (1519–21), an uprising of Castilian towns fearful of losing their privileges and goaded by the abuses of the young emperor's Flemish counsellors; and finally, it enjoys an incomparable geographical situation. On the Mediterranean front, Castile abuts Aragon, taken in the widest sense, which includes among other things Barcelona, Valencia, and the Balearic Islands; it also faces toward Italy—in particular, toward Milan and Naples—and Sicily. On the Atlantic front, it opens toward the immense American space discovered half a century earlier, then gradually charted and conquered and just entering the colonial era: in this year of 1547, the generation of conquistadores comes to an end with the death of Hernán Cortez, and the systematic exploitation of the mines at Potosí begins.

Did Castile actually choose this peerless destiny? If the *comuneros* had carried the day, she would have limited her ambitions, under their influence. She doubtless had at her disposal the resources that would permit her to stay in the forefront. But at the outset, it was circumstances that led her to cast her lot with the empire, even though nothing predisposed her to join it. For seven centuries she was only an outpost of Western Christendom. Concentrating all her strength on an interminable Reconquest, indifferent to the concerns of the rest of Europe, she remained in many respects closer to Islam, whose vassal she was for so long, than to her neighbors beyond the Pyrenees. Progressively regaining lost territory, surviving the civil wars that tore her apart in the fifteenth century, at the end of the Middle Ages she still continues to embody a unique model: that of a pluralistic Spain, where in spite of tensions and conflicts, Jews, Moors, and Christians managed to invent an original form of coexistence that was respectful of their differences as well as of their complementarity. Suddenly the union with Aragon, sealed by the marriage of Ferdinand and Isabel, then confirmed in 1479 at their accession, opens new prospects for Castile. And thirteen years later, Castile deals the *coup de grâce* to her former invaders when she seizes their last redoubt, Granada, in the very same year that Columbus discovers America. Thirty years more roll by, and now the accession of Charles, the imperial election, the conquest of the New World, propel her into the four corners of the world: a prodigious leap for a nation still young. Rudely torn from her medieval past, diverted from her peninsular inclinations, Castile presides over the birth of the modern age.

In order to withstand the shock without weakening, it is not enough for Castile to play her best cards: the resources of her soil, the ardor and audacity of her sons, the gold and silver extracted from the bowels of the Indies. It is necessary for her to hold her course in total awareness of the stakes and the means. For a nation that has scarcely reached majority is going to steer this enormous venture, in which the less robust pilots—the Low Countries or Aragon—will quickly become exhausted. She might have borne the burden of it more easily if Charles V, in exchange for the effort demanded, had chosen to be a Castilian monarch. But in forty years of rule, he makes only brief stays in the Peninsula, entrusting it most of the time to his subordinates: a detrimental absence, at the time when the victory of Christian Spain, consummated with the end of the Reconquest, has broken the balance of social orders. In this society of the Ancien Régime, compartmentalized among clerics, nobles, and commoners, and where money is introducing its own cleavages into each order, a new line of division is established between Old Christians—the class in the majority—and excluded people of every sort, whether they be of Jewish or Muslim ancestry. For these people, henceforth, the era of suspicion has begun.

In these middle years of the sixteenth century, the three hundred thousand Muslims remaining on the soil of the Peninsula are still under reprieve. Shielded by an ambiguous law that, in exchange for a purely formal conversion, permits them to keep their language, their habits, and their customs, they have managed to keep up, as in Granada, their network of family and tribal relations, or even to secure, as in Valencia, the support of their immediate overlords. The emperor, hostile to the proselytizing zeal of fanatical proponents of integration, tacitly promises them protection. It will not be retracted until the end of the reign, when the unassimilated population will be handed over to prosecution by its adversaries.

The case of the Jews is more complex. Those who out of loyalty to the faith of their ancestors had to choose the way of exile, following Isabel's decree, swarmed around the circumference of the Mediterranean. The *Sephardim* or Sephardic Jews are their descendants. The *conversos,* who preferred to play the game of assimilation, remained behind. Theologians, jurists, financiers, physicians, they are the proud elite of a nation to which they had furnished, during the Middle Ages, the personnel that she needed. Proud of the prerogatives that the trust of sovereigns, and their marital alliances with the aristocracy, had won for them, they become devout Catholics for the most part. Many of them, by the time their racial brothers were being expelled, had been good Christians for several generations. Certain princes of the Church—the cardinal primate of Toledo and even (it has been said) the first Grand Inquisitor—come from their ranks. That is enough to rouse the envy, indeed the hatred, of those who are jealous of a success all the less tolerable because it is not part of the scheme of the patriarchal society of former times.

So the reproach which afflicted the Jew is going to oppress the *converso,* whom his race as well as his conversion to the Christ crucified by his ancestors render doubly suspect. And the obsession with *la mancha,* racial taint, spreads among Old Christians, who boast of their freedom from contamination and proclaim it in the face of neighboring nations, which are disposed to consider eccentric Spain as a Semiticized country, infested with *marranos.* Thus an accusation which spares neither clerics nor nobles nor any of the great organizations of the state is instituted and duly authorized. And thus, in a bewildered desire to recover her problematical identity, Spain's vast turning inward upon herself is outlined. The impetus of an adventure conducted on a world-wide scale still masks this turning inward; but the reign of Philip II is going to reveal it. In 1547, to be precise, the chapter of the cathedral of Toledo enacts purity-of-blood statutes that prohibit *conversos'* access to ecclesiastical positions. The instigator of this measure? A humble peasant who became a cardinal and whose name, Guijarro, which means *pebble,* was latinized to *Silíceo.* Safe from any taint by an unimpeachable lineage, he succeeds by sheer power in forcing the adoption of this discriminatory regulation. The crown, then Rome, will wage in vain a rearguard action against it; but it will not take long to spread into general use. Backed in its plans by the Inquisition—it is also from 1547 that the first *Index* prohibiting seditious books dates—and sure of popular support, a Spain until then subterranean, the one that Pierre Chaunu justly calls "the Spain of rejections," is ready to be born: the same year as Cervantes.

ANCESTRY

OLD Christians on one side, New Christians on the other: in which of these two castes must one include the author of *Don Quixote?* To state the question in these terms is to take sides in the passionate debate that periodically agitates specialists. Usually the arguments put forward in favor of one hypothesis or the other are based on a slanted reading of the Cervantine texts. Those who see in Cervantes a representative of Spain's majority not only recall that he is said to be a *cristiano viejo* in the dossier that he took pains to compile after his return from Algiers; they also appeal—as if to courtroom exhibits— to the anti-Moorish diatribes in *The Dialogue of the Dogs* (Coloquio de los perros), *Don Quixote,* and *Persiles,* and to the ludicrous situations involving Jews in comedies about captivity. Their adversaries object that the man rescued from Barbary prisons was constantly rebuffed by people who should have rewarded his services and that he never produced tangible proof: the purity of his blood is accepted on mere hearsay evidence. They are less impressed by the vehemence of remarks against Jews and Moors than by the irony which lurks behind them, stressing *a fortiori* the derision aimed at dominant forms of behavior that bursts out in the interludes: thus *The Miraculous Puppet Show* (El retablo maravilloso) shows us a group of peasant dignitaries urged to applaud an imaginary show that is visible, someone tells them, only to people who are "without taint." Immediately they all shout their rapturous approval rather than let anyone suspect that they see nothing and expose themselves to taunts of impurity by their neighbors.

Did Cervantes want to be the defender of established values? Or was he, on the contrary, out of tune with his epoch? Whatever his choices may have been, to insist that they were dictated to him by his membership in one of the two castes is to fall into the trap of superficial determinism. In Cervantes, let us not forget, the doctrinaire never takes precedence over the artist, and the subversive power of his *oeuvre* transcends the design from which it seems, at first sight, to proceed. To know that the most illustrious writer of the Golden Age, the very symbol of Spain's universal genius, was a *converso* forced to conceal his origins may perhaps throw light on certain aspects of his mental universe, but it will never provide us with the key to its creation.

The documents gradually assembled, though they do not illuminate his ancestry completely, have at least put an end to the fantastic genealogies with which the author of *Don Quixote* has long been favored. Contrary to previous assertions, Cervantes does not descend from the ancient kings of León. Nor does he seem to be a relative of Cardinal Juan de Cervantes, an eminent patrician in the time of Isabel and Ferdinand. His surname, widely distributed in the Peninusla, is perhaps of Galician origin; but his immediate ancestors settled in Andalusia. His paternal great-grandfather, Ruy Díaz de Cervantes, was born about 1430. A cloth manufacturer during the epoch of the Catholic Rulers, he lived at Córdoba in comfortable circumstances with Catalina de Cabrera, his wife. Cervantes' grandfather, Juan de Cervantes, will manage to escape from this mercantile milieu: he will rise to the bar at the end of a circuitous career. Born around 1470, he studies law at Salamanca and at thirty marries a Cordoban physician's daughter, Leonor de Torreblanca, who will give him four children. Then, having become a *teniente de corregidor,* an assistant magistrate, he will spend twenty years as the agent of the central government in various municipalities. Named assistant to one of his uncles at Alcalá, he sees Rodrigo, his second son, the future father of Miguel, born there in 1509, the same year that Cisneros founds the university. Three years later, the "virtuous señor licentiate" is once more at Córdoba, whence he departs again for Toledo after having liquidated his father's business.

Two significant experiences are going to mark the progress of his career. In 1523 at Cuenca, he quarrels with his subordinates, who criticize his arbitrary actions. In 1527, at Guadalajara, he is a member of the council of the duke of El Infantado, Diego Hurtado de Mendoza. The duke, in his old age, takes a fancy to a pretty commoner named María Maldonado. In 1530 he marries her in secret, after having given her as dowry the tidy sum of two million *maravedís*.* One year later he gives up the ghost. Juan de Cervantes, his confidant and accomplice, must now face the wrath of the duke's sons, furious when they discover that their stepmother is inheriting a fifth of their father's estate. He has a particularly difficult encounter with the duke's bastard, Don Martín de Mendoza. This gentleman, a Gypsy on his mother's side (and an archdeacon into the bargain), had become the lover of the licentiate's own daughter, María, and had promised her a substantial dowry. Rudely dismissed, along with María, Juan de Cervantes takes legal action. His adversaries immediately counterattack. Incarcerated in Valladolid, in the same prison where his son Rodrigo and his grandson Miguel will one day be locked up, the licentiate succeeds in proving the falsity of the accusations brought against him. He obtains a favorable judgment. María de Cervantes, duly compensated by her ex-lover, brings into the world a child named Martina. María will hereafter call herself María de Mendoza.

In 1532 the licentiate is back in Alcalá, where he is going to live for five sumptuous years. The owner of a house on *la calle de la Imagen,* the Street of the Image, he also buys a house known as *la Calzonera,* nearby. He lives there in great style. Twenty years later, people will recall his horses, his servants, his expensive clothes, and they will recall that he mingled with the best society. Nevertheless, he soon takes up his itinerant existence again. We find him by turns in Ocaña, Madrid, Plasencia. These constant moves doubtless have to do with the posts that he occupies; but they are also evidence of growing dissension between him and his spouse. In 1538 a separation is arranged; and while Doña Leonor, who remains at Alcalá with her two sons, must face increasing financial difficulties, Juan de Cervantes returns to Córdoba, where he becomes an attorney for the Inquisition. He makes a few more sojourns at Baena, Cabra, Osuna, occasionally in the service of some great aristocratic name. Then he finally takes the road back to his native city, where he will end his days, rich and respected. The notarial documents that have come down to us tell us little about his private life; but at least they permit us to catch a glimpse of a

---

*See "A Note on the Spanish Monetary System" below, p. 000.

comfortable dwelling, a servant-mistress, a retinue of black and white slaves, and well-paid activities that will apparently cause various difficulties with his fellow lawyers.

A SURGEON FOR A FATHER

CERVANTES' grandfather is certainly a curious figure. Accused, perhaps wrongly, of venality, he was undoubtedly as lenient with the mighty as he was rigorous with the humble. Miguel is probably thinking of him when he puts disillusioned comments about officers of the courts in the mouth of one of his heroines. In any case, he owes to this grandfather his having been born on the banks of the Henares; for his father Rodrigo, second son of the licentiate, remained at Alcalá and settled there. We know little about this unobtrusive personage. Deaf from infancy, he had neither the tact of his elder brother Juan, who died prematurely in 1540, nor the abilities of the youngest, Andrés, who, having left for Córdoba with his father, will settle at Cabra after marrying a rich woman. But Rodrigo experienced success in those prosperous years before his parents' separation, when the Cervantes family lived in style in Cisneros' town. An amateur viol player and horseman, he took part in the tourneys and equestrian games where high society loved to show off. Alas, those days are over when, around 1542, he marries Leonor de Cortinas, from a family of rural landowners originating in Old Castile but settled at Arganda, in the environs of Madrid. His father's departure, his mother's financial disappointments, his elder brother's death, the duties of his new status, all force him to earn a living. Since his handicap prevents him from following the licentiate's footsteps, he resolves to become a *médico zurujano,* a surgeon, an occupation of low prestige at a time when Hippocrates' art was still in its infancy, in which the practitioner was scarcely more than a simple tradesman—and even a barber when the occasion required.

Did Rodrigo inherit his vocation from his maternal grandfather, Dr. Torreblanca, himself the offspring of a dynasty of reputable practitioners? Rodrigo's humble position at the bottom of the medical hierarchy suggests that he preferred to conceal that illustrious precedent. As to his marriage, we know nothing of the circumstances in which it took place. Very likely the parents of Leonor did not approve

of their daughter's choice. She had learned to read and write—a rarity
for the period—and doubtless very soon displayed that strength of
character of which she would give proof in adversity. Did they aspire
to a higher station for her? The fact is that none of their grandchildren
will see them present at their baptisms. This tacit disapproval echoes
the licentiate's indifference: he will not answer the letter when Rodrigo informs him of his decision to take a wife. It is not surprising
that none of the surgeon's three boys born during these years receives
the Christian name of Juan.

After Andrés, born at the end of one year of marriage and dead in
infancy, two daughters, Andrea (1544) and Luisa (1546), then two
boys, Miguel (1547) and Rodrigo (1550), are going to enlarge the
family circle in the space of six years. For a beginning practitioner
who is also committed to the support of his mother, it is a heavy
burden. Furthermore, competition is severe in a city where reputable
fellow doctors abound and where, as *The Dialogue of the Dogs* tells us,
there are two thousand medical students: consequently, "I infer," Berganza will say, "that either these two thousand doctors will have patients
to cure—which would certainly be a calamity and misfortune—or that
they will die of hunger." In order not to die of hunger, a novice like
Rodrigo must resign himself to the most humble tasks and accept as
clientele whoever comes his way. Students' brawls, work accidents,
gang fights bring him—for better or worse—a lot of fractures to set
and cuts to sew, with a plentiful number of bloodlettings into the
bargain; but it is altogether too little when there are so many mouths
to feed. Of course our surgeon occasionally moves away from student
boardinghouses and dubious establishments—the habitual scene of his
exploits—in order to concern himself with some noble patient, anxious about discretion or tight-fisted with his money. But these incur-
sions into high society are often a source of disappointment for him.
An incident that occurred while he was attending one of the sons of
the marquess of Cogolludo seems to have damaged his reputation.
Accused of incompetence by the young man's father and deprived of
his fees, Rodrigo tries in vain to take the case to court. Dissuaded
from proceeding further, discouraged by the difficulties encountered
in his practice, he dreams of moving away with his family.

The birth of his last-born child is going to precipitate his decision.
On the 10th of January, 1551, Juan de Cervantes authorizes María de
Mendoza to put the house on the *calle de la Imagen* up for sale. María

(whose daughter Martina has recently become the wife of Diego Díaz de Talavera, the chief clerk of the court of the archbishopric of Toledo) has prudently invested the settlement paid by her lover the archdeacon. Doubtless she decides on this transaction in agreement with Rodrigo; but before long, she will become estranged from her brother, the misfit in a family whose fate she will cease to share. Two months later, the Cervantes family, in full force, leave Alcalá for Valladolid, canceling out the past: forty leagues—a hundred and thirty miles or more—of wretched highways that the hired coach on which they have taken space with their baggage will require more than a week to cover, and each evening the miserable hospitality of a mediocre inn. They arrive at last, during the first days of April, on the banks of the Pisuerga, in the shadow of the court, where Charles V, absent for three years, is represented by his daughter, the regent Doña María, and by his son-in-law Maximilian.

Is this journey with no intention of returning the result of an impulsive act, as someone has said? Did Rodrigo set out in quest of adventure, in search of a better world, as Don Quixote will do in his own way? This theory confuses the concerns of the unsuccessful surgeon with the illusions of the Undoer of Wrongs. Valladolid, after all, was an entirely different world from La Mancha. With its thirty-five thousand inhabitants, it was one of the most prosperous cities in Old Castile: it was also a magnet for those who came to sue, petition, or intrigue in the halls of chancery or the antechambers of the councils. For Miguel's father, this new address meant prospects of a wealthier and more extensive clientele and, as a consequence, the hope of being protected, at last, from insecurity.

In reality, the departure from Alcalá inaugurates fifteen years of vagabondage that will take Rodrigo to the four corners of the Peninsula, until the day when he resolves to cast anchor in Madrid: fifteen years of incessant wandering that, if they call to mind Juan de Cervantes' thirty years of peregrinations, also prefigure the fifteen years during which the author of *Don Quixote* will, in his turn, trek across Andalusia. The unavoidable ups and downs of an impecunious life, someone will say to explain them. But the fact that they affected three successive generations makes one wonder what other constraints may have oppressed the men who experienced them: first Juan, the great instigator of lawsuits, related on his wife's side to a family of Andalusian physicians; then Rodrigo, an itinerant surgeon, whose marriage to the daughter of peasants was resented by them as a misalliance; and finally Miguel, whose war services no one will recompense and who, having become an agent of the royal Treasury, will have to travel through towns and villages in pursuit of recalcitrant debtors. Three professions, three wanderings, three destinies that, in view of the position of New Christians in the Spain of the sixteenth century, all appear to suggest secret membership in *converso* society. Nevertheless, fifteen statements produced by Cervantes allege the purity of his blood, while we have no decisive proof of a *mancha*. Rodrigo, when he makes his appearance at Valladolid, is not charged with the sins of Israel. In his dealings, he often refers to his father, and the name of the "virtuous senõr licentiate" is a source of honor for him. A few months later, he will invoke his noble status as an *hidalgo* in the law courts. But the man who claims this status is henceforth to be the loser in his encounters with adverse fortune.

DISAPPOINTMENTS AT VALLADOLID

EIGHT months are enough for Rodrigo to see his illusions vanish; and it will take him almost two years to get out of the trap he falls into one fine day. It must have been a severe test for this incorrigible dreamer, who (if one may judge from his household arrangements) believed from the very first that success would come effortlessly: upon his arrival, he installs himself in the Sancti Spiritus suburb, on the lower floor of a huge mansion rented by his sister María; he secures the help of an assistant, persuaded that clients will arrive in droves; he even hires a manservant.

Ill-considered expenditures? In fact, what he saw of the city was apt to nourish his hopes. Populated by some forty thousand souls, Valladolid, in the midst of expansion, had not yet come to terms with its growth. The chroniclers of the time like to speak of it as a vast encampment, deploring its often damp climate, scoffing at the hastily set-up offices and public services, describing the pigs that wallowed in the middle of the *Corredera de San Pablo*. But its churches with their elaborate façades, its palaces around the Plaza Mayor, were already the wonder of visitors. Ceaseless movement reigned in its commercial streets, well-known for their luxurious shops and skillful jewelers, alive with the incessant flow of people—gentlemen, businessmen, students, servants, monks, beggars, and slaves—who crowded between their walls. A Dutch traveler's amusing litany neatly summarizes the impression that this city of dubious character must have made on the visitor: it offered in profusion *pícaros, putas, pleytos, polvos, piedras, puercos, perros, piojos, y pulgas* ("crooks, whores, lawsuits, dust, stones, pigs, dogs, lice, and fleas"). In short, the confusion of a modern Babylon, but also the glamor of a real capital, where even the laborers were the best-paid in Spain.

Did Rodrigo sin on the side of optimism? Did he believe that he could successfully challenge his fellow doctors who already had their own establishments? Did he, in order to make a good impression, overspend on luxuries, counting on the financial support of a sister who must herself have lived in style? The fact remains that in November he is forced to borrow forty thousand *maravedís* in order to reimburse a creditor named Gregorio Romano. The usurious—and barely disguised—terms of this loan and the conditions of the contract suggest connivance between Pedro García, the lender, and María de Mendoza. When the loan falls due on St. John's Day of the following year, the debtor declares himself unable to honor his debt; he cannot even pay the rent. Jailed on July 2, 1552, Rodrigo learns two days later that his goods have been impounded. Meager booty, if one is to believe the inventory that has come down to us: a few pieces of furniture and hangings, a chest, a set of sheets, some clothing, a sword, a viol, two medical texts, a grammar book. If nothing has been concealed, it tells all one needs to know about the surgeon's destitution.

Doña Leonor de Torreblanca is going to salvage whatever she can by putting the attached goods in her own name. Giving up the ground-floor apartment, she installs herself and her family on the floor occupied by María. It is there that on July 22, her daughter-in-law will bring into the world her fifth child, a daughter who will be named Magdalena. Meanwhile, from the depths of his cell, Rodrigo has gone on the counterattack. Testimonies that he produces to defend his reputation prove that he and his father have honorable professions which are not given to commoners. It would appear that the *hidalquía* (nobility) of the Cervantes family, publicly acknowledged for two generations, has never been established by letters patent. Did Rodrigo present himself as a gentleman in the same way that his sister María makes herself out to be younger than she is, in the deposition that she has left us? It is noteworthy that the witnesses called by the surgeon all refer to the prosperous years at Alcalá and Guadalajara; no testimony emanates from Córdoba, where the paternal grandfather had founded a family. Was Miguel's father reluctant to specify his cloth-merchant ancestor's occupation? His silence about his Cordoban origins, his refusal to indicate his own profession, cast a shadow that troubles the historian.

In any case, Rodrigo's various ploys are going to run afoul of a judge who rejects his motions. His creditors, in fact, refuse to listen to anything until they have recovered what is owed. Freed on bail on November 7, Rodrigo, still insolvent, returns to his cell ten days later. In December of the same year, then in January of the following year, he is in and out of prison. It will be February before the unfortunate man leaves prison for good. He will still have to sell the furnishings of the house in Sancti Spiritus in order to collect sufficient money to settle his debts. There is nothing left for him but to take leave of a city where he must have known only frustrations and disappointments. In the spring of 1553 he once again loads his scanty baggage on a hired vehicle. Accompanied by the two Leonors, María, and his five children, he leaves the banks of the Pisuerga and returns, probably, to Alcalá. Does Miguel, who is about to turn six, retain memories of this bitter sojourn? His work shows no trace of it; but it will surely come back to him when he himself settles, half a century later, in Philip III's ephemeral capital. Unlike his father, he will enjoy the fruits of success, but he will also know, like Rodrigo, the damp straw of a jail cell.

If the surgeon does in fact return to his native city, he stays there for only a single summer: time to find temporary lodgings, supplied perhaps by his niece Martina and her clerk husband; time also to repair, to the extent possible, a shaky financial situation. Did Rodrigo try to re-establish his practice? Did he once again ask his sister María for assistance? Did he wait until Leonor received her share of revenue from wheat fields that the Cortinas family owned at Arganda? The only certainty: in autumn, he is on the road again, this time bound for Córdoba. He does not appear to have informed his father of his project: it is known that the licentiate had maintained only the slightest contacts with his family for fifteen years. This new departure is no less pregnant with meaning. It takes place, in fact, at the very moment when the kingdom's center of gravity is shifting from north to south, when the prodigious impetus that Seville had experienced is spreading

over all of the lower Guadalquivir valley, when Burgos and Valladolid
see their wool and cloth hit by the crisis in the textile industry. In his
own way, Rodrigo illustrates this change with his wanderings, in a
movement that his subsequent peregrinations will confirm, when the
time comes.

PILGRIMAGE TO THE FOUNTAINHEAD

THIS departure for Andalusia has inspired some emotional pages by
Cervantists. When the traveler who goes from Alcalá to Córdoba leaves
Toledo, he enters the vast stretches of La Mancha, which convoys of
former times had to cross in six or seven stages. How is it possible not
to imagine Miguel's emotion as one discovers under the October sky
the barren landscapes that his hero will one day traverse at Rocinante's
pace, the windmills that will inflame his imagination, the inns that
his madness will make him take for castles? This entirely romantic
celebration of the mental shock from which the masterpiece will one
day be born not only contradicts all that we know of *Don Quixote*'s
genesis; it also assumes that Cervantes did in fact make the journey
with his family. That, however, is a point which has yet to be established. For centuries, scholars have known practically nothing about
his years of infancy and adolescence: they lose track of him until 1567,
the year when he settles at Madrid. We owe to Astrana Marín the
discovery of Rodrigo's stay at Córdoba. It is attested to by a document
of October 30, 1553, several days after his arrival. Did the surgeon
come with his family? Nothing authorizes us to affirm it. Chastened
by his misfortunes, he may well have wanted to try his luck accompanied by his mother alone, leaving wife and children in Alcalá, under
the protection of his niece and sister. It has been verified that during
these years Leonor de Cortinas repeatedly found herself on the banks
of the Henares, with several of her children. Might not Miguel, still
quite young, have been one of their number? It is not absurd to think
so.

It would be interesting to know what the meeting of the licentiate
and his son was like. If Leonor de Torreblanca (who ended her days in
Córdoba) were also in the party, Juan de Cervantes, coddled by his
housekeeper, must scarcely have appreciated the reappearance of a wife
from whom he had been separated for so long. A domestic detail per-

mits us to see the extent of the old lawyer's sordid egotism: Rodrigo has hardly arrived in the Andalusian city when he buys several ells of linen and cotton cloth on credit. Could it be, as has been said, that he had no shirts? In any case, it was necessary for him to borrow the sum required for the purchase. That he is once again caught up in the vicious cycle of usury shows clearly that his father did not immediately give him the reception that he had a right to expect.

Doubtless more cordial relations gradually take the place of this initial coldness. It certainly appears that ties of kinship finally carried the day with Juan de Cervantes. Proof is the birth, around 1554, of the surgeon's last son, this time named Juan like his grandfather, though we do not know whether he saw the light of day at Córdoba or at Alcalá. The licentiate perhaps helped his son find lodgings in the lower-class quarter of San Nicolás de la Ajerquía, near the Guadalquivir. No doubt he recommended him to legal acquaintances, if, as seems probable, Rodrigo was looking for clientele. Miguel's father, having become a "familiar" of the Inquisition—that is, an informer—probably exercised his talents in the prison of the Holy Office, under the orders of a friendly physician; he might also have been attached to the hospital of La Caridad. Let us hope that he was able to come up to the expectations of his patrons and to supply the needs of his patients—and that his successes poured balm on his troubled heart.

Proud of her glorious past, Córdoba, who saw Seneca born and whose celebrated mosque still reminds us that she was once the capital of Muslim Spain, was too far away to be directly affected by Seville's activities. The exodus of Córdoba's inhabitants to Málaga, Granada, and even to the New World reveals a stagnation that will become more pronounced under Philip.II. With forty thousand inhabitants, a high number for the period, she will nevertheless remain an important relay station on the great axis which unites Castile to Andalusia. Her local commerce remained prosperous and her artisans, past masters in leatherwork, were the worthy heirs of the Cordovan leather craftsmen of the time of the Caliphs. Hence it is a still-active city that sees Rodrigo in harness again during the first months of a rainy winter marked by two sudden and spectacular floods of the Guadalquivir. Profiting by his past misfortunes, comforted by his father's support, he no longer has to dread the competition of eminent fellow surgeons, who in Alcalá or Valladolid, university towns, had the advantage. He is going to spend many years in the birthplace of his ancestors: years that one imagines sufficiently tranquil at last to encourage the surgeon, who had come to scout the territory, to summon his family. At least this hypothesis is the basis for Miguel's presumed stay in the Andalusian city. There, Miguel would have made three decisive discoveries: school, the theater, and the picaresque.

First of all, school: appropriate for a six-year-old boy at the right age to learn to read and write. Miguel is thought to have acquired the rudiments under Alonso de Vieras, a relative of the Cervantes family, whose "academy" was located in the Castellanos quarter. Was Miguel a child avid to learn? His passion for reading leads us to think so. He may later have become a pupil of those clever pedagogues the Jesuits, who were busy collecting under their stern direction the elite of Córdoba's youth. Did Miguel attend their Santa Catalina School, which after two years of provisional installation had recently moved into one of the handsomest palaces in Córdoba? Was he introduced on that occasion to grammar and rhetoric? Did he practice by translating Latin authors? So many questions remain unanswered. From the panegyric on the Jesuits of Seville pronounced by Berganza in *The Dialogue of the Dogs,* some have inferred that Miguel studied with their confreres at Córdoba: a specious argument at best, to which we will return when we consider Rodrigo's sojourn in Seville. Let us limit ourselves for the moment to crediting his son with the conventional knowledge of any young schoolchild.

Next the theater, for which he developed a taste early, if one is to believe his declaration on the subject. By theater, we mean the entertainments of a generation that was finding its way, in a period when the Spanish stage had no national existence and when permanent playhouses had not yet been born. Members of the closed circle of Andalusian high society must have applauded the allegorical plays, staged at Santa Catalina on special occasions by the good fathers, which their pupils acted before dignitaries and parents. These edifying comedies, written in a quaint Latin interlarded with Castilian, show us Man engaged with the Virtues and Vices; they must have made—in the opinion of some—a strong impression on young Miguel's mind. But nothing proves that this offspring of a humble surgeon was able to attend such performances, which he nowhere mentions.

More likely, during these years he experienced the revelation of puppet theater, for which a certain Sebastián Hay had established a reputation in Spain. In *Master Glass* (El licenciado Vidriera), Cervantes

will recall those "wanderers" who "stuffed all, or most, of the characters of the Old and New Testament into a sack and then sat on it to
eat and drink in bar rooms and taverns." One cannot appreciate Don
Quixote's pouncing on Master Peter's puppet theater and chopping up
the figurines brought to life by these mountebanks without discovering, behind his mad attack, the fascination which the young Cervantes
felt. And finally: did he observe, in some inn yard, the itinerant stage
of the great Lope de Rueda, whose talent he will celebrate in the
twilight of his life? Even though there is evidence of Rueda's presence
in Córdoba in 1556, what his admirer tells us suggests a later encounter, to which we will return.

With regard to that fringe of Spanish society where one meets thieves
and beggars of every sort in the troubled waters of vagrancy, delinquency, and prostitution: it holds such an important place in Cervantes' work that his initiation to what will later be called the picaresque
is sometimes dated from the Cordoban years. In this period, the *pícaro*,
properly so called, has not yet risen to the dignity of literature. In
fact, the term that designates him has a restricted meaning: it is applied
only to street porters and scullions. Beyond the word itself, nevertheless, one senses a new awareness of a phenomenon that is catching the
attention of theologians and jurists, who are beginning to concern
themselves with the increase in beggary, a theoretically legal way of
life. Their debates bring to the foreground a marginal world suddenly
dragged from the half-shadows where it stood. This parasitic world
has always existed. But that it should thus acquire, in mid-sixteenth-
century urban Spain, a visibility and prominence that no one suspected; that one discovers it as a backdrop for the adventures of Lazarillo de Tormes, the ancestor of the literary *pícaros:* these are the first
symptoms of a new conjunction and an evolution of attitudes.

Córdoba, an obligatory way station between Seville and Castile,
stands out quite early among the important places of the picaresque.
Near San Nicolás Church, the Plaza del Potro, which every tourist
today must visit, was in the Golden Age the meeting place of beggars
of every stripe. Cervantes recommends it, in *The Noble Scullery Maid*
(La ilustre fregona), to the novice *pícaro* anxious to start his apprenticeship. Did he himself visit it frequently in his early childhood,
during the hours of leisure that his teachers allowed him? Even if he
did risk going there, let us keep from foisting an unwarranted precoc-
ity on him. At the end of Philip II's reign, the author of *Don Quixote*

will repeatedly pass through Córdoba's environs, in the course of his
Andalusian travels; his dealings with the local underworld must therefore be those of a mature man.

Let us come back to Rodrigo, who seems to have adapted to his
new existence and whom two deaths in the family are suddenly going
to strike, one after the other. On March 11, 1556, the licentiate Cervantes departs for a better world. He is more than eighty years old, an
exceptionally advanced age for the period. One year later, it is Leonor
de Torreblanca's turn to die, at her son's house. Shortly before, she
had sold "a dark brown slave." Did she experience toward the end of
her life new reverses of fortune, after having recovered the affluence of
former years? From the reading of their respective wills, it is clear, in
any case, that the spouses were not reconciled. This double passing
marks the beginning of new vicissitudes for the surgeon. We lose track
of him for seven long years. Did he leave for New Castile again? Did
he there rejoin his family, which had perhaps remained on the banks
of the Henares? Did he take up his former life-style? Certain scholars
believe that instead he went south, in the direction of Granada, in
order to join his brother Andrés at Cabra. His presence in the duke of
Sessa's fief is not attested to until 1564. Had he stayed there previously, during these obscure years about which we are totally ignorant?
Did he take Miguel with him? So several biographers suppose; and
they advance two arguments: the protection which the duke of Sessa,
the future viceroy of Sicily, will later grant to the soldier of Lepanto,
a protection motivated, someone has said, by a relationship begun in
that remote period; and the repeated interest that. Cervantes' work
shows in the impressive chasm situated in the environs of this walled
town clinging to the outer foothills of the Sierra Nevada. But caution
is imperative here. The chasm at Cabra—presumed model for the cave
of Montesinos, into which Don Quixote descends—was not properly
speaking a tourist attraction; it was a folk motif, made familiar by the
Romancero. And a reference to it does not necessarily imply the memory
of an excursion to the place itself. With regard to the duke, governor
of Milan between 1558 and 1560, he would have had little leisure, in
the course of his short visits to his fief, to take an interest in an adolescent whose grandfather he had once employed, and no reason to
give him access to his library, as one scholar claims. It would be best,
then, to give up the appealing fantasy of an Andalusian pastoral with
Cervantes as the hero.

This seven-year parenthesis in the lives of the future writer and his father coincides, paradoxically, with a succession of important events. The same year that Juan de Cervantes disappears, Charles V, wasted by illness and cares, puts an end to a reign of more than forty years; to everyone's amazement, he retires to the monastery of Yuste, in the heart of Extremadura, where he will die two years later. His son Philip II receives as his share a domain that is less dispersed but almost as vast as Charles's: though it stretches as far as the Low Countries, it is centered around the Mediterranean. Castile, augmented by its Italian and colonial dependencies, plays up its already preponderant role there. The emperor had dreamed of another formula of division when in 1554 he married his heir apparent to Mary Tudor, Henry VIII's Catholic daughter. England and Flanders, Spain and Italy, and the American possessions would accordingly have become the major divisions of a more balanced whole. The death of Mary without issue, three months after her father-in-law's demise, and the accession of her Protestant sister Elizabeth destroy beyond repair this splendid project and are going to impose a different course on the fortunes of Europe. After 1560, Philip II confirms Castile's dominant position when without fanfare he permanently locates the court at Madrid. The same year, in conformity with the treaty of Cateau-Cambrésis, he makes a third marriage, to Elizabeth of Valois, the daughter of Henri II of France. In 1563, he starts construction on El Escorial. From there the king will attempt to impose his religion and his rule upon the world, while anchoring his power henceforth in the very heart of the Peninsula.

THE CALL OF SEVILLE

ABSENT, as he must have been, from the theater of events, Rodrigo de Cervantes does not reappear on the stage of our little drama until October 30, 1564. The setting has changed. We are now in Seville, where, according to a document we possess, the licentiate's son has for several months been managing rental houses. He carries out his activities in San Salvador, one of the wealthy parishes of the city; but he lives in San Miguel, a lower-class neighborhood. Two questions immediately come to mind. First, what motivated this change? Perhaps the initiative of his elder brother Andrés, who had been watching over the interests of the itinerant surgeon from his residence at Cabra.

Andrés, the owner of properties mentioned in the document, had probably taken his younger brother under his wing. Next: who accompanies Rodrigo this time? His daughter Andrea, without doubt. (We will speak of her again before long.) What about Leonor? The other five children? As in the case of Córdoba, we lack decisive proof that would permit us to answer. As a result, we are constrained, on the basis of a few hints, to allow Miguel a purely conjectural first experience of Seville, twenty years before the long sojourn which will mark his life and work so profoundly.

One can understand why Rodrigo, after so many disappointments, chose to try his luck, with no guarantee of success, in Seville, a city that united luxury with poverty, where swindlers abounded and where competition was keen, but with all the opportunities that a metropolis in full expansion could offer. Profiting simultaneously from fertile outlying districts, access to the Guadalquivir, and a monopoly on commerce with the Indies, the Andalusian capital had become the most dynamic and most prosperous city in the Peninsula. With almost a hundred thousand permanent residents and the constant influx of a floating population, Seville was experiencing an activity that was the marvel of visitors. In the midst of a building boom, according to the chroniclers, it was a paradise for real-estate speculations. Nevertheless, whether the ex-surgeon grew tired of his new occupation or was showing proof of his incompetence, he was not to remain in his brother's employ for long: all told, his stay will not exceed two years.

Miguel is eighteen, the age when the field of discoveries, interests, and emotions expands. The same biographers who have made him a pupil of the Jesuits at Córdoba readily inscribe his name in the registers of their Seville school, established in the very center of the city, in the district of Don Pedro Ponce. Anxious to see him finish a more-or-less normal schooling, they go to the length of advancing the date of his arrival to 1562 and of giving him Andrés' son Juan, his cousin, as a fellow student. Thus he can be made the classmate of Mateo Vázquez, Philip II's future secretary, whose path the author of *Don Quixote* will later cross. And so they also give him as a teacher Fr. Acevedo, whose plays were performed by students before the flower of Sevillian society, like those he had written previously at Córdoba. In the arrangement of these comedies, of which we have the manuscript text, several well-meaning scholars are inclined to see the matrix of Cervantes' notions about theater. The allegories that people the reverend father's psychomachies are said to foreshadow, in particular, the *figuras morales,* which the author of *Numancia* will one day boast of having invented. Furthermore, in the mysterious Miguel mentioned among the actors of the tragedy *Lucifer furens,* they recognize the surgeon's son, whose Christian name, they say, was uncommon in Seville. What an expenditure of imagination!

This handsome edifice rests on an extremely fragile foundation: the famous passage in *The Dialogue of the Dogs* where Berganza, in the service of a Sevillian merchant, recalls the teaching lavished on the merchant's children by the fathers of the Society of Jesus. This stirring eulogy of their pedagogy, long considered to be sincere, is perhaps in reality an inverted image, a ferocious denunciation of the order's worldly involvements. At least that is the way one student has recently interpreted it, in light of a lawsuit instituted against the Sons of St. Ignatius by one of their own, the great historian Mariana, one of the most lucid-minded Jesuits of the period of Philip II. Whichever it may be, dithyramb or diatribe, who is to say that this text reflects the author's personal experience? Supposing that Cervantes accompanied his father on his peregrinations, it is hard to imagine the parishioner of San Miguel sending one of his six children to benches occupied by the elite of the local youth. In the "Athens of Andalusia," where art and literature had always been held in honor, there were undoubtedly less exalted establishments where the surgeon's son could take up again—after how long an interruption?—the studies begun in Córdoba or Alcalá.

In any case, it is from these years that his love for the theater dates: "I have been fond of the stage," he will say, "since boyhood." And he will elaborate, shortly before his death:

> [I remember] having seen the great Lope de Rueda perform. He was a man outstanding for his acting and his intelligence. He was a native of Seville, by trade a "foil-beater," meaning one of those people who make gold leaf. He was admirable in pastoral poetry, and in this style, no one has excelled him either at the time or since then; and although in those days, being a boy, I was unable to judge confidently how good his verses were, nevertheless, because of some that have stayed in my memory, considering them now at the mature age which I have reached, I find that what I said is true.

Cervantes had a good memory. Besides the fact that he quotes in one of his own plays the verses that he remembered, he tells us very accurately what the eclogues, whose scanty decor he describes, were like. But the most vivid impression he had was of the farces that Rueda presented between the acts of his comedies, acting with equal talent the parts of black slave-women, pimps, simpletons, and Basques— four of the comic specialties in vogue in the *saynetes* (interludes) of the day.

At the appropriate time, we will examine the historical importance of this playwright, one of the fathers of the Castilian theater. For now, what is noteworthy is that at the very moment when Rodrigo de Cervantes was working for his brother, we find that he had Lope de Rueda as a neighbor. Rodrigo may even have been bound by ties of friendship to one of the members of Rueda's troupe—which we will meet in Madrid at a later date. Like the surgeon a parishioner of San Miguel, Rueda had his daughter Juana Luisa baptized there on July 18, 1564. It is therefore tempting to date from that very year the astonishment of a seventeen-year-old spectator. But—one may ask—what if Cervantes were not in Andalusia at that time? In that case, he might well have been able to see Rueda perform one or two years later, in Madrid or in Alcalá. Our knowledge, little better than fragmentary, of the playwright's touring calendar prevents us from being more precise.

The only properly documented episode in the course of Rodrigo's stay has as protagonist Andrea, the eldest of his children. A gentleman named Nicolás de Ovando, son of a magistrate of the King's Council and nephew of the vicar general of Castile, had become interested in the young woman, then in the bloom of her twenty years. According to the notarial documents that have come down to us, he must even have promised to marry her—a promise not kept, as might have been expected of a gallant from such a distinguished family. Did Ovando commit himself without due consideration, only to refuse the unequal union? Did Andrea really believe his oaths, designed to overcome her last resistance? Did she instead grant her favors freely, rather than having been duped by her suitor's beautiful words? What is certain is that she obtained—at least at the beginning—the financial reparations which she had a right to claim, according to the custom of the day. The birth of a daughter, Constanza de Ovando, will come just in time to prove the truth of her allegations.

A reading of these documents leaves us hungry for more information. What was the reality of this love affair, besides a matter of money— the mere surface of the episode? How did Rodrigo and his family live through the experience? How did Miguel feel about it? It has been assumed that he had met Ovando through his sister and by the same means had become friends with Mateo Vázquez, at that time the secretary (and, it is said, the favorite) of the uncle, the vicar general. After María de Mendoza and her Gypsy lover, Andrea adds a new link to the chain of illegitimate love affairs that mark Cervantes' life. The author of *Don Quixote,* as we shall see, will follow the tradition. A strange light illuminates this female universe—aunt, sisters, niece, and natural daughter—in which he will operate until the end of his life. What we know of the customs of the period, at least in a milieu like his, makes us think that, for him, their adventures were not synonymous with disgrace; but among all the Christian names that his heroines will bear, Constanza will be his favorite.

Indulgent with regard to seduced virgins, Spanish opinion was less so toward the unfaithful wife, especially if she were involved with an inferior. On January 10, 1565, all of Seville will attend, in San Francisco Square, the execution of an adulterous wife and her mulatto lover, performed by the husband himself, an innkeeper whose honor had been offended. Cervantes remembered this horrible scene, described in a chapter in *Persiles,* though one cannot be certain that he witnessed it himself. It is at about this time that Rodrigo returns to Alcalá. He there rejoins Leonor, perhaps, to whom three months earlier he had sent a power of attorney. On February 11 he attends the vow-taking of his daughter Luisa, who enters the Carmelite nunnery of La Concepción. With the name Luisa de Belén, she will one day become the prioress of this "little corner of God's earth," to use St. Teresa's image. On April 10, the surgeon's presence in Córdoba is again attested to. Was Miguel with him? Some maintain it: an allusion to the burial of Rueda, interred in the choir of the cathedral, has caused some to suppose that he was present at the funeral of the playwright, who died at the end of March.

In Seville again, Rodrigo finds himself involved once more in a suit over debts: during his absence, a creditor named Rodrigo de Chaves has demanded seizure of his goods. By an irony of fate, it is to Andrea that the surgeon is going to owe his salvation. Arguing that the sequestered goods are her personal property, she challenges the judge's decision and manages to prolong the case. Such presence of mind, such a sense of juridical fine points, are astounding in a young woman of twenty-two. It dissuades us from seeing her as the naive victim of an unscrupulous seducer. In any case, this new misfortune must have pushed her father to take leave of the Andalusian metropolis once and for all. Recalled to Alcalá by the sudden death of his mother-in-law, Elvira de Cortinas, he leaves again a few months later with his family for a place that he hopes will be more hospitable. His choice is fixed on Philip II's new capital. In the fall of 1566 he settles in Madrid.

THE MADRID YEARS

THE city to which Rodrigo has just moved his household—doubtless at the end of the preceding spring—has not yet recovered from its sudden metamorphosis. The seat of the monarchy for six years, Madrid still shows the signs of its modest origins. Once a fortified market town for the outposts of Christian Spain, it experienced its first period of growth at the end of the previous century, when the Catholic Rulers established their chancery there for a brief period. Eclipsed, under Charles V, by Toledo and Valladolid, more active and more populous, Madrid in fact owes its promotion to its geographical situation: from there, Philip II is going to be able to supervise more easily the work on El Escorial. For the fifteen years that the construction of the imposing monastery will last, the Spanish Empire will be governed from the banks of the Manzanares: an entirely provisional arrangement which the Prudent King's successors will confirm after a period of hesitation.

Madrid has far to go in order to be worthy of its new destiny. Its thirty-five thousand inhabitants leave it far behind Seville, whose prosperity and splendor Madrid has none of; however, compared with the eighteen thousand residents that it had twenty years earlier, Madrid's population bears witness to a strong demographic surge. The installation of the sovereign and his household in the old Alcázar, the transfer of councils and offices that accompany the royal ménage, cause the arrival of a mass of courtiers, functionaries, and petitioners, often flanked by a numerous domestic train, who frequently experience the greatest hardship in finding lodgings. The influx of a whole world of parasites, from high-flying adventurers to common mobsters, creates severe problems for the magistrates charged with public safety. To meet the challenge of its spectacular growth, to obtain needed wood, the city devours the forests that surround it. Nothing remains of these forests in our time except the Casa de Campo, whose holm oaks break for an instant the grandiose monotony of the Castilian plateau. These hastily assembled materials serve for building new quarters on the vacant lands that remain within the medieval enclosure. There is a proliferation of "tricky buildings," *casas de malicia:* houses with sloping roofs that skillfully mask, on the street side, the stories fitted out on the court-yard side, which allow their possessors to avoid the obligation of lodg-ing the innumerable functionaries of a bureaucratic king. Madrid will long preserve the signs of this town-planning-gone-wild: the network of lanes, the filth of the slums, the meager flow of the Manzanares will for a long time stimulate the wit of its detractors.

At that time, the city included fourteen parishes. In which did the Cervantes family choose to reside? We do not know, since Rodrigo describes himself simply as "residing in Madrid." A notarial document of December 2, 1566, provides us with the first indication of his pres-ence: it is a new power of attorney granted to Leonor by her husband, at the time of the settlement of Doña Elvira's estate. Fifteen days later, Leonor sells for seven thousand *maravedís* part of the estate, a vineyard located in Arganda. That she liquidates part of her inheritance so promptly tell us much about the surgeon's slim resources. Rodrigo appears to seek other means of livelihood, uninterested in taking up his former profession—perhaps unable to do so. A loan of eight hundred ducats granted by him to a certain Pedro Sánchez de Córdoba reveals the beneficial side effects of the Cortinas inheritance. Other notarial documents show him engaged in financial deals in company with Pirro Bocchi and Francesco Musacchi, two Italian businessmen. A third associate is also mentioned, one whose previous history and occupa-tions catch our attention: Alonso Getino de Guzmán, formerly a musi-cian and dancer attached to Lope de Rueda's troupe, who, after having lived in Seville for a time, has also made his way to Madrid. The official organizer of festivals and shows for the young capital, he must have enjoyed an enviable position compared with the common lot of actors. Certain documents seem to indicate that Rodrigo lodged the three men. Had he put his Sevillian experience to use in order to manage an apartment house for his brother? Should we imagine him rather as the keeper of a boardinghouse? We can only speculate.

The only thing we know for sure is that Nicolás de Ovando has disappeared from Andrea's life. Also settled in Madrid, he has suffered reverses of fortune: his father has died suddenly; his family has declared bankruptcy. A few years later he will become the chamberlain of Car-

dinal Espinosa, the Grand Inquisitor and president to the Council of
Castile. As for Andrea, she has found a new protector among the Italians that her father regularly visits. On July 9, 1569, Francesco Locadelo, a Genoese gentlemen with business interests, makes over to the
young woman an important gift, out of gratitude for care received
from Rodrigo and his daughter. The notarial document mentions
bandaging required for the rich merchant's sores and abscesses. It also
specifies the liberal gifts granted to the amiable nurse: lengths of cloth,
clothing, cushions and rugs, candlesticks and pewter plates, chairs and
writing tables—in short, enough to furnish a cozy apartment com-
fortably—in addition to a sum of three hundred gold *escudos*. A juicy
detail: the object of this gift is to permit Andrea to marry honorably.
The generous Locadelo will soon return to Italy; but Rodrigo and his
family, sheltered from want for a considerable time, will surely retain
fond memories of his stay among them. Did Miguel, twenty years old
at the time, know all about these transactions?

The presence of Getino de Guzmán under the paternal roof, on the
other hand, has a notable effect on his personal life: it marks the precise date of his literary debut. In October 1576, the birth of the Infanta
Catalina Micaela, second daughter of Philip II and Elizabeth of Valois,
is going to be celebrated with great splendor. And the director of the
festivities on that occasion is none other than Getino. On the triumphal arches erected under his supervision, he displays a number of
medallions decorated with poetic compositions. Among these compositions appears a sonnet by Miguel, prominently located:

> Serenest Queen, in whom is found
> All that God could give a human being . . .

It was believed for a long time that the autograph of this poem is
preserved in the Spanish manuscript collections of the Bibliothèque
Nationale in Paris. It is actually only a copy, discovered by accident
in the middle of the last century. This sonnet, to be frank, is not a
masterpiece by a precocious genius. It is a clumsy command performance, an occasional piece inspired by an unpublished poem dedicated
to the heir apparent, the famous Don Carlos, by Pedro Laínez, his
chamberlain. This homage by Cervantes to an established writer, whose
close friend he will become, is in conformity with the customs of the
age; above all, it tells us that the future author of *Don Quixote* has

recently begun to attend the literary salons of the capital. Besides Laínez, certain persons among those he rubs elbows with there offer him their friendship: López Maldonado and Gálvez de Montalvo, whose names will later be associated with his when he decides, after his return from captivity, to devote himself to the Muses. Perhaps he also goes to see *comedias* in the two newly opened permanent playhouses, the Corral de la Cruz and the Corral de la Pacheca. For the present, he has seen his verses engraved in letters of gold and presented to a curious but ephemeral public. He certainly aspires to a more durable success; and an opportunity will soon be offered to him to realize his wish.

FOUR POEMS

DID Philip II receive the tribute of verses dedicated to the young princess by his good and loyal subjects? It is doubtful, in any case, that he paid attention to those of the apprentice poet. He was occupied with other cares provoked by the tensions and difficulties of a time of crisis, cares that the painful ordeal of a family tragedy will sharpen.

In the eyes of a sovereign who considers himself the champion of the True Faith, any deviation, however minimal, is an attack on the monarchy, a blow leveled at a Spain that harbors in her bosom so many fringe elements and disenfranchised minorities. The discovery of clandestine Protestant groups at Valladolid and Seville in 1558 results immediately in a repression that will reach even the archbishop primate of Toledo, Carranza, accused of heretical tendencies. Punctuated by *autos-da-fé* of which Cervantes may have been a witness here or there, this discovery also strengthened the king in his determination to bar the way to pernicious ideas spreading across Europe and sowing discord in France and the Low Countries. Two prohibitions in 1558 and 1559 carry out and complete the three *Indexes* that the Inquisitor Valdés had published under the preceding reign. From these, historians have concluded rather too hastily that Spain was thenceforth cut off from foreign ideas, forgetting that there was never a breach in the exchanges with Philip II's other possessions, among them Italy and Flanders, which are two great centers of culture, more than ever. Antwerp in particular, with its remarkable printers, had become one of the principal distribution centers of Spanish books. There, in 1568, on orders from the sovereign, the humanist Arias Montano will direct the revised and enlarged edition of the Polyglot Bible of Alcalá.

Sixty years after Cisneros' edition, Arias Montano's enterprise has a different significance. Its object is to reply to the profanation of the Antwerp cathedral by Calvinists, and it appears at the moment when sympathy for the Reformation is spreading in the Low Countries. A symbol of a new crusade of intellects, it is the corollary of the crusade of arms launched at the same time against the Huguenot rebels. History has forgotten the peacemaking work of the regent Margarita of Parma, whose successful initiatives will contribute to pacifying the Catholic provinces of the south; she is remembered only for the ferocious repression led, from 1566 on, by the famous duke of Alba and marked by the execution at Brussels of Egmont and Horn. In spite of victories, the Spanish intervention soon takes on proportions that the duke had not foreseen. The war drags on and spreads; each camp seeks new allies, upsetting the balance of powers in Europe. The Flemish abscess, whose disastrous effects Cervantes will one day deplore, will suppurate in the flank of the great empire until the end of the century.

After 1556, Philip II was bent on showing that religious orthodoxy and purity of blood were thenceforth officially associated. The ratification of discriminatory statutes adopted nine years earlier at Toledo was followed by widespread repressive measures directed against *conversos*. One can understand the anxiety which the *moriscos*—Christians on the surface but Muslims in their hearts—inspire in the monarch. In the first stages, he decides to bring into the fold this important Andalusian community whose attachment to its traditions so greatly worries him. In 1566 the Moriscos of the kingdom of Granada are invited to give up their language, abandon their customs, and renounce their rites and practices. This policy of rapid assimilation, preached by Cardinal Espinosa, does not produce the results anticipated. It irritates the Moriscos, just as the hostility with which they feel themselves surrounded incites them to stiffen their resistance. Directly affected by the crisis in the silk industry, accused by public opinion of complicity with Barbary pirates, their property expropriated without compensation, they decide to take immediate action. On Christmas night 1568, they attempt to seize Granada. The attempt fails, but the rebellion spreads like wildfire. For three years a merciless war ravages the Alpujarras mountains. In order to put an end to the revolt, it will be necessary for the king's half-brother, Don Juan de Austria, to take over the operations. Don Juan will describe in poignant terms, in a letter to his brother, the solution taken: the scattering of the Andalusian community. But the Morisco question will nevertheless appear again thirty years later, on a Peninsula-wide scale. Cervantes, with singular perspicacity, will be able to give us a sense of its magnitude.

But even before the war at Granada breaks out, rumors in Madrid echo a drama which this time strikes a blow at the king's personal life. On January 15, 1568, Philip II has prayers said in all the churches that God will assist him in a decision which he is about to make. On January 18, accompanied by several members of his council, he enters the chamber where the Infante Don Carlos, the heir to the throne, is sleeping. Without warning, he notifies the prince of his permanent seclusion in this room, which becomes thenceforth his cell: a terrible decision motivated by the behavior of an unbalanced personality who had gone so far as to oppose his father with violence and who was suspected of conspiring with Flemish rebels. This punishment, intended to set an example, and the death of the Infante, which ensues six months later, will inflame the imagination of the Romantics: Don Carlos' sympathy for the Protestant cause, his incestuous love affair with his stepmother Elizabeth of Valois, his poisoning by order of his father, are some of the legends upon which Schiller and Verdi will one day embroider. As for the king, he suffers the ordeal with the patience of Abraham: "With this arrest, I wished," he will write to his sister, "to offer to God the sacrifice of my own flesh and blood and to put His service and universal good before other human considerations."

One imagines Cervantes learning about the prince's tragic end, doubtless from the lips of his friend Pedro Laínez, the poet-chamberlain to whom a manuscript account of the arrest is attributed. Though we know nothing of his thoughts at the time, we can guess something about his feelings on the death of the queen in October of the same year, carried off at the age of twenty-three while bringing a stillborn child into the world. Philip II's sorrow will impress all the court, though the emotion of the citizens of Madrid will be no less sincere:

> When war left our Hispanic soil free,
> The fairest flower on earth, with sudden flight,
> Was transplanted up to heaven.

These unskillful verses in the funereal mode, recalling the event, are the work of Miguel's pen. They come from one of four poems included in the official *Relación* of the funeral published the autumn of the following year by the first printer established in the capital, four poems that the author of the *Relación,* Juan López de Hoyos, requested for the occasion from his "well-beloved pupil."

López de Hoyos, a respectable if not important humanist, owes to his illustrious pupil his having piqued the curiosity of scholars. He also owes it to the discreet Erasmism that stamps his writings, to his predilection for a Christianity that, though of strict obedience, puts the accent on inner piety, as against narrow respect for rites. These principles, it has been said, reappear in the work of Cervantes: in his allusions to divine grace (of very Pauline sensibility), in his more-or-less veiled criticism of displays of hidebound formalism, in his rejection of all intolerance. Here scholars see the "last glimmer of Erasmus" shine forth at a time when Spanish disciples of the Dutchman had completely lost their cause. This thesis, once defended by great minds, attributes a coherent plan to everything in the author of *Don Quixote* that is out of tune with official ideology. Perhaps it would gain something by being refined. Inner piety, which is often made a prerogative of the thinker of Rotterdam, is one of the constants of Franciscan tradition, one that has left its mark on Spain, as Teresa of Avila bears witness. Who knows whether Cervantes—one of whose sisters will enter the Carmelite Order—did not feel its influence? And how much should one attribute, in his reserve and reticence, to what derives strictly from the domain of religious "ideas" and how much to those emotions not subject to the action of the understanding? How, in short, is it possible to capture the spiritual depths of a man who has been dead for almost five centuries and who, unconcerned about revealing his secret ego to us, always hides behind fictional beings? To give a peremptory answer to these questions would be to fall hopelessly into error.

The career of López de Hoyos, vicar of the Madrid parish of San Andrés, poses for the historian fewer puzzles than the exact extent of his intellectual influence. On January 25, 1568, after a competitive examination, he was named rector of the city high school, the *Estudio de la Villa,* which prepared students to enter the university. Founded a century earlier under the aegis of the Catholic Rulers, this municipal secondary school had experienced diverse fortunes since then. Threatened by the arrival of the Jesuits, who intended to make of it a dependency of their own establishment, it had seen its teaching suspended, then restored by some unknown intermediary. López de Hoyos, chosen by a jury of professors from Alcalá and promoted over his fellow competitors not only for his personal qualities but also through the protection of Cardinal Espinosa, inaugurated his teaching career in February. How did Miguel become his pupil? The affectionate mention of which he is the object in the *Relación* cited above does not enlighten us on either the circumstances of his entry into the *Estudio* or on his exact status. Had he taken lessons from the grammarian somewhere else? Does he share the lot of his younger fellow students, though he himself has passed the age of attending school? Do his previous training and his twenty full years qualify him, instead, to be his teacher's assistant? If he does in fact take the courses that López de Hoyos offers, his schooling is going to last less than one year, in any case: he will in fact leave Madrid even before his four poems come off the press. But these four months will be long enough for the humanist to notice and appreciate the future writer; it is for this foresight, rather than for any other reason, that he has passed into posterity.

What can one say about Cervantes' compositions inspired by the premature death of the queen? That they illustrate, certainly, the meters and strophes popular at the time: an epitaph in sonnet form, ten-line *coplas reales,* an elegy. That the readers of the time undoubtedly enjoyed, like López de Hoyos, this model of "very elegant style" and garland of "delicate conceits." That they are, principally, trial runs by an admirer of Garcilaso, the great Spanish poet of the Renaissance—a novice admirer who faces the test of the public. Was he encouraged by his friends and fellow poets? When Miguel comes back from captivity, one of them will greet his return in eloquent terms, proclaiming in a sonnet that "Spain is recovering her long-lost Muses." Whether or not he fulfilled the expectations that his first efforts aroused, it is not until after fifteen years of absence and ordeals that the author of *Don Quixote* will take up his vocation again.

A MYSTERIOUS DEPARTURE

OCTOBER 1568: Miguel de Cervantes is in Madrid, polishing his elegy on the queen's death. December 1569: López de Hoyos' pupil is settled in Rome, three months after the publication of the *Relación* of the funeral. What has happened meanwhile? Why has he given up a life that is, after all, tranquil, and abandoned projects that seemed to be taking shape? Whatever the cause, an unexpected departure, the date of which we do not know and for which nothing permits us to guess the reasons.

Nothing—except for a surprising document discovered in the last century in the archives at Simancas, and which Cervantists have for a long time preferred to ignore. On September 15, 1569, a royal warrant commands the bailiff Juan de Medina to arrest a student accused of having wounded a certain Antonio de Sigura in a duel. Who was the victim? A master mason of peasant origin, probably illiterate, who reappears later supervising royal buildings, though it is impossible to tell whether this mishap favored his promotion or not. As for the accused, who had fled to Seville, he was condemned by default to having his right hand publicly cut off and to banishment from the realm for ten years. His name was Miguel de Cervantes.

The distress of the great man's admirers in the presence of this sword-wielding fugitive from justice is understandable; and one can imagine the arguments advanced to prove that we are dealing with a homonym. Cervantes, once he gets to Rome, will enter Cardinal Acquaviva's service. With such references, how could he have obtained a post? How could he have been recommended by the duke of Sessa and by Don Juan de Austria, at the end of his campaigns? How could he re-enter the service of Philip II after his return from captivity? To these objections, certain scholars less burdened with scruples reply today that time and distance, not to mention influence, must have removed numerous obstacles and permitted the formerly condemned man to recover his lost honor. In the present state of our knowledge, they observe, the Sigura affair, with its repercussions, is the only explanation that one might offer for Miguel's departure of Italy, as well as for the change of course that ensues. This explanation also makes it possible to clarify certain obscure points in his biography: the fact that the detailed certificate that he took the trouble to compile and then presented upon his arrival at Rome stresses his status as an Old Christian but says nothing, contrary to the rule, of his situation with regard to the law; likewise the fact that in his statement of government service, Cervantes untruthfully declares on two occasions that he enlisted as a soldier in 1568. With regard to the recommendations of Don Juan and Sessa, they must have been granted to permit him to take advantage of an amnesty, after his return to Spain. Since this

return does not take place until 1580, the statute of limitations doubtless prevailed, since the ten years of banishment had by then expired:
unless, quite simply, Sigura had pardoned his adversary.

On the basis of this laconic document, biographers have given free
rein to their imaginations. Some have seized upon lines in the *Journey
to Parnassus,* which in veiled language recall a youthful indiscretion,
the consequences of which must have changed the course of the writer's life; some have compared the Sigura incident to analogous episodes
in *The Gallant Spaniard* (El gallardo español) and *Persiles:* in particular
one that shows us a soldier named Saavedra (a family surname that
Cervantes will later assume), also forced to flee to Italy after having
wounded a man in a duel. In order to explain the unusual severity of
the sentence, the encounter is supposed to have taken place under the
colonnade of the royal palace. In order to reconstruct the itinerary
followed by the fugitive, some have appealed to the descriptions scattered throughout the novels and short stories, attributing to them,
under the circumstances, an autobiographical value. After having tried
to embark for the Indies, the author of *Don Quixote* would have left
Seville and would have departed for Valencia, avoiding on the way the
environs of Granada, held by the rebellious Moriscos. He would have
headed north as far as Barcelona, reached Genoa by sea, then turned
south toward the Eternal City. Other biographers prefer to see him
make his way by land, reaching Italy via Languedoc and Provence,
like his heroes Persiles and Sigismunda.

This abundance of exact details is more entertaining than convincing. Let us accept the fact that, even if such incidents will never be
repeated during his lifetime, the surgeon's son drew his sword against
Sigura, at the risk of seeing his right hand cut off—the very same man
who will lose the use of his left hand at Lepanto. Let us also admit
that he fled from the arm of the law: Quevedo and Calderón, though
from a different background, will later experience similar misadventures. But let us leave to the past its share of mystery: just as we know
that there were two Juans and two Rodrigos, perhaps a day will come
when someone will discover that there were two Miguels de Cervantes.

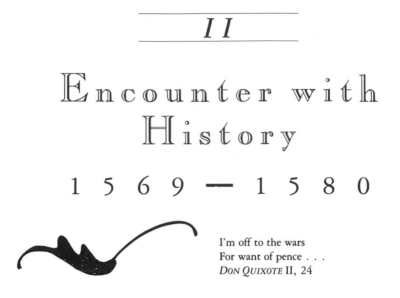

II

Encounter with History

1569 — 1580

I'm off to the wars
For want of pence . . .
Don Quixote II, 24

IN HIS MAJESTY'S SERVICE

WE now see Cervantes on the banks of the Tiber, far from his country and his family, as the Year of Our Lord 1569 draws to a close. What is he doing in the Rome of the Caesars and the popes? If we are to believe a statement that he will insert fifteen years later into the dedication of *Galatea,* he has become the chamberlain of Monsignor Acquaviva, a twenty-three-year-old Italian patrician who will soon receive the cardinal's purple. Acquaviva had come to Madrid the year before to offer Pius V's condolences to the king for the death of Don Carlos; there he made the acquaintance of our hero—or so some have imagined—perhaps through the offices of one of Espinosa's inner circle, and when he returned to Italy in December of 1568, he took Cervantes with him in his entourage. But this hypothesis does not fit with what we know about Miguel's stay. Even if he was not mixed up with the Sigura affair and left Spain on his own free will, it is hard to see why he would have waited until December of 1569 to have his father prepare a purity-of-blood statement. In fact, there is no doubt that he arrived in Rome during the last months of 1569 and entered the prelate's service, recommended perhaps by one of his distant relatives,

Cardinal Gaspar de Cervantes y Gaete. Someone then asked for his references, and on that occasion he must have had to produce the document that we possess.

On December 22, 1569, Rodrigo de Cervantes certifies before Duarte de Acuña, Madrid's *teniente de corregidor* (assistant magistrate), that Miguel was not born a bastard and that there were no Moors, Jews, converts, or persons reconciled by the Holy Office among his ancestors. This is the classic formula that we find in all these purity-of-blood certificates which (as one historian observes) took the place of our identification papers in the Spain of the time. Three witnesses corroborate the surgeon's statement. Their names are already known to us. The first is Alonso Getino de Guzmán, the former actor who had become the organizer of celebrations for Madrid and who is now an officer of the law, since he exercises the function of *alquacil* (bailiff) in the capital. If Miguel is indeed the man who wounded Sigura, then Getino de Guzmán's deposition is curious. Did he, a friend of the Cervantes family for more than eight years, according to his own words, put friendship before the duties of his office? Did he agree to give testimony out of leniency when he offered himself as guarantor of the honorable status of a fugitive from justice? To tell the truth, the *alquacil* limits himself to confirming the contents of Rodrigo's statements without referring to what we would today call Miguel's police record. As for the other two witnesses, Pirro Bocchi and Francesco Musacchi, they are Italian businessmen whom we have already met in the surgeon's circle. It is less surprising to see them appear in this document, because the Bocchi family were bankers at Rome, and their recommendation might be useful to a young man from Madrid on his arrival in the Eternal City.

Did Miguel comply with these formalities without resisting? In *The Dialogue of the Dogs* he gives Cipión hard words about the lords of the earth, who unlike the Lord of Heaven (he tells us) will not hire a servant until they "pick the nits out of his lineage, examine his abilities, observe the neatness of his appearance, and even want to know what clothes he owns." But the situation in which Miguel found himself did not allow him to make objections. Doubtless he took up his duties after the certificate arrived, toward February 1570. In May of the same year, he must have been one of the first to congratulate his master for his elevation to the rank of cardinal. But he does not seem to have remained in his service for long. Was he disappointed by the young prelate? The picture we have of Acquaviva lets us assume the opposite. Was Miguel tired of his new life? What we suspect about his occupation authorizes this supposition: contrary to what people think, the chamberlain in a great house was not his master's secretary, much less his confidant; he was a domestic, mainly, a *valet de chambre,* to be exact (as the etymology of the word suggests and as the handbooks of the time specify). It is possible that Cervantes, occupied with servile tasks most of the time, was admitted into the cardinal's intimate circle occasionally. The dedication to which we alluded above shows him to have been present at conversations between Acquaviva and his friend Ascanio Colonna, the very person to whom *Galatea* will be offered. But this promotion must have made his position even more ambiguous and consequently difficult to endure. This explains the brevity of his allusion to a past of which he might have been proud. It also clarifies the disillusioned words that the constraints of a servant's life inspire in his heroes: "I am not suitable for palaces," says Master Glass, "because I have a conscience and don't know how to flatter." And Don Quixote concludes his praise of freedom with an exclamation that speaks volumes: "Happy the man to whom Heaven has given a crust of bread without the need to be thankful for it to anyone but Heaven itself!" Leaving the marble halls of Rome behind, Cervantes is now going to make another decision: to embrace a military career. Perhaps he believed that his stay in the Acquaviva household would serve as a springboard to better things. If we can believe the page whom Don Quixote meets, "being a servant to the nobility has this advantage: for ensigns or captains often come out of the servants' hall." Unfortunately we know nothing about the circumstances in which he resolved to take this step. The data at our disposal are in fact contradictory. Cervantes' name does not appear on Philip II's army payrolls until 1572. On the other hand, the purity-of-blood inquiries conducted during his captivity in Algiers, in one case, and on his return, in the other, suggest that the future writer must have become a soldier in 1568. Yet all that we know of his activities during that year excludes the possibility that he donned a military uniform. We are forced to conclude that Cervantes and his father wanted to round out the length of his service either to cover up the Sigura affair or simply to give more weight to their request. It was a common practice at the time. Leonor de Cortinas, as we will soon see, will go quite a bit further along this route.

Must we, under these conditions, delay the real beginning of his service by two years? One of the witnesses of the 1578 investigation, Mateo de Santisteban, has Miguel say that at the time of the battle of Lepanto, he had been serving for two years under Diego de Urbina, a famous captain from Guadalajara mentioned in one of the interpolated tales in *Don Quixote*. He must therefore have enlisted in August or September, 1570. The problem is that, at that date, Urbina's company was still in Granada, engaged in the war against the Moriscos, and would not arrive in Italy until a year later. Hence it has been assumed that Cervantes first joined another unit in Naples (which at the time was decimated by a famine), the regiment of Don Alvaro de Sande. This gentleman, it is argued, had perhaps known Rodrigo thirty-five years previously, during the prosperous years in Alcalá. The major objection is that Don Alvaro (who never met our hero, so far as any proof exists) commanded a company of elite recruits, one of the famous *tercios* created earlier by Gonzalo de Córdoba that would make the Spanish infantry so redoubtable until the battle of Rocroi. It is hard to imagine the veterans who made up this unit welcoming into their ranks a greenhorn who we know will never wield the noble pike as they did but will be content with a common harquebus.

Furthermore, it is not yet time for the military preparations that the birth of the Holy League will require the following year. After the failure of the sieges of Orán and Malta in 1564–65, the Turks suspend all important naval operations. They change targets, at the accession of Selim II, Suleiman the Magnificent's successor, and turn toward a more accessible prey, the Venetian possessions of the eastern Mediterranean. In July 1570, they disembark on Cyprus, the most distant of the Venetian outposts, the most difficult to defend. But this invasion of a den of Christian corsairs who harass the maritime communications of the Ottoman Empire at first arouses only delaying tactics on the part of the Serenissima. Pope Pius V, who is disturbed by Islam's advance, urges Venice to become the spearhead of a confederation of Christian states; but she would prefer to come to an understanding with an adversary who at the end of a thirty-four-year peace remains her principal commercial partner. Inferior in resources and, even more, in manpower, handicapped by the over-extension of her bases of operations from the Adriatic to Asia Minor, dependent on wheat from the North Sea and spices from the East, she is anxious to re-establish good-neighborly relations with the Turk in order to preserve her essential interests.

After September, however, the extent of Turkish successes achieved on Cyprus makes the Venetians doubt the sultan's desire for peace. The idea of an anti-Turkish league is proposed in a formal pact with Spain and the Holy See. Philip II, freed from the cares of the Morisco war in Granada, calmed by the duke of Alba's victories in the Low Countries, assured of the financial support of his clergy, immediately approves it in principle; this leaves him free to broaden, at the proper moment, its objectives. But Venice, directly threatened, intends to impose her conditions. The negotiations drag on until the moment when the season is already too far gone to organize an effective response. The ill-prepared, ill-directed expedition sent in haste to relieve the island turns back after an abortive attempt at a diversionary action on Rhodes. While Famagusta, the last Cypriot bastion, valiantly resists the Turks' assaults, it is necessary to wait until spring returns in order finally to see the projected treaty conceived by the pontiff take form. On May 20, 1571, after the failure of negotiations with the enemy, Venice gives her assent to the establishment of the Holy League. She signs a three-year offensive and defensive pact with her allies and decides with them to begin assembling an armada, the command of which will be entrusted to Don Juan de Austria. A few days later, in order to provide the new admiral with all the resources of the Spanish possessions in Italy, Philip names Cardinal Granvelle viceroy of Naples.

In conclusion: even if Cervantes stated at Lepanto that he had previously fought on several occasions, as one of the witnesses at the first inquest says, we must take this secondhand declaration with caution, since it was made for a special purpose. It seems unlikely that the crisis of the summer of 1570 could have stirred up our hero's military vocation or could have led him, as some have assumed, to take part in the tragic campaign on Cyprus. One cannot infer, from the very free recreation of the capture of Nicosia by the Turks that *The Generous Suitor* (El amante liberal) offers us, that Cervantes found himself in the fighting. On the other hand, the events of the following spring had considerable repercussions in Catholic Europe. In Italy, they roused popular enthusiasm and caused a mass troop-levy, each village promising to send its contingent. In Spain, numerous men set out under the standards of Don Juan de Austria, prominent among them Pedro Laínez and López Maldonado, whom we have seen frequenting the same coteries as the author of *Don Quixote*. Other writers who will later become his friends took the same road: Rey de Artieda, Cristóbal de Virués. Even more significant: his own brother Rodrigo also lands in Italy in July 1571, with Diego de Urbina's company. Since it is precisely under Urbina's orders that the two brothers will fight at Lepanto, there is every reason to imagine Miguel meeting his younger brother in Naples that July and, inspired by his example, donning the showy garb that made people describe Spanish soldiers as "popinjays." A noble decision, assuredly, but one which we may suspect was dictated by need as well as by the call to glory. It is not surprising at a time when (as the Captive's father aptly recalls) an *hidalgo* had only three choices for a career: *iglesia o mar o casa real,* meaning entry into the religious orders, emigrating to the Indies, or His Majesty's service.

Before joining Rodrigo, Miguel probably spent more than eighteen months in Rome. It is not until after Lepanto that he will make the prolonged sojourn in Naples about which he speaks with such fervor in *The Journey to Parnassus.* It would be interesting, certainly, to learn what became of him after he left Acquaviva's palace. What were his pursuits at that time? What patrons did he find to support him in his need? So many questions remain unanswered! The indirect testimony of Cervantine fictions offers us, certainly, impressions of Italy that we will examine at the proper time; but it tells us nothing, or almost nothing, of the ex-chamberlain's daily existence. The only points of reference that we have are the events that occur in the Mediterranean at the moment when, having become a soldier of Philip II, the author of *Don Quixote* mounts the stage of history. His destiny, like that of his comrades in arms, is henceforth mixed up with that of the Holy League, toward which we will now turn our attention.

A SOLDIER AT LEPANTO

DON JUAN DE AUSTRIA, supreme commander of the league as of May 25, left Spain on July 20. He arrived at Naples on August 8, 1571, after putting in briefly at Genoa. His takeover of command six days later provided an excuse for an imposing ceremony. Cervantes, lost in the crowd, was surely present at it. On August 23, the Spanish squadron, with Juan Andrea Doria and Alvaro de Bazán at its head, set sail for Messina. There it joined Roman and Venetian contingents under the respective commands of Sebastiano Veniero and Marco Antonio Colonna, the father of Ascanio Colonna, to whom *Galatea* will be dedicated. Time had come for the united forces to review their troops before going to meet the Turk.

The armada assembled in the great Sicilian port is impressive: 208 galleys, 57 frigates—more than 300 vessels in all. And more than 80,000 men aboard: sailors, galley slaves, soldiers, auxiliaries, among whom are 26,000 combatants. All the ships, therefore, must be in perfect condition. The Spaniards make a good show, thanks to ten years of ceaseless rearmament; but the Venetians, suffering from their recent reverses, parade a row of galleys in very poor shape: some because of battle damage, others because they have just come from the ship-yards. An aggravating circumstance is that the Venetian soldiers are mercenaries, whose quality leaves something to be desired. Don Juan is going to have to deploy all his energies in order to fill the gaps and make a homogeneous whole of this ill-assorted fleet. He orders the Spaniards to reinforce the Venetian ships and man them with seasoned troops. By an irony of fate, one of Don Juan's subordinates, Don Pedro Portocarrero, is indirectly mixed up in the affairs of the Cervantes family. While the father is preparing to do his duty, his two sons Alonso and Pedro, still in Madrid, maintain close relations with two of Miguel's sisters: Andrea, rich in experience acquired with Ovando and Locadelo, and Magdalena, the youngest, who in spite of her six-teen springs already seems to be following in the footsteps of her elder sister. Alonso (who is married) is going to give two substantial gifts to his mistress, in August and in September, in the presence of a notary. They remind us of the liberal sums granted by Locadelo two years earlier—except that these payments are going to be the cause of a financial imbroglio and that Alonso, unlike the rich Italian, will be able at the opportune moment to evade his commitments.

Diego de Urbina, aboard the galley *Marquesa* with his men, is among those who are going to lend assistance to the Venetians. Like her sister ships, the *Marquesa* is a fast, streamlined craft more than one hundred and thirty feet long but no more than sixteen feet wide, designed for grappling. Fifty of these vessels, someone has observed, would fit eas-ily on the flight deck of a modern aircraft carrier. Onto this narrow vessel, surmounted by two castles, fore and aft, overshadowed by its two masts and mainsail, with thirty or forty banks of oars arranged on each side and taking up little space, are crammed more than four hundred individuals, in deplorable conditions of crowding and filth: two hundred rowers, captives or galley slaves for the most part; about thirty sailors engaged in navigation and upkeep; and finally about two hundred soldiers, among them a harquebusier of recent date who will one day write *Don Quixote*. No doubt the spectacle made a deep impression on the novice. He will remember, all his life—like Don Quixote and Sancho on the Bay of Barcelona—the rowers chained to their benches, attentive to the boatswain's pipe and exposed to the blows of his lash.

In early September, just when everything is in order, the fleet of the Holy League must wait out a storm that confines it to port. It finally leaves Messina on September 16. Don Juan directs his forces toward the Ionian islands, determined to seek out the enemy, whose squadron has harassed the estuaries of the Adriatic all summer and is attempting to catch its breath in the anchorages of the Peloponnesus. On September 26, the admiral puts in at Corfu, the "impregnable island," which has just repulsed an Ottoman raid with great difficulty. On the morning of October 6, he enters the Gulf of Corinth and comes within sight of the channel of Lepanto. Cervantes, aboard his galley, has approached the mythical shores once sung by Homer. North of the Ionian islands, he contemplated the imposing mass of the Acroceraunian mountains; off Corfu, he may have sighted Ithaca. But let us not imagine him dreaming of Ulysses' adventures in the romantic pose of Byron or Lamartine. Shaking with fever, he lies on a vermin-infested pallet in a space below decks that serves as infirmary: since the call at Corfu, seasickness and malaria have overwhelmed him.

The allied high command has just learned of the capture of Famagusta and the massacres perpetrated on that occasion by the Turks. Meanwhile, the squadron's lookouts have located the position of the enemy fleet, commanded by Ali Pasha and lurking twelve miles away, in the deep waters of the Lepanto channel. Opinions differ on what action to take. Don Juan decides to attack, against the advice of Andrea Doria, who favors a simple show of force. Ali Pasha resolves to come out of his lair. At dawn on Sunday the seventh, St. Mark's Day, the two fleets are in sight of each other. Deployed in combat order, they will advance slowly towards each other, banners to the wind, amid the flash of weapons and breastplates and the discordant concert of fifes, cymbals, and drums. In the course of a final inspection conducted aboard a swift frigate, the supreme commander exhorts his men, promising pardon to the galley slaves if there is victory; then, returning to the flagship, he and his men kneel to receive the papal blessing granted by Pius V. At midday, the first exchange of cannon fire signals the start of the battle.

The Ottoman right wing, relying on its knowledge of the channel's depths, tries to cut off the Venetians on their left and to drive them back toward the middle of the gulf. Supported by strong fire from the heavy galleasses, the heroic resistance of the Christians succeeds in limiting the effects of the maneuver. From the opposite side, in the middle of the waters, Doria's squadron takes on the forces of Euldj Ali, the *beylerbey* (provincial governor) of Algiers, a remarkable seaman, who launches a courageous attack and seizes the flagship of the Knights of Malta. His offensive is countered, not without loss; and it is the Venetian galleys on the left wing of the allied fleet that bear the brunt and return the best shots. Among them is the *Marquesa,* where Cervantes is fighting.

How does our harquebusier, whom we left on his sickbed, behave? The testimony of his comrades is explicit: in spite of his fever, he presented himself on the bridge before the engagement began; and, in response to his captain and his friends, who told him to take cover, since he was sick and in no condition to fight, he exclaimed

> that he would rather die fighting for God and his king than to go below deck and look after his health [. . .]; and so [. . .] he fought like a valiant soldier against the aforesaid Turks in the aforesaid battle, by the launch berth, as his captain had ordered him to do.

The launch emplacement, located at the front of the ship, was a particularly exposed combat post in case of grappling. Of Cervantes' courage there is not the least doubt. Nor did he retreat when, taking advantage of the favorable wind, the Holy League's troops in the center took their turn to attack. Don Juan's galleys, having removed the rams from their prows (which permitted a less constricted and more effective firing), throw themselves upon the enemy. Thereafter, any group tactics are impossible. The engagement is nothing less than a gigantic hand-to-hand combat that will throw together sixty thousand soldiers. "The battle was at that moment so bloody and horrible," writes an eyewitness, "that you would have said the sea and the fire were but a single thing." Marked by a succession of spectacular frontal attacks—Don Juan's galley will barely escape an assault by the Janissaries—it will be decided by frightful carnage.

Did our hero take part in a boarding action? Did he experience the anguish of the soldier that Don Quixote describes, standing on two feet of space, ready to leap from the prow of the attacking ship, with no other alternative to the enemy's blows than a mortal fall into waves red with blood? Judging by the losses—forty dead, including the captain himself, and more than one hundred and twenty wounded—the *Marquesa* seems instead to have endured the repeated assaults of the Turks. It is during these attacks that Cervantes will receive the three harquebus wounds that will remain in his opinion his greatest claim to glory. Two bullets struck him in the breast, the third rendered his left hand useless. This wound may look ugly, he will proudly say later, but

> he considers it beautiful, because he received it on the most memorable and exalted occasion that bygone ages ever saw or coming ages hope to see, fighting under the conquering banners of the son of that thunderbolt of war, Charles V, of blessed memory.

And in the twilight of his life, he will go further:

> If today someone should offer to do the impossible for me, I would still choose to have taken part in that prodigious action rather than to be healed of my wounds and not to have taken part in it.

And so is born *el manco de Lepanto* ("the one-handed veteran of Lepanto"), at the very moment when the fate of the battle begins to incline in favor of the allies, thanks to the superiority of the Spanish infantry. The death of Ali Pasha, wounded by a harquebus bullet and beheaded by a captive with a hatchet-blow, appears to mark the turning point of the battle. The defection of Euldj Ali's Berber galleys in the thick of the fight, then the revolt of ten thousand Christian galley slaves aboard the Turkish vessels, are going to hasten the outcome. By four in the afternoon the enemy defeat is consummated. The victors begin the pillage that will last until nightfall. The list of Ottoman losses is long: 110 ships destroyed or sunk, 130 captured, 30,000 men killed or wounded, nearly 15,000 slaves freed. The allies pay a no-less-heavy tribute to victory; for 12,000 of their men disappear in the fighting, including those who die as a result of their wounds. It is fortunate for us that Cervantes was not among their number.

The announcement of the news will call forth an explosion of joy in all the West, and its repercussions will be immense. All artists, all poets, will want to celebrate the naval battle *par excellence*. We have lost the play that it inspired in Cervantes after his return from Algiers. But one of the most beautiful pages from *Don Quixote* is the brief account of the engagement given by Ruy Pérez de Viedma, captured by Euldj Ali in the midst of the fighting: by mixing the glorious memory of the victory with the bitter memory of captivity, his description rises above the pieces of cold eloquence that Lepanto has too often inspired. In a different vein, in oral tradition, an entire florilegium of anecdotes attests to the legendary aura that quickly surrounded the event. People recall even today the miraculous presentiment of Pius V, who interrupts an audience to give thanks to the Lord of Hosts at the very instant the two fleets come together. And historians often quote the Gospel phrase with which he greets Don Juan: *Fuit homo missus a Deo, cui nomen erat Joannes* ("There was a man sent from God, whose name was John"). They also recall, by contrast, the stony expression of Philip II, who learned of the victory during the office for All Saints and sat emotionless until the final *Te Deum*. Quick to laugh at these anecdotes, following Voltaire's example, historians of the last century stressed instead the opportunities lost in the days after the "prodigious action": Veniero's immediate return to Venice, depriving Don Juan of any hope of pursuing the Turks to the Dardanelles; the reconstitution, starting the next year, of an Ottoman armada comparable to the one that had just been reduced to nothing; the failure of two new maritime expeditions launched by Philip II's half-brother; the separate peace treaty signed by the Most Serene Republic. Had the mountain given birth to a mouse? Such is not the opinion of the Captive, for whom an essential objective was achieved on that glorious day in October 1571:

> [On] that day, which was so fortunate for Christendom, all the nations of the earth were disabused of their error in imagining the Turks to be invincible on sea—on that day, I say [. . .], Ottoman pride and arrogance were broken . . .

This is exactly the opinion of Fernand Braudel, whose work has restated the problem in new terms. Even if the Holy League did not survive the pontiff who imposed it and who will die six months later, even if

Ottoman naval power was not destroyed, it was, he believes, the myth of Turkish invincibility that sank with all hands at Lepanto. Henceforth Spanish galleys will become bolder and show themselves everywhere on the sea instead of entrusting their safety to the cannon of Corfu, Malta, and Messina. In the theater of maritime operations, Turkish expansionism marks time; Christian Europe takes the initiative.

The facts remain, however, that Europe was unable to exploit its advantage and that the obliteration of the Ottoman fleet is matched by the disappearance of Europe's own fleets. Soon the day will come when naval engagements will desert the Mediterranean and when the Mediterranean itself will disappear from the foreground of history. But for the moment, the West has lived out its last dream of a Crusade. Cervantes shared this dream intensely; before long, he will awaken from it.

IN THE WAKE OF A VICTORY

ON the evening of October 7, the hero who had revealed himself on the bridge of the *Marquesa* is in no condition to deduce lessons from the event. He is simply a wounded man racked by fever again, being cared for with the means on board by the surgeons of the period, wondering whether he is going to increase the number of the dead. Attended by his brother, Cervantes sees the victorious fleet once again en route to Corfu. After the division of the booty, the Venetian galleys head north, in an oblique line, in the direction of the Adriatic; Don Juan de Austria with the main body of his forces turns toward his bases. On October 31, after having endured the first storm of fall, the supreme commander receives at Messina the reception he might have expected. That same day, Miguel enters the city hospital with his companions in misfortune.

In that grim place, which has nothing in common with our modern hospitals but the name, he will gradually recover from his wounds. His convalescence lasts several months, while Don Juan, following his brother's instructions, settles into his winter quarters in Sicily, cold and bored as he waits for the return of spring. One would like to imagine the author of *Don Quixote* allowing himself to dream, read, write poetry, if the deplorable sanitary conditions where he finds himself, the lack of privacy imposed on him, relief from his suffering, leave him the strength for it. One pictures the supreme commander at his bedside, come to show his concern for those wounded at Lepanto. Does Cervantes deserve the congratulations of *"señor* Don Juan," who according to one of the witnesses at the first inquest was informed of Miguel's brilliant conduct and increased his salary by four ducats? Does the admiral reward him with a few words of cheer? Only one thing is certain: between January and March 1572, on three occasions, Miguel receives, like his comrades, a grant of twenty ducats, the price of the care that has been administered to him.

When he leaves the hospital on April 24, Cervantes apparently no longer suffers from the two harquebus shots that had struck him in the breast. But he has lost the use of his left hand. Nevertheless, he returns to active duty. Perhaps it is at this time that he is promoted to *soldado aventajado*—elite trooper—with a monthly salary of three ducats; perhaps he also joins, until the end of winter, Diego de Urbina's company, which during that period is bivouacked in Calabria. But before long he is transferred to the command of a different captain, Don Manuel Ponce de León, who belongs to one of Don Lope de Figueroa's *tercios.* This change of assignment is recorded among the preparations for a new campaign—preparations which, to tell the truth, drag on indefinitely. The death of Pius V on May 1, at the age of sixty-eight, effectively deprives the Holy League of its principal mover. The new pontiff, Gregory XIII, vainly declares himself ready to carry on the work begun; but the allies no longer have the indispensable arbiter of their differences that his predecessor had been. What is more, this unfortunate state is aggravated by the hesitation of Philip II: the Prudent King, worried by the flare-up of troubles in Flanders and by the spread of Barbary piracy, is reluctant to launch against the Turks an offensive that will leave their vassals unpunished. With the backing of the Italians, the supreme commander manages to overcome all resistance. On July 7, 1572, the allied vanguard, 140 galleys strong, under the command of Marco Antonio Colonna, leaves Messina. Cervantes appears among the soldiers who ship out with it. On August 2, Don Juan finally receives from his half brother, reassured by the duke of Alba's victories, authorization to assume command again. But when he reaches Corfu eight days later with 65 galleys, his lieutenant commander has already headed south without waiting for him. Marco Antonio has gone in search of the enemy, disturbed by the ravages inflicted by the Turk. He encounters Euldj Ali southeast of the Peloponnesus but is unable to maintain contact, out-maneuvered by the skillful Turk, and he must return to his base.

It is not until September 1 that the two allied squadrons, reunited at last, set sail for Modon, off the southwest of the peninsula. It is already too late to carry out the plan conceived by Don Juan: to blockade by land and by sea the Turks that have retreated to the Gulf of Navarino and force them to surrender. To understand the reasons for its failure, let us listen to the Captive once more:

> The following year, which was the year seventy-two, I found myself at Navarino rowing in the leading galley with the three lanterns [i.e., the flagship]. There I saw how the opportunity of capturing the whole Turkish fleet in port was lost; for all the marines and Janissaries that belonged to it were sure that they were about to be attacked inside the very harbor. They had their kits and *pasamaques,* or shoes, ready to flee at once on shore without waiting to be attacked, in so great fear did they stand of our fleet. But Heaven ordered it otherwise, not for any fault or neglect of the general who commanded on our side, but for the sins of Christendom and because it was God's will and pleasure that we should always have instruments of punishment to chastise us. As it was, [Euldj Ali] took refuge at Modon, which is an island near Navarino, and, landing his forces, fortified the mouth of the harbor and waited quietly until Don Juan retired.

This imaginary eyewitness account, seen from the enemy camp, permits the author of *Don Quixote* to give us his feelings about this sad affair. In the 1590 petition in which he recalls his periods of service, he will limit himself to indicating his presence at Navarino, the year after Lepanto. But under the cloak of fiction, he openly criticizes the way the expedition was conceived and carried out, cautiously softening his statements by references to the will of Heaven.

On October 7, the anniversary of Lepanto, the heavy autumn rains force the Christian fleet to leave these inhospitable latitudes and retire to Zante. Only Alvaro de Bazán will save his honor by seizing, with his galley *La Loba* (She-Wolf), the vessel called *La Presa,* commanded by Barbarossa's grandson. Ruy Pérez de Viedma has left us a gripping account of the corsair's death:

> The [grand-] son of Barbarossa was so cruel and treated his slaves so badly that when those who were at the oars saw that the *She-Wolf* galley was

bearing down upon them and gaining upon them, they all at once dropped their oars. They seized their captain who stood on the stage at the end of the gangway shouting to them to row hard, and they passed him on from bench to bench, from the poop to the prow, biting him, so that before he had got much past the mast, his soul had already gone to hell.

Let us not conclude as some have done that Cervantes participated in this seizure. But we can wager that the man who will one day analyze this abortive campaign so lucidly was, during those weeks, an attentive observer of the vicissitudes that marked it.

When Colonna's galleys leave the main body of the fleet on October 29, in order to return to Civitavecchia, Don Juan returns to Messina. From there he departs for Naples, where he will make his winter quarters, in conformity with orders from the king of Spain. It is there that on February 11, then on March 6, 1573, he authorizes two pay orders, in the sum of thirty *escudos,* for Cervantes. Did he wish to reward him for brave conduct at Navarino? We would need to know whether our hero took part in the landing operation: his wounds, scarcely healed, would not have allowed him to hold a harquebus and put himself, as at Lepanto, on the front line. The draft for the two payments suggests, instead, back pay, deposited with the delay habitual in the accounting services of Philip II's armies. With regard to the garrison life that he may have led during these months of inactivity, it remains wrapped in mystery.

With the return of spring, it is not long before Miguel becomes active again. This time the allies arrange a rendezvous at Corfu as early as April 15, in order to undertake without delay a campaign that they hope will be decisive. Several weeks before that date, however, Venice secretly signs a separate peace treaty with the sultan, to whom she cedes Cyprus. On April 4, she makes the official announcement of it to her indignant allies. As the Captive accurately observes, the treaty came in response to Venice's wishes even more than to her adversary's. This about-face—called treason by Spanish historians—is explained by the heavy sacrifices suffered by the Serenissima during the last three years, by the weight of her commercial interests, and finally by the uncertain outcome of the conflict to which she had committed herself on the initiative of Pius V.

Yet when all is said, this defection could not but please Philip II, who had no desire to see his galleys venture beyond Corfu every year, far from their Italian bases, with the sole object of defending the Venetian frontier. His principal concern is not the Turkish squadron but the Barbary privateering that is increasing its raids on the coasts of Spain and Italy and is filling the *bagnios*—slave prisons—of North Africa: Christian captives "rained on Algiers," a petition of the time tells us. But regular operations against the corsairs are rarely effective; they are above all very expensive, since they require a permanent fleet the maintenance of which comes to more than four million ducats per annum. The recruitment of rowers, necessary in greater numbers as ships become faster, is said to be harder day by day. The obvious conclusion: a blow at the enemy's head, by seizing the pirates' den from which the raiding parties sally forth. But which one? For Alvaro de Bazán—as once for Charles V, as for Cervantes a little later—the choice is clear: Algiers. Don Juan, on his own, argues for a different objective: Tunis. To this recommendation the king finally throws his support. In the sovereign's mind it is a matter of a limited operation aimed at restoring a faithful vassal, Muley Hamida, dethroned three years earlier by Euldj Ali. By this means, the fortress at La Goleta, occupied since 1535, will be protected; and by this means a decisive blow at Algiers can be more easily dealt, when the time comes. Don Juan, on the other hand, cherishes an entirely different dream: to carve out for himself a kingdom on the flanks of the Maghreb, two steps from Malta and from Sicily; to assume the crown to which he aspires— this royal bastard to whom his half brother obstinately refuses the title of "highness." A dream which certainly does not enter into the plans of the Prudent King.

Three months of haggling will be necessary for the supreme commander to make his point of view prevail. It will take another three to assemble the 170 ships and 20,000 soldiers necessary for the operation. Starting from Messina, with calls at Palermo and Trapani, the Spanish galleys finally sight the Tunisian coast. On October 8, 1573, the day after the second anniversary of Lepanto, Don Juan orders his forces to land. The rest is nothing but a triumphal march: the entry into Tunis, deserted by its inhabitants; the naming of a Muslim governor, Muley Mohammed; the capture of Bizerta: everything is in order in less than a week. On October 24, Philip II's half brother departs for Sicily. But instead of dismantling the forts, as the king had commanded, he strengthens their defenses, putting La Goleta in the charge of Don Pedro Portocarrero, whose two sons are still involved with the Cervantes sisters.

Miguel, for once, is going to escape misfortune. Instead of remaining behind with the garrison in the fortress, he embarks with Don Lope de Figueroa's soldiers. He will perhaps spend part of the winter in Sardinia, where the *tercio* with which he serves is posted. But his name appears twice, at Naples, on the Treasury books: in February and March 1574, he receives sixty *escudos,* in two payments, for his good and loyal service. In May he proceeds to Genoa with the squadrons from Naples and Sicily.

Don Juan, who is striving to obtain the title of king of Tunis from the pope, has been sent by Philip II to Lombardy on the pretext of putting a stop to French intrigues in the north of Italy. During this time, the Turks are preparing their revenge. On July 11, a fleet of 240 vessels, with 40,000 soldiers aboard, appears before Tunis under the command of Euldj Ali and Sinan Pasha. It is the last important operation that the Sublime Porte will conduct in the western Mediterranean. The defenders of the forts, inferior in numbers, capitulate on August 25. Tunis surrenders in turn, on September 13. Informed of the danger, Don Juan begs Granvelle, vainly, for assistance that the king, dealing with a grave financial crisis, is in no condition to grant. Leaving from La Spezia in great haste, he calls at Naples on August 7; but scarcely have his galleys put out to sea when he runs into two storms, one after the other, and finds himself blocked in the port of Trapani, in Sicily, where he will learn of the disaster. There is nothing for him to do but return to Palermo, where he lands on October 16. Cervantes participated in this sad escapade. Perhaps he learned after his return that Acquaviva had given up the ghost in late July at Rome, barely twenty-six years old.

In his petition of 1590, Miguel has left us a laconic reference to the events that he experienced: after Navarino, he states in substance, "I was present at Tunis and at La Goleta." In contrast, the Captive in the novella interpolated in *Don Quixote* is far more eloquent. In his account, he does not limit himself to telling us what happened between the October 1573 expedition and the catastrophe that occurred in August of the following year. He devotes two sonnets to the fall of the fortress, mourning, in passing, the heavy losses incurred on that occasion. He alludes to the tragic fate suffered by the principal defenders of La Goleta, especially Don Pedro Portocarrero—a "wretched soldier" in Don Juan's opinion—who was made prisoner by the Turks and died of grief on the way to Constantinople. He finally extracts the lesson of that badly managed operation. Certain people, he tells us, maintain that it would have been possible to save the fortress even if it had not received help:

> But many thought, and I thought so too, that it was a special mercy and favor which Heaven showed to Spain in permitting the destruction of that source and hiding place of mischief, that devourer, sponge, and moth of incalculable sums, uselessly wasted there to no other purpose except preserving the memory of its capture by the invincible Charles V. As if to make that eternal, as it is and will be, these stones were needed to support it!

Clearly Cervantes does not wish to cite those at fault by name. But in the final reckoning, and from his lofty vantage point, he approves abandoning a place without true strategic value and the liquidation, however painful it may be, of a utopian and useless conquest. So Philip II, whose conduct is not questioned here, also reasoned, whatever commentators may have said to the contrary. Ultimately, Don Juan was responsible for the disaster. If Miguel remains ever faithful to his memory, his admiration is not blind, and he can, on occasion, point out Don Juan's mistakes.

Miguel will spend the whole autumn in Sicily. On November 15, 1574, he is still at Palermo, where he receives another pay order, in the sum of twenty-five *escudos*. A valuable detail: the pay order mentions for the first time his rank as a *soldado aventajado,* and it is signed by the duke of Sessa. The lord of Cabra, former patron of Juan de Cervantes and of his son Andrés, has been in fact since the spring of 1572 the supreme commander's adjutant. He supports Don Juan but also strives when necessary to moderate his enthusiasm. No doubt he is charged with spying on Don Juan discreetly. With the return of winter, and as Miguel, still under Figueroa's orders, is leaving Palermo for Naples (where he rejoins Rodrigo), Don Juan reaches Madrid, to give the king an explanation of the Tunis affair. Don Juan will not return to Italy until June of the following year, with the title of lieutenant general, but without the princely dignity of which he dreamed. That summer, the galleys of Spain will not leave on campaign against the Turk. For Cervantes, the hour is near when he must say good-bye to the soldier's life and face the harshest trial he is ever to experience: captivity. At least he will take with him, when he leaves Naples, a rich vision of that Italy whose presence permeates his works. The time has come to examine it closely.

IMPRESSIONS OF ITALY

IF Italy left its mark on Cervantes, it is first and foremost because of
the amount of time he spent there. He was not an isolated case, in
that respect. In a century when almost all of Italy (with the exceptions
of Venice, Savoy, and the Papal States) was a Spanish possession,
gentlemen and magistrates, sailors and soldiers, clerics and students,
tramps and vagabonds, flocked from Barcelona, Valencia, Cartagena,
fascinated by its brilliant civilization, attracted by a way of life unknown
in Castile, lured by the easy living offered to its denizens. But where
our hero stands out among his compatriots is in the diversity of his
Italian experiences, a diversity growing out of the vicissitudes he experienced beginning with his arrival at Rome and, to an even greater
extent, out of the comings and goings that his military campaigns and
the succession of quarters force upon him. His service record tells us
nothing about this splintered, fragmented stay. We have to appeal to
the oblique testimony of his fictional works. Among them, the *Journey
to Parnassus* has always held the interest of biographers. Though it is
imaginary, this burlesque escapade, which takes the poet from his
hovel in Madrid to Apollo's sanctuary, surprises the reader with the
impression of actual experience that emanates from it. The memories
of scenery from Genoa to Messina that it stirs are no less convincing.
But the *Journey to Parnassus* is not a travel diary; it is a spiritual testament, with an air of autobiography.

The biographical implications that one can extract from *Galatea,*
the *Exemplary Novellas,* and *Persiles,* which are more abundant and varied, demand the same cautious analysis. Between the soldier from
Lepanto's wanderings and the aging writer's transposition of them,
there is not only a time-lapse that is occasionally as much as forty
years; there is also the weight of literary influences and conventions,
the element of novelistic elaboration, the point of view of the characters and the bias that it implies. It is not the lover of real experiences
but the perceptive reader of Boccaccio and the *novellieri* who places the
action of *The Man Who Was Too Curious for His Own Good* (El curioso
impertinente) at Florence and the adventures of *Signora Cornelia* (La
señora Cornelia) at Bologna, makes *The Generous Suitor* a native of Trapani, and sends the hero of *The Call of Blood* (La fuerza de la sangre) to
Naples. With regard to the description of Italian cities that are one of

the ornaments of *Master Glass* (El licenciado Vidriera), they are not
the curious traveler's unretouched descriptions of what he liked; they
are in fact bravura passages that conform to contemporary rhetorical
canons. Examples are the accounts of Genoa, where Tomás Rodaja
observes its "admirable beauty" and houses that seem "set into the
cliffs like diamonds in gold," and his praise of Florence, which enchants
him "not only because of its agreeable site but for its cleanness, its
sumptuous buildings, its cool river, and its peaceful streets." These
are skillfully joined recollections whose symbolic function constantly
shows through and which put before the reader a series of emblems,
not a succession of settings.

It would nevertheless be an insult to this stylized Italy to reduce the
details of its composition to a gathering of commonplaces. If Italy
appears so often as a backdrop for the novellas, it is mainly because
she is the place par excellence for adventure, where Miguel had experienced his own with particular intensity before his characters also felt
her call. Hence certain pages, which are so close to us, quiver with
life. Even in *Galatea,* dependent upon pastoral conventions, we experience with Timbrio his astonishment before the Ligurian Riviera,
"full of elegant gardens, white houses, and shining spires that, when
struck by the sun's rays, reflect such intense rays that one can scarcely
look at them." But where the author's voice breaks through most clearly
is in the seductive picture that the captain paints for Master Glass,
when he catalogues the charms of military life:

> He praised the way soldiers live; painted a lifelike picture of the beauties
> of Naples, the easy ways of Palermo, the wealth of Milan, the feasts of
> Lombardy, the splendid meals in the inns; he sketched for him pleasantly
> and accurately the "*aconcha,* innkeeper," "come here, *manigoldo,*" "bring
> on the *macatela, li polastri, e li macarroni.*" He praised the soldier's free life
> and easy living in Italy to the skies . . .

The persuasive speech of an old trooper in search of recruits? Certainly.
But behind the captain's glibness one senses the nostalgia of a Cervantes still on the road, who has rediscovered the "shabbiness" and
"discomforts" of the inns and taverns of Spain but can still hear the
inflections of Dante's language and taste the flavor of Italy's foods and
the bouquet of her wines:

The smoothness of Trebbiano, the vigor of Montefiascone, the strength of Asperino, the nobility of the two Greek wines from Candia and Samos, the greatness of Cinque Vignole, the sweetness and pleasantness of "my lady" Guarnaccia, the countrified flavor of La Centola . . .

Nostalgia for a refined civilization, of course, but also for the *dolce vita italiana* that offers to a foreigner capable of appreciating them an infinite gamut of seductions.

Two significant moments marked his stay. First, his arrival in Rome. The majestic spectacle of the Eternal City will inspire the pilgrims in *Persiles* with one of the most beautiful sonnets embedded in the novel; and it also awakens in Tomás Rodaja, the licentiate made of glass, a thoroughly sane admiration:

He visited her churches, worshipped her relics, and admired her great size; just as one comes to know the size and ferocity of a lion by the size of his claws, so he deduced the size of [ancient] Rome by its fragmented marbles, statues partial and entire, its broken arches and demolished baths, its magnificent porticoes and great amphitheaters, its famous and sacred river, always filled to its banks with water [. . . ,] its bridges, which seem to look at one another, and by its streets, that with their names alone assume authority over the streets of all the other cities in the world: the Via Appia, Flaminia, Giulia, and others of that sort.

One thinks of Du Bellay's examination of Rome's antiquities. Rodaja's scrutiny becomes tinged with discreet irony when he turns his gaze from the city of the Caesars to the city of the popes:

He also noted the splendor of the College of Cardinals, the majesty of the Supreme Pontiff, the concourse and variety of peoples and nations. He saw everything, noted everything, and put everything in its proper perspective. And after having visited the seven churches, made his confession to a penitentiary, and kissed His Holiness's foot, loaded down with Agnus-Dei [seals] and rosaries, he decided to go to Naples . . .

Is it Erasmus's disciple, hostile to the practices of superstitious devotion, who uses Tomás's visit as a pretext for this sly dig? Likelier, perhaps, Acquaviva's ex-chamberlain, who still remembers the intrigues of the Vatican.

But it is undoubtedly the sum of his experiences while living in

Naples "for more than a year" that marked Miguel most strongly. Rodaja will bluntly say about the capital of Spanish Italy—"by the seashore" and "crowned by castles and towers"—that she is "in his opinion and in the opinion of all who have seen her, the best city in Europe, indeed the world." This enthusiasm is understandable if one assumes that of all the Italian cities, Naples reserved the warmest welcome for Cervantes. There he felt the excitement that the birth of the Holy League stirred up. There he also tasted the peace of the winter months between two campaigns. There, in all probability, he was able to break out of the routine of garrison life with amusements besides taverns and courtesans. Otherwise, it is difficult to comprehend the melancholy recollection of that stay found in the *Journey to Parnassus* and the keen disappointment that he will experience half a century later when the count of Lemos, named viceroy of Naples, does not take him along, after encouraging his hopes.

Ought one to go further and date from this epoch an unhappy love affair that seems to have left a bitter memory? Some scholars detect allusions to a betrayal by a mysterious Silena in the statements of Lauso, one of the shepherds in *Galatea,* behind whom (they say) the writer may be hiding. Lauso recalls Silena in his sorrowful stanzas. Other scholars even suppose that a child was born of this liaison, the same person that Miguel, in the *Journey to Parnassus,* sees appear in a dream in Naples and whom he greets with emotion:

> And then, with hesitation, there approached
> A friend called Promontorio—a young man
> In years but a great man in the soldier's craft.
> My wonder grew to find I was in Naples,
> Beyond all doubt . . .
> My friend embraced me with affection, and
> With arms about me said it hard to believe
> That I was there. He called me father, and I
> Called him my son: which was no more than the truth . . .

Nevertheless, it is hard to imagine our poet revealing in the twilight of his life the existence of a bastard, whose strange surname—attested to at Naples, apparently—makes one think instead of a literary joke. With regard to the pathetic verses put in Lauso's mouth, they remind us above all that between the personal anecdote and its lyric translation, poets of the Renaissance always interpose the filter of inventive imitation. Perhaps Cervantes, during his stay in Naples, did escape the venal love affairs that were the common lot of his companions. But the lover deceived by Silena could well be nothing more than a self-portrait of the artist that he chose to give us upon his return from captivity.

AT THE WELLSPRINGS OF CULTURE

THE Italy that Cervantes sets before our mind's eye is the fruit of direct experience. It is also, thanks to the power of words, an imaginary world where fictional beings move about. As a consequence, his fiction occasionally reflects, in this confluence of Life and Literature, the tensions caused by the Spanish occupation that the Italian Peninsula endured for three hundred years. These tensions were always present: on the eve of Lepanto, the memories of the two pillages of Rome carried out by Charles V's troops (whom Pope Paul IV considered a pack of Jews and Marranos) were still vivid. A little later, Miguel's friend Gálvez de Montalvo will complain about the Romans' hostility towards him: "They have the manners of mule-drivers," he will say, "chanting insults at us all their lives." This same hostility shows through in the relationships between Italians and Spaniards in the Rome of *Persiles*.

Castilian bureaucrats and Catalan merchants, quick to take advantage of the country, were as hated as His Majesty's soldiers, who habitually lived off the land during their campaign movements. The warm welcome accorded to Spaniards by a free city like Lucca was surely the exception, as is evident in the remark by one of the heroes of *Persiles:* "The reason for this," he declares, "is that [the Spanish] are not in command there but must ask for what they want; and since they do not stay there for more than a day, they have no opportunity to show their temperament, which is considered arrogant." Anti-Spanish feeling is expressed in the Italian theater of this period, through the grotesque character of Captain Matamoros. It will later reassert itself with extraordinary violence during the riots that several times bloodied Genoa, Florence, and above all Naples until the end of the Hapsburg domination.

In contrast with these unscrupulous predators, Cervantes was a representative of a noble tradition, embodied in the writers and artists who from the beginning of the Renaissance made their way to Italy in order to drink from the very wellsprings of humanism: Juan del Encina, considered the father of Castilian theater; Garcilaso de la Vega, the poet of the *Eclogues* that transfigured the pastoral heritage with their lyricism; Torres Naharro, who displays the satirical humor of Roman customs in his plays. The author of *Don Quixote* followed their example, except that he never led the life of a professional writer in the Italian Peninsula. He will first learn to handle Tuscan for his daily needs— once in a while he quotes a phrase of it—and the Ingenious *Hidalgo* occasionally comments on the subtlety of Italian. Cervantes, a self-taught man, explored the masterpieces of Italian literature with the ardor of a person fond of reading "even the scraps of paper in the streets." Was he ever able to quench this thirst for reading? On two occasions at least: first at Rome, during the free moments doubtless allowed by his functions in Acquaviva's household; then at Naples, where his friend Laínez seems to have introduced him into several literary salons.

What did he read, in fact? Or rather, what did he retain from his readings? The best of a rich, abundant literature, which sometimes leaves its mark on his writings but which he wanted to surpass rather than to imitate: the lyric poets, chiefly Petrarch, whose works he studied in the original but also by way of Garcilaso; even more, the great chivalric poems and their world of adventures—Boioardo's *Orlando innamorato,* Ariosto's *Orlando furioso,*—with a clear perception of the specific quality of each of these masterpieces and a marked preference for the *Orlando furioso,* whose fantasy and humor could hardly fail to enchant the future creator of Don Quixote; Boccaccio's *Decameron,* with its extraordinary variety of characters and situations. If the author of the *Exemplary Novellas* did not copy the style of the *Decameron* closely, he nevertheless learned a lesson from it: without sacrificing his own originality, he transposes its formula so successfully that his contemporaries will nickname him "the Spanish Boccaccio." And we should not forget the pastoral, consecrated in antiquity by Theocritus and Virgil, which Sannazaro's *Arcadia* adapted to the sixteenth century and which Tasso's *Aminta* brought to perfection. Under their influence, Cervantes will, ten years later, invent the shepherds' world of *Galatea*—not, as critics have sometimes said, by idealizing Sardinian shepherds that he observed during a hypothetical stay of some months on their island.

We could add to this list indefinitely by simply identifying reminiscences that appear in Cervantine texts. While making such an inventory, which clearly would extend beyond the period that we are here considering, we would discover other names, the enumeration of which is of no interest. But let us keep the name of León Hebreo, whose successful *Dialoghi d'amore* played an appreciable role in the genesis of *Galatea,* as an important number of direct borrowings attests. Let us also retain, without attempting to be exhaustive, the commentators of Aristotle's *Poetics:* Castelvetro's reflections on the verisimilitude of the story and the purposes of poetry will guide the author of *Don Quixote* in working out his esthetics and fine-tuning his craft as writer. But as we see it, what is essential is the way Cervantes managed to assimilate this heritage: not like "some scholar anxious to store up knowledge"—as the late Pierre Guénon rightly observes—but with an acute sense of what we will one day call "the pleasure of the text." As proof we have what Don Quixote tells us about the translations he admires but to which he confesses he prefers the original. As he says to anyone who cares to listen,

> Still it seems to me that translation from one language into another, except from the queens of languages, Greek and Latin, is like looking at Flemish tapestries on the wrong side; for though the figures are visible, they are full of threads that make them indistinct, and they do not show the smoothness and texture of the right side.

This enlightened reader's discernment is perfectly consistent with Cervantes' perpetual desire to escape from the narrow circle of books. We have already seen it expressed in his early youth in his passion for the theater, a passion that during these Italian years must have found plenty to satisfy it to the fullest: the learned tragedies of Dolce or Giraldi Cinzio, inspired by Seneca's works; Miguel will meditate on their formula when he starts to write his *Numancia:* or the *commedia dell'arte,* new-hatched at the time but already organized around its main characters; their *lazzi* will fecundate the Cervantine interludes: and finally the peasant farces in dialect that he undoubtedly saw and applauded in the environs of Siena; *La guarda cuidadosa* (The Vigilant Guard) develops one of its time-tested plots. If his taste for shows was awakened in the days of Lope de Rueda, it is quite certainly the Italian example that fostered the development of his vocation as dramatist and that will induce him to try his luck when he returns from captivity.

Did he have the same interest in the artistic treasures of the cities through which he passed? Did he, who was so manifestly fascinated by their architecture, examine the canvases that decorated their palaces? Biographers sometimes show us Cervantes under the vaulted ceiling of the Sistine Chapel, lifting his eyes toward the *Creation* and *Last Judgment*. The pilgrims in *Persiles* will not fail to visit and admire the pictures of "the pious Raphael of Urbino and [. . .] the divine Michelangelo." Above all, we would like to know whether Cervantes limited himself to accumulating the readings, the images, the memories in this fashion, or whether he took advantage of his free time to start writing again. He had taken his first steps as a writer in lyric poetry, under the guidance of López de Hoyos. The prestige of his favorite models (Petrarch, Bembo, Garcilaso, Herrera), the poetry contests of the Neapolitan academies, the encouragement of Laínez and Figueroa, both distinguished poets, undoubtedly prompted him to persevere in that direction. A good number of the poems inserted in *Galatea*—notably those that refer to Silena—must have been written during the years in Italy. But our imperfect knowledge of Cervantine chronology does not permit us to identify them with certainty. Moreover, for Miguel, such sacrifices to the Muses could only be a pastime, squeezed in among the more serious occupations demanded by His Majesty's service. But at the beginning of 1575, spring returns without the usual military preparations. Don Juan comes back from Spain in June with no instructions or precise projects. Our hero, forced to do nothing, condemned to a routine, feels the spirit of adventure stirring inside. And once again Destiny is going to answer his prayers, far beyond his expectations.

FAREWELL TO ARMS

WHEN did Cervantes make up his mind to leave Italy? We do not know. On the other hand, we have some idea of the motives that could have dictated his decision. He could hardly consider himself repaid, as a *soldado aventajado,* for the three wounds received at Lepanto, three expeditions against the Turk, four years spent in uniform. What can he expect from his leaders when the prospects of a new campaign are beginning to fade? He is tired of life as resident of a foreign country, discouraging for anyone who meets with nothing but indifference or hostility outside the narrow circle of the garrison. One senses a little of this disappointment in the disillusioned picture that Tomás Rodaja paints of a soldier's itinerant life when he describes

> . . . the power of commissaries, the foul temper of certain captains, the diligence of billet officers, the deviousness and tight-fistedness of paymasters, the complaints of towns, the trade in billets, the insolence of new recruits, the quarreling of innkeepers, the requests for more pack-animals than necessary, and finally the unavoidable need to do all the things that he observed and disapproved.

Berganza will show this same obvious disapproval when he contemplates the spectacle of the hardened, shameless soldiers who "committed insolent crimes in the towns we passed through, which made people speak ill of a [ruler] who did not deserve it." And the lesson that he draws from it betrays a disenchantment that our hero must have shared:

> For even though [the ruler] may want it and strive for it, he cannot correct these ills, because all or almost all aspects of war bring with them hardship, cruelty, and inconvenience.

Cervantes can no longer sing, like the page in *Don Quixote,*

> I'm off to the wars
> For want of peace.
> Oh, had I but money,
> I'd show more sense.

He is as usual without a cent, in spite of the *escudos* from the duke of Sessa; but he can no longer go to war, at least not to fight against the Turk. At the end of June 1575, a rumor begins to circulate about Don Juan's departing for Flanders as a replacement for the duke of Alba, whose cruelty has not produced the anticipated results. Did Miguel hope to leave Italy under Don Juan's command? He seems instead to have felt the call of his native land rather than the lure of northern fog. The news that he has been receiving from his family is more and more worrisome. His parents have been struggling with money problems again, for at least two years. Bocchi and Musacchi, the two Italians, doubtless found partners besides the ex-surgeon. As for Locadelo's generous gifts, they have long since gone up in smoke. Once more the specter of usury haunts the Cervantes household, as an IOU for debts signed by the couple to a Madrid secondhand clothier suggests. For their part, Andrea and Magdalena are still involved with Alonso and Pedro de Portocarrero, the sons of the unfortunate governor of La Goleta; but their relations have turned sour. Alonso, who has just inherited his father's fortune, finds new ways of evading, instead of keeping, his promises. A series of notarial documents, the first of which dates from May 7, 1575, records a sum of one thousand ducats due from the two brothers, as well as the delay of payments requested and consented to, and claims presented by the two sisters. A waste of time. Alonso, widowed in 1576, will marry, the following year, a girl of the highest nobility, without having fulfilled his obligations to Andrea. A last appeal filed by her in 1578 will be also doomed to failure.

Miguel, now sure that the fleet will not set out on campaign, decides to return to Spain. He obtains from Don Juan and from the duke of Sessa two letters of recommendation in support of his service record. With what object, specifically? Is it to apply for a captaincy, upon his return to Madrid? This is what his friend Castañeda will declare in his 1580 deposition, adding that Cervantes hoped to see himself put in charge of one of the companies being formed to be sent to Italy. But with his useless left hand, could he honestly continue to dream, as in the days of Acquaviva, and to expect a promotion rarely granted to anyone with less than ten years of service to his credit? The letters that he carried with him when he left Naples have not survived, but we can guess their content from what the duke of Sessa says in the certificate that he will send to Leonor de Cortinas three years later. The duke, more evasive than Castañeda, says only that his protégé, crippled in the left hand, has requested permission from Don Juan to return to Spain in order to ask for compensation for his service: *a pedir se le hiziesse merced*. As for Leonor, she will be even more laconic: her statements suggest a discharge for her son, pure and simple. Perhaps Miguel, handicapped by his wounds, aspired to a civil appointment instead. A job as magistrate *(corregidor)*, for example, like his grandfather the licentiate or his uncle Andrés. In fact, he will apply for one in a petition to the Council of the Indies fifteen years later. Simpler yet—if one admits his duel with Sigura and his conviction by default in 1568—perhaps he hoped to benefit by a stay of proceedings, pleading his seven years of exile, his acts of bravery, and the satisfaction of his superiors.

The fact remains that during the early part of September, our *sol-dado aventajado* embarks at Naples on the galley *El Sol.* Commanded by Gaspar Pedro de Villena, it was one of four vessels making up a flotilla preparing to weigh anchor for Barcelona, under the orders of Don Sancho de Leiva: a late departure because during the entire summer the assignment of these ships has been the object of a dispute between Don Juan de Austria and the marquess of Mondéjar, viceroy of Naples. With Miguel, besides his brother Rodrigo and some of their friends, several prominent personalities take their place. Our hero prepares to endure an uncomfortable crossing, equal to Master Glass's voyage in one of "those seagoing houses where most of the time bedbugs annoy, galley slaves steal, sailors pester, mice destroy, and the surge nauseates." It will above all be a dramatic crossing. A storm scatters the galleys after a few days. Three of them finally reach port safely; but the last one, *El Sol,* will be attacked by Barbary corsairs and its passengers taken to Algiers as captives.

On the strength of divergent statements, supplemented by the more-or-less amplified accounts provided by Cervantine fictions, some scholars affirm that the flotilla in fact endured two storms. The first probably caused it to veer toward Corsica; the second must have scattered it off Toulon. For others, there must have been only one storm, occurring in the Gulf of Lions. Cervantes' galley must have detoured toward Corsica by itself. But in both hypotheses, she probably attempted to rejoin the flotilla by hugging the French coast. Then, on September 26, she must have been boarded by corsairs near the Three Marys—in other words, off Saintes-Maries-de-la-Mer.

This version of the facts is still the most widely held; but today it is no longer acceptable: it mixes purely novelistic details with the data drawn from an all-too-often hasty reading of the documents. One of the experts on the question, Juan Bautista Avalle-Arce, has made a careful analysis of the sources available to us and has shown that scholars have confused the different crossings made by *El Sol* in the course of these years. Three essential points stand out in his study. First, Cervantes did not leave Naples on September 20, as people have believed for two centuries, but on the sixth or seventh of that month. Next, the flotilla, which had been hugging the coast of Italy and Provence, as was customary at the approach of autumn, was dispersed by the storm off Port-de-Bouc on the eighteenth of September. Finally, the capture—which did occur on the twenty-sixth—did not take place near the Saintes-Maries but lower, along the Catalan coast, not far from Cadaqués or Palamós. The desperation of the unfortunate passengers was all the worse, since they were almost at the end of their voyage.

Who was the perpetrator of this brilliant feat? An Albanian renegade, as his name indicates, Arnaut Mami, at the head of three galleys. His lieutenant, another renegade of Greek origin, was called Dali Mami; we will soon hear of him again. Refusing to surrender, the Spaniards resist their assailants for several hours; a number of them, including the captain, perish in the course of the fighting. Finally, overwhelmed by numbers, the survivors are transferred, tied hand and foot, to the Barbary ships. The operation has scarcely been completed when the rest of the Christian flotilla appears on the horizon, forcing the corsairs to abandon their prize and flee in haste with their captives. Three days later, Arnaut Mami's galleys arrive in sight of Algiers:

> When I arrived, a captive, and saw this land,
> Ill-famed in all the world, whose bosom conceals,
> Protects, embraces such a throng of pirates,
> I could not keep from weeping.

So speaks Saavedra, in *Life in Algiers* (El trato de Argel). The author of *Don Quixote* will carry this arrival engraved in his memory from now on. Nor will it be his only souvenir of captivity: far from it.

THE BAGNIOS OF ALGIERS

WHEN the twenty-eight-year-old captive disembarks with his fellow prisoners in chains on that September day, he experiences mixed emotions: mingled with his despair at finding himself in the hands of corsairs that he has only recently been fighting is anguish over the trials that await him as well as astonishment at a remarkable spectacle. When he expected to find nothing but a nest of pirates, he discovers a city of 150,000 inhabitants, more populous than Palermo or Rome, whose bustling streets remind him of Naples. He will soon pick out, as a keen observer, numerous signs of the prosperity that contemporary eyewitnesses all stress: a port full of activity, with its lighthouse, breakwater, and warehouses; constant movement around the different markets, through narrow streets whose irregular network masks the careful arrangement of houses and quarters; a multitude of mosques, baths, and palaces whose hidden patios echo with the murmur of fountains; and beyond the ramparts that protect the city, a profusion of gardens overlooking the sea, to which the hills that loom above it descend stepwise. In short, he sees all the symptoms of a vitality that will raise the city to its apogee, fifty years later.

Algiers owes this vitality above all to privateering, a substitute for all-out war but also an ancient and widespread industry whose origins are lost in the mists of time. The Maghrebi corsairs, consummate technicians and tacticians, have raised it to a level of perfection that Christian privateering, vigorously carried out from Leghorn and Malta, will never reach. Fast, handy, perfectly maintained, the Algerian galleys—about thirty in Cervantes' day—are the spearhead of its economy. Capturing hundreds of Christian ships each year, carrying off, by the thousands, captives from the coasts of Spain and Italy, they enrich the entire city with traffic in slaves and commerce in plundered merchandise. Their return to port is always an occasion for merrymaking. As one eyewitness says, "All they do is eat, drink, and make merry." One can readily picture Miguel and his comrades exposed to outbursts of this rejoicing as they are led to the slave market where captives were sold to the highest bidder, after careful examination by prospective buyers. Perhaps our hero is spared that humiliation, since he is going to fall to the lot of Arnaut Mami's first mate, Dali Mami, called *El Cojo,* which means "the cripple." The prestigious signatures on the letters of recommendation found in Miguel's possession explain this privilege. The corsair, convinced that he is dealing with an important personage, will demand as the price of ransom the considerable sum of five hundred gold *escudos.*

This is the first piece of information that has come down to us regarding Cervantes' sojourn in Algiers. It is a five-year-long stay that we know rather well in its broad outlines and prominent incidents, thanks to depositions collected during the two inquests of 1578 and 1580; thanks also to the records of steps taken by the writer's family to obtain ransom for him and his brother; and thanks, finally, to the testimony of Fray Diego de Haedo, whose *Topography and General History of Algiers* (Topographía e historia general de Argel), published in 1612, teems with bits of information about the Barbary city. It also makes special mention of Cervantes, among the prominent Christian captives. Still, it is necessary to handle this evidence, direct and indirect, with caution: the testimony of his companions because it was produced at Cervantes' request, to refute the slanderous statements made against him by his enemies; the account that we owe to Haedo because it is inseparable from the charges made by that author against the city and its pirates in order to awaken Spanish public opinion from its indifference and to stimulate the work of ransoming captives.

Furthermore, however precious they may be, these sources are virtually silent on what constitutes in our eyes the essential point: how Cervantes lived within that experience; the relations that he established with Muslims and Christians; the way he viewed a civilization different from his own. So we are tempted to appeal to the literary projection of his captivity in order to complete these data: besides the two plays with suggestive titles, *Life in Algiers* (El trato de Argel) and *The Bagnios of Algiers* (Los baños de Argel), there is the "Captive's Tale" interpolated in *Don Quixote,* the importance of which we have already begun to appreciate. These transpositions are very free, but they are irreplaceable, nevertheless. Behind the incidental elements of convention and novelistic elaboration, they restore to us, in fact, the fragments of an exceptional adventure and, even more, the personal feelings of the man who experienced it. Let us listen to the Captive:

In this way I lived on, shut up in a building or prison called by the Turks a *baño,* in which they confine the Christian captives, the king's as well as those belonging to private individuals, and also what they call those of the *almacén,* which is as much as to say the slaves of the municipality, who serve the city in the public works and other employments. Captives of this kind recover their liberty with great difficulty, for, as they are public property and have no particular master, there is no one with whom to bargain for their ransom, even though they may have the means. To these *baños,* as I have said, some private individuals of the town are in the habit of bringing their captives, especially when they are to be ransomed. There they can keep them in safety and comfort until their ransom arrives. The king's captives also, those that are going to be ransomed, do not go out to work with the rest of the crew, except when their ransom is delayed. For then, to make them write for it more urgently, they compel them to work and go for wood, which is no light labor.

I, however, was one of those held for ransom, for when it was discovered that I was a captain, although I declared my scanty means and lack of fortune, nothing could dissuade them from including me among the gentlemen and those waiting to be ransomed. They put a chain on me, more as a mark of this than to keep me safe, and so I spent my life in that *baño* with several other gentlemen and persons of quality marked out as held for ransom. Though at times, or rather almost always, we suffered from hunger and scanty clothing, nothing distressed us so much as hearing and seeing at every turn the unexampled and unheard-of cruelties my master inflicted upon the Christians. Every day he hanged a man, impaled one, cut off the ears of another, and all with so little provocation, or so entirely without any, that the Turks acknowledged he did it for its own sake and because he was by nature murderously disposed toward the whole human race.

Did all captives suffer these cruelties and tortures? It is doubtless necessary to make distinctions. As historians of privateering have established, those most at risk were the humblest, generally employed as house servants, agricultural workers, or laborers in the quarries and arsenals. Among them, the strongest were certainly to be pitied most: assigned as rowers in the galleys during the summer, in winter they were used on land as stevedores or rented by the day. More enviable was the fate of specialized shipyard workers: armorers, metal-casters, carpenters, naval architects, caulkers. Indispensable to the Barbary sailors, they were at a premium on the market; on the other hand, their special skills robbed them of any hope of ransom; thus they were inclined to become renegades. Young boys and girls had of course a right to special consideration. But they most often inspired in their companions in misery nothing but scorn, since they were destined to be instruments of pleasure, urged by their masters to embrace Islam. There remain, as the Captive indicates, the people of quality or those thought to be so. As captives for ransom, they escaped all these constraints; in exchange, they became the object of speculative transactions, either between their different owners or between the Turks and the monks—Trinitarians and Mercedarians principally—who had come from Spain and Italy to negotiate their freedom.

During the first months of his captivity, Miguel was relatively unoccupied. Confined in the *bagnio* from dusk to dawn, during the day he undoubtedly played up his infirmity to obtain freedom to come and go across the city, rubbing elbows with a world of people whose practices and customs he was unaware of until then. As a consequence, the novelistic adventures that he assigns his characters unfold in a setting and an atmosphere that bear the stamp of keen observation. It is not only the rites of privateering and the slave trade that compose the backdrop of these adventures; it is also a whole political organization whose machinery he shows us: around the *Pasha,* the sultan's delegate, who is assisted by the *Divan,* his council, he gives us glimpses of the *Odjaq* (the Janissary militia) and the *taifa* of the *rais* (the corporation of corsairs), the two feudal organizations that fought each other for the real power in Algiers.

What he uncovers for us—with a light touch, never descending to didactic exposition or mere depiction of quaint customs—is the functioning of an extremely open society, perfectly suited to the "Noah's ark" that the city had become: an extremely divided society, in which the distinctions appear based less on occupation or wealth than on religious or racial alliances. At the top of the pyramid, the Turks, who form the administrative and military framework in Algiers; with them the corsairs, natives from all around the Mediterranean basin and representing almost "all the Christian nations." At the bottom of the ladder, the mass of captives, which Haedo estimates to be twenty-five thousand souls at the end of the sixteenth century, without counting black slaves. Between these two poles, a whole series of communities, in which a Jewish colony is highly conspicuous amid the dubious and motley world of Morisco artisans, renegade shopkeepers, Christian merchants, and Kabyle day laborers. These colonies maintained complex relationships among themselves, and Cervantine fictions present to us, behind the play of conventions, a vision of them without Manicheanism. It is quite true that antagonism between individuals occasionally becomes exacerbated; that in the course of action or intrigue, Moors and Christians call each other dogs and scoundrels; that the buffoon in *The Bagnios of Algiers,* the sacristan Tristán, is free with insults for the Moorish children who make fun of him and with jibes directed at the Jew whom he amuses himself by tormenting. But love affairs between masters and their slaves, the love shared by the Captive and the beautiful Zoraida, the daughter of the renegade Agi Morato, allow us to glimpse, beyond their literary implications, what Inquisitorial Spain knew nothing about: the peaceful coexistence of these communities.

So, though Cervantes is moved by the fate of his companions, victims of irascible masters or playthings of their libidinous desires, he also gives us an infinitely subtler picture of the Muslim world than the caricature-like distortion to which we are more often exposed in the

polemical writings of his contemporaries. Let us not make him an
expert on the Koran. His witnesses, to a man, saw him

> . . . live as a good Christian, zealous for God's good name, confessing
> and taking communion when Christians customarily do so; and if he occa-
> sionally had dealings with Moors and renegades, he always defended the
> Holy Catholic Faith, and he strengthened and inspired many not to become
> Moors or renegades.

No doubt. But in contact with these Moors and renegades, Miguel
learned to go beyond prejudices, to renounce ill-considered opinions.
In his works, he castigates those who renounce the Faith of Christ out
of weakness or inertia; and he exalts, in contrast, the heroism of mar-
tyrs true to their convictions, like Miguel de Aranda, the Valencian
priest who was stoned and burned, doubtless under Cervantes' very
eyes. But he also knows that Muslims who impose conversion on their
slaves are rare; they do not hesitate—in self-interest—to "return
Christians to Christianity with a beating," in order not to be forced to
emancipate each new convert, as the law required. As for Cervantes'
curiosity about Islam, it not only shows up in the abundance of Arabic
terms and expressions that he employs but is reflected in his allusions
to Muslim greetings, to the muezzins' calls to prayer, to the marriage
rites of the Moroccan sultan Abd-el-Malek. It is likewise proved by
the impartial homage that he pays to the relative tolerance shown by
the Turks toward their captives. As it says in *The Bagnios of Algiers,*

> [It is surprising, but]
> These faithless dogs allow us, as you see,
> To keep our own religion and to say
> Our mass, even if only in secret.

Cervantes will surely recall this tolerance on the day when the Spain
of Philip III decrees the massive and final expulsion of the Moriscos.
In that regard, his Algerian experience must have been precious to
him.

THE CAPTIVE'S TRIBULATIONS

THE image of Islam that Cervantine fictions present is all the more
fascinating because it was distilled over a period of years, as the prod-

uct of a long process of artistic elaboration. In the heat of the action—
or rather of inactivity—our hero felt little inclination to look about
him with the serene gaze of the impartial observer. Once the immediate desperation born of his capture had passed, his only concern, like
that of a good number of his companions, was to leave Algiers and its
bitter delights as quickly as possible. Doubtless he notified his relatives at once. But considering the price of his ransom, could he really
hope to see them collect the necessary sum? The feelings that he then
experienced must have been on all points identical to those that he
attributes to the Captive in *Don Quixote:*

> In Algiers I resolved to seek other means of effecting the purpose I cher-
> ished so dearly, for the hope of obtaining my liberty never deserted me.
> When in my plots and schemes and attempts the result did not answer
> my expectations, without giving way to despair I immediately began to
> look out for or think up some new hope to support me, however faint or
> feeble it might be.

Just like his *alter ego,* Cervantes is going to think of nothing but escape,
in spite of the difficulties and risks of such an enterprise. As early as
January 1576, in the very heart of winter, he sets in motion the first
attempt, in the company of several of the men who will later testify
in his favor. To risk one's life on the high seas in such a season would
have been folly. He chooses therefore to set out for the nearest fortress,
about four hundred kilometers west of Algiers:

> He found a Moor who could lead him and other Christians to Orán over-
> land; the Moor led them out of Algiers and, after having traveled for
> several days, deserted them; so it was necessary to turn back to Algiers,
> to the same enclosure where he was before; and thereafter, he was more
> mistreated than before, with beatings and chains.

However severe it may be, this treatment cannot be compared with
the fate usually reserved for recaptured fugitives: one has only to read
Haedo's description of the atrocious punishments inflicted on such
people. Cervantes must have been spared because of the profit his master expected to get out of ransom payments for a protégé of Don Juan
de Austria. Two of his companions in the attempted flight, Castañeda
and Antón Marco, will also escape punishment. They will even man-

age to benefit from it, seeing that as early as the month of March they paid their ransom and left for Spain. It is probably through their mediation that Miguel and Rodrigo inform their parents. In early spring, in fact, the surgeon takes the first steps of which we have preserved a trace. On two occasions, in April 1576, then in February of the following year, he strives without success to recoup eight hundred gold ducats that the licentiate Pedro de Córdoba has owed him for almost ten years. In April he also proceeds to sell off goods belonging to him, without our knowing what sort of profit he made on them. A little later, he addresses to the Council of Castile, then to the King's Council, a petition for a subsidy—in vain. On November 9, 1576, he presents a new request, supported by a certificate of purity of blood, now lost; but the financial aid for which he applies is refused again. Then it is Leonor's turn to apply to the Council of the Crusade. Making use of a pious lie, doubtless at the instigation of her guarantor, the ever-present Getino de Guzmán, she passes herself off as a widow. The maneuver succeeds: on December 16, she receives, on certain conditions, a loan of sixty ducats for the ransom of her two sons.

In the interval, three Mercedarians have been designated by their order to carry out a redemption of captives. When they complete their preparations, the three monks—Fray Jorge de Olivar, Fray Jorge de Ongay, and Fray Jerónimo Antich—depart for Algiers, where they disembark on April 20, 1577, "with a great quantity of money and other means in merchandise." Had they received an adequate sum from the surgeon and his wife? Surely not, because upon their arrival Dali Mami raises Miguel's ransom to five hundred ducats. Miguel then makes a decision which does him honor: renouncing his right as first-born, he convinces the ransomer-monks to buy his brother's freedom first. The pasha, Rodrigo's master, is asking three hundred ducats. Had Miguel given up all hope of returning to Spain? Quite the contrary: his determination is unshaken, and Rodrigo's liberation will provide the opportunity he intends to seize in order to achieve his objectives.

Though standing aside in favor of his younger brother, Miguel was secretly developing a precise plan. Rodrigo, after his arrival in Spain, was to contact one of the audacious frigate-sailors who went off at night in search of Christian captives along the Barbary coast and, at their own risk, brought them back to Valencia or Mallorca: a dangerous enterprise, certainly, but common enough and often rewarded with success. He was also to procure the cooperation and funds necessary for its realization. To that end, Rodrigo was supposed to secure the support of local authorities, thanks to letters of recommendation that two Knights of Malta, Don Antonio de Toledo and Don Francisco de Valencia, themselves recently liberated, had given him. Early in the month of May, Cervantes sets his plan in motion. Taking advantage of Dali Mami's absence, he leads out of the city "fourteen of the most important Christian captives that were in Algiers at the time" and hides them in a cave located in the *alcaide* (warden) Hassan's market garden, three miles to the east of Algiers. With the complicity of the gardener, a Navarrian slave named Juan, the fourteen captives are going to spend five months concealed in their hiding place, fed and encouraged by Miguel, during the wait for the ship that would save them. Five interminable months, during which the Turks seem not to have noticed their disappearance, incredibly enough!

Why such a long wait? Quite simply because the kingpin of the operation, Rodrigo de Cervantes, is forced to wait patiently all summer before making his way back to Spain. In July 1577, Rabadan Pasha, his former master, leaves Algiers to return to Constantinople at the expiration of his term of service. In his place the governor Euldj Ali—him again!—names another of his protégés, of whom Ruy Pérez de Viedma has left us a suggestive portrait. He was, Viedma tells us,

> . . . a Venetian renegade who, when a cabin boy on board a ship, had been taken by Uchalí and was so much beloved by him that he became one of his most favored youths. He came to be the most cruel renegade I ever saw. His name was Hassan Pasha, and he grew very rich and became king of Algiers.

Haedo, too, informs us about the physical appearance of the personage, whom he describes as

> . . . tall in stature, lean of body, with large, cruel, shining eyes, a long, sharp nose, thin lips, a rather thin beard, chestnut-colored hair, and a bilious hue that tended to yellow: all signs of his evil character.

When he takes up his duties, Hassan attempts to seize all captives already ransomed, and he doubles the total of their ransom. Francisco de Valencia and Antonio de Toledo will be among the few who escape in the nick of time. It will be necessary for Fray Jorge de Olivar, one of the three ransomer-monks, to offer himself as hostage to the new governor in order to persuade Hassan to authorize the departure of the first convoy of 106 captives on August 24. Rodrigo is among their number. He has scarcely arrived in Spain when he gets to work. Within the space of four weeks, he has a frigate ready at Mallorca. Commanded by a former captive named Viana, she sets out to fetch Miguel and his companions, who expect her to arrive September 28; but on the appointed day, she is not at the rendezvous. What appears to have happened is either that the Mallorcans judged it too risky to land; or they were discovered and forced to weigh anchor; or perhaps they were simply captured. The fact remains that one of those whom the fugitives had taken into their confidence, a renegade from Melilla nicknamed *el dorador,* the gilder, became frightened and revealed everything to Hassan. Caught in their cave by the Turks on the morning of the thirtieth, the unfortunate captives were unable to put up the least resistance. It was on this occasion, according to the principal witnesses, that Miguel showed extraordinary courage. He immediately declares himself to be the only guilty party, his companions having done nothing—according to him—but follow his advice and instructions. He will persist in this account during his appearance before the pasha, in spite of insults and death-threats. And so he will manage to exonerate not only those he had taken with him but also Fray Jorge de Olivar, who had remained as hostage and whom his jailers accused of complicity.

But at what price? The affair will produce only one victim, the unfortunate gardener, who will be hanged on October 3 and will die in atrocious suffering. As for Cervantes, he escapes capital punishment again on this occasion: loaded with manacles and chains, he will be imprisoned in the king's *bagnio* for five months. Such leniency on the part of the Venetian renegade is astonishing. All the documents describe him as a cruel man, and Cervantine fictions show him decreeing beatings, tortures, and other punishments for the luckless escapees that are brought back to him. It is true that his victims were generally poor wretches, while our hero, for the reasons we have seen, was considered an exceptional captive. Doubtless Hassan was also impressed by Cervantes' determination and sangfroid: at least that is what Haedo suggests and what we are led to believe by the pasha's admiration for the loyalty and indomitable courage of Spanish captives in *Life in Algiers.*

Indomitable Miguel certainly was, for in March of 1578, five months later, he repeats the offense:

> While he was in prison, he secretly sent a Moor to Orán with a letter to the marquess, Don Martín de Córdoba, the commander of Orán and its forces, and to other important people whom he counted among his friends and acquaintances at Orán, asking them to send one or more spies and trustworthy persons who could return with the aforesaid Moor to Algiers and help him and three other important gentlemen whom the king held confined in his *bagnio* to escape.

Our hero will meet failure once again:

> The aforesaid Moor, carrying the aforesaid letters to Orán, was caught by other Moors at the entrance to Orán; and because the letters that they found on him roused their suspicions, they seized him and took him to Algiers, to Hassan Pasha. The latter, having examined the letters and seeing the name and signature of Miguel de Cervantes, had the Moor impaled. He died courageously without revealing anything. And [the Pasha] ordered the aforesaid Miguel de Cervantes to be given two thousand blows.

Two thousand blows? That meant certain death. But one of the witnesses adds, *si no le dieron, fue porque hubo buenos terceros:* "if they did not flog him, it was because there were powerful intermediaries." For the third time, Cervantes saved his neck. It would be satisfying to know more about these mediations. The Captive Captain is astonishingly discreet on the subject and is content to echo our own surprise: recalling the exploits of one of his companions, he says simply that

> . . . a Spanish soldier, a certain de Saavedra by name [did] things that will dwell in the memory of the people there for many a year, and all to recover his liberty. [But to this man Saavedra, Hassan] never gave a blow himself, or ordered a blow to be given, or addressed a hard word . . . For the least of the many things he did we all dreaded that he would be impaled, and he himself was in fear of it more than once.

What supporters could Miguel count on? Someone has suggested that Dali Mami, now an admiral and disinclined to see the pasha sacrifice a valuable slave, approached Hassan. Another biographer has posited the existence of a mysterious Moorish woman enamored of Cervantes, just as the daughter of Agi Morato falls in love with the Captive. To tell the truth, the real conditions of life in Algiers were hardly propitious for such idylls: a Christian slave caught in the act with a Muslim woman was doomed to certain death unless willing to convert to Islam. Another hypothesis seems more plausible: an intervention bound up with diplomatic negotiations. Agi Morato—Hayyi Murad—of whom Cervantine fictions have left a picture that is as novelistic as it is touching, was in fact an important personage in the Maghrebi capital. This Slavonian renegade, a native of Ragusa on the Dalmatian coast, was famous for his wealth. But he also owed his prestige to his status as a *hadji* (he had made the pilgrimage to Mecca), as well as to his influence with the Grand Turk, of whose diplomatic corps he was a *chaouch,* an envoy. His daughter, whom Cervantes will make one of his heroines, had first married Abd-el-Malek, the sultan of Morocco. Exiled to Algiers by a palace conspiracy, the sultan had reconquered his throne in 1576. Two years later, he was killed during the victorious battle of Alcazarquivir against King Sebastian of Portugal, and after his death his widow would marry none other than Hassan Pasha, in 1580.

Exactly what role did Agi Morato play in Algiers? He was the Grand Turk's emissary. On two occasions, in March 1573 and again in August 1577, he will make the first secret overtures to Spain: ambiguous overtures, certainly, but preludes to the Constantinople negotiations that will produce the great Hispano-Turkish truce of 1579–81. The Spanish archives speak of discreet contacts made with Philip II by means of divers intermediaries: Valencian merchants; a ransomer-monk known to Cervantes, Fray Rodrigo de Arce; the viceroy of Valencia, involved by Rodrigo in the escape attempt of 1577; finally Don Martín de Córdoba, whom we have seen in connection with the aborted project of March 1578. The documents even allude to a proposition for an alliance, under the terms of which Don Juan de Austria would have received the governance of the Venetian States. But let us not exaggerate the significance of this proposition, all the more preposterous since the victor of Lepanto, sent to the Low Countries by his half brother, was going to perish prematurely at Namur, a victim of typhus, on October 1, 1578:

> *Non rescatar, non fugir,*
> *Don Juan no venir,*
> *acá morir.*

[No rescuing, no escaping,
Don Juan not coming,
dying here.]

So goes the sarcastic refrain that Moorish children will henceforth shout in the ears of captives, in that *lingua franca* cross-bred from Spanish and Italian that took the place of Esperanto in Algiers. Yes, there was assuredly a portion of bluff in Agi Morato's offers. But there is no reason to exclude the possibility that Cervantes, protected by his high-placed contacts, real or imaginary, should have been summoned to the inner sanctum of the *chaouch* in order to back up the official informants. It would then be possible to understand why he was twice pardoned by Hassan.

Meanwhile, the surgeon and his wife have begun their rescue efforts again. In March 1578, at the very moment when his son suffers his third failure, Rodrigo senior (brought back to life for the occasion) presents to the Council of Castile a new subsidy request, supported by the investigation whose contents we have already exploited. It appears to have had no effect whatever. We would like to know whether Miguel's sisters joined their efforts to those of their parents: twelve years later in his request to the Council of the Indies, the ex-captive will state that his two sisters sacrificed their dowries for the ransom of their brothers, a touching statement invented to meet the circumstances but which must be taken with a grain of salt. With regard to Magdalena, she seems to have been in financial difficulties comparable to those she had experienced earlier. Between 1578 and 1580, a certain Fernando de Lodeña (whom we will soon meet again) and then a Basque gentleman named Juan Pérez de Alcega will make promises to her that they do not keep. At the same time, Andrea takes up dressmaking in order to support her daughter Constanza, who is now in her custody. She seems to have managed her affairs with more discretion than her younger sister—and with more savoir faire, as her life-style in this period proves: her rent, for example, is five times higher than her parents' payments. It is probably she who through the mediation of the Mercedarian monks will turn over to the Valencian merchant Hernando de Torres, in June 1578, the essential one hundred ducats that represent the contribution of the two sisters to the common enterprise. But Torres, who was then supposed to go to Algiers in order to negotiate the ransom of a group of captives, will not accomplish his mission.

But it is the captive's mother who shows the greatest initiative, as in the past. In order to collect the necessary funds, she contracts for a share in a commercial venture: in July 1578, she asks the Council of War for permission to export to Algiers eight thousand ducats' worth of merchandise from the kingdom of Valencia. In support of her request, she submits an affidavit from the duke of Sessa. In November, she receives from the king a license for a much lower value—only two thousand ducats—"for the ransom of the aforesaid Miguel de Cervantes." Did she put her project into action? It appears in fact that she was unable to find the guarantor needed in such circumstances. Furthermore, Leonor had not yet at that date repaid the advance of sixty ducats that the Council of the Crusade had granted her the previous year. In March 1579, she will still not have settled her debt, and she will be threatened with seizure of her property and that of her guarantor, Getino de Guzmán. She will have the utmost difficulty in obtaining postponement of the date of payment.

Was Miguel kept abreast of these difficulties? Did he conclude from them that he would never be ransomed? Whatever his state of mind, he has no option but to spend his fourth winter in Algiers. With the return of spring, new hopes will revive; new tribulations are also in store for him. They will perhaps be the cruelest of all.

THE PRICE OF FREEDOM

"IT would be possible to make a separate story of the life and exploits of Miguel de Cervantes in captivity," Haedo will say later. But unfortunately we know almost nothing about his activities from March 1578 to September 1579, during which time eighteen months roll by. The only bit of information that has come down to us from that period is a petition addressed to Hassan in October 1578, to obtain freedom for Fray Jorge de Olivar, who was still being held as hostage. At the bottom of this document, our hero's signature appears among others. One must conclude from this that while he undoubtedly enjoyed prestige among the captives, his credit with the Muslim authorities was also still intact. It may even have increased when they saw that the jail routine inflicted on him by the pasha was quickly relaxed.

Must we go further and turn Cervantes into a man with nerves of steel, who never experienced confusion or doubt? His hagiographers have eagerly spread this fable by interpreting the testimony of his companions in a biased manner. It does not diminish his merits to imagine him occasionally in the slough of despond, a prey to contradictory feelings that make his acts of courage seem even more admirable. No doubt he often shared the emotion of those Christians that he puts on the stage in *The Bagnios of Algiers,* who from high on the ramparts of the city contemplate the sea's horizon while they sing of their longing for their lost homeland:

> *Cuán cara eres de haber, oh dulce España.*
>
> ["How costly you are to possess, oh sweetest Spain!"]

There is no doubt that those Muslim authorities for whom he served as a secret informant invited him to join them, with the prospects of a brilliant career as a reward for his conversion to Islam, as often happened in such cases. The number of renegades who appear in Cervantes' work, the roles he gives them, the carefully drawn image of them that he presents, all show not only that he was motivated by an enlightened curiosity but that he was deeply moved by the drama of thousands of children lost in the clash of two civilizations. On rereading the long scene from *Life in Algiers* where the soldier Saavedra persuades one of his companions, tempted to become a Turk, that he should not apostatize, we can readily agree with the keen observation of one critic, who sees in the discussion that brings the two characters into conflict a projection of an authentic inner debate. Placed in that context, Cervantes' dealings with Moors and renegades, his stirring defense of the Catholic faith, are illuminated with a new light, one that makes him more accessible, more human, and—in a word—more real.

How did he manage to endure, not to give in to temptation or despair during those long months? Thanks no doubt to friendship, poetry, and prayer. One of the witnesses who will depose in his favor after his liberation speaks of his contacts with the elite of his companions: priests, magistrates, monks, gentlemen, officers, and other servants of His Majesty. One of them, Dr. Sosa, to whom Haedo probably owes part of his documentation, will fully confirm that deposition, indicating that Miguel

. . . often spent time composing verses in praise of Our Lord, his blessed
Mother, and the Most Blessed Sacrament, and other holy and pious subjects, some of which he discussed with me in private and sent to me so
that I could examine them.

This statement has given rise to numerous suppositions. Did the author
of *Don Quixote* start work at that time on *Life in Algiers,* which ends
with a prayer to the Virgin Mary recited by a chorus of captives? Did
he begin to work on *Galatea* or, at the very least, compose some of the
poems scattered throughout the work? It is hard to exclude the two
possibilities. On the other hand, it is not justifiable to infer from Dr.
Sosa's declaration that the famous "Epistle to Mateo Vázquez" is
authentic. This ardent plea for a punitive expedition against Algiers,
addressed to Philip II's secretary, supposedly, was discovered in the
last century. It is probably nothing more than a forgery made from
bits and pieces, including a fragment of the speech from *Life in Algiers*
that Saavedra addresses to the king of Spain, adjuring him to seize the
Barbary city. Cervantes in all probability continued to cultivate the
lyric muse, along the lines of his previous efforts. This is what the few
vestiges of his Algerian output that we still have attest to: the two
sonnets dedicated to his fellow captive, the Italian jurist Bartolomeo
Ruffino di Chiambery, which he must have composed after 1576; and
the *octavas* that he will offer three years later to the Sicilian humanist
Antonio Veneziano, captured by the Turks in the spring of 1579.

His contacts with these elite personages must surely have provided
him with sorely needed consolation. When he sends Veneziano his
poem, accompanied by a dedicatory letter dated November 6, 1579,
Miguel has just lived through some trying weeks. The hopes that he
had cherished for an instant, he tells us in that letter, prevented his
putting the final touches to his verses: fallacious hopes, whose disappearance condemns him to wait for better days. In plainer language:
he has attempted for the fourth time to escape, and he finds himself
checkmated again. The plan that he had devised during the course of
September was a variant of the one he had conceived two years earlier
with the assistance of his brother. This time it involved outfitting
locally a twelve-bench frigate and returning to Spain with sixty passengers, "the finest flower of the Christian captives in Algiers." Two
key personages took part in the enterprise: the supplier of funds, a
Valencian businessman named Onofre Exarque, who we know pledged

thirteen hundred doubloons for the purchase of the ship; and the actual buyer, an Andalusian from Granada called the Licentiate Girón, who, having become a renegade under the name of Abderrahman, aspired to return to the bosom of the Church. All was ready for the departure when, in early October, another renegade, of Florentine origin, a man named Caybán, went to see Hassan and told him everything. His statements were immediately confirmed by the real author of the betrayal, Dr. Juan Blanco de Paz. This Dominican, born in Extremadura of Judeo-Morisco parents, and a fugitive from the law because of having broken an edict of exile, appears to have acted out of pure jealousy or out of spite at not having been selected to join those who planned to escape. He will receive as the reward for his denunciation one *escudo* and a pot of grease.

Onofre, terrified, now offers to ransom Cervantes with his own money and to dispatch him on the first boat leaving for Spain. But Miguel, with his habitual courage, refuses to agree to this proposition. He decides to assume full responsibility for the affair, in order to save an innocent person unjustly accused by the pasha. Leaving the safety of the house where he is hiding, he appears before Hassan, hands bound and a noose around his neck. Once again the pasha grants him his life, but only after allowing him to believe that he is going to be hanged. Our hero will remain incarcerated in the king's palace itself for five months. An interesting particular: when Dali Mami returns to Algiers, Hassan will buy his slave from him at the price fixed by the corsair, five hundred gold *escudos*.

The account of this escape attempt that has come down to us is as usual extremely laconic. According to one of the witnesses, Cervantes owed his salvation to a friend of the pasha, the Murcian corsair Morat Rais, called *Maltrapillo,* "Ragamuffin." May one also assume an intervention by Agi Morato, who was in a fair way toward becoming the king's father-in-law? We can only ask the question. Another explanation recently advanced suggests that Hassan, whose habits we know, felt the fascination that Miguel exercised over everyone around him. Hence the pasha's magnanimity; hence also the fact that he buys Miguel with his own money before doubling the price of his ransom six months later. Reciprocal attraction? Without going so far as to affirm it expressly, certain scholars have noted that once out of captivity, the author of *Don Quixote* was the object of accusations the substance of which we do not know but to which he had to respond with an inquiry into his morals. These critics have at the same time underlined the importance that homosexuality assumes in the plays inspired by the experience. They have observed that the heroic Francisquito of *The Bagnios of Algiers,* put to death for having repulsed the advances of a Muslim judge *(cadi),* is merely the reverse image of young Juanico in *Life in Algiers,* who gives in to the desires of his master, seduced by sweets and fine clothing. They have also pointed out the recurrence of the name Andrés in Cervantine fiction: the very name that Hassan bore before apostatizing (but also, let us remember, the name of the writer's uncle and older sister). Is it necessary to see in this obsession the sign of an unacknowledged penchant in an individual reputed "chaste and reserved," a penchant so repressed that it assumes the guise of intense repulsion? At least that is what certain clever analysts of Cervantine *eros* suggest. We will speak of this matter again when we reach the delicate subject of the love affairs of the author of *Don Quixote.* Let us state for the moment that if one can trust the portrait that Haedo draws of the sallow pasha, then Cervantes was surely less sensitive to his physical attractions than to the charisma that even his detractors saw in him.

At the same time that these events were occurring in Algiers, Leonor de Cortinas was sending her last troops into the battle that she had been waging for four years. In March of 1579, she obtained from the Council of the Crusade another delay for the repayment of the sixty ducats borrowed three years earlier. On July 31 of the same year, once again a widow for the occasion, she sends to Fray Juan Gil, procurator general of the Order of the Trinity, the sum of three hundred ducats for the ransom of her son Miguel, "who is thirty-three years old, crippled in his left hand, and has a blond beard." It was all that she herself and her family were able to show for their efforts. To this total, the Trinitarians were going to add forty-five ducats, deducted from the subsidies obtained by them in readiness for the mission they were preparing for the following spring.

On May 29, 1580, Fray Juan Gil arrives in Algiers at last, in company with one of his fellow monks, Fray Antón de la Bella. He finds a city barely recovered from a terrible winter and decimated by a famine that has killed more than five thousand persons. Weary of the proconsulate of a pasha whose arbitrary acts are uncountable, Algiers is uneasy at the gathering of Spanish troops summoned to Badajoz and Cádiz, which raises (ill-founded) fears of an armada to be sent against the city. Upon their arrival, the two monks enter into the first nego-

tiations with Hassan. But the discussions go nowhere because privateering is in full swing at that time and the principal corsairs are at
sea. In August, the two ransomer-monks succeed in buying a hundred
captives; Cervantes, however, is not among their number. Hassan,
whose term of office is ending, then offers Fray Juan Gil the pick of
his captives and slaves; he sets the ransom at 500 *escudos* a head, with
the exception of a certain Jerónimo de Palafox, valued by him at 1,000
escudos. Since the Trinitarian cannot pay such a sum, he decides to
ransom Miguel at the indicated price: he adds to the 280 *escudos* still
at his disposal 220 *escudos* taken from the general fund. On September
19, 1580, while the pasha is preparing to set sail, with his slaves
already chained to the benches of his galley, Fray Juan Gil deposits in
Spanish gold *escudos* the ransom-price: Cervantes is free at last. He had
almost left for Constantinople with his master; perhaps he would never
have returned from there.

One can imagine his joy. "To my mind," Ruy Pérez de Viedma will
say, "there is no happiness on earth to compare with recovering lost
liberty." Nevertheless, before leaving Algiers, our hero intends to settle his accounts. He is going to have to face a slander campaign mounted
against him by Blanco de Paz. We do not know the content of the
statements spread about him by this "slanderous, back-biting, haughty
man, a person of evil inclinations." Was Cervantes accused of immor-
ality with Hassan or compromising relations with Agi Morato? The
testimony available to us speaks only of "vicious, ugly matters." The
threat was serious, because Blanco de Paz claimed to be no less than a
commissioner of the Inquisition. This claim explains why Miguel,
now the house-guest of another ransomed captive, his friend Diego de
Benavides, wanted to cut the malicious rumors short. On October 10,
he arranges an inquest, to which we owe the clearest information relative to his captivity. In the presence of Fray Juan Gil and Pedro de
Rivera, Apostolic notary in Algiers, twelve witnesses, including
Benavides and Dr. Sosa, are going to confirm the statements made at
the inquiry on "the captivity, life, and habits" of the plaintiff. They
will show, on that occasion, that the accusations made by the unworthy priest and self-styled commissioner are groundless. Fourteen days
later, our captive embarks with five other ransomed persons on board
a ship belonging to Master Antón Francés. On the twenty-seventh,
Cervantes is within sight of the coast of Spain. His captivity has lasted
five years and one month.

Miguel's captivity ends like the one depicted in *Life in Algiers*. The

chorus of captives presented in that play learns, like Miguel, of the
imminent arrival of Fray Juan Gil; like Miguel, the group offers a
fervent prayer of thanks to the Virgin. On the other hand, the Captive's adventure—like his homologue Don Lope's in *The Bagnios of
Algiers*—illustrates the writer's ability to distance himself from his
tribulations: both the Captive and Don Lope actually escape by sea,
thanks to a renegade more loyal than El Dorador or Caybán, and they
succeed with a flight that our hero attempted several times in vain.
But it is the wandering students in *Persiles* who will have the last
word. These con men pretend to be ex-captives, hoodwinking peasants
in a Castilian village with the phony account of their sufferings among
the Barbary Moors. Unmasked by the mayor of the village, who is an
authentic escapee from Algiers, they will learn from him details that
will enable them in the future to give their story convincing realism.
This final irony shows us how completely Cervantes, in the twilight
of his life, has abandoned his former dreams. But what he will never
deny is the lesson that he learned from his Algerian experience. It not
only revealed new horizons to him, it helped him, in the face of adversity, to reveal his true self to others as well as to himself. In that
regard, Algiers, after Lepanto, was the forge where his personal destiny was wrought.

III

Shadowy
Love Affairs
1 5 8 0 — 1 5 8 7

There are times for recreation, when the
troubled spirit may rest.
EXEMPLARY NOVELLAS, PREFACE

DISILLUSIONMENT AFTER THE RETURN

The next day, they saw before them their longed-for, beloved homeland.
Joy revived in their hearts; their spirits became excited with new contentment, among the greatest one can have in this life: to return after a long
captivity, safe and sound, to one's fatherland.

SUCH are the sentiments that Cervantes attributes to Ricardo and his
companions in *The Generous Suitor* (El amante liberal) at the moment
when, in flight from Cyprus and the Turks, they finally catch sight of
Sicily. Such were the feelings that he himself must have experienced
at dawn on October 27, 1580, when he saw the coast of the Levant
north of Alicante appear on the horizon. Three days later, Miguel and
his comrades, who disembark at Denia, will make their entry into
Valencia. There they get the warm reception traditionally reserved for
freed captives. At the Trinitarian monastery, they receive the care and
refreshment they greatly need. Then, on All Saints' Day, they march
in procession to the cathedral for a thanksgiving ceremony described
for us in *The English Spanish Lady* (La española inglesa).

Now a waiting period of more than a month begins for our hero,

according to a deposition made at Madrid on December 9 by two of
his friends. Perhaps he asked them, through an intermediary, to testify on his behalf to aid him in obtaining a subsidy from the Council
of Castile that would permit him to repay the loans granted to his
family at the time of his ransoming; such at least is the object of the
steps taken by his father eight days earlier. Perhaps he wanted to
assure himself before returning to Castile that he would not be held
accountable for the Sigura affair, now more than ten years old. Whatever the reason, Cervantes took advantage of the delay to enjoy the
charms of Valencia, in praise of which he has left us an enthusiastic
account in *Persiles:* "the grandeur of its site, the excellence of its citizens, its pleasant surroundings, . . . the beauty of its women, and its
extraordinary and charming language." Some believe that he made
contacts among the Valencian poets to whom he will pay homage in
Galatea and that during his stay he visited the workshop of Timoneda,
the publisher of Lope de Rueda's comedies. In *The Bagnios of Algiers,*
there is an allusion to the vigorous old age of this bookseller-writer,
who will die three years later at an advanced age.

In mid-December we finally see Miguel in Madrid, after twelve
years of absence, joyfully embracing his family. A moving reunion, no
doubt, but overshadowed by the disappointments that had accumu-
lated in the interim: the melancholy of the ex-surgeon, immured in
his deafness, burdened with years and with debts, without a useful
occupation; the worries of Leonor, tired of struggling with adverse
fortune and of inventing humiliating lies; and, finally, the repeated
mortifications of the sisters—these trials must have perpetuated a morose
atmosphere in the family dwelling. One can understand why Rodrigo
junior, who had come back from captivity three years earlier, chose to
pursue a military career and had left for Flanders to serve under the
duke of Alba even before his older brother's return. Andrea, we have
seen, probably lived with a protector, whose name we do not know.
As for Magdalena, who is still involved with Juan Pérez de Alcega,
court clerk of the queen, Ana of Austria, she now calls herself Doña
Magdalena Pimentel de Sotomayor. Since the period of Charles V, the
mania for the title *don* had been spreading in Spain, and our writer,
not without humor, will confer it upon the Knight of the Woeful
Countenance. By means of this title, the rejects of a society dominated
by the aristocracy gave themselves the appearance of respectability, in
a country in the grip of inflation, where fortunes appeared and disappeared.

Upon his arrival, Miguel addresses to the Council of Castile the petition that he had not been able to present to it five years earlier, this time provided with two new testimonials. We have not preserved the council's answer, but it must have been negative. At a time when Spain was present on all battlefields, former combatants in search of pensions swarmed in the streets of the capital, like the ragged soldier that the interlude *The Vigilant Guard* presents with such skill. To complete his misfortune, our harquebusier could no longer appeal to the supporters who had so strongly impressed his Barbary jailers: the duke of Sessa had given up the ghost one year earlier, three months after Don Juan. To whom can he appeal from now on? Two names came to mind: Antonio de Toledo, whose intervention at the time of Cervantes' second escape attempt we recall, and who had become *escudero mayor*—royal equerry—at court; and Mateo Vázquez, who stood in the shadow of Philip II and supervised the execution of his orders and the implementation of his policies. Writers have often spoken of the friendship that the author of *Don Quixote* must have felt for this son of a Corsican adventurer and a woman once held captive in Algiers. Friendship is too strong a word, since, as we have seen, Cervantes was certainly not his classmate at the Jesuit school in Seville, and the poetic epistle which he is supposed to have dedicated to Vázquez is probably apocryphal. If there were contacts between the two men, they can only have been made through the mediation of Ovando, Andrea de Cervantes' former lover, who had become Cardinal Espinosa's chamberlain at the time when Vázquez himself was the cardinal's secretary.

When Espinosa died in 1573, Mateo Vázquez went into the service of Philip II. He will be involved henceforth in the factional disputes over influence waged in the sovereign's entourage. One of the instigators of these intrigues was the king's all-powerful secretary, Antonio Pérez, the lover of the duchess of Eboli. Pérez, hostile to the party of Don Juan de Austria, in January of 1578 planned the assassination of Juan de Escobedo, the secretary of the victor of Lepanto, no doubt with the tacit consent of the monarch, who was irritated by his half brother's self-serving schemes and saw in Escobedo Don Juan's evil genius. Vázquez, a declared enemy of Antonio Pérez, whose dissolute habits he disapproved of, is among those who the following year will publicly denounce Pérez's machinations and, by putting pressure on the king, will contribute to his disgrace.

Whoever his intercessor may have been, at the end of a winter of useless efforts Cervantes decides to present himself at court in order to plead his own case. But at the moment when he makes up his mind, Philip II and his entourage are no longer in Castile. The king in fact has left El Escorial in the month of March, to assume the crown of Portugal. He is gathering the fruits of the cunning policy he has been pursuing since his unstable and fanatical nephew Sebastian launched the fatal conquest of Morocco. Sebastian, obsessed with the idea of a crusade against the infidels, refused to heed those who attempted to turn him from his mad project. He had scarcely disembarked in Tangier, on August 4, 1578, when he and the flower of his nobility were massacred on the sands of Alcazarquivir. His successor, the cardinal-king Don Henrique, his uncle, died in January 1580, designating as his heir Philip II. Philip's sister Juana was Sebastian's mother; the Prudent King's rights were undeniable, and he saw to it that they prevailed. But his accession would mean direct control by a powerful neighbor that already held Portugal in economic and financial bondage. By necessity the higher clergy, nobility, and merchant bourgeoisie back Philip's candidacy, which is supported by the Council of Regents. On the other hand, the people and lower clergy prefer a bastard of the king's, Don Antonio, Prior of Crato, who proclaims himself king at Santarém. Philip II now decides on military intervention. For that purpose, he assembles at Badajoz and Cádiz the forces that had so disturbed Hassan Pasha and the Barbary peoples. At the end of a four-month campaign, directed by the duke of Alba, Don Antonio is forced to take ship for Calais. His rival's cause is victorious throughout the realm, as well as in its vast possessions beyond the sea. Only the Azores will resist for a few more months.

Philip II summons the Portuguese *Cortes* (parliament) to Thomar, where he swears allegiance and where Cervantes no doubt catches up with him, without, however, getting the hearing that he hoped for. Antonio de Toledo has died in the interval, and Mateo Vázquez is preoccupied with other cares. As for the king, whom petitioners continually importune, he has sworn to respect the laws and customs of the Portuguese "dominion"; he is trying to give preference to his new subjects. Miguel will be granted, as a consolation, the right to a short mission to Orán, which he will carry out in May–June 1581. He mentions it in his service record, and it is attested to also by an order for payment in his name, dated May 21, that gives him an advance of fifty *escudos*. What was the exact object of this mission, which was undoubtedly dangerous? To assure himself of the loyalty of the Portuguese fortresses in North Africa? To obtain information on the movements of the Turkish fleet, which was then causing fears of a raid on the western Mediterranean? In his petition of 1590, the ex-combatant of Lepanto speaks only of contacts with the *caid*—warden—of Mostaganem, without specifying their nature. What is certain is that his reunion with the Maghreb must have been a moment of intense emotion for him. It is easy to imagine what his sentiments must have been both as he entered Orán, to which he had on two occasions attempted to flee during his captivity, as well as when he introduced himself to the governor of the fort, Don Martín de Córdoba, once a prisoner of the Barbary pirates, like himself. One detects, in addition, the echo of this stay in the stage directions for *The Gallant Spaniard* (El gallardo español), whose action has as backdrop the heroic defense of the city against the Turks in the spring of 1563.

Having departed from Cádiz on May 23, Cervantes is going to return by way of Cartagena. He disembarks on June 26, probably, and there receives the remaining fifty ducats that had been promised to him. He soon reaches Lisbon, where the king has been in residence for some time, in order to give an account of his mission to the proper person. He finds the city in a holiday mood. In *Persiles,* he will describe its incomparable site, with its vast anchorage covered with "the moving forests formed by the masts of ships." He will, it appears, remain until winter. Perhaps it is there that he wrote his *canción* (song) to Larsileo that he will include in book 4 of *Galatea.* Certain critics have at least supposed so, stressing the fact that Larsileo was the literary pseudonym of Mateo Vázquez, about whom the novel says that "in affairs of court, he has long, practical experience." Did our hero also find love in Lisbon? No evidence lends itself to such a hypothesis, besides the conventional homage that he pays—still in *Persiles*—to the women of Lisbon, whose "beauty astonishes and captivates." As for his supposed participation in the expedition against the Azores led by Alvaro de Bazán, it has been inferred from an ambiguous phrase from the petition of 1590, in which Miguel's service record is confused with his brother's. Only Rodrigo has the honor of taking part in a campaign that will end with the defeat of the Prior of Crato and of the French squadron called to the rescue. At the time of the fleet's triumphal return to Lisbon, in September 1583, it had been almost two years since Miguel had departed for Castile, without having received the recompense to which he believed he had a right.

Did he stop at Salamanca on the way home with the object of renewing studies interrupted thirteen years earlier? Certain critics have said so, arguing that Cervantes brings Diego de Carriazo and Juan de Avendaño, the heroes of *The Noble Scullery Maid* (La ilustre fregona), to the banks of the Tormes. And in fact the two youths bear the names of two students whose traces university records preserve for the very years 1581 and 1584. However pleasant the coincidence is, the argument is too fine-spun to make such a supposition admissible. Today, the writer's admirers agree that Cervantes, unlike Góngora, Quevedo, or Calderón, did not take his degree. They are no longer shocked by his occasional lapses when he cites Horace. And they agree with Berganza "that it is as much a fault to quote Latin to a person who does not understand it, as to quote it without understanding it yourself." All the more so, when they see his rivals taking their classical references from one of the handbooks and alphabetized collections of sayings at which the preface to *Don Quixote* pokes fun. Miguel, as we have seen, had a passion for reading; but above all, he lived in contact with reality. His education was less bookish than his colleagues', but his culture nevertheless compares favorably with theirs; and considering the complexity of the problems that it poses, his *oeuvre* is worth as much as their learned treatises.

Cervantes finds himself in Madrid once again on February 17, 1582. From there he addresses a letter to "the illustrious Lord Antonio de Eraso, member of the Council of the Indies, at Lisbon." The manuscript was discovered about thirty years ago in the archives at Simancas. It is one of the few documents from his hand that have come down to us:

> Illustrious sir: Secretary Valmaseda received me as I expected, in view of the favor that Your Grace was going to do for me. But neither his consideration nor my diligence can overcome my bad luck. The bad luck that I have had with my affairs is that the post I applied for is not being filled by His Majesty; so I am forced to wait for the dispatch vessel [from the Indies] to see whether it brings news of some vacancy. All those posts that were vacant are already filled, according to what *Señor* Valmaseda has told me. I know that he has really tried to find out about anything that I might apply for. I pray Your Grace to express to him the gratitude that he deserves for his good offices, so that he will know that I am not ungrateful . . .

So not only has Miguel not been able to find a post in the Indies, in spite of backing from Eraso, he has not succeeded, even with Valmaseda's support, in obtaining the Madrid sinecure that would have satisfied him, in default of the other. Like Tomás Rodaja, he could say, decidedly, that palaces were not his world. This double rejection is going to cause him to withdraw from the antechambers of power for a long time. Perhaps he was expecting such a rebuff; but it certainly did not catch him idle. His letter ends with two phrases that tell us what activities were occupying all his attention:

> In the meanwhile, I am entertaining myself by bringing up Galatea (which is the book that I told Your Grace I was writing). When she has grown a little, she will come kiss Your Grace's hands and receive the polish and improvement that I have not been able to give her.

So it is to his *Galatea* that Cervantes is devoting himself assiduously, during these months punctuated by moves, requests, and intrigues. Behind the petitioner's mask we discover the face of the poet again; the moment has come to examine his features.

RETURN TO THE MUSES

AT the end of 1581, when he rejoins the paternal household that he had left eight or nine months earlier, Miguel once again encounters the vexations that had spurred him to set out in the first place. His brother Rodrigo, stationed in Portugal, continues to serve the king there. At the close of the Azores campaign, in September 1583, his bravery in combat will win him promotion to *soldado aventajado* and, soon afterwards, to the rank of ensign. So it is incumbent on the eldest son to help the surgeon and his wife, always in the grip of money problems. As for Andrea, she has faded into the background, though her brother must have thought of her with gratitude when he liquidated the last of the Locadelo gifts in September 1585. Magdalena, lastly, who is going on twenty-five, sees the plans that her liaison with Juan Pérez de Alcega undoubtedly inspired go up in smoke. The ex–court clerk of Queen Ana (who had died in October of 1580) was aspiring to the post of steward in the Infantas' household, and the prospect of a misalliance must not have appealed to him. This explains why he went back on his promises, forcing his victim to file a claim with the vicar general of Madrid. The outcome of the affair will be consistent with family tradition: on August 12, 1581, Pérez de Alcega agrees in the presence of the notary to give to the plaintiff as a form of compensation three hundred ducats payable in three installments, within the term of one year. History does not tell us whether he kept his word; but the young woman, cured of her illusions, will gradually withdraw from the world; Doña Magdalena Pimentel de Sotomayor will one day become Sister Magdalena de Jesús.

It would be interesting to know how Miguel came to the assistance of his family, how he helped them pay off debts contracted in order to meet his ransom. Did he resume his duties with López de Hoyos, who was still head of the *Estudio de la Villa?* He must surely have had an emotional reunion with his former teacher; and it is perhaps through him that there came into Cervantes' hands a manual of devotion that had just come off the press, bearing an *aprobación* by the aging humanist. But even had Miguel been capable, after so many years, of becoming López de Hoyos's assistant again, playing at school-pedant could only have been a last resort. Besides, López de Hoyos was going to disappear in early summer 1583, without our being able to gauge the effect of this death on the life of his former pupil.

It is unlikely that in conversations between the headmaster of the *estudio* and his "well-beloved" disciple, Lepanto, Tunis, and Barbary pirates were the only subjects. Leafing through the *Relación* of Elizabeth of Valois's funeral, which had appeared after his departure for Rome, seeing his first poems in print after a lapse of twelve years, Cervantes would quite naturally have been led to entertain López de Hoyos with his Italian readings and his works in progress, in the forefront of which stood *Galatea.* Naturally he does not make López his only confidant regarding his projects. Renewing his attendance at salons in the capital, he will gradually enlarge the circle of his literary friendships. Among his elders, Pedro Laínez, "an old and true friend," is the man to whom he feels closest. Repatriated from Italy like Cervantes, Laínez is now an official censor. But our poet equally admires Francisco de Figueroa, whom he occasionally visits at his retreat at Alcalá. Relations with his contemporaries are also very cordial; they are particularly close with Gálvez de Montalvo, Pedro de Padilla, Juan Rufo, Luis de Vargas Manrique, Gabriel López de Maldonado, Lucas Gracián Dantisco. Who are these men in the republic of letters? Lyric poets, mainly, who cater to contemporary taste while drawing inspiration from the work of their illustrious predecessors Garcilaso, Herrera, Fray Luis de León. Cultivating without special preference both

Castilian forms—traditional eight-syllable verses in quatrains, five-line stanzas, and ballads, called *redondillas, quintillas,* and *romances*—and strophes imported from Italy—sonnets, elegies, *canzone*—they struggle against poetry's "disfavored" state (to use Cervantes' word). So they make an effort to perpetuate the vogue of themes made fashionable by the Renaissance: the despair of the rejected lover, the pain of absence, tranquillity in the presence of a harmonious and smiling Nature.

Relations between Miguel and his fellow writers will soon begin to intensify. Starting in 1583, collections of verses that these poets publish are generally graced by a preliminary sonnet by Cervantes. In return, in 1585, three of these writers pay him their respects in verses included among the pieces written for the occasion that appear in the first pages of the edition of *Galatea*. Miguel soon repays their compliments: the "Song of Calliope," 108 octavas (eight-line stanzas) inserted into book 4 of his romance, is a garland of enthusiastic eulogies offered to his favorite writers. Let us not misinterpret these reciprocal praises: in the twilight of the sixteenth century, just as in our waning twentieth century, people knew how to express genuine fraternal respect—to the benefit of everyone, naturally. The real question is whether what we have here is nothing more than a document that illustrates the literary customs of the day, or whether it proves that Cervantes was recognized by his peers. The reader of today feels ill equipped to decide. What is left of Cervantine literary production that is contemporary with his return to Madrid—essentially, the poetry inserted in *Galatea*—certainly reveals estimable talents; but it is nevertheless the work of a second-rank poet, an honest disciple of Petrarch and Garcilaso. Cervantes himself seems to have been well aware of his limitations, as he will reveal in the *Journey to Parnassus,* in the phrases of a strophe that is not without humor:

> I who always work through sleepless nights
> To counterfeit the poet's talent that heaven
> Chose not to give me . . .

Nevertheless, some years later public opinion will hail him as one of the two or three best authors of ballads *(romances)* that Philip II's capital can boast. But the majority of his compositions are no longer available to us, either because they circulated in the form of manu-

script copies now lost, or because they were published anonymously
in collections by various authors, and we are now unable to identify
them.

Miguel quickly enters into the literary milieu of *la Villa y Corte*.
The warm reception that he receives surely gives him the burst of
energy necessary to complete the writing of *Galatea*. Besides, he has
an example close at hand to give him courage: the publication in 1582
of Gálvez de Montalvo's *Fílida's Shepherd,* an autobiographical fable
that transfigures the poet's ill-fated passion for one of the ladies in
Elizabeth of Valois's retinue, Doña Magdalena Girón, and gives it a
bucolic setting. In imitation of this model, no doubt, Cervantes tries
his hand at the game of pseudonyms and literary disguises, to which
he refers obliquely in the preface of his romance. If one can trust a
table of concordances discovered thirty years ago among the manu-
scripts of the National Library in Madrid, the author put himself into
the fiction behind the mask of Lauso, while presenting Pedro Laínez,
Francisco de Figueroa, Gálvez de Montalvo, Mateo Vázquez, and Don
Juan de Austria himself under the names of Damon, Tirsi, Siralbo,
Larsileo, and Astraliano, respectively. But such autobiographical possibilities are only an accessory reason for Cervantes' infatuation with
shepherds' idylls. His fondness for them is part of a much vaster and
deeper movement; it reflects the vogue that the pastoral genre enjoyed
throughout the Renaissance and all over Europe. Today this vogue
surprises us—heirs that we are (without always admitting it) of the
nineteenth century, which invented photography and raised to the
level of an esthetic ideal the slice-of-life and picture-of-customs. But
behind the conventions that make it tedious—eternal spring, absence
of any material constraints, the lover's complaint, the beloved's indifference—in the trappings of Greco-Roman antiquity, the pastoral
expresses some of the aspirations common to all periods: the dream of
a Golden Age; the return to nature; the quest for an impossible harmony of body and soul, immune to the passage of time, safe from the
attack of old age and death's scythe.

After 1530, Charles V's Spain recreated the idyllic scheme of Sannazaro's *Arcadia* on the banks of the Tagus: in the music of Garcilaso's
verses, the *locus amoenus* of his *Eclogues* becomes the setting for melancholy lyrics that describe love's pangs, in surroundings of an idealized
Nature. The generation of Philip II will remember the lesson well.
But in the slow rhythm of prose interlarded with verses—woven from

the melancholy and tears of shepherds isolated in a world of innocence, with no other god but Eros—the harmony of nature is out of tune with the discord of their hearts. This particular modulation of the pastoral, inaugurated by Montemayor toward the middle of the century, is going to achieve a dazzling success: between 1559 and 1600 twenty-six editions of his romance *Diana* appear, not counting sequels, imitations, and adaptations. The reasons for such a success are easy to understand. The aristocratic and courtly public demanded a new kind of escape literature; after the great undertakings of the imperial period, it is faced with the critical expansion of a changing society and lives in an age that sees the triumph of money and the loss of patriarchal values. The romances of chivalry, so dear to the contemporaries of Charles V, with their naiveté, obscenity, and incoherence, no longer satisfy their concerns or taste. But the tribulations of shepherds suited their frame of mind exactly, while revealing new vistas of amorous introspection, punctuated by a discreet appeal to the reader's complicity. The appeal of this genre is all the stronger because the pastoral expresses a coherent conception of perfect love as the universal principle of action. Perfect love as universal energy is a concept nourished by the Neoplatonic ideas spread by Baldassare Castiglione and León Hebreo. Its undeniably secular roots will call down the fulminations of high-minded moralists. Wasted effort: despite censure and warnings, young people and women of all ages gave their support to *Diana,* with unshakable loyalty. As for the bucolic trappings, they are so well suited to perfect love that they are accepted with no hesitation whatever. "It may be that people speak better in the city," Fray Luis de León will aptly say, "but refinement of feeling belongs to solitude and to the countryside."

Such is the bestseller that Cervantes will take as his model. Doubtless he had been reading pastoral romances since adolescence, when he received his initiation into poetry under the guidance of López de Hoyos; but at that time he was not yet dreaming of fathoming their secrets. In order to do that, he would, in the course of time, have to enlarge the field of his readings, to meditate on Petrarch, Sannazaro, and León Hebreo, and to ponder the mysteries of love, thanks to experiences that were not altogether bookish. So, after his return to Spain, it was with different eyes that he reread *Diana,* whose vogue had not diminished. The pastoral romance, with its interpolated poems, was the most suitable way to frame the compositions that he sought to

have printed—not without difficulty—under his name. At the same
time, while he was following in the footsteps of Montemayor and of a
writer closer to him, his friend Montalvo, Miguel aimed less at con-
forming to fashion than at exploring the possibilities that prose narrative provided to an intelligent connoisseur of the resources of Castilian.
The writing of *Galatea,* begun during his first stay in the capital,
when he was reunited with his family, then taken up at Lisbon after
his mission to Orán and continued in Madrid all through 1582, will
bring him to the summer of the following year.

In all likelihood, Cervantes submitted his rough drafts to those men
whose opinion he valued: Antonio de Eraso, the addressee of the February letter; Laínez and Figueroa, "both worthy of eternal, endless
praise"; Gracián Dantisco, titular censor but also an experienced reader
of the literary production of his day. Cervantes is going to choose the
bookseller Blas de Robles, originally from Alcalá, like himself, as his
publisher. On June 14, 1584, he grants to Robles the rights to his
manuscript, "a book of prose and verse containing the six books of
Galatea, which he has written in our Castilian language." Actually,
the contract must have been negotiated some time earlier. Payable in
two installments, the sum agreed to by Robles—120 ducats—was
quite acceptable; besides, a novice poet, as Cervantes was at that time,
would have been ill advised to create difficulties.

As for the patron, whose support was indispensable to him, he will
be (as we have already seen) Ascanio Colonna, the friend of Cardinal
Acquaviva and son of Marco Antonio Colonna. Though titular bishop
of St. Sophia, Colonna resided at that time in Alcalá. Some years later
he will become the viceroy of Aragon and will himself receive the
cardinal's hat. Acquaviva's ex-chamberlain must have met him in Rome;
perhaps he renewed his acquaintance through the offices of Montalvo,
whose debut Colonna had sponsored. Thanks to Colonna's patronage,
Galatea will be printed at Alcalá during the summer of 1584, provided (in February) with an *aprobación* by Gracián Dantisco and with a
royal copyright signed by Eraso. In autumn, Miguel addresses the
dedication of his book to Ascanio, whose father has just died. In March
1585, a volume of 375 octavo folios goes on sale at Robles's shop in
Madrid: it is entitled *The First Part of Galatea, Divided into Six Books.*
Cervantes, who by his own admission had not wanted "to keep it put
away for himself alone any longer," is now a full-fledged writer. The
time has come for him to hear the reader's verdict.

A PASTORAL RHAPSODY

LET us imagine the first impressions made by *Galatea* on a reader in Philip II's Madrid. As soon as he opens the book, without stopping at the unfamiliar author's name, he finds a setting, a passion, a language that are already familiar to him:

> While mountain, meadow, plain, and river send back
> The sad and mournful accent of my song's
> Ill-tunèd sound with weary spirit's bitter
> Echo . . .

The unhappy Sireno, whom Montemayor showed us at the foot of the mountains of León recalling his love affair with the incomparable Diana, is transformed into the unfortunate Elicio, on the banks of the Tagus, lamenting to all the echoes Galatea's coldness. Cervantes does not use this deliberate homage to his predecessor simply as a way to introduce the subject. It is visible, in the course of the narrative, in everything that reveals his obviously scrupulous respect for the conventions of the genre: the verdant grove embellished by the murmur of a flowing brook, where shepherds live protected from cold and hunger; the divers instruments on which they accompany themselves while singing their complaints; the courtly greetings exchanged by two rivals who sigh in vain for the same shepherdess; the alternation of antiphonal strophes of strictly Vergilian cut; the shepherds' devotion to the woman chosen by their hearts; their ardor, inhibited by the very perfection of the beauty that she radiates; the purity of the intentions that motivate them, comparable only to the reserve and the modesty that Galatea and her companions display in all circumstances; finally, their passionate interest in their own feelings, as if the only adventure worthy of being experienced is that which leads to the depths of their souls.

It is not only the list of themes but also the structure of the romance itself that attests to the success of the formula made popular by the author of *Diana*. The fifty-some-odd shepherds who populate the Cervantine pastoral all experience disappointment in an equal number of overlapping cases of unrequited feelings—attraction, aversion, or simple indifference—toward fellow shepherds and shepherdesses. Before the eyes of the reader passes a succession of microcosms of love, bound together by the play of balances and contrasts, in a narrative whose slow progress is periodically interrupted by long parentheses. Inspired by León Hebreo, the main points of these disquisitions, which Cervantes goes to lengths to justify in his preface, are expanded upon by Tirsi and Damon, two wise shepherds who have managed to break love's chains and are consequently invested with a symbolic role in the general economy of the work. The repeated insertion of interpolated novellas, the regular alternation of poetry and prose, are more clear signs of the debt Cervantes owes to his predecessors: an unavoidable debt, since every pastoral brings into play, within a universe pervaded with literary culture, a system of reminiscences, of which one finds traces in the speeches of different characters.

But let us take a closer look at the inventory of literary debts. It is quite true that the melancholy and delicate Elicio is consistent with his predecessors when, as a sort of preamble, he confides his suffering to the woods and rocks. But the appearance of Galatea's other suitor, Erasto, introduces an unexpected note into what was nothing but a concert of harmonious moans:

> Erasto arrived accompanied by his mastiffs, the faithful guardians of the innocent little sheep that with such protection were safe from the blood-thirsty fangs of ravening wolves; he was playing with them and calling them by their names, giving to each the description that his temperament and spirit deserved: he called one Lion, one Hawk, one Hardy, one Spot. And they, as if they were endowed with reason, shaking their heads and running toward him, expressed the pleasure that they felt at his pleasure.

These mastiffs very nearly wag their tails; only the narrator's regard for propriety restrains him. The rustic Erasto, however, who is quick to conjure the "fatal rabies and cruel mange" that threaten his "playful kids and young lambkins," seems ready to venture outside the bucolic setting; he foreshadows, though timidly, the Castilian peasants of *The Dialogue of the Dogs* (El coloquio de los perros) and *Don Quixote*.

In the fleeting encounter of the two shepherds, we see sketched out, very summarily of course, the confrontation of the two kinds of truth distinguished by Aristotle, the truth of poetry and that of history: a confrontation that the ongoing dialogue between the Ingenious *Hidalgo* and his squire will develop on a new scale and with new breadth. It is what gives a new sound to the symphony of pipes and viols that the pastoral had previously offered. And other modulations combine to give Cervantine music a color that belongs to it alone: for example, Galatea's steadfast rejection of her numerous suitors. This is not the stereotyped behavior of the indifferent beauty; it is the coherent expression of an autonomous heroine's desire for freedom, in a person who obstinately refuses to be a mere love-object. As a consequence, the universe of *Galatea* tends to emancipate itself from inherited conventions. But it does not close in upon itself, even so. From the first pages, Italian-style novellas are inserted into the plot—as a result of various shepherds' arrivals and encounters—in a skillfully guided narration. Lisardo and Crisalva, Timbrio and Silerio, Darinto and Rosana, bring violence and death into the verdant grove; they force the shepherds to tear themselves away from their sufferings in order to learn to take action; and they open up the Cervantine Arcady to new vistas: the court and its intrigues; the city and its spell; the sea, with its dangers of piracy. This contamination not only enlarges the field of pastoral fiction; it opens the way that will lead Cervantes to the subtle and daring orchestrations of his *Exemplary Novellas* and *Persiles*.

At the same time, this universe, operating by its own logic, cannot admit anything that might deter the natural progress of the story or alter the motivations that explain it. None of those nymphs or satyrs that occasionally show up in *Diana* and that will reappear later in Lope de Vega's *Arcadia*. No situation resolved by supernatural intervention, like the water of oblivion that the sorceress Felicia makes Montemayor's heroes drink in order to extricate them from an impasse—and get the narrator out of trouble. In the scrutiny of Don Quixote's books, the Priest will tell us what we should think of this device:

> To begin, then, with the *Diana* of Montemayor. It is my opinion it should not be burned, but that everything about the sage Felicia and the magic water should be removed, together with almost all the longer pieces of verse. Let it keep, and welcome, its prose and the honor of being the first book of the kind.

It is a man in his late fifties, with the objectivity of age and experience, who attributes this language to the Priest—an objectivity that explains the judgment this same spokesman offers on *Galatea* and its author:

> That Cervantes has been for many years a great friend of mine, and to my knowledge he has had more experience with reverses than in verses. His

book is not without imagination; it presents us with something but brings nothing to a conclusion. We must wait for the second part that he has promised . . .

The matter-of-fact tone, the half-veiled criticisms, refer in part to the unfinished aspect of his romance. As it has come down to us, the story is interrupted at the moment when Galatea is forced to leave for Portugal, and we have no way of knowing what the outcome of her adventures will be. But the Priest's remarks take on a totally different shade of meaning in the light of Berganza's discourse in *The Dialogue of the Dogs,* when he ironically recalls all those books "that talked of shepherds and shepherdesses" and that he learned were the delight of his master's lady-love. If the dog-narrator pokes fun at pastoral fiction, it is because the shepherds whose flock he guarded have left him quite a different mental picture. Unlike Elicio, his shepherds sang,

> not with delicate, resonant, admirable voices but with hoarse voices, so that, by themselves or together, they seemed to be not singing but shouting or growling.

The inverted stylization presented to us here is quite as arbitrary as the idealization proper to the classical pastoral, whose heroes do *not* spend most of the day "delousing themselves or mending their sandals." If Berganza takes pleasure in sharpening the contrasts, it is in order the better to demystify bucolic conventions. He tells us by way of conclusion:

> From that, I came to understand what I think everybody must believe: that all those books are things dreamed up and skillfully written for the amusement of people with leisure, and are not true at all. If they were, there would have been among my shepherds some vestige of that most happy life, of those pleasant meadows, vast forests, sacred mountains, beautiful gardens, clear brooks and crystalline springs, and of those gallantries as chaste as they are well-expressed, and of shepherds fainting here and shepherdesses fainting there, of one player's pipes sounding here, some other's shawm there.

No, the pastoral is not true, as history is true. History tells things "as they were, without adding or taking anything from the truth." But does the pastoral offer to us another kind of truth, the subtle truth of those "mendacious fables . . . suited to the understanding of the reader" that make the impossible seem believable? At a distance of thirty years, Miguel doubts that his *Galatea* has really succeeded in doing so, with its overly abstract characters, its too-frequent digressions, and its interminable declamations. To be sure, *Galatea* receives quite a favorable reception when it comes off the press. Admired in literary salons, praised by Lope de Vega, it will appear in a second edition, five years later. Published again in Paris in 1611, in the wake of the success of *Don Quixote,* it will be much appreciated at the French court, where, we are told, ladies and gentlemen knew it "almost by heart." One of its fervent readers will be Honoré d'Urfé, whose *L'Astrée* proves that in the days of Richelieu and Corneille, these "dreamed-up" stories will continue to amuse people of leisure. Nevertheless, in spite of the compliments and praise, Cervantes cannot bring himself to publish the *Second Part,* though he announces it on four occasions, and even on his deathbed. In the end, his favorite Arcady is the one he will incorporate in *Don Quixote.* Spread across various episodes, it will grow strong from challenges to its reality, so to speak. The first case is the Arcadia that the student Grisóstomo invents to amuse himself: the son of a rich peasant, he has read Montemayor at Salamanca, and he takes it into his head, when he returns to his village, to dress up as a shepherd. In order to play the bashful lover, he becomes infatuated with Marcela, whose only attachment is to her independence. Caught in the trap of a passion with no hope of success, he finally kills himself. Then there is the case of the Arcadia recreated for their own amusement by some cultivated readers of Sannazaro and Garcilaso who have a refined sense of stage setting: it is a pastime for courtiers who are well aware that it is purely artificial. And finally, there is the Arcadia that Don Quixote dreams of creating at the conclusion of his wanderings, in order to forget an ignominious defeat that prevents him thenceforth from going about the world. He succeeds—for the space of a discourse—in making Sancho share his longing for this Arcadia of the Word, until the wall of incomprehension that separates their respective desires is revealed by the turn of a phrase. *This* is the pastoral romance that even today continues to attract and fascinate us. It would never have seen the light if Cervantes had not taken up the challenge of *Diana;* but it also relegates *Galatea* to the semi-obscurity of the archeology of its creation.

THE LURE OF THE THEATER

DID Miguel, balked in his quest for a post at court, seek bittersweet
consolation for frustrated ambition in the peace of bucolic literature?
Biographers have often given in to the temptation of opposing dream
to reality: according to them, Don Quixote's father, facing an indifferent or hostile world, showed his hero a way out. But let us be
careful not to attribute to an author the face that he will one day give
to his most illustrious creation. Cervantes did not remodel the real
world to suit his fancies, pastoral or chivalric. At a time when the
profession of writer had not yet been invented, he had tried to obtain
the only kind of position that would permit him to continue to write.
Laínez, Figueroa, Gálvez de Montalvo were there to serve as examples
and to urge him to take such a course. Failing to obtain the post that
he coveted, the author of *Galatea* then sees himself obliged to try the
impossible: to live by his pen, however modestly. The ducats received
from Robles were not enough, by themselves, to permit him to stay
afloat, however numerous the readers of his first book. How then to
expand his public? By trying to satisfy a passion that he himself had
felt from his earliest youth, that was sweeping Spain, and that would
not soon leave her: the passion for the theater.

The Madrid that Cervantes had left fifteen years earlier, at the time
of his unexpected departure for Italy, had just provided itself with a
building intended for presenting plays. Miguel still preferred the
makeshift productions organized by Lope de Rueda. A year before his
death, as we have seen, Cervantes left a fond, rather bantering description of Rueda that is worth quoting:

> In the time of this celebrated Spaniard, all of the impresario's stage prop-
> erties fit into a sack and were little more than a few white sheepskin coats
> decorated with gilt leather and a few beards and wigs and shepherds'
> crooks. The plays were dialogues like eclogues, by two or three shepherds
> and a shepherdess; they were embellished and lengthened with two or
> three interludes about black servant-women, pimps, fools, Biscayans . . .
> At that time there was no stage machinery or fights between Moors and
> Christians on foot or on horseback; there were no characters that would
> come out, or appear to come out, of the center of the earth, through the
> hole in the stage, which consisted of four benches set in a square, with
> four to six boards on top of them. . . . And there were certainly no clouds

descending from heaven with angels or souls. The decoration of the theater was an old quilt—drawn by two ropes from one side to the other—which made what they [now] call the "tiring room." The musicians, without a guitar, stood behind it, singing some ancient ballad.

This recollection, imbued with bookish allusions, does not of course aspire to the rigorous exactitude of an erudite reconstruction; but one can sense nostalgia for the repertory performed on movable boards set up in an inn-yard or, once in a while, even in the open air: comedies in prose, inspired by Plautus, Terence, or the Italian Renaissance, that set daring suitors, suspicious graybeards, and inventive lackeys against one another (as Molière will do later in *Les Fourberies de Scapin*); pastoral fables *(églogas),* closer to Christmas playlets than to Virgil or Theocritus's eclogues, which for a long time were enough to satisfy the theatrical urges of Seville or Valencia's bourgeoisie; and comic interludes, pervaded with folklore, which deal with the same themes in a humorous way, like a countermelody.

These plays, written in a picturesque, lively, and spontaneous language that always fits the character, generally took the talents of the actors into consideration. But their popularity could not continue indefinitely with the repetition of the same situations, the same schemes, the same tried-and-true procedures. When Cervantes returns to Spain, he observes that they no longer come up to the public's expectations. The audience has changed. As Madrid supplants Seville and Valencia, a nobility both bureaucratic and courtly takes the place of the merchant bourgeoisie and imposes its values and its taste. At the same time, conditions of play-presentation are transformed. Wandering troupes of actors continue, no doubt, to lead a difficult, hazardous existence in the course of their tours, "running from town to town and from inn to tavern, like perpetual gypsies." But the troupes are now larger, their full complement attaining as many as fifteen players, including women and children. Their craft is also improved in the school of the Italian actors who crisscross the Peninsula. Most important, they have become an essential link in the system set up by philanthropic religious societies that give money to support hospices and hospitals in every town, thanks to profits from sponsored performances. This veritable "entertainment industry" gives a decisive push to religious mystery plays *(autos).* The *autos,* in the line of medieval morality plays, aim to complete, in visual form, the catechesis revived by the Counter-Reformation. At the same time, the entertainment industry contributes to the rise of secular theater by encouraging the construction of the first *corrales,* permanent stages set up in the inner courtyards of buildings and adapted to the needs of dramatic spectacle.

Thus, between 1578 and 1582, Madrid sees the Corral de la Cruz and the Corral del Príncipe built, with the help of Italian actors. During the same years, Seville, Valencia, Granada, Toledo, Valladolid, and Zaragoza inaugurate or remodel their own theaters. Everywhere we find the same ground-floor courtyard, between two structures, framed on the sides by stepped rows of seating, above which are grill-protected windows, and overhung in the back by a gallery called the "henroost" *(cazuela).* Privileged spectators took their places on the sides; the *cazuela* held women of modest means; and the pit was reserved for the turbulent throng of groundlings *(mosqueteros).* With regard to the stage, it has nothing in common with the boards of former times. It is a rectangular platform, about twenty-two feet by thirteen feet, which backs up to a two-story façade. Flanked by two side doors, extended toward the rear by a dressing room concealed behind a curtain, surmounted by a gallery provided with openings that could serve as windows, this stage platform communicates with the basement by a trap door: in all, four complementary areas that permit the simultaneous presentation of multiple places.

Such is the space in which a style of performance evolves whose development Cervantes traces, after his fashion; we see its effects in the stage directions of his own plays: drum rolls, the rumble of thunder, the appearance of horses on the stage, sudden "discoveries" managed thanks to the tiring-room curtain, the unexpected arrival of a messenger from heaven, propelled by a windlass. Let us not be misled by these rudimentary tricks, which recall medieval mystery plays far more than they prefigure the complex techniques of the Italian-style stage: at the end of the sixteenth century, dramatic space, the *lieu scénique,* is still an abstract space which contains neither scenery nor the objects to which the "closed box" stage has accustomed us. Its power of evocation rests above all on the text and to a lesser extent on the declamation and movements of the actors charged with embodying the text. Thus the platform can be a room, a street, or a field, one after another; the gallery can become a balcony, a mountain, or a rampart: an austere system, but one to which spectators accommodate themselves perfectly and which will be used by Lope de Vega and his generation; during almost half a century, people will go to *hear* and not to *see* a play. Not until the reign of Philip IV will Calderón and his collaborators adapt at court an imported Italian theater with stage machinery, where ostentatious performances are reserved for the king and the aristocracy. But at the moment when Cervantes turns his attention to the *corrales,* the conventions on which dramatic spectacle rests exclude the illusion of reality as well as *trompe-l'oeil* stage effects.

What in fact becomes clear, during these years when the Spanish theater is still finding its way, is the desire to break with the empiricism of Rueda's heirs, mere followers content to repeat their master's recipes in order to provide cheap amusement for a public eager for novelty. Working separately, Argensola at Zaragoza, Rey de Artieda and Virués at Valencia, and Juan de la Cueva at Seville simultaneously express this desire for a break. A single ambition spurs them: to rise above the limitations of such a consumer-oriented art, to give the stage the dignity it lacks. Where will they seek their models for this objective? From all indications, not in the directions already explored by their predecessors. They do not appeal to *Celestina,* the tragicomic study of a divided world that today appears to us to be the work that laid the foundations of modern theater. In this period, no one considers it for performance, since it was conceived to be read aloud, with its twenty-one acts, its slow pace, its long speeches. They likewise turn away from the early Castilian playwrights—Juan del Encina, Gil Vicente—whose *autos* and eclogues, composed at the beginning of the century, still bear the mark of liturgical themes and scriptural texts. Their rural inspiration was once the delight of the salons of the worldly and educated, but they now belong to a bygone era. The new playwrights are unaware of the remarkably original productions of Torres Naharro, whose secular comedies reveal a very lively sense of dramatic movement and of theatrical possibilities; but Torres has spent the most illustrious part of his life outside Spain, in the cosmopolitan milieu of the Roman Curia.

The precedent they return to is Seneca's drama, which is the currently prevailing model throughout Europe and which they reread often through his Italian disciples of the Cinquecento, Dolce and Giraldi Cinzio. In Seneca's wake, they strive to wear the tragic buskin, refurbishing allegories, heroes from antiquity, legendary figures of the Reconquista; they adopt lofty-sounding poetry, use and abuse rhetorical bombast. This preference for "Seneca the Spaniard" explains the tendencies of a repertory in which Aristotle's precepts are constantly flouted, in which complicated plots pile one adventure on another, while mixing times and places. In its way, this humanist drama expresses, if maladroitly, the intuitions that the creator of the *comedia nueva,* Lope de Vega, will formulate. But its major weakness is that it was invented by scholars for scholars; so it will fail, lacking a trained public, lacking adequate material conditions, and lacking a writer of genius capable of creating characters, of making an action live, of inventing a language; a writer who is not content with mere horror and violence, heaping up bodies, and making blood flow.

Cervantes followed the efforts of these creators of an abortive renewal with sympathy. He read Argensola's tragedies and will later praise them by the mouth of the Priest in *Don Quixote.* He was doubtless familiar with Cueva's plays, which their author had presented in Seville and will publish in 1583. And finally, in all likelihood he had met Virués during his passage through Valencia: in the "Song of Calliope" he celebrates this estimable poet, who like himself had fought at Lepanto and whose courage, talent, and learning he praises. But he does not, for all that, neglect professional entertainers, who were the only persons who could open for him the doors of the *corrales.* Two intermediaries must have been valuable to him. The first is Alonso Getino de Guzmán, who, as we have seen, sponsored his literary debut and intervened several times on behalf of his parents. Having become an *alquacil* (bailiff), the ex-dancer from Rueda's troupe and former master of revels for the capital seems to have participated closely in the activities that led to the opening of the Corral de la Cruz. The second intermediary is Tomás Gutiérrez, associated with Miguel's family for several years, an actor himself, and Miguel's close friend; we will meet him later in Seville.

To be introduced by professionals was Cervantes' "Open, Sesame." In a period that did not recognize literary property, the poet—as far as actors were concerned—was simply a collaborator on an ephemeral production, the furnisher of an extremely perishable commodity. The director of the troupe (or as they said at the time, symptomatically, the *autor de comedias*), once he had acquired the manuscript of a text, could alter or transform it at will. To protest was useless: "Take my advice and never meddle with actors," Sancho will say to his master, "for they are a privileged class." Fortunate the writer who received a decent sum as the price of his labor, like the forty ducats that Gaspar de Porres will agree to pay Miguel in 1585 for two plays, of which we have only the titles: *Life at Constantinople* (El trato de Constantinopla) and *The Mix-up* (La confusa). Even if he was never a mercenary author, our hero could hardly be indifferent to these shiny metal arguments, fit to conjure the specter of poverty; and while *Galatea* was the fruit of patient labor, the *comedias* that he planned for the stages of Madrid would require less effort than cleverness if he could find a formula that would please the spectators.

And so Cervantes and the theater make contact. Did the meeting take place on his return from captivity? It is doubtful. First, because (as we know) the author of *Galatea* had other worries at that time: anxious to claim his reward for service, he would soon join the court in Portugal. Furthermore, the death of Queen Ana, which occurred in the autumn of 1580, shortly before his arrival in Valencia, forced the Madrid theaters to close as a sign of mourning; they would not re-open until December of the following year. On the other hand, during the time that Miguel was putting the finishing touches on his pastoral romance, after his return from Lisbon, the circumstances were more favorable for trying his luck with actors. He will not forget that experience.

TWO PLAYS LOST AND FOUND

And this is a truth that no one can gainsay, and here is where my going beyond the limits of modesty comes in: the theaters of Madrid saw the performance of *Life in Algiers,* which I wrote, and *The Destruction of Numancia* and *The Naval Battle,* where I dared to reduce plays from the five acts they used to have to three. I revealed (or to be more precise, I was the first to present) the soul's imaginings and hidden thoughts by putting allegorical figures on stage, to general and satisfied applause from the audience. At that time I wrote about twenty to thirty plays, all of which were recited without anyone's offering gifts of cucumbers or other missiles; they finished their runs without hissing, booing, or uproar.

THE tone is set. At the hour of reckoning, Cervantes is unconcerned about the more-or-less worthy motives that caused him to take up playwriting; he wants only to record his appreciable, if not decisive, contribution to the progress of the Spanish stage. Some critics have challenged his claims, arguing that others before him had written plays in three acts and introduced allegories into their creations. The objection falls flat if one observes that here it is a question of practices at Madrid, at a time when Madrid, Seville, and Valencia were very much independent cultural microcosms. For example, the allegorical characters—*figuras morales*—in *Life in Algiers* illustrate perfectly our poet's claim. They are not, like traditional allegories, personified obstacles that embody the antagonistic forces with which the individual is supposed to be struggling; they take part in the action in order to exteriorize the interior debate of the character present on stage, without ever exchanging words with him or attempting to take his place. One can understand why Miguel is anxious to establish his paternity of this original technique.

No, Cervantes is not one of those people who deck themselves out with borrowed plumage. On the contrary, what is striking about his recollection of an experience that affected him deeply is the contrast between the vigor with which he describes the innovations he introduced and the ambiguous, evasive way he describes the reception of his plays. Only *The Mix-up* seems to have received favorable treatment, for he tells us in the *Journey to Parnassus* that this play was judged "admirable": another reason to deplore its loss. Cervantes' account of his success with the public in the capital (at a time when the *corrales* were scarcely beginning their careers and the Spanish stage was not yet really a national institution) is obviously perceptive, if not rigorous.

Can we, in the light of this account, measure the historical importance of Cervantine theater, which preceded the birth of the *comedia nueva* by fifteen years? The difficulty rests on both the partial loss of the dramatic literature of that transitional period and the almost total disappearance of the "twenty to thirty" plays alluded to in Cervantes' account. The number is in itself not excessive, in view of the hundreds of plays that Lope de Vega wrote in the course of a truly long and fecund career. Besides, Cervantes was quite the opposite of a born improviser, and he had distinct reservations about the glibness of his young rival. We have, thanks to the "Postscript" (Adjunta) to the *Journey to Parnassus,* the titles of ten of these hypothetical plays. Three of them are also mentioned in the text quoted above. But only *Life in Algiers* and *The Siege of Numancia* (El cerco de Numancia) have come down to us, in defective manuscript copies rediscovered in the eighteenth century under layers of library dust. As for *The Naval Battle* (La batalla naval), obviously inspired by Lepanto, we must mourn its loss, too.

Critics have often condemned *Life in Algiers,* a work saturated with the ex-captive's painful memories. The episodic scenes that this play strings together follow one another apparently without order, and at first acquaintance they disconcert the reader. The plot around which these scenes are arranged—the thwarted love affair of Silvia and Aurelio, two Christian slaves subjected to the advances of their respective owners—injects a purely conventional situation taken from Greek romances and Italian *novelle* into a setting about life in captivity. The novelistic vicissitudes that spring from this plot are quite out of tune with the realistic episodes—involving the selling of slaves, apostatizing, ransom, cruelty, torture—that make up the backdrop, whose documentary interest often surpasses its artistic value. And the approximately forty roles that it requires, out of proportion with the resources of a troupe of actors—all these elements tell us that the play is a beginner's first try.

Consequently, indulgence is all the more necessary since the only text at our disposal is a defective one, mutilated by cuts made by an unscrupulous adapter. In spite of its undeniable faults of construction, *Life in Algiers* deserves more than mere condescending mention. Even though the tension between life and literature that informs it up to its dénouement is weakened by startling changes of tone, this play nevertheless represents something quite new in the theater of the day. Cervantes is the only writer of his generation who boldly depicts on the stage an irreplaceable autobiographical experience, placing it in the immediate present: allusions to current events, the announcement of the landing of the ransom party, the participation of a captive named Saavedra (the author's true *alter ego*), the appearance of Hassan Pasha, at the end, as a sort of *deus ex machina,* are all evidence of personal experience. At the same time, in transposing his experience, he does not present us with either an unretouched document or a slice of life. Proof is his selection of data in view of what the action needs: their insertion into a purely fictive chronology; their contamination with literary reminiscences that echo Virgil, Lucan, and Seneca as readily as Heliodorus, Boccaccio, and the *Romancero;* their presentation, in conclusion, in a way that combines allusion, story, and setting, so as to satisfy the essential demand for effectiveness.

The word may seem a little strong applied to a play whose coherence has been challenged. But let us say it anyway: the theatricality of *Life in Algiers* is unquestionable. But it is necessary to uncover the thematic and symbolic connections uniting the apparently disconnected sequences that pass before our eyes, impelled by the trials and tribulations of the hero and heroine. The confusion of Aurelio's companions, torn between their sorrow over the martyrdom of one of their number and their hope for the providential arrival of Philip II's ships, corresponds to Aurelio's own situation. The separation of a family dispersed by slave auction echoes the distress of Silvia, torn from her loving family by pirates. By this means, the author creates a dialogue between the one and the many, between the individual and the collective, among the various destinies presented to the spectator, refracted as through a prism. But this dialogue, underlined by variations of vocabulary and style, as well as by the alternation of meters and strophes, is not compatible with the limitations of the Italian-style stage (though this incongruous reference to the theater *a la italiana* explains certain ill-thought-out criticisms). It was conceived from the beginning for the plural space of the *corral;* and it might perhaps be adequately transferred to the stage today, given the resources of modern stagecraft.

Instead of making the play a historical set piece, such an adaptation—and here is the hard part—would have to be capable of putting the action back into the unfolding historical moment; the juncture where the suspended time of captivity without immediate hope of escape is situated; the moment remodeled by the captives' hopes and desires, when they see warning signs of a Spanish expedition against Algiers in what are actually the preparations for the Portuguese campaign. After his return to Madrid, Cervantes realized that an attack on Algiers—a utopian idea, we hasten to add—would never come to pass. Philip II's Spain now turns toward the Atlantic West, concerned with new objectives as a result of the unification of the Peninsula, the revival of tensions with England, and France's interior difficulties left from the Wars of Religion. Renouncing all African ambitions, Spain confines herself, vis-à-vis the Barbary pirates, to a strict defense of her Levantine and Andalusian coast. But *Life in Algiers* does not limit itself to recalling, for the benefit of Spanish public opinion, the importance of the activities of ransomer-monks; at the very moment when the Mediterranean begins to lose its historical importance, Saavedra's imaginary appeal to Philip II to deliver Algiers exalts the illusory importance of a naval operation whose time has passed. Hence the gap between the image painted by impatient captives, of a city in desperate straits, ready to fall like a ripe fruit, and the image created piecemeal as a setting for the fiction, of a prosperous city under a strict political and military order, enriched by daring corsairs and the growing sea-trade they control, the preferred place for the exchanges perpetually transacted between Christendom and Islam. In the play there is no lack of symbols for this extraordinary commerce; or for the complex relations established in the course of the action between masters and servants; or for the ambiguous attitudes that both groups adopt in the face of unforeseen events, ignoring the conventions of a Manichean universe that would set in opposition the good and the bad. The message of *Life in Algiers* is, then, subtler than appeared at first sight. It is up to theatrical professionals to tell us whether it comes across. As for the biographer, he cannot help pointing out the first significant break between the illusions of the hero of Lepanto and Algiers and the disappointments of the captive returned to his native soil.

Numancia, the only Spanish tragedy to have survived for posterity, seems just as ambiguous to us today, but for other reasons. Its theme is well known: the collective suicide of a Celtiberian city, encircled by Scipio's legions, that chose to sacrifice itself rather than to consent, under the sway of famine, to an ignominious surrender. This historical event, which occurred in 133 B.C., had been recorded and exalted by the chroniclers of imperial Spain. Cervantes not only rehabilitated it, he succeeded in enriching the outline borrowed from his sources with original episodes taken from legend or his favorite authors. From antiquity Virgil and Seneca, from peninsular tradition Ercilla and the *Romancero,* furnish him with elements for a sweeping recreation that emphasizes the high points of the action: the initial appearance of Scipio, haranguing his troops; the invocation of infernal powers by the besieged, who are looking for omens; the final agony of the defenders; the spectacular death of the last survivor. At the same time, as in *Life in Algiers,* each separate destiny refracts in some way the fate of a city that identifies itself with the unanimous will of its inhabitants. As the city marches toward its ineluctable end, warriors, women, and children, each on his own scale, are set against the siege, famine, and death, composing the grandiose or pathetic tableaux for what Robert Marrast rightly calls "the great fresco of horror" of *Numancia.* Finally, at regular intervals, the dialogue between Spain and the River Duero, the reply of the infernal gods by the voice of a messenger from beyond the grave, the appearance of War and Famine, the concluding speech by Fame, introduce an allegorical counterpoint that, after the fashion of the ancient chorus, gradually separates and makes explicit the meaning and far-reaching significance of the event.

Put into this perspective, the action opens upon vistas for which one would vainly seek the equivalent in Argensola, Virués, or Cueva. The efforts of the defenders to avert an evil fate meet the requirements of pure tragedy, which is accomplished when Numancia, thwarting Roman schemes, chooses the way of sacrifice and decides to accept her destiny freely. Simultaneously, speeches by the allegorical figures place this unheard-of act of bravery in an expanded time frame, before eternalizing it in the mythical mode. Opposing Scipio, a god-sent hero who symbolizes the knowledge of warfare and who wants no other guide but glory, the Celtiberian city appears at first to embody a scandalous, stubborn challenge to all-powerful Rome. But in the light of prophecies by the Duero and by Fame, her resistance and suicide become the first stage in a journey that links, one after another, the occupation of Spain by Roman legions, the fall of the Roman Empire under the blows of the barbarians, the sack of papal Rome by the duke of Alba's troops, and, finally, the temporal and spiritual hegemony of Philip II's Spain at the time of Portugal's reincorporation into the crown. Reexamined from this angle, the sacrifice of Numancia not only robs Scipio of his victory, it foreshadows the future apotheosis of the Hapsburg monarchy, the heir of both Numancia and Rome: the audience is invited to ponder the significance and meditate upon the meaning of its apogee.

It is conceivable that *Numancia* received, if one can believe its author, a favorable reception in the *corrales*. But one should also observe that, at that period, it was *Spanish* armies that were imposing their iron law on those who refused Iberian hegemony. The Moriscos of Alpujarras, the Flemings who defended Haarlem, Leyden, and Antwerp, saw Don Juan de Austria, as well as the duke of Alba, as a new Scipio come to make them bow the neck. Cervantes is an attentive observer of this painful present; and, in the setting that he creates, Fame's prophecy makes a strange, almost discordant, sound. A dissonance intended by the author? We cannot be sure. But what is certain is that in our day we are no longer responsive to that exaltation of imperial Spain that, as far as we are concerned, belongs to the musty past; whereas the collective sacrifice of Numancia retains its universal significance.

Whether analogous to our own historical situation or not, it continues to touch us directly.

Impressed by the epic inspiration of *Numancia,* the German Romantics were the first to rediscover the play. Goethe and Schopenhauer, in particular, do not hesitate to compare it to *The Persians* and *The Seven Against Thebes.* A century later, in the middle of the Spanish Civil War, Rafael Alberti in Madrid and Jean-Louis Barrault in Paris, neither aware of the other's activities, are responsible for its resurrection on the stage. Barrault's production, respectful of the text, attempts to underline its subversive force as an apology for resistance against an oppressor. Rafael Alberti will go even farther: his "modernized" adaptation of the tragedy, performed during the siege of Madrid, will explicitly identify Franco's troops and their Italian allies with the Roman attackers. We are still fascinated by the heroic gesture of these beings who prefer death to slavery and who reveal their courage in the exercise of their freedom. If we still admire their aspirations for independence and justice, it is because their choice is not inspired by past examples but sets itself up as its own model and offers itself as a pattern for future ages, as a seed waiting to sprout, in the course of time. Thus the message of death that *Numancia* provides is also a message of life: it teaches the ever-possible revenge of the weak on the strong.

ANA FRANCA

THE letter to Eraso from early 1582 lets us see a discouraged, bitter Miguel, who has no illusions about the success of his patrons' efforts. At least he still had, deep in his heart, that passion for writing that made him devote all his attention to his *Galatea.* Two years later, he has obviously given up the idea of going to the Indies, and he no longer talks about the improbable sinecure that for a while he had been led to expect. He now has other satisfactions besides those provided by conversations with his literary creations: his plays are being produced on Madrid's stages; he is about to see *Galatea* come off the presses. Cervantes is on the way to becoming a name in the world into which he has chosen to thrust himself.

To what extent was his personal life affected by this change? Were his parents aware of his success, or did they view it as merely a stopgap? Doubtless they would have preferred for the survivor of Lepanto and Algiers to receive, like his brother Rodrigo, a reward for his services. As a royal functionary in Madrid or Alcalá, he would not only have been safe from want, he would have brought them financial aid as well as protection and support in their squabbles with debtors and creditors. Instead, his only resources are unpredictable profits from aleatory contracts, in a century that could not conceive the possibility of writing as a profession. (Lope de Vega, even at the peak of his fame, and in spite of the favor of publishers and of the public, will never manage to live by his pen. As the secretary of a Maecenas fond of the fair sex, he will have to agree to act as a go-between.) Miguel must surely have given his family some kind of subsidy during these prosperous times; but we know nothing of the amount or how it was spent. One thing is virtually certain: neither the *escudos* received from the actors who produced *Numancia* nor the ducats paid by Blas de Robles permitted him to reimburse the Trinitarians for the sum that Fray Juan Gil had advanced for his ransom. In order to do so, it will be necessary for his mother to receive the profits—finally—from the two thousand ducats' worth of merchandise she had previously received authorization to export to Algiers. She will finally settle her debt in November 1584.

Another question comes naturally to mind: what kind of life does our hero lead from day to day when he leaves the silence of his study to mingle with his fellow writers and theatrical people? What kind of image does he present to those who approach him? Should we picture him with the traits of one of those poets that the *Exemplary Novellas* depict without mercy? One thinks, for example, of the "student, to all appearances," whom Berganza describes in the throes of creation:

> He was busy writing in a notebook, and from time to time he would slap his forehead and bite his nails, staring at the sky; at other times he would become so pensive that he moved neither foot nor hand, nor even blinked, such was his concentration. Once I approached him without his noticing me; I heard him mumbling under his breath, and after a good while he shouted, "By God, this is the best octave I've ever written in my life!" And writing rapidly in his notebook, he showed signs of great satisfaction.

This description is too obviously a bravura passage to be considered a self-caricature by *Don Quixote's* author. One can say the same about the scribbler that Master Glass describes to us, always ready to inflict his latest sonnet on whoever will listen:

> At which point he purses his lips, arches his eyebrows, and digs around in his pocket; and from a thousand dirty, half-torn pieces of paper, on which there are another thousand sonnets, he extracts the one he wants to recite, and finally he repeats it in a sugary, coy tone.

An exercise in style? No doubt. It would be pointless to play "guess who?" and try to give a name to these entirely imaginary puppets. Even so, Cervantes' zestful caricatures are not untrue to the habits of the republic of letters or the failings with which his fellow writers must often have appeared to him to be afflicted. Even though he shared their occupations and practiced their rites, he was only too aware of the ridicule to which their desperate rivalries and petty ambitions exposed them, and he will not hesitate, when he considers it warranted, to stand aloof.

Disinclined to provide topics for gossip in Madrid's literary salons, as Lope de Vega will manage to do some years later, the author of *Galatea* is no less reserved on the subject of his love life. We do not even know whether he dedicated his verses to some inaccessible muse, like Garcilaso, Herrera, or Gálvez de Montalvo: it is upon Don Quixote that he will one day impose the burden of hopeless adoration for Dulcinea. Nor do we hear of any of those tumultuous adventures that contributed so much to Lope's notoriety. Only a few allusions, as discreet as they are belated, extracted from the austere prose of notarial documents reveal to us a love affair that Cervantes had at the age of thirty-five. The fruit of this liaison was an illegitimate daughter, Isabel, whom his sister Magdalena will take in when she reaches the age of fifteen, when she is orphaned. Miguel will give her his name after his final return to Madrid.

Unless one believes the tales in the *Journey to Parnassus* and makes Promontorio a flesh-and-blood person, Miguel does not seem to have had another child besides this one, who will one day become Isabel de Saavedra and of whom we shall hear again. But who was her mother? A certain Ana de Villafranca, also called Ana Franca de Rojas, about whom the Cervantine archives are almost silent, but whose traces historians have succeeded in discovering by roundabout ways. She was the daughter of Juan Villafranca, a wool merchant, and was born twenty years earlier in Madrid. Still quite young, she entered the service of an aunt, whose husband, the bailiff *(alguacil)* Martín Mújica, will be mixed up six years later in the escape of Antonio Pérez, the king's ex-secretary. At the death of her aunt in 1579, she received a bequest of one hundred ducats, intended to permit her to set up housekeeping. Had someone already found a match for her? The fact is that, whether pressured or of her own free will, at the age of sixteen she marries, on August 11, 1580, Alonso Rodríguez, a semi-literate Asturian trades-man. With the help of mysterious patrons, the couple waste no time in finding a house of their own, because they are going to keep a tavern on Tudescos Street, frequented by impresarios and actors. It is doubt-less there that the author of *Numancia* makes the acquaintance of the young woman, who was already the mother of a little girl named Ana. Since her daughter was born in mid-November, their love affair must have begun at the latest around the beginning of 1584, at the time of the negotiations with Blas de Robles. In the deposition that she will make in Valladolid in June of 1605, on the occasion of the Ezpeleta affair, Isabel will say that she is twenty.

Such at least is the commonly held version. One scholar, Herrero García, sees in this mysterious paternity a scheme devised by Cervantes: Isabel's real mother was his sister Magdalena (according to this theory), and her father was a certain Juan de Urbina, of whom we will speak when the time comes. Ana Franca merely lent her name so that Magdalena could conceal her lapse. On the death of the tavern-keeper's wife, Miguel then took over and recognized as his daughter a girl who was in reality only his niece. Magdalena, by taking the young woman into her service, paid her dues by playing guardian, in order not to admit that she was the mother.

This hypothesis, proposed forty years ago, is in keeping with what we know about the loose life of Cervantes' sisters, which marked the birth of both Constanza and Isabel with the same illegitimacy. But no document provides explicit proof for it. Certainly nothing permits us to maintain that Magdalena de Cervantes was the mistress of Juan de Urbina, who (as we will see) does not appear in the life of *Don Quixote*'s author before 1606. So we can, without fear of contradiction, stick to the letter of the notarized documents and let ourselves ponder the guilty love affair of Miguel and Ana Franca. Was the young woman pretty? Had she deceived her husband before? Did she make the first move to overcome the scruples of an admirer whom his companions in captivity called "chaste and reserved"? The curiosity of biographers is in proportion to the reticence of Cervantes regarding this adventure; and theirs is all the more lively because the liaison with Ana Franca is, in every respect, the very opposite of the ethereal love affairs experienced by the shepherds in *Galatea*. To call this contrast schizophrenic is, however, to make an unwarranted judgment. On Miguel's relationships with women, we have only the testimony of the archives: a family milieu marked by a series of emotional failures and persistently tainted with an air of illegitimacy by Martina de Mendoza, Constanza de Ovando, and Isabel de Saavedra; a single authenticated liaison, almost casual, that seems to have lasted no more than a few months, without either partner's having exaggerated its importance; and finally a marriage, which we will soon see also has its share of enigmas. None of this authorizes us to maintain, for patriotic reasons, that Cervantes' sexuality was as healthy as any normal Spaniard's of his period; or, conversely, to put him on the analyst's couch in order to diagnose some repressed desire, to be filed in the dossier with Juan Blanco de Paz's slanders.

What remains is the essence, that is to say, the literary figures of Cervantine *eros*, in a whole gamut of situations that go from the mercenary intrigues of *The Fraudulent Marriage* (El casamiento engañoso) to the absolute devotion that Don Quixote gives to the lady of his thoughts. In this area, it is quite true that the extremes prevail, as if there were no place for more moderate behavior between the shamelessness of Maritornes and the irreproachable chastity of Constanza, the noble kitchen wench. The novelistic mode is certainly better adapted to out-of-the-ordinary events than to the peaceful delights of conjugal harmony. *The Call of Blood*, to cite but one example, illustrates this principle to perfection: the novella opens with the kidnapping of a heroine who is carried off before the eyes of her family and then thrown into the street after having been raped by her kidnapper. The fact is that deviant, not to say perverse, attitudes attract Cervantes' attention as much as, if not more than, the amorous ardor of seducers and fallen women—the necessary ingredients of Golden Age stories. Describing, in a rather abstract way, the supreme power of carnal love, *Galatea* already means to warn us against the innumerable disorders to which those who submit to the sway of desire abandon themselves:

> That desire . . . that incites a brother to seek the abominable embraces of his beloved sister, the stepmother those of her stepson, and, worse still, the father himself those of his own daughter.

A fine program for our Spanish Boccaccio! But he is too great an artist to follow it and content himself with the depiction of such misbehavior. Against the backdrop of these "abominable embraces," other tendencies show up—propensities on which Cervantine fictions cast a singular light: the ill-advised curiosity of Anselmo, the *curioso impertinente,* who, aware of the disaster that he is about to provoke, pushes his friend Lotario to test the fidelity of his own wife, Camila, to the point of surrender; the folly of old Carrizales, the jealous Extremaduran, who, because he wants to preserve his innocent young wife Leonor from all temptation, shuts her up in a gilded cage, where she and her attendants play with dolls, and where he tastes the overripe fruits— "neither pleasant nor disagreeable"—of this aberrant union; the obstinacy of the Knight of the Woeful Countenance, the distracted worshipper of an idol who unites "all the impossible and imaginary attributes of beauty that poets give to their mistresses." Do we find in this preference for the unusual nothing but the commonplaces of platonic and courtly love, transposed into a different key? Might Miguel not also be projecting his own inhibitions into it? Was he not occasionally obeying some obscure compulsion, as when he condemns Rosamunda in *Persiles* to the worst punishment, that "impure rose"—*rosa inmunda*— who wanted to be the high priestess of sex and who withers away because she cannot sate her instincts? The fantasies of a writer reveal our own enigmas.

THE ATTRACTIONS OF MARRIAGE

SEPTEMBER 1584: Ana Franca is about to bring into the world a female child whose real father only she and Miguel know. How did he receive the news? Distressed at times, one imagines, by a paternity that he must suppress; embarrassed in the presence of the husband; prudently reserved with his family; then, on the contrary, delighted by a secret that is harder and harder to conceal as the fateful day approaches. It is probable, in any case, that he did not accept it with the indifference that seducers in Golden Age Spain so often affected toward their bastards: whether because he was aware of the futility of a relationship that he could not make legal, or because he refused to make it official in the guise of a *ménage à trois*.

Such must have been his feelings when, toward the middle of the month, he leaves Madrid again, taking the mule-drawn carriage that connects the capital with Toledo each week. This time, he is not leaving for some distant destination. After a brief stop halfway, at Illescas, a large commercial town (where fifteen years later El Greco will paint the two admirable portraits that to this day decorate the altars of the monastery of La Caridad), he turns obliquely toward the east. He passes through one more town, and he is at Esquivias. We know the object of this journey. It had to do with Cervantes' carrying out for his friend Pedro Laínez, who had died six months earlier, a project that Laínez had not had time to finish: to publish the now-posthumous works that his widow Juana Gaitán retained in her possession in manuscript. This capable woman is a curious personality. Of Morisco ancestry, she married Laínez late in his life, in spite of the difference in their ages; and she will remain in close touch with our hero until her death. She had been living in Esquivias, her home town, in retirement since the death of her husband; but she had not vowed to live the solitary life. Diego de Hondaro, the young son of a Burgos businessman, barely twenty-two, had arrived to comfort her with his presence. On June 12, Juana Gaitán took the youth as her second husband. We still have the marriage contract. There is no mention of the husband's *escudos,* but there is a detailed description of the poet's property, the use of which is left to the discretion of his widow. There is also a matter of Laínez's *Cancionero* (collected lyrics), valued at 120,000 *maravedís,* as well as of another collection of verse and prose entitled—oh, irony of fate—*The Illusions and Disillusionments of Love.*

Cervantes, who had just successfully concluded his negotiations with Blas de Robles, was well prepared to help the passionate Juana profit from his experience and to enlighten her with his counsels. So it is that at the approach of grape harvest, he will make his entry into Esquivias, whose "noblest wines" and "noble families" he will celebrate later in the preface to *Persiles.* Situated at the edge of La Mancha, amid the hills that border the Sagra plain, Esquivias was indeed proud of its vineyards. As for its families, they were no less eminent: of the 175 families listed in a contemporary census, 37—more than a fifth—claimed to be *hidalgos* and displayed their coats of arms on the portals of their houses.

Miguel undoubtedly examined his old friend's papers carefully. On September 22, Juana Gaitán will officially, in the presence of a notary, entrust the attorney Ortiga Roza with the task of finding a publisher.

That this contract, countersigned by Cervantes, came to naught is due
no doubt to the reluctance of booksellers, who had no interest in publishing a posthumous collection of lyrics at a time when poetry "was
in such disfavor." But that is another story, which at that moment
was of no concern.

How had the noble families of Esquivias accepted the Hondaro
household? Without excessive cordiality, probably, in view of the air
of scandal that floated around a too-hasty marriage, and in view of the
suspect ancestry of the newlywed bride. One can easily picture the
haughtiness of the upper-crust matrons, after the portrait that Teresa
Panza, Sancho's wife, draws of the snobs she meets in her own village,

> . . . who think that because they are gentlewomen the wind must not
> touch them, and they go to church with as many airs as if they were
> queens, no less, and seem to think they are disgraced if they look at a
> farmer's wife.

Nevertheless, though remarried under dubious circumstances, Juana
Gaitán was still the widow of a chamberlain of the prince, Don Carlos,
and she cannot have failed to dazzle her neighbors with her connections.

Among the people whose friendship she seems to have cultivated,
Catalina de Palacios soon emerges. She lived in a house very near Juana's
and had also recently lost her husband. This sad coincidence may have
favored their closeness, even if Catalina did not have the manners or
temperament of the beautiful Morisca. Concerns different from those
that agitated Juana were more than enough to fill the widow's time:
the administration of her own patrimony, consisting basically of vineyards and olive groves, as well as two or three houses at Toledo and in
the vicinity; the settlement—complicated, to say the least—of the
estate of her spouse, Hernando de Salazar Vozmediano, who had died
leaving a profusion of debts; the future of her two minor sons, Francisco and Fernando, reared under the tutelage of her brother Juan de
Palacios, the priest of Esquivias, who will themselves become priests
in time; and, finally, the education of her only daughter, Catalina de
Salazar, born in November 1565, who had not yet celebrated her
twentieth spring.

In her mourner's weeds, this young woman is going to attract Miguel's attention and before long become his wife. Was he expecting to

meet her? Determined to accomplish his pious duty, he did not intend
to let himself be distracted from his task. But, as he will confess later
in the preface to the *Exemplary Novellas,* "One is not always attending
to affairs, however important they may be; there are times for recreation, when the troubled spirit may rest." And meeting Catalina was
one of these moments of relaxation. Did it take place in the street, at
church, or in some house in Esquivias? Was it the result of chance, or
did Juana Gaitán enjoying playing marriage broker? No one knows.
In any case, our poet will not wait long to take the plunge and make
his proposal of marriage. Two months after his arrival in Esquivias,
on December 12, 1584, in the Church of St. Mary of the Assumption,
Juan de Palacios hears the vows of the bride and groom in the presence
of three witnesses.

One feels somewhat frustrated by the laconic style of the document
preserved in the parochial archives of Esquivias. We would like it to
tell us a little more about the hero of the day and in particular about
his young bride. Was she blond, like Galatea? Did she have instead—
as is likely—the olive skin and dark hair of the daughters of La Sagra?
We know nothing about the charms which, we hope, contributed to
Miguel's speedy decision. The only information that has come down
to us concerns, essentially, her ancestors and her age; it also reveals to
us that she could read and write, and it leads us to believe that she
had some Jewish blood in her veins.

We would need more information to clarify the motives that pushed
a mature man to bind his fate so hastily to that of such a young woman:
at the age of thirty-seven, he was almost twice her age. Romantic souls
like to speak of love at first sight, though they have given up—the
chronology forces them—making Catalina the model for the heroine
of his pastoral romance: *Galatea,* let us remember, was on the point
of being printed and will appear three months after the sacramental "I
do." Cynics, on the other hand, attribute less exalted motives to the
author of *Don Quixote* and suspect him of marrying for money: he did
not discover, presumably, the limitations of her inheritance and the
extent of debts left by his late father-in-law until after he became
Catalina's husband.

Between these two extremes, one can see in Cervantes a man who
has given up the illusions of his youth and, in addition, aspires to
distance himself from the bohemian literary world, all the more disposed, consequently, to embrace the state of marriage. Accidental cir-

cumstances make him believe that he has found at Esquivias the haven of which he had been dreaming without realizing it. There were certainly plenty of reasons to support him in this belief: the distance from Madrid and Ana Franca, the warm welcome from Juana Gaitán, the memory of his dead friend, the pleasant neighborhood of the Salazar family, the sweetness of September's golden days, the bucolic charm of the Ombidales spring and the oak groves that tower over Esquivias, the peaceable life of a big Castilian town at grape-harvest time. Let us also hope that there entered at least partially into the decision of this artist so sensitive to beauty the charm of an adolescent still shy but already capable of ravishing all the senses and of making Miguel glimpse "a happy fulfillment of his desires." As for Catalina, we would like to know what attracted her: the glory of the combatant of Lepanto, the tribulations of the captive from Algiers, the renown of the poet from Madrid? Perhaps simply the smooth brow, the lively eyes, and the still-blond beard of the man whose companions said that "he had to a high degree a special grace in everything [he did]"? At least one thing is sure: in the chill of a December morning, she said "I do" for better or for worse.

LIVING AT ESQUIVIAS

THE visitor who decides to stop at Esquivias can still see the house that once belonged to the Salazar family: a huge, austere dwelling, quite near the church, with its wide portal, windows ornamented with grills, column-lined patio surmounted by a wooden balcony, cellar and pantry where oil and wine were stored each year.

Cervantes is going to take up residence there in early 1585, to taste the joys of home life and to manage his wife's property. Did he do it with the blessings of his new in-laws? Some biographers have their doubts, arguing that the marriage was celebrated too quietly, if not in haste, and alleging that eighteen months went by before Miguel finally saw the promised dowry paid. These arguments are less convincing than the biographers are willing to admit. At the time of her marriage, Catalina was still in mourning for her father, and consequently it was not possible to give her a brilliant wedding. As for Miguel, his parents were old; however strong their desire to be present at Esquivias, they were in no condition to endure the fatigue of the journey. With regard to the delay that appears to have been imposed by Catalina's family, it occurs because Cervantes himself was slow to pay the hundred ducats he was required to deposit. Nothing proves, consequently, that Catalina de Palacios was getting a shrewish mother-in-law into the bargain or that the uncle-priest, who was an educated man, was unimpressed by the vocation of his niece's husband.

The break with the active life of the *Villa y Corte* must have been sudden. Madrid is in the grip of numerous rumors. Relations between Spain and England are more and more strained because of the support Elizabeth is giving to her fellow heretics, the Dutch rebels. Along the coast of Andalusia, Francis Drake's raids spread terror and help poison relations between the two countries. Philip II, his attention directed more and more toward the Atlantic, wants to put an end to an adversary whose initiatives run counter to his own policies. People begin to talk insistently about a project that Don Alvaro de Bazán, the conqueror of the Azores, had submitted to Philip three years earlier and that is once again under consideration: to send a massive naval expedition into the heart of the British Isles, which would force the Virgin Queen to surrender.

Another rumor runs through the streets of the capital: the court will soon move to El Escorial, finished at last, after twenty-three years of work. The citizens of Madrid dread what the departure will cost; but the "tone setters" among them make no effort to keep the king in Madrid by adopting his irreproachable habits and austere deportment. Moralists vie with one another in denouncing the insolent triumph of easy money and excessive luxury. They thunder against the licentiousness that so impresses foreign travelers. In December of 1585, a jumbled series of decrees prohibits blasphemy, disturbances at night, duels to the death, card games, speculation on the food supply, and schemes by prostitutes to promote the sale of their charms. These draconian measures, completed and expanded less than a year later, do not seem to have had the hoped-for effect.

In comparison with this brouhaha, the silence of Esquivias, made more palpable by the rigors of the Castilian winter, must have given Miguel the impression that he had changed planets. Were the company of his young wife, the evenings by the fire with the Salazar tribe, the neighborliness of Juana Gaitán, enough to fill the free time left after seeing to the olive groves and vineyards and the affairs of a father-in-law whom he had never met? There were, assuredly, chats with upper-class *hidalgos,* many of whom had served in the armies of the emperor and the Prudent King. They certainly welcomed the soldier from Lepanto with friendship. But when your name is Cervantes, and you prefer to entrust the best of yourself to your pen, you grow tired of recalling, even over a pitcher of noble wine, His Lordship Don Juan, the wounds received aboard *La Marquesa,* the desertion of La Goleta, and the hardships of Algiers. There is nothing to do then but imitate Teresa Panza and comment on the trifling events of the day: the marriage of La Berrueca's daughter to a good-for-nothing painter who has given up the brush for the spade and now is working the fields "like a gentleman"; the disappointments of Pedro Lobo's son, who wanted to become a priest and had received the tonsure but whom Mingo Silvato's daughter, pregnant because of him (she says), has just taken to court; the passing of a company of soldiers that carried off three girls when it left; the secret anxiety that grows week by week because "there are no olives this year, and there is not a drop of vinegar to be had in the whole village." Certainly Esquivias was a little less rustic than the Manchegan town from which Don Quixote and Sancho will one day set out, the name of which Cervantes prefers to leave unmentioned. But with minor exceptions, life was not so different there: our novelist must surely have recalled, when he amuses himself for an instant in the character of Teresa, the gossip of a remote corner of darkest Spain.

And then let us not forget an essential fact: the new denizen of Esquivias has not broken ties with his native city. In February of 1585, less than two months after his marriage, he sees himself extolled in his friend Padilla's *Spiritual Garden* as one of the most famous poets in Castile. On March 5, he signs with Gaspar de Porres, the *autor* (manager), the contract about which we have spoken. A few days later, *Galatea* comes off the presses of Alcalá. The conclusion is obvious: Miguel, for professional reasons, frequently covers the twelve leagues that separate Esquivias from Madrid. For family reasons, too. Doubtless after New Year's he takes Catalina to the capital to introduce her to his family. He will probably return there at the end of spring when his father dies, on June 13, at the age of more than seventy-five. In spite of his handicap and his failures, the ex-surgeon succeeded in attaining a respectable age. We have his will, dictated on June 8, from his deathbed, by which he names his wife and the mother of his daughter-in-law executors. This mark of confidence is all the more touching because the unfortunate Rodrigo has almost nothing to leave. At least he will be able to proclaim, with his head held high, that he has paid all of his debts; when one knows how heavily they weighed on him during his life, one understands the significance of this proud declaration.

We have evidence of another stay of Miguel's in Madrid, during which he signs, on August 1, a promissory note as witness. The creditor was Inés Osorio, wife of the celebrated actor Jerónimo Velázquez; their daughter Elena was at the time Lope de Vega's mistress. From this, people have concluded that Lope and Cervantes were on intimate terms. It would be better to speak of cordial relations. The author of *Galatea* puts the young prodigy, who had just celebrated his twentieth birthday, among the poets mentioned in the "Song of Calliope": he pays him an almost paternal homage and takes pleasure in hailing his promising debut. Two years later, Lope will separate from Elena after an exchange of defamatory libels which will cost him a noisy lawsuit and will force him into exile at Valencia. By that time, Cervantes will have resumed his itinerant life; their paths will not cross again for ten years.

Without giving up his trips to Madrid, Miguel was little by little widening the radius of his movements. He is often at Toledo, where, as we have seen, the Salazar family had interests. He will later make Toledo the setting of several of his novellas. In *The Call of Blood,* in particular, he devotes several heartfelt lines to the pleasures one can enjoy on the banks of the Tagus, and takes satisfaction in praising the pleasant disposition of Toledans. One also meets him, on at least two occasions, further south, on the banks of the Guadalquivir. On December 2, 1585, there are indications of a stop at Seville, where he apparently lodges with his friend Tomás Gutiérrez, the former actor, who, after taking leave of the theatrical world, keeps a boardinghouse on Bayona Street, near the cathedral. In Seville Cervantes busies himself with mysterious transactions on behalf, it seems, of Diego de Hondaro, the young husband of Juana Gaitán. We have a note signed by his hand in which he promises to reimburse within six months the sum of two hundred thousand *maravedís* that a certain Gómez de Carrión lends him "at his behest and request, in order to accommodate and be of service to him." Two other documents, one of which is a letter of exchange, show him handling important sums. Was it a question (as a power-of-attorney granted to Hondaro by his wife suggests) of amassing the money necessary for the printing of the famous *cancionero?* Or did Miguel, as Astrana Marín supposes, pay some sort of compensation to Ana Franca de Rojas as the price of his separation from her? No one knows. At Christmas, he returns to Esquivias, where he attends the wedding of a nephew by marriage, Gonzalo de Guzmán Salazar, to the niece of the priest of Santo Tomé at Toledo, the man who a year later commissioned the *Burial of the Count of Orgaz* from El Greco, and who appears in the center of the picture as the officiant. Astrana Marín, whose imagination was never at rest, asks whether Cervantes did not also pose for the painter: El Greco, he suggests, gave Cervantes' face to one of the gentlemen attending the burial. If this were true, we would owe to El Greco the only authentic portrait of the author of *Don Quixote.*

In June 1586, we find our hero in Seville again, still doing business with the same partners. Whatever the outcome of his transactions, he does not seem to have prolonged his stay in Andalusia, because on August 9 he is present in Esquivias, to receive in due legal form Catalina's dowry. In turn, he pays to her the hundred ducats promised. The inventory drawn up on this occasion reveals a decent patrimony, matched with a no less decent trousseau; the whole is valued at a little more than four hundred ducats. The list includes land, a kitchen garden, olive trees, vines, hens, a rooster: "I am satisfied with little, but I desire much," Miguel will say in the *Journey to Parnassus*. In any case, Cervantes' mother-in-law Catalina de Palacios fulfilled her obligations. She went even further: on the same day, she grants her son-in-law power to administer the family property. Some have seen this gesture as proof of trust. One can also ask whether, acting in this way, the widow of Hernando de Salazar did not hope to keep Cervantes, who is more and more absent from the conjugal domicile, in Esquivias. If such was her intention, her effort is going to fail; in what circumstances, we shall see.

THE SEVILLIAN MIRAGE

THE sudden decision that led Miguel to take leave of his wife after less than three years of life together remains tinged with mystery. There is, to be sure, no lack of signs, during those twenty-eight months, of his repeated infidelities to the illustrious pedigrees and noble wines.

But his farewell to Esquivias is also a farewell to Madrid: it means a new life.

The first piece of evidence: Cervantes is tired of his Arcadia. He was not playing at operetta shepherd, like Grisóstomo. It is true that his shepherdess, though less cruel than Marcela, did not have "great wealth," like Marcela; but she was similarly "in the care of an uncle of hers, a priest who officiated in our village." Catalina's family owned houses; but the bulk of her inheritance, besides the few acres of which her mother had the usufruct, was nothing but a mass of debts—to which our writer could see no end. If Hernando de Salazar had not, like his father Gonzalo, deliberately lied in writing, he had nevertheless demonstrated plain irresponsibility in the administration of his property. In the twilight of his life, his difficulties had made him unable even to pay the wages of his employees. One can understand why his son-in-law, grappling with a hundred creditors, could think of no solution but locking up the account books that had been bestowed on him.

The incidents of village life were insufficient to banish his bad humor. Talk of rain and fine weather, comments on wine prices and olive-oil quotations, were subjects whose charms he had exhausted. There were assuredly the pleasures of the table; but they were in accord with proverbial Castilian frugality. Excepting important occasions—the marriage of Gonzalo de Salazar after Miguel's return from Seville or, some months later, the baptism of a child of Simón Hernández, a wine merchant and next-door neighbor—the usual fare was what Don Quixote will make do with: "A stew of rather more beef than mutton, hash most nights, bacon and eggs on Saturdays, lentils on Fridays, and a pigeon or so extra on Sundays." After the table was cleared, it was customary (as it was throughout Spain) to examine and "delouse" the most illustrious pedigrees. There were numerous *hidalgos* who counted *conversos* among their ancestors, starting with the Salazar family. They owed this taint to their connection with the Quijadas, one of whose ancestors clearly piqued Miguel's curiosity. He was a monk who had died more than half a century earlier and who had a reputation as a great reader of romances of chivalry. One can still see his house today, next to Catalina's. His name was Alonso Quijada, and we will hear it mentioned again.

These are minor inconveniences, you will say, for a person who had lived hand to mouth for so long and was henceforth assured of a roof and a place to sleep and of being coddled by a diligent wife. But was

that true happiness? We must understand that Catalina was undoubtedly a devoted wife; she will prove it, furthermore, when her husband
returns to live with her. But perhaps Cervantes rediscovered his anx-
ieties, his demons, after the honeymoon; and an adolescent from the
depths of La Mancha, even though she was an *hidalga* and knew how
to read and write, could not compete with them. Did she also get
wind of the guilty love affair with Ana Franca and of the offspring
that was the result of it? It is possible that she accepted the situation,
knowing of quite comparable cases all around her. Her paternal grandfather, the same Gonzalo de Salazar whose unscrupulousness we have
mentioned, had a natural son; and her uncle Luis de Salazar, a little
later, followed Gonzalo's example. But it is probable that she will not
discover until later the parentage of Isabel de Saavedra, when Isabel
comes with her aunts to share the Cervantes household at Valladolid.

Catalina, a prisoner in a family milieu that must have oppressed her
vagabond husband, and frustrated in her desire for motherhood, must
quickly have felt herself irrelevant to the aspirations of a man who
spent so little time with her: "As long as a wife is not foolish, stupid,
or simple-minded, that is enough," as Rodolfo will say in *The Call of
Blood.* Perhaps. But is this Cervantes speaking, through the mouth of
Leocadia's seducer? We would wager that Miguel thought differently,
but that Catalina, for her part, realized what her husband lacked in
order to hold his own in the little world of Esquivias. Some critics
think they see her *alter ego* in the shrewish Guiomar, in *The Judge of
Divorces* (El juez de los divorcios), who throws her disappointments
and resentment in her scrawny husband's face:

> I mean, I thought I was marrying a normal man, but after a few days I
> discovered that I had married a blockhead . . . [who] doesn't know right
> from left, or try to find ways and means to earn a little money to help
> support his home and family . . . He tosses restlessly all night. I ask him
> what's wrong. He answers that he is composing a sonnet in his head for a
> friend who has asked for it; and he is determined to be a poet, as if it
> weren't the poorest profession in the world.

This caricature reveals both the limitations of the subject and the conventions of the genre, the interlude. But there is a *je ne sais quoi* that
troubles us in the disillusionment of this irreproachable woman, who
takes cover behind her virtue in order to express her grievances. *The*

Judge of Divorces is of course a late work, written after the poet's final return to Madrid. But the odds are against Cervantes' having waited until his fiftieth year to discover the first cracks in the fragile edifice of his happiness:

> Love and fancy easily blind the eyes of judgment, so essential in choosing one's way of life, and the matrimonial choice is very liable to error, requiring great caution and the special favor of heaven to make it a good one. The man who sets out on a long journey will, if he is wise, seek some trusty and pleasant companion to accompany him before he departs. Why, then, should not a man do likewise for the whole journey of life down to the final halting place of death, more especially when the companion has to be his companion in bed, at board, and everywhere, as the wife is to her husband? The companionship of one's wife is no article of merchandise that, after it has been bought, may be returned, or bartered, or changed. It is an inseparable quality that lasts as long as life lasts; it is a noose that, once you put it about your neck, turns into a Gordian knot. If it is not severed by the scythe of Death, there is no untying it.

Fine, powerful words, that do honor to the person who utters them. But how to reconcile these noble principles with the mediocre realities of daily life? The compromise devised by Miguel—to divide his time between Madrid and Esquivias—could not last indefinitely. If he were deprived of permanent contact with his fellow writers, booksellers, and actors, our writer risked being supplanted by better-connected rivals, always ready to show up whenever and wherever necessary. Lope de Vega already understood the situation perfectly.

And then, in fact, Miguel seems to have undergone a crisis and to have doubted his vocation. His authentic production during these years amounts, all in all, to three occasional sonnets. Two of them, published in 1587, were doubtless written shortly before: a meager showing. That he never finished his *Galatea* is proof of dissatisfaction—of a case of writer's block, we would say—whose origins perhaps go back to this period. As for the *corrales* of the capital, one wonders whether they confirmed the welcome that the success of *The Mix-up* had augured. Indeed, we do not even know whether he fully honored his contract with Porres, since he tells us nothing about what became of *Life at Constantinople* (El trato de Constantinopla). Could it be that the formúla he invented no longer pleased audiences and that he sensed with

foreboding the appearance of a younger rival, who was also more popular with the public? Whatever the case, for twenty years he is going
to exile himself from the republic of letters, of which he had hoped to
become one of the figureheads: "I found other things to occupy me,
and I laid down my pen and gave up writing plays." Late in his life,
Cervantes will recall, in these suggestive terms and with his customary
discretion, a decision that he could hardly have made lightly.

All that remained was an excuse, not to say the pretext, to justify—
in his own as well as in his family's eyes—what must be called his
desertion. His business in Seville, his meetings with Tomás Gutiérrez
in the shadow of La Giralda, must have given him some foretaste of
an existence freed from the slavery of Esquivias; they gave him a glimpse
of occupations more consistent with his desire for independence, which
was all the stronger because he felt that he was sponging off his wife.
Perhaps he learned through Gutiérrez that the naval expedition against
the English that Alvaro de Bazán had been demanding for three years
had just been approved. Exploiting the indignation roused by Mary
Stuart's execution on February 18, 1587, Philip II had resolved to set
the project in motion. At the beginning of April, a member of his
council, Antonio de Guevara, was named commissary general. Charged
with preparations for the operation and in particular with the wheat
and olive-oil supplies, he ordered his deputy, Diego de Valdivia, to
set up headquarters in Seville. To carry out this mission and to proceed
to the indispensable requisitions throughout Andalusia, Valdivia needed
an entire army of subordinates. One of those who will request a job as
commissary officer will, in fact, be Cervantes.

Miguel will actually receive this commission in Seville in September. But he had already returned to the banks of the Guadalquivir five
months earlier, in early May. We have information on the circumstances of his departure. On April 25, Toledo celebrates with splendor
the transfer of the relics of St. Leocadia, patroness of the city, from
Flanders. The king himself honors the ceremonies with his presence.
Two or three days earlier, the cortège had stopped at Esquivias. Did
Cervantes join it there? Everything suggests that he took part, along
with several of his friends, in the festivities, of which one can hear
echoes in *Persiles*. On April 28, at Toledo, in the presence of the notary
Ambrosio Mexía, he signs a document conferring power-of-attorney
on Catalina. Rather than pass through Esquivias again in order to hand
it to his wife in person, he sends it to her with the witness, her nephew

Gaspar de Guzmán. The next day, the Bay of Cadiz will be the theater of a spectacular raid by Drake, "the greatest pirate in the West." On the same day, Miguel finds himself once again on the roads of La Mancha. Through Ciudad Real, Argamasilla, Almodóvar, and Alcudia, at the rate of eight or nine leagues a day, he crosses the expanses that Don Quixote will one day immortalize. Ten days later, he is again the guest of Tomás Gutiérrez. It is certainly not a final farewell to Catalina, the noble wines, and the most noble families; but it looks like running away, all the same. It is, in any case, the beginning of a new stage in his life, under the sign of a wandering that will last almost fifteen years.

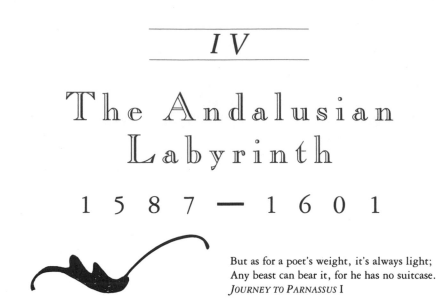

IV

The Andalusian Labyrinth

1 5 8 7 — 1 6 0 1

But as for a poet's weight, it's always light;
Any beast can bear it, for he has no suitcase.
JOURNEY TO PARNASSUS I

FIRST COMMISSIONS

Disembarking at Seville in the early days of June, before the dog days pounce on Andalusia, Cervantes perhaps recalled distant memories of his adolescence; but he was re-entering a city that had become familiar to him, particularly since his recent missions on behalf of Juana Gaitán. No doubt he went immediately to the quarter over which the cathedral looms. There, as we know, on Bayona Street his friend Tomás Gutiérrez kept a luxurious boardinghouse greatly esteemed by noble travelers. Gutiérrez was pleased to count among his clients "princes, dukes, counts, and gentlemen," who fled the discomfort of ordinary inns. Did he, as is often claimed, offer hospitality to the refugee from Esquivias? At the very least he must have housed Cervantes upon his arrival, to give him time to find lodgings. It is quite likely that he also introduced Cervantes to Diego de Valdivia, the deputy of council-member Guevara, and that he acted as the guarantor without whom Miguel would never have obtained the employment for which he had applied.

On September 18, 1587, after three months of enforced idleness, the new commissary officer for the provisioning of the king's galleys leaves the banks of the Guadalquivir. He undertakes the first of a series of circuits that for five years are going to require all of his energies and take up most of his time. First, he goes to Ecija, a picturesque, prosperous town famous for its Roman past and its Moorish ruins, and especially proud of the Gothic churches and Renaissance palaces built by noble families of the first rank. Located about twenty leagues from Seville, in the heart of the wheat country that extends as far as Córdoba, it was an obligatory stop for a collector of stores sent to requisition grain—in exchange for a promissory note—destined for the fleet. In theory our commissary officer had full powers to start proceedings for unavoidable seizures. But in fact, his ability to maneuver was as limited as his travel allowance: twelve *reales* a day, a laughable sum in proportion to his responsibilities, which would have justified his demanding three times as much. Furthermore, that money served only to cover his ordinary expenses; his real salary was not to be paid until the completion of his mission, in the form of back pay. Farmers, too, were not paid for the levied wheat until it had been deposited in storehouses, often after months of waiting. All this was more than enough to confuse the accounts, and Cervantes, with the best will in the world, will eventually lose his way in this tangle.

On his arrival in Ecija, the author of *Galatea* will at least have the pleasure of being welcomed by the town's *corregidor,* Mosquera de Figueroa, a distinguished poet for whom he has the highest esteem and whose talent he had praised in the "Song of Calliope." Mosquera might have been a valuable intermediary with the municipal authorities. But he is, unfortunately, at the end of his term of office, and before long he will leave the scene. So from early October Miguel is going to find himself alone again among influential persons who are ill-disposed towards him. Suffering from a bad harvest that was aggravating the food crisis that Andalusia was then experiencing, they were all the more uncooperative because they had not yet been paid for a previous series of requisitions. After a week of fruitless discussions, the farmers decided to approach Valdivia directly, over the head of his subordinate. When Valdivia refused to consider their demand to suspend the requisition, Cervantes had no other way out but to execute his orders and seize the wheat where he found it: in the granaries of rich land-owners *(terratenientes),* among whom were several noble canons-prebendary. It was a risky operation, and the response was quick to come: the excommunication of the commissary officer by the vicar general of Seville.

In the last century, this incident greatly impressed all those who saw the author of *Don Quixote* as a precursor of freethinking, an irreverent spirit whom his Andalusian misadventures must have strengthened in his struggle against obscurantism. We need to reduce matters to their correct proportions: in sixteenth-century Spain, excommunication was frequent because it was the only arm at the Church's disposal in conflicts which periodically set it against civil powers. Charles V and Philip II, let us not forget, both had similar experiences, and on two occasions. Our writer's unpleasant encounter nevertheless gives a certain bite to a half-bantering comment from the Knight of the Woeful Countenance, when he realizes that he has broken the leg of an unfortunate cleric whom he took in the darkness for a supernatural apparition:

> "I forgot to mention," said [the cleric], "that your worship is excommunicated for having laid violent hands on a holy thing [. . .]."
> "I know that I did not lay hands, only this pike" [replied Don Quixote]. "Besides, I did not think I was committing an assault upon priests or things of the Church, which, like a Catholic and faithful Christian, as I am, I respect and revere, but upon phantoms and specters from the other world."

Don Quixote's good faith is certainly undeniable, but his creator's mischievousness is no less so, even if it aims at the customs and practices of certain members of the Church rather than at the institution. And no one will be surprised to learn that Spanish anticlericalism has made a proverbial expression of the famous exchange between master and servant when they enter the slumbering town of El Toboso in search of Dulcinea and bump unexpectedly into a tall tower:

> *"It's the church we have come upon, Sancho,"* he said.
> "So I see," said Sancho, "and God grant we may not come upon our graves."

The dialogue is too heavy with double meanings to be entirely innocent, and it makes one think that on their way to El Toboso, Don Quixote and Sancho have made a detour through Ecija.

The excommunication was enough to make Valdivia, conscious of the difficulties that his envoy was having, appear in person in early November. By means of a compromise with local authorities, he will succeed in having part of the wheat that he had authority to requisition handed over. Then Cervantes, in Valdivia's company, betakes himself to La Rambla, a large market town in the farmlands *(campiña)* of Córdoba, where the welcome will be distinctly cool. Eight years earlier, in fact, La Rambla had been plundered by unscrupulous commissary officers, and the promised compensation had not yet been paid. This meant that the announcement of requisitions was badly received and that, in the absence of his superior, who had immediately departed on a new mission, Miguel would have to do things the hard way: arresting recalcitrants, meting out prison sentences, which were confirmed and increased by Valdivia when he returned: in short, the habitual arsenal of repressive measures, without which the orders issued would remain a dead letter.

December sees Cervantes crisscrossing the province, which was the real breadbasket of Andalusia, in order to institute new seizures: at Castro del Río, where he commits a stubborn sacristan to prison and is excommunicated again, by the vicar general of Córdoba this time; at Espejo, overshadowed by the Mudéjar castle of the dukes of Osuna; finally at Cabra, the fief of the dukes of Sessa, where the *corregidor* had for a long time been Andrés de Cervantes, the elder brother of the surgeon. There Miguel finds his cousin Rodrigo, then twenty-three years old, who will assist him for a while in his functions. At the approach of Christmas, Miguel returns to Seville, reversing direction on the road he had followed when he left. A disappointment awaits him there: Madrid has not yet deposited the promised funds; so he cannot touch the thirteen hundred *maravedís* owing to him as the price of his good and loyal services. By way of consolation, he receives congratulations from Valdivia and beguiles his frustration with the latest news of the *Villa y Corte*. Doña Leonor, in spite of her widowhood, appears to be safe from need at last. Ana Franca, a widow herself since October, now keeps the tavern on Francos Street by herself and devotes what free time she has to raising her two daughters.

The eye of the public, indifferent to the fate of these two humble women, prefers to follow the escapades of Lope de Vega. He has broken with his mistress Elena Osorio and spreads satirical libels about the young woman and her family. Elena's father, the actor Jerónimo Velázquez, as well as her new protector, the rich financier Perrenot de Granvelle, are the principal targets. These defamatory pasquinades are clearly the favorite topic of local gossip; some even suspect Cervantes, briefly, of having written them. Lope is arrested on December 29, 1587. After a noisy trial, he is convicted of being the author of the libels and is exiled from the capital for eight years. He shouts from the rooftops that he is going to embark on one of the ships of the Invincible Armada, and with that in mind he makes his way to Lisbon. Did he really take part in the expedition? It is still a point of argument. The only certainty is that he will spend his years of exile in Valencia, and he will invent the theater of the Golden Age.

But what about the Invincible Armada, the war machine that is to break British pride and that Miguel, in the depths of Andalusia, is helping to put into action? Between the king's plans and their effective realization, the gap, to tell the truth, appears to be considerable. Assembled at Lisbon, the ships that make up the immense fleet are far from ready to put out to sea. The armaments, stores, recruitment of troops and crews, weigh heavy on the Spanish economy: the budget for the enterprise rises to more than seven million ducats. The departure scheduled for January 18 must be pushed back to February 15; improvisation is the rule everywhere. Even Cervantes experiences this in his modest way. When the commissary general, Antonio de Guevara, finally arrives in Seville, he sends Miguel a testimonial of satisfaction for the way in which he has carried out his task; but Guevara does not include any *maravedís* with it. Instead, he bestows a new commission on Miguel, on January 22, at the very moment when Philip II, to put an end to the disorganization, entrusts the coordination of preparations to the count of Fuentes. This appointment does not take into account the vanity of the project's instigator: Alvaro de Bazán, embittered by this royal decision, even though designated by the king as commander of the expedition, dies of apoplexy on February 9. The last of the admirals of Lepanto disappears with Bazán, the "thunderbolt of war" to whom Cervantes will dedicate a post-mortem sonnet. In Bazán's place, the sovereign names one of his own relatives, the extremely rich duke of Medinasidonia, nicknamed the "duke of tuna fish" in reference to the profits he received each year from his Andalusian fisheries. A good administrator, Medinasidonia had no experience of the sea. He attempts to decline the honor that falls to him, arguing that he is not competent. Wasted effort: Philip II has made his choice. The odyssey of the Invincible Armada has just begun, as has Miguel's.

NEW DISAPPOINTMENTS

CERVANTES has begun his wanderings again. From January to May 1588, he divides his time between Ecija and its environs, in the heart of the *campiña* that he traverses in all directions. In the wings of the world's stage, while living an apparently wretched existence, he accumulates a fund of observations and experiences that later will fuse together in the *Exemplary Novellas* and in *Don Quixote*. This time he is requisitioning olive oil from farmers. He flatters himself that he understands their behavior better and better and occasionally penetrates their motives. From contact with them he derives valuable knowledge of the peasant world in which a large part of the adventures of the Knight and his Squire will take place. It is a far cry from the shepherds of *Galatea*, from their exquisite courtesy and refined sentiments. Our commissary officer ascertains to his cost, like his hero, that "there is no peasant who will keep his word if he finds it inconvenient to do so." He discovers tensions and conflicts that are harsher in Andalusia than elsewhere because the land-owning aristocracy exercises an almost feudal power over its vassals, power that must constantly be guarded in order to protect aristocratic interests. Under these conditions, one can see why Cervantes is determined not to blunder, compounds with his clients, and reduces his demands by half. The rich farmers of Ecija will be grateful to him for this, and when the occasion arises, they will put him in charge of collecting taxes that the Treasury is demanding from them: a fine testimonial of confidence but one calculated to put Cervantes in the most ambiguous of positions.

Back in Seville at the beginning of spring, Cervantes receives the announcement of his mother-in-law's death, which had occurred on May 1. He will soon learn that Catalina de Palacios had taken steps to reserve exclusively for her own descendants the income from her legacy—80,000 *maravedís*—while sparing her son-in-law the trouble of settling her debts—200,000 *maravedís*—and the care of administering her estate. From the evidence, it appears that she never forgave him his sudden departure from Esquivias. Miguel must certainly have received the news without excessive grief. Other more immediate concerns are monopolizing his attention. He has received only a single installment, to date, of the ten months' salary that he has a right to claim. He is unable to pay the indemnities promised to the farmers from whom he has requisitioned stores, and his debts have risen to 120,000 *maravedís*. The only way out: to take to the road again, as he does on June 12, provided with a third commission from Guevara. By that date, the "invincible" Armada has finally left Lisbon. Postponed until March 20, then May 20, the departure could not take place until June 10. It is an impressive fleet that sails north: 130 ships, 30,000 men, soldiers and sailors; nevertheless, it is smaller than initial expectations and as a consequence insufficiently equipped to deserve its nickname and guarantee its success. Under full sail, it goes blindly to meet an adverse destiny; and the fate that awaits Cervantes is hardly more enviable or inspiring, relatively speaking.

By the beginning of summer, our commissary officer has established his quarters at Ecija again. This time, he must not only store the requisitioned wheat, but he must also have it ground and made into biscuit. Needless to say, he comes up against the ill will of his suppliers, to whom he can promise only fine words. It is not until the end of July that the first subsidies finally arrive from Madrid, at the very moment when Miguel learns that the archbishop of Seville has lifted the excommunication imposed on him: small consolation in view of the obstacles he faces. The more he strives to convince the farmers in the heart of *la sartén de España* ("Spain's frying pan": Andalusia in the hottest part of summer), the more the difficulties multiply. As the last straw, the wheat requisitioned the previous year has not been properly stored: infested with weevils, it is spoiled and unsuitable for consumption. This is a severe blow to the commissary officer. In addition, he discovers that the assistant who now accompanies him, Miguel de Santa María, has a right to identical emoluments. He feels somewhat bitter about it, particularly since he is obliged to pay his current expenses from his own money. We have the statement of expenditures that he incurred during this period. This detailed inventory attests to the scrupulous honesty of a man who is going to reject the cheating habitual among his colleagues: "I ne'er set foot where lying, fraud, deceit / Do travel," he will proudly say in the *Journey to Parnassus*. It also reveals his total incapacity for juggling figures: an examination of his accounts actually reveals an error in addition that he commits to his own detriment. A little later, during his troubles with Treasury officials, we will have confirmation of his lack of skill.

It is at Ecija that Cervantes is going to meet the most stubborn resistance; there, the rich farmers, most of them *hidalgos,* are the most determined to see that their rights prevail, as one would expect. Chosen by them to defend their interests, the *regidor*—councillor—Luis Portocarrero tries to multiply delaying tactics. Reluctant to use force, Miguel appeals for arbitration from Guevara, who gives partial satisfaction to the plaintiffs. Emboldened by this initial success, Portocarrero tries to push his advantage: in the absence of our commissary officer, who had left for Marchena at the end of the month of August, Portocarrero accuses him of embezzlement. When Cervantes returns to Ecija, warned by Guevara that an order from the king has been issued against him, he immediately goes on the counter-attack. His adversaries stand behind their accusations. Cervantes must issue a formal refutation of the charges. A magistrate comes to inquire into the quantity of wheat and barley that Cervantes has taken from the town:

> As the aforesaid inquest is being conducted to the detriment of my honesty and the faithfulness with which I have carried out, and continue to carry out, my office; and to spare the aforesaid *regidor* the trouble, I offer the list which accompanies this [deposition], according to which it will be seen that the quantity [of grain] that I have removed does not amount to a thousand bushels of wheat and barley; and so that it may be seen and verified that this is true, I request and pray the city [fathers] to announce in the square and at the gates of this city that all may come to declare how much wheat and barley I have taken from the aforesaid inhabitants.

After long months of bitter arguing, the notables will end by withdrawing the lawsuit brought against Cervantes, acknowledging that he has acted "in the best way and with diligence."

During the time that this unpleasant quarrel was becoming more venomous, various rumors were beginning to circulate in Madrid and Seville concerning the Armada. Battered by a severe storm after departing from Lisbon, the fleet was to make port at La Coruña, before heading north again in July. Some weeks later, all of Spain thrilled to the sound of the first news. Hope fills all hearts: Medinasidonia, they say, has made his rendezvous with Alexander Farnese, the governor of the Low Countries; Drake has been killed and the British fleet scattered; Philip II's forces have set foot on the English coast. But as the days of waiting drag on, nothing comes to confirm these brilliant successes; uneasiness follows joy; people begin to talk of reverses. The ode that Miguel composes, between two commissions, echoes the confusion in the public's mind. The poet presses Fame, with all the necessary eloquence, to confirm the long-awaited triumph:

> Beat, swift Fame, your rapid wings;
> Break through the North's dark mists;
> With hastening feet come and destroy
> Confusèd rumblings of evil news,
> And with your light disperse the shadows
> From Spain's good name . . .

The mediocre quality of these verses (the authenticity of which has been doubted, furthermore) would suffice to prove that Cervantes had entirely abandoned the pen to devote himself to "other occupations." But this anguished appeal reflects, even so, the confusion that had taken hold of the realm.

In autumn the truth will finally be known. Medinasidonia, having arrived within sight of England during the last days of July, has not succeeded in engaging the enemy squadron in battle. His adversary, a better tactician, stole away after a few skirmishes, forcing the Spanish to put in at Pas-de-Calais. Exposed to attacks by English fire-ships, blocked by Dutch ships that prevent it from making its rendezvous with Farnese, the Armada cannot remain indefinitely on the Flemish coast, which lacks deep-water ports. So, because he is unable to retrace his steps, Medinasidonia decides to return to Spain by the northern route, skirting the British Isles by way of Scotland. Caught in the first assaults of bad weather, decimated by cold, hunger, and epidemics, harried by the enemy from the rear, the impressive fleet that Philip II put into action at the beginning of summer is going to lose in successive waves half of its complement of ships. At the end of an interminable voyage, about sixty of the ships at most will manage to reach, in scattered ranks, Santander and La Coruña.

As the whole country goes into mourning, Cervantes is going to dedicate a second ode to this defeat, perceived as a veritable disaster because of the size of the forces involved and the outcome that no one had anticipated. This time, it is the homeland that he addresses and tries to comfort:

> Think it no disgrace, O Spain, our mother,
> To see your sons returning to your bosom,
> Leaving the sea so full of their mishaps;
> For no enemy's right hand has turned them homeward:
> The irresistible gale has brought them back.

The king, in the presence of his closest advisers, will show his indignation at God's allowing the defeat of Spanish arms. Historians of the last century blamed the ineptitude of the admiral instead. Today they admit that Medinasidonia was not as incompetent as people once said. The enterprise, as it was conceived, might have succeeded, but only on condition that everything should unfold according to the plan envisioned. As soon as obstacles and unforeseen delays began to multiply, the failure was increased tenfold by the very importance of the means in play. Spain's offensive capacity was certainly not destroyed, and Philip II will answer the call of those who, like Miguel, urge him to take up fate's challenge: as early as the following year there will again be talk of a landing in England, and there will be an effort to gather the necessary forces. But like its fleet, the Iberian monarchy has ceased to be considered invincible. An aggravating circumstance: the financial liability of the operation was as great as the emotional ordeal. Even though gold—or rather silver—continued to flow into Seville, to launch a new armada presupposed a gigantic effort that the nation no longer had the strength to make. The projected expedition, constantly postponed, will end up vanishing into thin air. It was time to be on the defensive; ten years later, it would be time for peace.

For the present, however, the determination displayed by the king imposed renewed zeal on the commissary officials. Reconfirmed in his post, Cervantes takes up his Andalusian rounds again in the middle of a grim winter that contributes to a rise in prices. As for his superiors, the hour has come for them to present their accounts. Guevara, called to Madrid in January, is invited to explain his management of public funds. A long inquest begins, rendered more difficult by the complexity of payment procedures and by lacunae in the vouchers; it is an inquest in which all of the council member's agents are going to find themselves involved. Miguel will see his turn come a little later.

For the moment, he abides by the instructions that have been given to him. From January to April 1589, he spends most of his time between Ecija and Seville; his troubles with Portocarrero are doubtless nothing but an unpleasant memory. In June he reappears in the Andalusian capital identified as a resident, if we are to believe the documents where his name is mentioned. On June 26, with Tomás Gutiérrez and Miguel de Santa María, he engages in financial operations that have made biographers suspect an unforeseen win at cards. In fact, a reading of the great Cervantine texts reveals, if not a passion for gambling, at least an interest in its vocabulary and a taste for the metaphors that derive from it. On the day when he offers to the reader his *Exemplary Novellas,* he will compare them to a "billiard table to which everyone may come to entertain himself without risk." And when he is telling his age, he turns again to a gambling image to state it indirectly: "I beat fifty-five years by nine and win the hand." As far as knowing whether he was really a habitué of gambling establishments, let us leave the last word to the governor of Barataria. To his notary, who advises him that it would be better to close the second-rate dens rather than the gambling houses maintained by people of quality, Sancho replies with a phrase that speaks volumes about his reservations: "I already know, notary, that there is a good deal to be said on that point."

Were these transactions at Seville a prelude to an impromptu departure? The fact remains that we completely lose track of Cervantes for seven months. We do not see him surface until February 12, 1590, at Carmona, where Don Felipe de Africa, the famous nephew of the sultan of Morocco, who had abjured Islam, was then living. During this long eclipse, the author of *Don Quixote* must have renewed contacts with his family, first at Esquivias, then at Madrid. Did he obtain his wife's pardon? Did he set his mind at rest regarding his mother's condition? Did he find his sisters bent over their needlework, under the wing of some protector? Did he, finally, see Ana Franca again, and their daughter Isabel? The mystery remains unsolved.

A TIME OF SUSPICIONS

ONE thing is certain: Miguel is tired of traveling the roads on the back of an old mule,

> Of grayish hue and stumbling gait . . .
> Large of bone and small in sturdiness . . .

He can no longer face the muddy winters and sultry summers, balked by the refusal of farmers, the calumnies of local magnates, and the hostility of the clergy. Commissioned by Miguel de Oviedo, Guevara's recent substitute, to collect the four thousand *arrobas* (about 16,000 gallons) of olive oil that Carmona and its region are supposed to furnish, he exhausts himself with arrangements, negotiations, compromises. At least he has the consolation of receiving part of his salary in May, just as his tour comes to an end. But this existence weighs him down, though he refuses, out of pride, to air his grievances—except on one occasion. What to do, then, in order not to return home, with his tail between his legs, to sponge off his wife or sister?

Cervantes decides to stake everything on one play. On May 21, 1590, he sends a petition to the Council of the Indies. Delivered by Magdalena, probably, it is accompanied by a detailed account of his service, deliberately mingled with his younger brother's service record. It reveals a commissary officer attentive to shifts in government employments:

> Sir: Miguel de Cerbantes Sahavedra [. . .] requests and begs with all humility that Your Majesty will deign to reward him with one of the three or four posts that are at present vacant in the Indies: viz., the auditor's office in the kingdom of New Granada, or the governorship of the province of Soconusco in Guatemala, or the post of accountant of galleys at Cartagena, or magistrate of the city of La Paz; and he will accept any of these posts that Your Majesty may grant as a favor, because he is a capable and competent man, deserving of Your Majesty's favor; because his desire is to continue, now and to end his days, in Your Majesty's service, as his ancestors have done; and in this matter he will receive the greatest benefit and favor.

Miguel, let us note in passing, henceforth adds to his surname the name Saavedra. He undoubtedly took this second surname, which none of his direct ancestors bore, from a distant relation, Gonzalo de Cervantes Saavedra. By a curious coincidence, this Gonzalo was forced to flee Córdoba in 1568 after a bloody duel: he had shipped out in Don Juan's galleys, and perhaps he too had fought at Lepanto. He appears among the poets mentioned in the "Song of Calliope"; so the author of *Galatea* knew him personally.

Whether he made Gonzalo a role model or not, Cervantes was fascinated by the name Saavedra, borne by a heroic captive in the *Romancero*, who had become a mythical personage. Cervantes will give it to the Christian slave in *Life in Algiers* who is his spokesman and who dissuades one of his companions from converting to Islam. And he will likewise bestow it on the brilliant defender of Orán who propels the action of *The Gallant Spaniard*. Finally, he will baptize his own *alter ego* with the same name in one of the tales interpolated in *Don Quixote*—the exemplary Christian slave whose unshakable resistance in the face of Hassan Pasha's threats rouses the admiration of Ruy Pérez de Viedma, the captive captain. The choice of a second surname, which the writer substituted for Cortinas, his mother's last name, and which his natural daughter Isabel will bear exclusively for several years, has never ceased to intrigue biographers. A recent student, Louis Combet, goes so far as to interpret it as an indication of masochistic behavior: lacking the power to rid himself of the patronymic imposed by civil law, Miguel doubled it, on a social and symbolic level. This fascinating hypothesis rests on inductions, not to say intuitions, rather than on formal proofs. As for the phenomenon that is diagnosed as masochism, it interests us less from a clinical point of view than because of its connection with its "secondary" effects: it is under the name of Cervantes Saavedra that, fifteen years later, the author of *Don Quixote* will achieve success, then immortality: a remarkable sublimation of all the failure-producing behavior maintained hitherto by an individual who managed to impose himself on posterity.

Let us return to the Year of Our Lord 1590. For the last time, Cervantes tries to obtain for himself the sinecure of which he dreamed on his return from captivity and which had seemed a prospect at the time of *Galatea's* appearance. Had he obtained a post, would he have departed accompanied—or not—by Catalina, with no intention of returning? Would he have been lost to literature? Perhaps not. But one can hardly imagine Don Quixote and Sancho coming into the world under the skies of Colombia or Guatemala. At the very least, their profile would have been different and their renown would certainly have suffered as a result.

Did this humble subject of the Prudent King really believe that his application might succeed? Besides the rebuffs he had already experienced, his handicap, his age, his somewhat suspicious origins, his zeal in the service of a council member whose financial practices were being examined with a fine-toothed comb, were not qualifications to invoke if he wished to achieve his objectives. Whatever the hopes he entertained for his request, he must have asked himself many a time, as he contemplated the ships on the Guadalquivir ready to set sail, what destiny awaited him in those Indies to which he will send his hero Carrizales. The Jealous Extremaduran tells us that America is the refuge and shelter of Spain's desperate, a church for those seeking sanctuary, a safe-conduct for murderers, a place to cheat without discovery for the cardsharps called *ciertos* ["safe bets"] by those skilled in the art, a great lure for loose women, a delusion for many in general and salvation for few in particular.

If he were condemned to vegetate in some obscure province far from Mexico City or Lima, the two intellectual capitals of the New World, he risked disappearing in the anonymity of the tropics, just as Mateo Alemán, the author of *Guzmán de Alfarache,* will disappear. Fortunately—or unfortunately—he will be spared this fate. On June 6, Dr. Núñez Morquecho, the secretary of the council, jotted in the margin of his request this lapidary annotation: *busque por acá en que se le haga merced.* Roughly: "Let him look around Castile for some kind of government post." In plain language: "Let him apply elsewhere."

With no post overseas and with disappointment in his heart, Cervantes is going to make an effort to recover the sums he has been laying out for the last two years. The Treasury, of course, grumbles: some of the commissary agents have not been honest—far from it—and have conspired to make illegal profits. Lumped with these crooks, the author of *Don Quixote* receives an offer of 55,000 *maravedís,* half of what he expected to recover. His protestations have no effect; or rather, they encourage Madrid to summon our commissary agent to explain his handling of his requisitions: a disturbing summons because at that moment Guevara, whose financial activities are looking more and more suspect, has just been relieved of his functions. His former deputy at first refuses: he alleges that he hasn't a cent—*muy sin dinero*—and that as a consequence he has quite recently had to borrow ten ducats in order to repair the state of his wardrobe. Since his means do not permit him to make the journey, he requests in December that Juan Serón, Guevara's secretary, appear in his name. After that, he reiterates his claims and again demands the settlement of his back pay. On March 12, he finally wins his case: Juan de Tamayo, the Treasury pay-officer assigned, pays him 110,000 *maravedís,* or almost all of his salary due. An enormous concession at the very moment when the thunderbolts of justice are about to fall upon the palace clique whose activities Guevara, perhaps unknowingly, concealed: he is accused of fraud; his assistant, Benito de Meno, is arrested. A new commissary general, Pedro de Isunza, arrives in Seville to put an end to these deplorable practices. Miguel must have greeted the arrival of an administrator of integrity with joy; but it will require more than that for him to manage to pull his own chestnuts out of the fire.

Reassigned to his duties by Isunza—at ten *reales* per day instead of twelve—Cervantes, innocent in his honesty, must have believed that he had really finished with the interference of Madrid bureaucrats. He will soon know better. In May 1591, he leaves for Jaén, to the north of Granada, to requisition olive oil and wheat. There he spends all summer, extending the radius of his operations as far as Ubeda and Baeza, where St. John of the Cross is soon to die. At the beginning of autumn, he is at Estepa, looking for wheat and barley. In December, he stops at Montilla, which owed its fame to a pair of witches, mother and daughter, called "the Camacha women." Not long before, the Inquisition had a bone to pick with the two, because, among other talents, they were thought to be able to change a man into a horse, as if it were child's play; they restored damaged maidenheads, and they had fresh roses in their garden in mid-December. They will reappear in *The Dialogue of the Dogs,* remembered by their sister-witch and rival Cañizares on that memorable night that Berganza spends with her at Montilla.

A few days later, because of irregularities connected with a seizure, Miguel's assistant, Nicolás Benito, clashes with Salvador de Toro, the steward of the royal granaries in the town to Teba, near Málaga. Protesting the arbitrary act committed by Benito against him, Toro appeals directly to Isunza and demands an indemnity of 600,000 *maravedís* in damages. Cervantes, in spite of his efforts, is held responsible for his assistant's blunder. The prompt intervention of Isunza, who guarantees the honesty of his commissary agent in a letter of January 1592, addressed to the king, apparently wins a suspension of charges for Cervantes.

The return of spring sees him pursuing his rounds, this time between Andújar and Jaén. On this occasion he attends the pilgrimage of Nuestra Señora de la Cabeza; he will describe its solemnities to us in *Persiles.* Back in Seville, he finds himself without a cent again and sick to boot; he has to ask his friend Gutiérrez to furnish him a place to stay. At the beginning of summer, Salvador de Toro, who has meanwhile betaken himself to Madrid, brings suit against Isunza, with the object of obtaining reimbursement from his adversary's funds. Cervantes, directly implicated in the affair, spends the rest of the year preparing his defense.

As the last straw, while all this is going on, the Council of War enjoins him to settle without delay the 27,000 *maravedís* he owes the Treasury. It is the notable citizens of Ecija, asked to vouch for him, who pull him temporarily out of these difficulties, at the precise moment when—oh, irony of fate—he himself acts as guarantor in a settlement case involving the Valencian merchant Juan Fortuny.

In early September, the author of *Don Quixote* starts a new tour. On the nineteenth, he is in Castro del Río. There, the warrant for his arrest for the illegal sale of wheat, issued by Francisco Moscoso, the *corregidor* of Ecija, catches up with him. Moscoso did not actually have the authority to proceed in this way. But the situation could not have been more favorable to him: Guevara, suspended in April, had been placed under temporary arrest; he will die in Madrid on September 27, before the commission of inquiry publishes its conclusions. Even worse, Benito de Meno, Guevara's assistant, was about to go on trial. In December he will be hanged with four of his accomplices, at Puerto de Santa María. In spite of the fact that Cervantes was completely ignorant of the swindle committed by these individuals, he was nonetheless in a difficult position. He is put in prison at Castro del Río without delay and is not released until Isunza intervenes again. He has barely left for Ecija, where we find him again in October, in the process of requisitioning olive oil, when he is accused by the Tribunal of Seville of a new irregularity in his accounts. This time it is a question of 128,000 *maravedís*, the value of a year's salary, corresponding no doubt to the wheat that Moscoso accused him of having sold without authorization. So our commissary agent, summoned to the capital to explain his part in the Teba incident, takes the road to Madrid in order to join Isunza there. In an admirable deposition, Cervantes claims entire responsibility for the irregularities committed by Nicolás Benito to the detriment of the royal granaries, thus clearing his superior of the accusation of fraud lodged against him by Toro. Isunza, profoundly affected by this calumny, will die six months later; but his adversary Toro, although the case is dismissed, will try for ten years to obtain a posthumous revenge, with a determination worthy of a better cause.

Seville's accusation of irregularity in his accounts, as well as the events at Teba, Ecija, and Castro del Río, inevitably call the attention of high government agencies to Cervantes. Nevertheless, the Council of War, to which he appeals, issues a judgment against Moscoso. When

Cervantes returns to Andalusia in mid-December, he remains inactive for six months. In July of 1593, he receives a new commission from Miguel de Oviedo, charged with settling Isunza's estate. He is active all summer long in the environs of Seville, trying to help solve a food crisis that a severe winter has caused in the city. In autumn, on October 19, Doña Leonor suddenly dies at the age of seventy-three, just as she is beginning to see the specter of poverty disappear. The documents relative to her funeral and estate allow us, in fact, to glimpse a relative prosperity, of which we would like to know the source. It might well be the effect of a match between Andrea and a mysterious Florentine named Santi Ambrosio, doubtless a businessman like a good number of his compatriots living in Madrid, who will die before 1605 without our knowing the date of the marriage. In all likelihood, Miguel deeply felt the death of a mother who had tried everything to free him from Barbary prisons. Perhaps he is thinking of her when he sketches, in *The Call of Blood,* the portrait of Doña Estefanía, that other mother in whom, "as a woman and an aristocrat . . . , compassion and mercy are as natural as cruelty in a man."

The disappearance of Doña Leonor, preceded a little earlier by the demise of his uncle Andrés, the *corregidor* of Cabra, coincides with a turning point in Cervantes' Andalusian peregrinations. He returns to Seville; but his life as a commissary agent is coming to an end. How is he going to occupy himself all through the coming winter? We do not know. We know only that in April 1594, Miguel de Oviedo, on instructions from the king, closes down the vast operation set up by Guevara and continued after him by Isunza: the commissions have run their course and with them the complex system, so often challenged, that had made Miguel's life miserable. In June, the author of *Don Quixote* sees his accounts finally approved. He has not managed to put a single *maravedí* aside; but he is no longer held responsible for the sums formerly demanded from him. Once again in Madrid, where this time Catalina has joined him, he may possibly have thought that he had said good-bye to government service. In fact he will soon return to Andalusia, there to face new trials. As a consolation for these hardships, he will master all the contrasts of the modern Babylon whose adopted son he has become.

ON THE BANKS OF THE GUADALQUIVIR

ALL during his tours of duty, Seville has been Cervantes' one and only home port. In this haven he tries to recover his strength between commissions, to vindicate his rights, to prepare his defense against those who put his competence and honesty in doubt. The sum of his stays in the Andalusian capital amounts probably to half of these six years of coming and going and worry. What we know about the machine of which he was a cog, about its numerous restraints and its way of working, explains why he needed periodically to return to the place whence all decisions emanated: to the center of the web that Guevara, on instructions from the monarch, had cast over the whole of southern Spain in order the better to imprison it in his nets. But even if the growing demands of the Castilian bureaucracy made them heavier, the duties of his post would not by themselves have been able to bring him back incessantly to the banks of the Guadalquivir and to keep him there for months each time. This city fascinates him and holds him, enough to dissuade him from returning to Esquivias and settling there.

Quien no ha visto Sevilla, no ha visto maravilla, says a Spanish proverb: "He who has not seen Seville has never seen a wonder." And this was never so true as at the moment when Spain, in spite of the failure of the Armada, was still at the peak of her power. The traffic with the Indies that had so impressed foreign travelers, even at the beginning of the reign, later experienced an extraordinary surge. Merchant vessels and galeasses discharged cartloads of silver from the mines of Potosí and dumped on the *Arenal*—the sandy embankment along the river— the articles and products that the New World exchanged with old Europe. Lope de Vega, in *The Strand at Seville* (El Arenal de Sevilla), evokes the forest of masts that covers the Guadalquivir and its banks and paints a picturesque scene of the lively activity that prevails there:

> All of Spain and Italy and France
> Live along this strand, for it's the marketplace
> Of the world for trading and for profit.

This "marketplace of the world" was beginning to worry perspicacious observers: behind the fabulous growth of the king's income, revealed by this influx of merchandise from all parts of the world, they undoubtedly perceived Spain's growing dependence on the foreign products with which she was incapable of competing. But in the eyes of most, this permanent fair was the very sign of the prosperity of a city that had doubled its population in less than half a century and that, in this period, was reaching 150,000 inhabitants.

As a result of its prodigious growth, Seville's physiognomy was being profoundly altered. Of course the remains of Muslim occupation still left their mark on the urban landscape, from the Giralda (once the minaret of the former mosque, now the bell tower of the cathedral) to the Tower of Gold, whose crenellated mass one could see on the river bank. But it was no longer only the Gothic churches that broke the uniform whiteness of patio-centered houses. Sumptuous Plater-esque palaces proclaimed the luxurious life-style of a powerful feudal aristocracy, while imposing monuments in Renaissance style reflected the essential function of the city as "the only emporium for commerce with the western Indies": the Aduana and Moneda—Customs House and Mint—built under Charles V, would soon be surpassed by the magnificent Lonja—the Exchange or merchants' loggia—constructed at the insistence of the clergy to drive the moneychangers from the temple, or at least from the immediate vicinity of the cathedral, their preferred place of business.

There is no dearth of evidence for the astonishment aroused by the silver shops in the Alcaicería or by the luxury articles crammed into the *calle de los Francos*. But those quickest to go into ecstasy were without any doubt transient visitors. In the presence of this flood of riches, Sevillians by birth or adoption affected a certain detachment. A calculated detachment in the merchants and ship owners—often Genoese, Portuguese, or Flemings—who, as Cipión will say, "live modestly," but whose ambition and wealth "explode in their chil-dren," whom they treat "as if they were the children of some prince." An insolent detachment in all the speculators, who in a more-or-less legal fashion made profits on the windfalls from a "speculative com-merce" as apt to create sudden fortunes as to precipitate similarly sud-den bankruptcies: "For silver flowed in people's dealings," Mateo Alemán will say, "as copper circulated elsewhere, and they spent it freely with little concern." Hence the splendor of the houses, the luxuriousness of clothing, the magnificence of religious festivities and secular celebra-tions; hence also the numerous slaves, white and black, whose sight astounded foreigners, causing one of them to say that "the inhabitants of Seville resemble the pieces of a chess game."

Cervantes must occasionally have caught sight of some of the great names of Sevillian aristocracy. Nor could he have failed to observe the habits of the merchants humorously described by Cipión, whether through the intermediation of Guevara or Isunza, whose birth and position opened all doors, or with the aid of Tomás Gutiérrez, who had an observation post of the first order at his disposal on Bayona Street. Was he admitted into their inner circle? His origins and station make that rather doubtful. At least he never tried, like so many scribblers, to hitch his fate to theirs and, using patronage as an excuse, become their toady. His examination of them is clear-eyed but fleeting. On the other hand, he reveals from within the motley crowd that populates public places. Readers will later be able to judge this in the admirable portrait that he draws, in *The Jealous Extremaduran*, of the black porter (assigned by Carrizales to guard his dwelling) who, because he is mad about the guitar, allows himself to be tricked by a rogue who has sworn to get into the house.

Did our commissary agent, in many respects a man on the fringe of society, profit from his moments of leisure to renew acquaintance with his fellow writers? Even if there never was, in the true sense of the term, a "Sevillian school," the Spanish Athens in the decade that followed Lepanto was home to a constellation of humanists and poets who contributed greatly to its renown. It was Miguel's bad luck that when he arrived in Andalusia, the count of Gelves's salon, which under the guidance of the "divine" Herrera once set the tone for the rest of the city, had closed its doors eight years earlier. Juan de Mal Lara was dead; Herrera, so admired by Cervantes, was ending his days retired from the world; Juan de la Cueva, like many others, had left for Madrid; Mosquera de Figueroa, whom we glimpsed at Ecija in the exercise of his office, was often required by his post as *corregidor* to be absent. Perhaps it was he who, during one of his stays, introduced the author of *Galatea* to the estimable Baltasar del Alcázar, the Sevillian Martial. Perhaps it was Alcázar who brought Cervantes to the two or three local academies where he would later read some of his verses; perhaps Alcázar took him to the bookshops of Díaz and Clemente Hidalgo before introducing him to the celebrated sculptor Martínez Montañés. But Cervantes, subject to the unpredictability of an itinerant life, must not have been a regular visitor in this society of literary men: Francisco

Pacheco, though praised by Cervantes in the "Song of Calliope," does not even mention our hero in his gallery of illustrious Sevillians.

With regard to his literary works, those that can be dated from these years are limited to a handful of poems. First, there are the two odes to the Armada, contemporary with the expedition but discovered and published at the end of the last century. Their grandiloquence occasionally recalls Herrera's manner; but they also tremble with the patriotic inspiration that already permeates *Numancia*. Next, published anonymously in 1593, is the ballad entitled "The House of Jealousy" (La morada de los celos), an allegorical piece that will give its title to one of the plays Miguel will later hand to the printer. Its theme, not long since sounded in *Galatea,* will be reorchestrated in quite a different key in *The Jealous Extremaduran.* A short balance sheet, one might say, in comparison with the results of seven years spent in Madrid and Esquivias. But the circumstances, let us not forget, had changed considerably. It may well be, besides, that between jobs Cervantes began work during this period on some of the great texts that he will publish in the last ten years of his life. Thus "The Captive's Tale," thoroughly impregnated with memories of Algiers, is thought to have been written around 1590, before being revised in order to become one of the interpolated novellas in the first part of *Don Quixote*. Some scholars date the two exemplary novellas *Rinconete and Cortadillo* and *The Jealous Extremaduran* from the same period, since there has come down to us an unpublished first draft of these stories, earlier than the definitive version published three years before the author's death.

Scholars at the beginning of this century, unconditional admirers of their idol's "realism," made that the criterion of Cervantes' maturity, without duly considering the late character of the fantasies of *Persiles* or the constant attachment that Miguel shows for the pastoral. They concluded that the Cervantes of the great period could not have written his masterpieces except from life: hence their determination to date from his years at Seville those stories whose action unfolds on the banks of the Guadalquivir. Today we are reluctant to associate, in so mechanical a fashion, personal experience and literary creation: otherwise, it would be necessary for us to spread over ten years the writing of *The Dialogue of the Dogs*, which takes us by turn to Seville, Montilla, and Valladolid. It is better to stick to the few facts available to us on the subject: our commissary agent, overwhelmed by the drudgery of his depressing occupation, was above all nostalgic for the time when he had been able to devote himself to literature whenever he pleased.

His passion for writing was too deeply embedded in his soul to permit him to give up the pen forever, even for a hypothetical post in the Indies. And there emerge, from the jumble of accounts and notarial acts, a few significant indications that attest to a love for literature that, as we have seen, will make him say one day that he is "fond of reading even scraps of paper in the streets." In July 1590, taking advantage of a respite between two tours, he attends the auction of a recently deceased bibliophile's collections. For the sum of fifty *reales* he acquires "four little books with gilded bindings, in French print," as well as a life of St. Dominic, handsomely bound.

What was the subject of these four works that could have attracted his attention? Could they have been the *Histoires tragiques* of Bandello, adapted by Belleforest and Boaistuau, widely circulated in Spain at that time? Whether he knew French or not, we can be sure that he was not simply attracted by their market value. As for his devotion to the founder of the Inquisition, is it perhaps connected with the genesis of *The Saintly Scoundrel* (El rufián dichoso), an edifying play that he will write later? Its hero, a Sevillian of the worst sort, repents one fine day and ends his life as an official in the Order of Preachers.

Cervantes has not burned all his bridges to the theater, either. Two years later, on September 5, 1592, as he leaves his lodging in the Magdalena quarter in order to return to his friend Gutiérrez's hotel, he signs a curious contract: in return for three hundred ducats, he engages to write "as soon as he can" six plays for Rodrigo Osorio, one of the most prominent actors of his generation and the director of a troupe besides. Did he keep his promise? Everything seems to suggest that he did not. It has even been claimed that the contract was a worthless scrap of paper, a half-hearted gesture made by a once-successful author who wants to persuade himself that he still has the talent. The fact is that Miguel never refers to this project anywhere. It is hard to see, in truth, how he could have completed it during the worst of the incidents that occurred at Ecija and Teba. Perhaps he simply sketched the outline of one or two of the eight "never performed" *comedias* that he will publish on the eve of his death.

One thing is certain: although he may visit some famous actor when the occasion offers, the author of *Numancia* now lives remote from the stage. Contrary to Lope and his followers, he never becomes part of the system of production whose workings we described earlier and which, in the interval, had given birth to a veritable show business industry. His intermediary with Osorio must have been, once again, the inevitable Gutiérrez. The innkeeper of Bayona Street, however, was trying to put distance between himself and his former milieu. At a time when theologians and moralists, disturbed by the success of secular performances, sought to obtain the closing of the *corrales*, he aspired to a respectability incompatible with his histrionic past. Indeed in 1593 we see him apply for membership in the Confraternity of the Most Holy Sacrament, a religious organization that welcomed into its ranks the cream of Sevillian society and held a choice spot in the Holy Week processions. At first his application will meet with rejection: what is more, the applicant, an actor and innkeeper—two notorious defects—was suspected of having Jewish blood. Only after fifteen months of stubborn negotiations, marked notably by the excommunication of recalcitrant members, will the application be accepted. These vicissitudes would be without great interest for us if Cervantes' testimony did not appear prominently among those produced by Gutiérrez. In his deposition, Cervantes does not limit himself to defending actors and praising his friend of ten years; he identifies himself, oddly enough, as a native of Córdoba and a son and grandson of familiars of the Holy Office: a double lie aimed at helping the candidate's pretensions succeed but that nonetheless adds a contradictory document to the dossier on our writer's origins.

Did Miguel hope to reap some benefit from his presumed connections with the Inquisition? Whatever the case, he who during his rounds had crossed swords with the Church is going to take revenge of sorts: in the spring of 1595, he participates in a poetry contest organized by the Dominicans of Zaragoza in honor of the canonization of St. Hyacinthus (San Jacinto), the Apostle to Poland. These literary "jousts" were common in the Spain of the day, and the greatest poets did not hesitate to enter. Such was not the case at Zaragoza, where only a few middling writers answered the call. The author of *Don Quixote* thus easily wins the laurels for a *glosa*—variations—on four verses of doggerel set for the inspiration of the contestants. The prize: three silver spoons that will turn up again later in his daughter's inheritance. But the happy laureate does not go to Aragón to receive them with his own hands, for at the same moment, during the first days of May, he is in Toledo for the ordination of one of his brothers-in-law.

Eight days later, misfortune once more swoops down upon him. Against all expectation, he finds himself involved in the bankruptcy of a financier in whose bank he had deposited his money. This unfortunate incident not only adds a link to the chain of his disappointments, it is a prelude to the greatest trial that he is yet to experience: imprisonment.

A TROUBLESOME BANKRUPTCY

TO understand how Cervantes became involved, it is necessary to go back two years, to the period when he had finished his commissary tours. In August of 1594, while he is vegetating in Madrid for three months in search of a new post, he receives an unexpected offer from Agustín de Cetina, Oviedo and Isunza's ex-treasurer, who has meanwhile become an *oidor de justicia*, an official of the law courts. The post required Cervantes' presence in Granada and its region in order to collect 2.5 million *maravedís* in back taxes. Our writer accepts this mission without hesitation, provided with a daily wage of five hundred *maravedís*, to be subtracted by him from the sums collected. But first it is necessary for him to produce a bondsman. The man that he proposes to Cetina, Francisco Suárez Gasco, is an adventurer suspected of trying to have his wife murdered, whose "disorderly conduct" inspires the gravest doubts. Miguel succeeds in having him accepted, with some difficulty; but to make up the four thousand ducats guaranteed by Gasco, Cervantes is forced to use his property as well as Catalina's as collateral.

In early September, we see him take the road for Andalusia again, leaving the *Villa y Corte* behind. One can sometimes imagine him looking like the appointee whose bantering portrait the soldier in *The Judge of Divorces* sketches: one of those

> sly, restless little men, with a staff-of-office in his hand, on a small, scrawny, vicious rented mule, without a mule-boy to accompany him, because such animals are never rented except by themselves and when they have no companion; his little saddlebags on its haunches, with a shirt and collar in one and half a cheese, his loaf, and his leather wine bottle in the other; wearing over his street clothes—in order to turn them into traveling clothes—nothing but some leggings and a single spur; and with his com-

mission in his pocket and ambition in his heart, he leaves by the Toledo bridge, moving briskly in spite of the lazy mule's tricks; and before long, he is sending home a ham, a few yards of rough linen, in short, those things that are cheap in the towns in his commission-district; and in this way the sinner supports his household as best he can.

This description reveals a keen sense of observation; but it is first and foremost a bravura piece that includes a large dose of fictionalizing: the mission entrusted by Cetina to Cervantes was far more important than the one undertaken by his wretched *alter ego* in this passage. As for Catalina, one can hardly imagine her celebrating, like Guiomar in the interlude, this new departure: whatever consolation she might derive from the salted ham and rough cloth, the noble descendant of the illustrious families of Esquivias would hardly have appreciated seeing her ex-commissary agent playing the role of tax collector.

Miguel pays no attention to these annoyances. By way of Toledo, Jaén, and Ubeda he reaches the kingdom of Granada and soon arrives at Guadix. His tour, planned to last barely two months, is going to keep him busy until winter: a jaunt though mountains and valleys that undoubtedly makes an impression on his literary work, but of which we hear only indirect echoes. The author of *Don Quixote* is not a romantic traveler, avid to transcribe what he sees. None of the emotion that he must have felt in the presence of the Alhambra or the Generalife rises to the surface; nothing—or almost nothing—shows through of his impressions of this journey through a country marked by eight centuries of Muslim occupation, where the memory of the Alpujarras revolt was still vivid. On the other hand, from time to time we catch sight of shapes that reveal his interest in a civilization so different and yet so like that of official Spain: the Morisco gardener from the environs of Granada who takes in and shelters Berganza for more than a month; the sorceress Zenotia, originally from Alhama, whom *Persiles* shows us practicing her witchcraft on those she pursues with her hatred; Gypsies, wandering in bands along the highways of Andalusia, in spite of the authorities as well as of public opinion irritated by their obstinate refusal of any form of assimilation.

Berganza will become the mouthpiece for this hostility. Denouncing "their numerous tricks, deceptions, and lies," he bares the ruses invented by these perpetual itinerants in order to disguise their misdeeds:

In order to conceal their laziness, they keep busy forging articles of iron, making tools with which they facilitate their robberies; so you will always see the men carrying pliers, drills, hammers through the streets for sale; and the women, trivets and fire-shovels. All of the women are midwives, and in this they have the advantage over our women, because they bring their children into the world without expense or attendants, and they wash the babies with cold water as soon as they are born . . . When these women beg for alms, they obtain them with tricks and coarse jokes rather than with devout prayers; they never work as servants, saying that no one trusts them, and they become lazy; and I have rarely or never—if I recall rightly—seen a Gypsy woman at the foot of an altar taking communion, though I have often gone into churches.

Coming from a dog, even a trained dog, this last detail is a witty touch. It adds a nuance to this diatribe tinged with irony, behind which one detects the author's mixed feelings. We gradually discover how much this "wicked race" fascinates him: this nomad people clever at getting around the law and ready on occasion to welcome misfits of all sorts, from escaped criminals to the prodigal sons of high society. It is in such a context that we must place the astonishing adventures of Preciosa, the pseudo-Gypsy heroine of *The Gypsy Girl* (La gitanilla), who captivates a young gentleman. Dazzled by the charms and virtues of his beloved, he is also carried away by the powerful lure of life close to Nature and by the irresistible call of freedom.

Cervantes does not appear to have encountered major difficulties during his first stages: neither at Guadix nor even at Baza, where he must have heard the name of one of the ex-prebendaries of the cathedral, Juan Blanco de Paz. His enemy from Algiers, excommunicated and sought by the law, had just been deprived of his post. But at Motril he is going to run into an unexpected complication: the money he was supposed to collect there had already by been paid to the Treasury, as the receipts produced by his clients seemed to attest. Apprised of the affair, the king immediately detects a fraudulent maneuver and enjoins Miguel to see that the sums due are paid. Meanwhile, our commissary agent has left for Ronda and Vélez Málaga, where, on two occasions, he must consent to a compromise, for lack of correctly prepared accounting documents. Back in Seville after an absence of four months, he turns over to the merchant Simón Freire the balance of the money collected—130,000 *maravedís*—including his own funds. Next he goes up to Madrid to report on his mission. In May, he is at Toledo,

without word from Freire, to whom he has written twice. Then he
learns of the bankruptcy of his correspondent, who has disappeared
and taken with him 60,000 ducats. Cervantes rushes to Seville to
attempt to recover the deposit. Alas, Freire's creditors have frozen his
assets. After several months of petitions and anxiety, Cervantes gets
possession of the sums destined for the Treasury; but he must renounce
his salary, swallowed up in the failure of a man in whom he had
imprudently put his trust. When the Canon in *Don Quixote* recalls his
friend Cervantes, he will say quite correctly that "he has more experience in reverses than in verses."

Since misfortunes never come singly, this business occurs at the
moment when both in Madrid and in Esquivias Miguel's family is
plunged into gloom. Constanza de Ovando has upheld the family tradition: following the example of her mother and her aunt, she has had
an affair with an aristocrat: Pedro de Lanuza, the brother of Juan de
Lanuza, the chief justice of Aragón. Juan had been decapitated four
years earlier at Zaragoza for having helped Antonio Pérez, Philip II's
ex-secretary, escape to France. The young Pedro de Lanuza, assigned
to live in Madrid, there had met Constanza—five years his senior—in
circumstances of which we know nothing. For four years, their love
affair goes smoothly, until the day when the suitor, declared innocent
of any complicity with his brother, is restored to his rights. That is
all it takes for him to abandon his mistress, granting her an indemnity
of 1,400 ducats, payable over seven years in twelve installments. Was
this compensation, duly accepted in the presence of a notary on June
5, 1595, actually paid? Nothing allows us to say so. At a distance of
forty years, Andrea de Cervantes was reliving through her daughter
her own disappointments.

A month earlier, Juan de Palacios had given up the ghost in Esquivias, after having bequeathed his goods to his niece and young neph-
ews. As expected, Catalina will receive only a small portion of the
estate: two vineyards, a few olive trees, two French tapestries, a set of
bedclothes, and a small barrel. Doubtless she was paying for her husband's desertion. The punishment was all the more severe because the
young woman now found herself without a guardian and dependent
on her two brothers' goodwill. Miguel seems to have taken advantage
of his business in Madrid to join her for a short stay. There is indeed
proof of his presence at Toledo on May 18, for the ordination of his
brother-in-law Francisco de Salazar Palacios. But did he bring Catalina

the support that she needed? His mix-ups with debtors and creditors, his troubles with the royal bureaucracy, unfortunately suggest the opposite. It is easier to imagine him, after his misadventure with Freire, departing without delay for Seville, where, as usual, his friend Gutiérrez was expecting him. At least this is what the little information we have suggests about his occupations during the twenty months that pass between the Freire affair and his new troubles with the Treasury: twenty months during which we are completely or almost completely ignorant of his activities; twenty months, at the end of which the trap closes on the unfortunate commissary agent, without his having any inkling of the disaster that was waiting for him.

Once his contention with Freire had been settled, Cervantes in fact should have returned to Madrid one more time, to present a detailed balance-sheet of his commission. Why did he neglect to do so? Did he believe that he had completed all the required formalities? And did he conclude from this that his accounts would speak for themselves? His superiors, in any case, understood the matter differently and are going to demand from him the 80,000-*maravedí* tax reduction that he had granted the agents for Vélez Málaga: apparently the Treasury could not find a trace of the report from the commissary agent. So his bondsman in Madrid, Suárez Gasco, is informed that Miguel must appear before his superiors without delay. Suárez Gasco, fearing that he will be required to pay if his client defaults, requests a twenty-day delay before appearing in court. On September 6, 1597, the judge, Gaspar de Vallejo, one of the magistrates of the tribunal of Seville, is appointed to notify Cervantes that his guarantors must undertake to settle his debts, whatever the sum; in default of which, he is to be taken to Madrid at his own expense and put under lock and key until further notice. By mistake or malice, Vallejo then commits an incredible abuse of power. Instead of charging Cervantes for the actual sum that the Treasury was demanding from him—the 80,000 *maravedís*—he demands the two and a half million that Cetina had commissioned him to collect, and the bulk of which our commissary agent had already turned over to the state. No one, of course, could guarantee such a sum, even with the resources that Suárez Gasco had at his disposal. There was nothing left for the judge but to arrest our hero. In spite of his instructions, Vallejo now decides to incarcerate Cervantes on the spot, instead of sending him to Madrid. Perhaps he would have acted differently if the accused had bought his cooperation or, to talk like the innkeeper in *The Noble Scullery Maid*, if he had the funds necessary to "grease all of the ministers of justice; because if they are not greased, they groan louder than ox-carts." For failure to do so, Miguel is going to discover Seville's prison, twenty years after the *bagnios* of Algiers. It remains to determine the exact meaning and extent of this decisive experience.

THE PRISONS OF SEVILLE

WHEN he crossed the threshold, much against his will, of the royal prison, Cervantes was entering one of the important places in the Andalusian capital and one of its most notable monuments, if we are to believe one of the chroniclers of the day:

> Visible . . . at the entrance to Sierpe Street, coming from San Francisco Square, and next to the square, is the Royal Prison, which stands out among other buildings and is easily identified even by complete outsiders not only because of the innumerable throngs of people that come and go through the main entrance at all hours of the day and take shelter there at night, but also because of the signs it has on its huge portal, with the royal arms and the arms of Seville.

Such a crowd bears witness to what this prison had become at the end of the sixteenth century: a veritable monster, where almost two thousand detainees resided permanently; which means that it had a capacity greater than that of all of the other penal establishments in the Peninsula, including Madrid's.

This importance is hardly surprising. Seville, by far the most populous city in Spain, was at that time also the rendezvous of adventurers of all sorts, attracted like Guzmán de Alfarache to this "land of Jauja, where everything abounds and the streets are paved with silver." Shady characters from every region of the country swooped down on a city administered by corrupt magistrates, where monopolists, assured of the protection of local authorities, speculated all year long on the price of foodstuffs. As Guzmán will say, "You can sell whatever you have to offer, because there are buyers for everything": all of which makes the pusillanimous quake but the audacious dream of avidly seizing their share of that fabulous banquet, even if only to gather up the crumbs and disappear at the first sign of trouble, "their pockets bursting at the seams with the weight of *escudos* and *reales*."

Cervantes was certainly not of that breed. What we know of his Andalusian tours, his complicated accounts, and his troubles with his creditors would suffice to clear him of any suspicion. Still, the vicissitudes of his impecunious life gave him many opportunities to associate with this tainted element. His friendship with Tomás Gutiérrez, his relations with Suárez Gasco, his mysterious financial transactions, his passion for cards and gambling, reveal his attraction to this society beyond the fringe. How could he resist the ambiguous enticements of a city whose insidious charms softened the sternest souls? As St. Teresa confesses,

> I do not know whether [it is] the climate of the region, for I have always heard tell that there devils have more power to tempt, which God must give them; and they certainly harassed me, for I never saw myself weaker or more cowardly in my life than when I was there: indeed, I did not know myself.

Whether Cervantes knew himself or not, the fact is that he fell under the spell of the Andalusian Babylon, "shelter of the poor and refuge of outcasts," like so many others. Seville, in fact, was not only the meeting place for ambitious or humble *pícaros*. It was also a magnet for all those alienated from honest labor by the stagnation of cloth manufacture, the decline of the craftsman class, the mediocrity of life in the country, the scorn that all Spaniards, nobles and commoners alike, felt for the mechanical arts and productive activities. The city was to an even greater extent the capital par excellence of delinquency and crime, where all the specimens of picaresque fauna came together to form a veritable anti-society, with its hierarchy, its rules, and its jargon: crippled or blind beggars, grouped into duly recognized brotherhoods; vagabonds pretending to be porters or scullions, in order the better to conceal their pilfering and thievery; sharpers skilled at fleecing the too-trusting clients of gambling houses; cut-purses and *capeadores*, past masters in the art of stealing capes and cloaks; pimps drawing their revenues from the prostitution that flourished on all levels: and finally, bullies and professional killers ready to sell their services to anyone wanting to rid himself discreetly of a rival or an annoyance.

We owe to the author of the *Exemplary Novellas* the most colorful picture of this Sevillian underworld that exists. Cervantes preserves for us its types, customs, and exploits: a realistic picture, it is sometimes said. This is to misunderstand completely a technique of evocation that, by playing skillfully on the contrast between Being and Seeming, transfigures the real instead of copying it. As one historian of the Golden Age correctly observes, the picaresque world that Cervantes offers us is the very opposite of the closed universe, locked into its codes and rites, being described at that very moment in books about underworld life that flourish all over Europe, for example *La Vie généreuse des mercelots, gueux et bohesmiens* (The Noble Life of Thieves, Beggars, and Gypsies), published at Lyons in 1596. Cervantes' world is, on the contrary, an open one, where air circulates, where one constantly inhales an astonishing perfume of freedom.

Of course this regenerated picaresque world would not be credible were it not rooted in an authentic experience that impregnates even the stock setting in which our writer places his pimps and bullies: the Huerta del Alamillo outside the walls; the Compás del Arenal by the river; the sinister slaughterhouses at the base of the ramparts; the Court of Elms and the Court of Oranges beside the cathedral, off-limits to ordinary officers of the law. No one, on the basis of this experience, has done a better job of revealing the compromises of Audiencia magistrates or the complicity of beggars and policemen than Berganza, though the ending that the dog gives his story—the ruin of a corrupt bailiff thrown by a stolen horse—is more than sufficient to separate it from a banal police report. With regard to the beggar Monipodio's Academy, whose uses and customs Rinconete and Cortadillo discover during their stay in Seville, it is certainly no ordinary crime syndicate; it is the unexpected setting—bathed in brilliant light—for a brotherhood of the highest type. Nevertheless, the statutes that govern it are strangely similar to those of a contemporary association of malefactors about which Luis Zapata speaks and which, he tells us, had its prior and consuls, like a tradesmen's brotherhood. The extraordinary scene that we contemplate with the eyes of Rincón and Cortado is consequently based on a very precise knowledge of Andalusian delinquency; but it is the exceptional quality of the writing expressing it that instantly captures the reader's sympathy and elevates the *pícaro* to the category of myth.

This knowledge would have been incomplete if Miguel had not had the privilege of perfecting it during his detention. Regarding this confinement, we are ignorant of its exact duration, though it lasted several months. The author of *Don Quixote* is not generous with details;

and the *Interlude of the Prison at Seville* (Entremés de la cárcel de Sevilla), which certain scholars formerly attributed to him solely on the basis of his incarceration, is uncontestably by another writer. We nevertheless have some idea of what his stay must have been, thanks to a detailed account that we owe to one of his contemporaries, the procurator Cristóbal de Chaves. Familiar with the place thanks to his functions, Chaves opens the three doors of the prison for us, one by one: the golden door, the copper door, and the silver door, so named because whoever wanted to pass through them free of chains was required to spend gold, copper, and silver. Traversing the chambers and galleries in order, we come to the heart of the penal universe, "a true picture of hell on earth," if one is to believe an eyewitness, because of the stench, confusion, and tumult that prevailed in the enclosure day and night. Guided by our procurator, we discover practices established by the underworld that have acquired the force of law there: the initiation that old-timers imposed on the newly detained, to test their courage; the advantages granted to the privileged, who could, for money, receive expensive clothing, fine food, and lovers; the sometimes fatal quarrels that set faction-leaders against one another; the cheers that greeted the brave man capable of undergoing torture without denouncing his accomplices; the litanies of mourning and the funeral cortège of prisoners who accompanied those condemned to death to the place of their execution.

Within this motley world ruled by corruption, vice, and violence, debtors surely formed a separate group. But if their lot was less rigorous, their daily existence was still no more enviable, because their destitution prevented them from winning the benevolence of judges or the favor of their jailers. With no known resources, Cervantes finds himself condemned to the mixed company of the dormitories and the meager rations of persons who lack the wherewithal to improve their daily fare. Put in irons thanks to an iniquitous judge, he must have relived—at least at first—the bitterness he had experienced in the jails of Hassan Pasha. Still, however grave the charges that weighed upon him, the stakes were certainly no longer the same. This time it was not a question of obtaining his freedom by paying ransom but of seeing justice done. Did he find the necessary supporters for this objective? Presumably Agustín de Cetina occupied himself from Madrid, using his contacts in high places in order to plead Miguel's case. On the other hand, it appears that Cervantes could not count on the support of Tomás Gutiérrez. Tired, perhaps, of coming to the aid of a starving wretch, the innkeeper disappears from his life without leaving a trace. We know only that he will die in 1604. "Between the rich and the poor, there can be no lasting friendship," one of the heroes of *Persiles* will admit with melancholy, "on account of the inequality that there is between wealth and poverty."

In the grip of adversity, the ex-commissary officer, faithful to himself, does not allow himself to despair. He has scarcely entered prison when he writes to Philip II to denounce the arbitrary procedures of which he is a victim. We have lost the text of his petition, but we still have the king's reply, dated December 1, in which he enjoins Vallejo to free the prisoner so that he may present himself in Madrid within thirty days. In default of his appearance before the Treasury, the monarch says specifically, Cervantes is still to remain free, whether his guarantors settle his outstanding debt or not, because there is no justification for detaining him any longer. This is tacit recognition of our commissary officer's innocence. But between his incarceration and the royal judgment, two long months drag by. Vallejo could obviously do nothing but obey. When did he act? In the spring of 1598, says Astrana Marín on the basis of a now-lost document, according to which Cervantes is supposed to have received in March, while still in prison, a new summons from the Treasury. This time they wanted him to explain his actions on his commission of 1591–92 and, more particularly, on the Nicolás Benito incident. It is possible to conclude from this document, as Astrana does, that the judge imposes on our hero so large a bond—the royal summons authorizes such a measure—that, lacking the power to deposit such a sum, he remains in prison until April. According to the evidence available, he will not reappear on the streets of Seville until that date. Are these meager bits of evidence sufficient in spite of everything to prove that, for three months, Vallejo was able to invent delaying maneuvers? It is just as possible to conclude that he immediately complied and that Miguel was set free in January, without informing posterity on the subject. One thing is certain, in any case: he will never go to Madrid to offer the explanations for which the officials were waiting. As for the Treasury agents, they will finally give up, after having planned, without much conviction, two new attempts; the question of the fantastic accounts of Vélez Málaga will not arise again for several years.

THE URGE TO WRITE AGAIN

WE must not reproach certain biographers for having unduly prolonged Cervantes' detention. Their eagerness to do so is the result of a
little phrase in the preface to *Don Quixote* that has caused a lot of ink
to flow and provoked a debate that is not yet concluded. Miguel,
offering to his reader the fruit of his late-night efforts, starts by con-
fiding his dream that his book should "be the fairest, gayest, and
cleverest that could be imagined." An impossible dream, he immediately adds, with bitterness:

> But I could not counteract Nature's law that everything shall beget its
> like; and what, then, could this sterile, uncultivated wit of mine beget
> but the story of a dry, shriveled, eccentric offspring, full of thoughts of
> all sorts and such as never came into any other imagination—just what
> might be begotten in a prison, where every misery is lodged and every
> doleful sound makes its dwelling?

Cool-headed Cervantists tell us that this is a protestation of unworthi-
ness that conforms to the conventions of the genre, touched with a
humor that dissuades us from taking the statement literally. Hot-
headed Cervantists refuse to take this caution into account: they can
see only the uncomfortable, noisy, sinister prison, where—according
to the author's avowal—the masterpiece was conceived: a real, live
prison, they insist, and not a metaphor for some spiritual or moral
seclusion that Cervantes must be recalling here in imagistic terms.

So be it. But where are we to locate this gloomy place? The romantics were the first to put it in Argamasilla de Alba, alleging without
other proofs that this Castilian town was the true homeland of the
illustrious Knight. The writer Hartzenbusch, who will later become
the director of the National Library, goes so far as to transport an
entire printery to Argamasilla in order to set up, on the straw-littered
floor of the dungeon, the edition of *Don Quixote* on which he put his
name. Certain more circumspect scholars, at the beginning of this
century, favored Castro del Río, where in 1592 our commissary agent
had been momentarily detained as a consequence of a blunder by one
of his assistants. Their hypothesis is ingenious: if we recall that all the
books that make up Don Quixote's library are earlier than 1592, then

one may be tempted to conclude that at that date Cervantes began to work on the first chapters of his novel. That is to forget, however, that his detention was too short to allow for it and, above all, that his incessant troubles with farmers and canons hardly left him the leisure. So there remains only the prison at Seville, where the atmosphere, such as Chaves describes it, is very like what the novelist suggests. Forced into inactivity at the moment when he feels himself seized again by the desire to write, Miguel could well have conceived the basic idea for a book that, eight years later, will provide him with delayed fame.

The basic idea, we said. We take that to mean the mad project of a Manchegan gentleman with his mind deranged by the adventures of Amadís, who, believing that he is reviving knight-errantry, goes out to travel the world and attack windmills: a project too rich in meaning for Cervantes not too have brooded over it for hours, for days. But those who in the interest of their theories delay the author's liberation from prison by several months make him take up the pen immediately and sketch the Ingenious *Hidalgo*. Yet nothing authorizes us to claim (as is sometimes done) that Cervantes sketched him from life, using the silhouette of a "spare, gaunt-featured" fellow prisoner. Nothing permits us to affirm that to refresh his memory he had his nephew bring him the romances of which his book offers us a parody. Nothing proves that during the time of his imprisonment he tossed off a simple novella that will not take on the dimensions we are familiar with until later. This first rough draft leaves us, in fact, skeptical, as do the efforts expended to deduce its exact physiognomy. Does it correspond to the five chapters of Don Quixote's first sally, before he casts his lot with Sancho? Or should we instead extend it to the scrutiny of his library, or indeed as far as his combat with the Biscayan squire? Even supposing that in some first stage Cervantes limited himself to drafting a short story, the revisions that he made on it are so skillful that it is impossible to detect the working outline of it in the full narration that has come down to us. From the very first chapters, we see the appearance of the major themes, around which the structure of the entire novel is ordered: the hero's madness, his preparations, his dubbing at the inn, his return to the village in search of a squire, his departure with the squire for new adventures—all are quite plainly the first stages of an epic of vast proportions. Don Quixote *engendered* behind bars? Why not? Don Quixote *born* in a prison in Seville? That is a conjecture that we cannot risk.

What seems plausible to us, on the other hand, is that once he was free, Miguel set himself to work without delay. Besides his prolonged joblessness—we know of no occupation from now on—his reluctance to return to Madrid was strong enough to keep him in the shadow of La Giralda, or at least to confine him to his lodgings in the San Isidro quarter. What little we do know of his activities during the last two years of a century that had been a glorious one allows us to glimpse, again, a life of expedients. In September 1598, he must buy eleven rods of black cloth on credit. Two months later he is mixed up in an obscure affair over the sale of biscuit. Perhaps this difficulty will resolve itself at the beginning of the following year, when he is reimbursed for eighty ducats owing to him.

A return to *la vie bohème,* if you will; and a return to literature, though we cannot follow the progress of his labors as a writer with any certainty. Clever critics who have analyzed the composition of *Don Quixote* have discovered here and there slips of the pen; they have even found small inconsistencies: for example, during the penance that the hero carries out in the Sierra Morena, Sancho's ass is at one minute present on the scene and the next is said to have been stolen. The result of hasty revision? No doubt. An indication of a revision started in Seville, then suspended for several months only to begin again under different skies? That is what the construction of the novel suggests, in any case. Instead of a linear narration, issuing from a pre-established pattern, it is an expanding universe, gradually shaped by the polyphony of the different narrators; and in the course of the wanderings of master and servant, it is enriched with adventitious episodes. In all likelihood, at least one of these interpolated tales—"The Captive's Tale"—is, as we have seen, contemporary with the first commissions Miguel carried out for Guevara. Another novella—"The Man Who Was Too Curious for His Own Good"—was perhaps written some years later. Even if their inclusion in the body of the novel was not decided until afterwards, they nevertheless make up a portion of a creativity, long concealed, that will not come into full bloom until after 1605.

Anyone who goes further discovers once more the lacunae in an unsure chronology, in need of precise criteria for dating. Some presume that Cervantes wrote the first chapters of *Persiles* at this time, then at the end of his life resumed the project, which would not be published until after his death. Others maintain likewise that after *Rinconete and Cortadillo* he must have composed *Two Young Ladies* (Las dos doncellas) and *Signora Cornelia,* two novellas in the Italian taste. This hypothesis, which lacks convincing arguments, is extremely fragile. In the same order of ideas, various critics for a long time insisted that *The Generous Suitor,* modeled on Byzantine tales, was conceived in the same period, along the lines of the interpolated tales in *Galatea;* today we would be rather inclined to delay its genesis by twenty years.

In the twilight of the sixteenth century, the exposed part of the Cervantine iceberg is capped with two short poems that were not published until well after the writer's death, though their instant success assured their diffusion by mouth and manuscript. The authenticity of the first one has again been contested: it is a sonnet on current events, which, when it was read at a meeting of wits, must have delighted the audience. Under the joint command of Thomas Howard, earl of Effingham, and the earl of Essex, Queen Elizabeth's favorite, the British fleet captured Cádiz in July 1596, sacking it with impunity for three weeks. Charged with defending Andalusia, Medinasidonia, the hero of the Armada, hastily formed companies of soldiers who spent their time parading before the ramparts of Seville but wisely abstained from moving against the enemy:

> In July we had a second Holy Week
> Thronged by certain Brotherhoods
> Called "companies" by the soldiers,
> Who terrify the people, if not the Englishman. . .
>
> Earth rumbled, heaven grew dark and threatened ruin;
> And finally, after the Earl had taken his leave,
> The great Medina entered Cádiz in triumph,
> With perfect calm, without a trace of fear.

This sonnet, as one can see, drips with sarcastic irony. Cervantes seems to have lost his illusions in the school of hard knocks; but he has found a new tone, a register in which he will soon become past master.

The second poem is one that Miguel will consider, in the *Journey to Parnassus,* as the best of his writings. It presents two swaggering bullies, who make us witnesses of their astonishment:

> "I swear to God, its size amazes me;
>   I'd give a doubloon to be able to describe it.

Who wouldn't be astonished and astounded
By this structure, this magnificence?

By the living Jesus Christ, each piece is worth
More than a million, and it's a disgrace it won't last
A century, O great Seville, new Rome in victories,
In courage and in wealth.

I'd wager that the soul of the departed
Has left high heaven, where he enjoys eternal
Bliss, to enjoy this place." A bully, hearing this,
Replied, "What Your Honor says is true, sir soldier,
And whoever says it's not, lies like a dog."
Whereupon he clapped his hat upon his head,
Checked his sword, looked furtively, and left.
And that was that.

Carried away by the vigor of the writing, the uninformed reader soon asks himself, "What is this marvel, and who is the departed soul? And what is the meaning of the sudden collapse of tone, suggesting that the mountain has given birth to a mouse?" Let us clear up the mystery without further delay: it is a funeral monument set up on November 24, 1598, to honor an illustrious personage in death; and it is to the king himself that the Audiencia—the court of appeals—and the Inquisition were paying this homage, after a quarrel about precedence. Two months earlier, on September 13, Philip II had returned his soul to God.

WITNESS OF THE END OF A REIGN

THE death of the Prudent King did not really surprise a public that had seen the signs of his approaching end grow more numerous. For at least three years, the chronic afflictions from which the monarch suffered had been becoming more severe: dysentery, gout, malaria confined him to his invalid's chair, which he left only for his bed of pain. At seventy years of age, he was a toothless, fever-racked old man, whose physical and mental faculties were considerably diminished and who spent hours sunk in unhealthy torpor. Nevertheless, even while he watched the court preparing itself for the final outcome, he did not intend to follow his father's example and renounce the exercise of power while he was still alive. The most he would do, as a consequence of his illness, was to modify his system of governing. Mateo Vázquez, who had died in 1591, was no longer there to assist with his counsels. A sort of cabinet, the Junta, had inherited the secretary's duties; audiences were at first in the charge of the king's nephew, Archduke Albert, then of his successor to the throne, the future Philip III. The sovereign still continued to sign all documents that were submitted to him and to follow affairs of state closely. His interest extended to minor questions, like the condition of the thousand Jews who were still living in Lombardy, or the rebuilding of the center of Toledo, destroyed by fire. But though he considered himself, as ever, the champion of orthodoxy, his primary concern henceforth was to put an end to the different conflicts that set the Peninsula against her neighbors: on this heading at least he echoed one of the grievances of the *Cortes* and was in line with his subjects' wishes.

Forty years of warlike enterprises had exhausted Spain. If the Ottoman Empire had ceased to be a menace, the Low Countries, England, and France were equally stubborn adversaries over whom Spain could on occasion achieve a victory but whom it was impossible to destroy. The failure of the Invincible Armada had sounded the knell of projects to invade the British Isles. Hope of crushing the Dutch Protestants was an illusion. As for France, long torn by the Wars of Religion, she had put an end to her dissension. With the conversion of Henri IV to Catholicism, it was no longer necessary for Philip II to preserve the League against the Huguenots; Henri IV—the *Vert-Galant*—was a redoubtable partner whom one could not treat with contempt. To maintain war on all fronts was thus to see the twelve million ducats that carrying out operations required each year disappear into a bottomless pit: an effort that the finances of the realm could no longer afford at the end of the century. Though the Indies supply a quarter of the crown's resources, the essential part comes from taxes—in particular, the famous *millones*, which pays for Spain's armies—the weight of which has doubled in twenty years and which Castile, the principal contributor, is no longer in condition to bear. At this juncture, agriculture, which has long been the major source of the country's wealth, now handicapped by unproductive soil and a series of severe winters, becomes inceasingly inadequate. The concentration of land in the hands of an aristocracy indifferent to their use; the exorbitant privileges granted to the Mesta, the brotherhood of stock-breeders; the accumulation of contributions and taxes that hit the peasant: all these circumstances accelerate the exodus from the countryside and hasten the decline of the *campo*—to the despair of *arbitristas* (self-proclaimed "advisers"), who dream of a dynamic elite of rich farmers.

Lacking a gentry capable of taking the economy in hand, Philip's monarchy could have used a bourgeoisie worthy of that name. But history decided otherwise. Because it fails to modernize, the Castilian cloth industry, a conglomerate of family workshops, is unable to withstand foreign competition. It makes even less of an effort because the ingots unloaded at Seville make everyone believe that true wealth is what the galleons are discharging; there is no need to manufacture or produce what one can buy abroad cheaply. This ruinous thinking leaves the nation that has just invented world marketing at the mercy of her neighbors. "Spain, who has the Indies," the more perceptive will say, "is an Indies for foreigners." Only merchants and bankers like those whose way of life Berganza recalls save their capital, because of their place in the gold circuit, and they forsake true commerce in merchandise for the money-traffic. But the education they give their children, their determination to make them rise above the commoner class, clearly show their concern for escaping their original condition as quickly as possible. In a Spain where the Jew, converted or not, symbolizes the spirit of lucre, in a Spain that views with suspicion all activity connected with finance or business, how was it possible that the bourgeoisie should *not* tend to betray its vocation? Following the example of a nobility that subscribes to these sterilizing attitudes and accumulates government offices and prebends, the bourgeoisie turns from the mechanical arts to more sedate occupations, putting its revenues into land, pushing its sons toward canonries or the magistracy. In the dialogue on arms and learning, one of Don Quixote's great speeches, it is learning that wins: a sign of the Ingenious *Hidalgo*'s anachronism.

This desertion by the elite classes reveals a wasting disease that a thousand symptoms confirm. The wandering of vagabonds throughout the territory, the plethora of rogues and beggars on the streets of Madrid and Seville, proclaim the triumph of idleness—*ocio* as opposed to *negocio*—that all the moralists outdo each other to condemn and that the picaresque novel will soon interpret in its own way. But there are other signs of the profound sickness from which Spain was then suffering: the chronic famines, prolonged by a cycle of disastrous harvests; the rise in prices, stimulated by speculation at Seville, that will attain record figures; the permanent budget deficit, long masked by usurious loans contracted with Genoese bankers, that ends in the spectacular bankruptcy of 1596; the growing trade imbalance at a time when traffic from the Indies endures assaults by enemy corsairs and the effects of foreign contraband; the once-growing population, now out of breath and declining, severely struck by the terrible bloodletting—half a million dead—of the great plague of 1599–1601.

Must one conclude, as has sometimes been done, that the Spanish Empire is now entering its decadence? It is too hasty to accept as fact, forty years in advance, a decline that will not become irremediable until after Rocroi. In 1598, there are still numerous options. The Iberian monarchy, strong in its possessions in Europe and America, is still the greatest world power, and though its adversaries contest its hegemony, they are not yet in any condition to quarrel over this primacy. So it is an honorable peace that Philip II and Spanish public opinion rightfully seek, and it is in this spirit that on May 2, 1598, the Prudent King signs with Henri IV the Treaty of Vervins. It appears to be a return to the *statu quo ante*, as it had been defined at Cateau Cambrésis. In fact, Spain will soon discover that France is once again a neighbor to be reckoned with. For the moment, however, this accord gives hope to the partisans of a negotiated solution in Flanders. On May 6 of the same year, Philip II abdicates the government of the Flemish States to his daughter Isabel, his favorite, to whom he gives his nephew, Archduke Albert, for a husband. This *de facto* autonomy granted to the Catholic Low Countries augurs a truce with the Protestant rebels. England remains hostile to peace; but the death of Elizabeth three years later will facilitate the opening of negotiations.

Meanwhile, the Spanish sovereign had departed for a better world, after having begged God's pardon for his sins, given his son his last pieces of advice, and arranged the ceremonies for his own funeral. In spite of what his detractors—the instigators of the "Black Legend"— have said, a great reign came to an end with his disappearance, the reign of the first sovereign to have governed on a worldwide scale; but it ended with a crisis, a crisis of power and a crisis of identity, from which a lesson was to be drawn. Its gravity did not escape the author of *Don Quixote*. The death of the Prudent King dictated to him not only the sonnet that we quoted above; it also inspired a curious funeral eulogy whose solemnity is unequivocal. The poet bows low before the illustrious departed, in accordance with the conventions of the genre:

> Where shall I begin to ponder your honors
> After I have called you "father of religious orders
> And defender of the faith"?

But this apparent deference is soon tinged with irony:

> Without doubt I shall have to call you "a new and peaceful
> Mars," since you conquered most of what you wanted
> In peacetime . . .

A veiled allusion to the military reverses of the bureaucrat-king, echoed a few verses further on in the undisguised mention of the financial débacle:

> That the chests (where the gold they say you collected was locked
> Away) are empty, shows us that you hid your treasure
> In heaven.

Cervantes is not easy on a monarch who has roused admiration and hatred but of whom it cannot be said that he was not equal to his mission. The drama of Philip II is the result of a divorce between the principles on which his action was founded and the results he finally achieved. In an eminently unstable period that prohibited long-term strategy, an ambitious and intransigent policy like Philip's was doomed to failure. Did Miguel resent this intransigence? Did he instead reproach Philip, recalling Lepanto, for having abandoned the Mediterranean for the Atlantic and the seas of the North? No one knows. But he judged the king on his actions, and he did so bluntly.

FAREWELL TO ANDALUSIA

ON February 10, 1599, Cervantes signs at Seville a receipt in which he acknowledges having lent eighty ducats to a certain Juan de Cervantes, who may well be a distant relation. After this, we hear of him only sporadically. Some claim that at the approach of summer, he flees from the plague that is laying the city low, and that in October he attends the solemn entry of the new sovereign, Philip III, at Madrid. We find him still on the banks of the Guadalquivir, however, between

March and May 1600, summoned to appear in court as a witness for
Agustín de Cetina. On that occasion, he calls himself a parishioner of
San Nicolás, thus giving us to understand that he continues to reside
in Seville, even though he comes.and goes more or less regularly between
Andalusia and Castile.

Did he strengthen the ties with his family? It seems, at least, that
he had a good understanding with his sisters, to judge by something
that happened two years earlier, the consequences of which will produce repercussions in his later life. On May 12, 1598, Ana Franca de
Rojas had joined her husband in the grave, four months before it was
Philip II's turn to disappear. It is not known whether this death took
her close relations by surprise. In any case, Ana left two daughters in
the care of an attorney from Madrid, who the following year, on August
9, 1599, will be named guardian of the two orphans. Two days later,
on August 11, Isabel, the younger, enters the service of Magdalena de
Cervantes. By the terms of the contract, the latter promised to provide, for two years, room and board, to teach Isabel to sew and to keep
house, and to pay her, as the price of her labor, the sum of twenty
ducats. A revealing detail: the notarial act, though it indicates that
the young woman is the daughter of the late Alonso Rodríguez, nevertheless calls her Isabel de Saavedra, while our old friend the licentiate
Juan de Cervantes is mentioned in the same document in his capacity
as grandfather. Miguel thus indirectly acknowledged a paternity that
had probably ceased to be kept secret for some time. So it is as a niece
that the young woman goes to live with Magdalena, establishing at
the same time close relations with Constanza, the daughter of Doña
Andrea: the best possible company, arriving at the moment when
Constanza must console herself over her broken love affair with Pedro
de Lanuza.

One senses that during all this time Cervantes lived like the rest of
the kingdom, waiting for the new king's first decisions. It is at this
precise moment that Spain, gripped by doubt, finds an outstanding
interpreter in the person of Mateo Alemán. The son of a surgeon, like
his contemporary Miguel, and like him a functionary of the Treasury,
this native Sevillian, an admitted *converso,* brings out at Madrid in
March 1599 *The First Part of Guzmán de Alfarache* (La primera parte de
Guzmán de Alfarache). The work was an immediate success: twenty-
three editions in six years; and the reception given the *Segunda parte* in
1604 will confirm this success.

Who is Guzmán? If not the author's *alter ego,* at least his spokes-man. He is the son of a failed banker whose wanderings we follow: from his native Seville, he betakes himself first to Madrid, then to Genoa and Rome, before retracing his steps by successive stages to the banks of the Guadalquivir; there he is finally arrested and finds himself leading the life of a galley slave. He is, in short, an adventurer who sets himself up as the *pícaro* par excellence. Chapelain, the French translator of Alemán, will judiciously rebaptize him *le gueux,* "the sponger." How did this person from the fringes of society, whom his creator places under the aegis of *Lazarillo de Tormes,* his illustrious precursor, impose himself so quickly as the very image of the modern man? How did the readers of *Guzmán* come to recognize themselves in him? To the extent that they allowed themselves to fall into the trap of first-person narrative. What the *pícaro* sets before us, in fact, is not only the story of a downfall experienced with ill-got and ill-spent money; it is, in the form of an autobiography interrupted by long moral meditations, a destiny that could quite as well be our own, however little the circumstances lend themselves to it and however little we give in to temptation.

It has been said of this exemplary novel, which for the first time paints a large-scale picture of "real" life, that it is a documentary. The *pícaro* is certainly our neighbor, our brother; we meet him on every street corner, something inconceivable with either the shepherds of *Diana* or the knights of *Amadís.* But we must beware of the *pícaro*'s discourse, with its rhetorical apparatus that subjects to the constraints of traditional themes and norms a deceptive reality that has turned into a universe of swindling. Rather than the mirror of an epoch, Mateo Alemán gives us a spectrum analysis of a society whose avowed values and false appearances he reveals; an analysis that the device of the two Guzmáns—the unscrupulous hero and the repentant narrator— permits, in a profound dialectic of sin and redemption.

Today we ask ourselves what the author's purpose was. Did Ale-mán, by means of the destiny of an unsuccessful bourgeois—Guz-mán—mean to deliver the most violent indictment of money, banking, and business that classical Europe has produced? Did he not aspire instead to question, in the guise of an allegorical fable, the dominant mentality, responsible for the *pícaro*'s deviant behavior and failure? Behind the conventional debate concerning sin and grace one would thus see emerging a modern-style parable, concerning a new merchant class freed from the idleness of the *rentier* class, living off investments. In other words, the final conversion of the hero, liberated from the galleys, would in its way represent the conversion of the Castilian elite classes to the virtues of investment and savings. This shows the breadth of the horizons revealed by this book, where the game of Being and Seeming is the *basso continuo* above which one can separate the successive avatars of the hero and the vicissitudes that develop from them. Whatever interpretation the reader may retain, one fact becomes evident to him in the course of his reading: the crushing burden of dishonor that weighs on the *pícaro* until he is illumined by grace, *in extremis*. In vain does the repentant Guzmán ceaselessly demand the exercise of free will, a possibility he eventually demonstrates; this freedom does not become effective until the end of a career that inexorably leads Guzmán the sinner from thievery to fraud and makes him plumb the depths of abjectness.

Now it is precisely this implacable mechanism that Cervantes is going to question, for complex reasons that bring into play at the same time the aims of literature and the image of the human condition that literature gives us. The author of *Don Quixote* has obviously tested the validity of the picaresque formula in the light of Aristotle's *Poetics,* rediscovered by the Italian Renaissance, on which Dr. López Pinciano had three years earlier published—in Spain—a rich commentary. Cervantes' meditation led him to reject what he regarded as the arbitrary nature of Alemán's formula. He is going to take as his interpreter— not without malice—Ginés de Pasamonte, one of the prisoners that the Ingenious *Hidalgo* encounters on his path and that to his sorrow he helps free from their chains. Like the galley slave Guzmán, the galley slave Ginés declares to any who will listen that he has written the story of his life:

"Is it that good?" said Don Quixote.
"It's so good," replied Ginés, "that it will show up *Lazarillo de Tormes* and all that kind that have been written or ever will be written. All I will say about it is that it deals with facts, and facts so neat and amusing that no lies could match them."
"And what is the title of the book?" asked Don Quixote.
"*The Life of Ginés de Pasamonte,*" replied the subject of it.
"And is it finished?" asked Don Quixote.
"How can it be finished," said the other, "when my life is not yet fin-

ished? All that is written is from my birth to the point when they sent
me to the galleys this last time."

"Then you have been there before?" said Don Quixote.

"In the service of God and the king I have been there for four years
before now, and I know by this time what the biscuit and the lash are
like," replied Ginés. "And it is no great grievance to me to go back to
them, for there I shall have time to finish my book. I still have many
things left to say . . ."

It matters little, under the circumstances, that Ginés de Pasamonte
borrows his surname from Jerónimo de Pasamonte, an adventurer whom
Cervantes undoubtedly knew personally and who also left us a considerably novelized account of his life. What counts here is the message
the Ginés delivers for our benefit: by affirming his existence before
others and proclaiming himself the author and hero of a true as well
as amusing story, Ginés exposes, in his own way, the double artifice
upon which *Guzmán* rests. The pseudo-autobiography written by Mateo
Alemán assumes that the author is neither the abject beggar nor his
repentant double; so it does not depend upon either the truth or verisimilitude. As for the backward look the *pícaro* is supposed to cast
upon himself: when all is said and done, it is a deceptive look because
it is provisional: only death can give meaning to a completed life.
Thus, against the closed structure of *Guzmán* Cervantes will prefer to
set the open structure of his novellas, where vagabonds take up the
picaresque adventure as a game, without our knowing whether they
will manage to escape from it or not. Some, like Rinconete and Cortadillo, become skilled in the ways of Sevillian delinquency before
disappearing from sight one fine day. Others, like Carriazo and Avendaño, the two friends in *The Noble Scullery Maid*, reveal their status as
gentlemen when the time comes, but only after having become so
expert in the picaresque métier that they would have been qualified,
we are told, "to give lectures on the subject to the famous Alfarache."
These characters who invent their being and their lives before our eyes
thus affirm (along with their creator) the ultimate freedom: a freedom
that the act of will by which Alonso Quijano is soon to baptize himself
Don Quixote expresses in the highest degree.

This lucid reconstruction of a picaresque literature freed from any
sort of system is not born of bias but of a deepening reflection on
"lying fables" and the status of prose fiction. Miguel is going to con-

tinue this reflection, begun during his imprisonment and incorporated
little by little into the substance of his great book, under other skies.
When does he finally take leave of Seville? In the summer of 1600,
certain scholars believe, at the moment when the "the disease is coming down from Castile," as Guzmán says—the terrible Black Plague
that had decimated Spain a year earlier and was increasing in strength
in Andalusia. Other scholars think that he prolonged his stay on the
banks of the Guadalquivir by several months before heading north
toward Toledo and Esquivias. Whatever the case, this departure marks
another turning point in the life of Cervantes, now a man in his fifties.
Ten years of wandering and trials that seemingly brought him nothing
but disappointments are over; in fact, they are ten years of irreplaceable experiences, in the course of which he imperceptibly forged the
weapons that will permit him to immortalize his name.

V

The Ingenious Gentleman

1601 — 1606

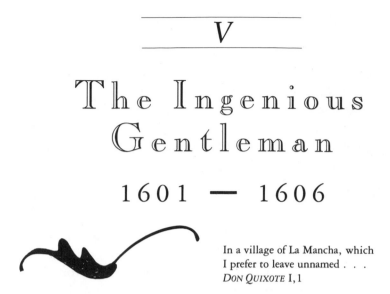

In a village of La Mancha, which
I prefer to leave unnamed . . .
Don Quixote I, 1

A NEW REIGN, A NEW ERA

A LITTLE more than a year after Philip II's death, the glorious century that saw Spain impose her supremacy on the world comes to an end: scarcely fifteen months, but enough time to show Spain what to expect of the dead king's successor. Philip III cuts a rather pale figure in comparison with the men who preceded him on the throne. Though he inherited from his father a religious fervor that will win him the nickname Philip the Pious, he differs from Philip II in his reluctance to exercise power. During almost half a century, the Prudent King had devoted himself without respite to affairs of state. Anxious to examine all the documents submitted for his approval, he normally spent eight to nine hours a day at his work-table, not counting the time spent on audiences or with his ministers. But the new sovereign, from the beginning of his reign, shows everyone that such habits no longer prevail. To this very young man, who has just celebrated his twentieth birthday, to rule means, essentially, to put in an appearance and then to flee from the somber monastery where the defunct king had voluntarily secluded himself in order to weave a better web. The official mourning-period has scarcely ended when, in April of 1599,

the marriage of Philip III and Margarita of Austria becomes the excuse
for sumptuous celebrations organized in the four corners of the realm
in honor of Their Majesties. Henceforth everything will be a pretext
for amusements and festivities calculated to show the love that his
faithful subjects bear toward their monarch.

In marrying his cousin, Philip III is merely fulfilling his father's
last wishes. His sister, Isabel Clara Eugenia, upon whom (one may
recall) the government of the Low Countries has devolved, will plight
her troth to the Archduke Albert on the same day. But—a sign of the
times—this double wedding is not going to be celebrated at El Escorial or in Madrid but in Valencia, a more agreeable site in early spring
than the Castilian plateau, whipped by winds from the sierra. Lope de
Vega has left us a detailed description of the ceremonies he attended
as secretary of the marquess of Sarriá, the same person who, having
become count of Lemos, will one day be Cervantes' patron. If Lope
describes with a certain amount of pride the entertainments he arranged
in honor of the newlyweds, he passes over in silence what other accounts
report to us: his own participation in a Mardi Gras parade, costumed
as a retainer of Sir Carnival, mounted on a mule from whose trappings
hung rabbits, partridges, and pullets. Nor does he tells us anything
about a play that scholars have occasionally attributed to him, and
which seems likely to have been performed before the sovereigns. Entitled
Captives in Algiers (Los cautivos de Argel), it is taken largely from *Life
in Algiers*, the first play written by Miguel on his return from captivity. This adaptation, in accordance with the canons of the *comedia
nueva,* must have been written without Cervantes' knowledge; and no
doubt he felt some resentment when he got wind of it. He may perhaps have concluded that the public was ready to give him its approval,
in spite of his refusal to follow current taste. Was he inclined to change
his style? Judging by the conversation between the Priest and the
Canon in the First Part of *Don Quixote,* one can presume that he had a
rather low opinion of fashionable *comedias*. We will return to that debate
at the proper time.

Besides the mildness of its climate, Valencia held two other trumps.
It was the logical terminus of the newlyweds' voyage. Margarita and
Albert came by sea from Italy, following the shortest route. It was
also the city closest to Denia, where Cervantes, on his return from
Algiers, had landed not long ago, and where the happy couples were
soon going to be received in splendor by their host, Francisco Gómez

de Sandoval y Rojas, marquess of Denia. When the marquess arranged festivities more brilliant even than the Valencian ceremonies, he intended not only to show publicly the gratitude of a man whom the young king had taken as mentor, and whom he had liberally showered with gifts; he aimed above all to proclaim before the world his prerogatives as reigning favorite, promoted at the will of the monarch to the highest responsibilities. Philip II, with his usual sagacity, had perceived the influence that this aristocrat of illustrious lineage, whose affable manners ill concealed his boundless vanity, wielded over the timid, apathetic prince. "Ah Don Cristóbal! I fear that *they* will govern *him*," the old king had exclaimed one day when Cristóbal de Moura, his faithful counsellor, was recalling in his presence the tasks that awaited the heir to the crown. Indeed the Prudent King had scarcely given up the ghost before the marquess exerted himself to prove that he was the real master. He removes Moura and Vázquez de Arce, close collaborators of the late sovereign, from court. He makes his brother-in-law Miranda president of the Council of Castile. Some months later, he will have his uncle, Cardinal Sandoval y Rojas, named archbishop of Toledo. (Let us say in Cardinal Sandoval's defense that he will show himself to be an enlightened patron for Cervantes.) Philip III gives his minister a free hand. Having become duke of Lerma, Sandoval y Rojas is going to preside over Spain's destiny for nineteen years, inaugurating at the same time an era of "favorites."

At first glance, Lerma's system appears to mark a return, pure and simple, to the rule of favorites, *privados* and *validos*, that Castile had known at the end of the Middle Ages, a practice to which Isabel the Catholic had put an end and which the personal government of the first two Hapsburgs had relegated to the shadows of prehistory. In fact, the administrative machinery put into place by Charles V and perfected by his successor had attained such a degree of complexity that even a monarch as filled with a sense of duty as Philip II could no longer aspire to control its workings. Having neither the energy nor the capacities of his father, the new sovereign was thus forced to put himself in the hands of others. Unfortunately for the country, Lerma was not up to his mission. Of indolent temperament, subject to frequent fits of melancholy, he was apt to lose interest in public affairs for days on end, in order to spend his time at parties or hunting. He deserves credit for an attempt to reform the bureaucratic apparatus: small committees, analogous to the juntas that assisted Philip II toward the end of his reign, are going to take over the examination of numerous questions, relieving the royal councils, which were bogged down in routine administration; and they will also permit the duke and his collaborators to fend off the high aristocracy, anxious to recover within the agencies of state the influence that it had lost more than a century ago. For Lerma to act effectively, he would have needed to surround himself with a competent team. But his principal advisers, Pedro Franqueza and Rodrigo Calderón, were opportunists who will be found guilty of embezzlement. The first, in charge of finances, will be exposed in 1607. Arrested and subjected to torture, he will have to restore the sums he had misappropriated for his own profit. The second will manage to keep himself in power for more than twenty years; but, a casualty of his patron's disgrace, he will be dragged down in Lerma's fall and, at the accession of Philip IV, will end his days on the block.

The duke, let us emphasize, does not limit himself to covering up the peculations of his subordinates. Profiting shamelessly by the position that the king's favor confers on him, he will accumulate a colossal fortune in less than three years: named *Comendador* of Castile by Philip III, recipient though his own efforts of numerous fiefs and substantial prebends, authorized to deduct each year an appreciable part of the gold for the fleet, by 1602 he has at his disposal an annual income of two hundred thousand ducats. This spectacular attainment of wealth by a man whose revenues had until then been modest is rightly viewed as scandalous, at a time when Spain is in a period of economic stagnation and when the situation demands quick action. But Lerma and his advisers will be incapable of defining a coherent fiscal policy. Anxious to reduce the weight of taxes that burden Castile, they soon encounter the resolute opposition of the other provinces, all the more hostile to a new division of the tax load because the sums originally granted by Catalonia and Valencia have been squandered in pensions for the privileged. The crown, deprived of part of its resources by the exhaustion of silver lodes in America, is reduced to finding new expedients: the systematic sale of posts and offices, a demand for subsidies from Portuguese Jews, decrees authorizing the minting of copper money—in short, the whole arsenal of schemes to which a government facing bankruptcy has recourse.

It is in this atmosphere of improvisation that a decision—one that marks in a symbolic way the break with the preceding regime—is going to be taken: the transfer of the court to Valladolid. On the first of January 1601, the first convoys leave Madrid for the banks of the Pisuerga, thereby confirming rumors that had been circulating for almost a year about the impending departure of the sovereign. The reason officially given: Philip III's delicate health, weakened by the rigors of Madrid's winter, will benefit by the air of Valladolid, where (someone added) living is cheaper. In fact, Lerma has to get the king away from the influence of his grandmother, the empress María of Austria, who had retired twenty years earlier to the Reformed Carmelite convent in Madrid, and who cordially loathes the favorite. The duke, mindful of his total interests, will not fail to extract considerable profit from this moving operation: four hundred thousand ducats paid by the authorities of the new capital as the price of his influence. Less fortunate than he, all those who live in the shadow of the palace, whether in court and chancery employments or in business activities, are going to have to exile themselves to a city where finding lodgings, in view of the influx of the new arrivals, is a matter of luck. In this exodus, which in the course of weeks empties Madrid of its substance and affects it in its vitals, Andrea and Magdalena de Cervantes will inevitably be carried along. As for Miguel, he will delay a while in joining them; but the moment he makes up his mind, he will see his career as writer take a new direction.

A RETURN TO CASTILE?

BETWEEN the summer of 1600, when it appears that Cervantes takes leave of Seville forever, and the summer of 1604, when his presence at Valladolid is duly attested to, four years elapse during which we are almost completely ignorant of his activities. Only a few rare indications let us glimpse a still-itinerant life, marked, however, by more frequent stays in Esquivias and its environs.

In this dawn of the seventeenth century, Spain, tired of fighting on all fronts, aspires to a peace, modeled on the treaty signed by Philip II and the king of France, that will put an end to the war she has been waging for so many years with England and the Low Countries. At this point an event occurs that rudely plunges Miguel's existence into mourning and reminds him that this desire for peace is still nothing but a pious wish: on July 2, 1600, Rodrigo de Cervantes is killed in the battle of the Dunes, won by Maurice of Nassau over the troops of

Archduke Albert. Thus ends the career of soldiering that had taken the last of the surgeon's children to Lepanto, Italy, the Azores, and Flanders. It was a heroic death, undoubtedly; but this man who fell under enemy fire had not managed in eighteen years of campaigns to rise above the rank of ensign. We will never know why Rodrigo did not rise higher in the military ranks or why it will take his heirs more than half a century to recover—only in part—his arrears in salary. But these wretched details are consistent with the tone of an epoch disabused of its former illusions.

Where did Cervantes hear the news? Perhaps in Toledo, where on August 19 of the same year his brother-in-law Fernando de Salazar Palacios, at the age of nineteen, was to take the Franciscan habit with the name Fray Juan de Salazar. The young man left his possessions to his sister and to his elder brother Francisco, while Miguel was designated testamentary executor. So from this fact one can infer that Miguel attended the ceremony in order to fulfill his responsibilities.

We must wait until January 27, 1602, to see him reappear, in Esquivias, for the baptism of the daughter of a family friendly with the Salazars. There he assumes the duties of godfather with fellow sponsor Juana Gaitán, the friend who had not long ago welcomed him. Did he come especially for the occasion? Twelve days earlier, his wife had sold a piece of land to her neighbor and relative Gabriel Quijada de Salazar for the sum of 10,200 *maravedís*. We know nothing of the precise reasons for the sale, but Catalina had done it by proxy, in her husband's absence.

We would like to know what was happening to Cervantes during the fifteen months that separate Fernando's taking of the habit and the baptism at Esquivias. Perhaps he was present at the family reunion that took place in Toledo in December of 1601 for a different ordination, that of Francisco de Palacios, the oldest of his brothers-in-law. It would appear that during all this time, Miguel was having trouble with his creditors. On September 14, 1601, the Treasury accountants had in effect renewed the charge and demanded from him, in vain, the eighty thousand *maravedís* from Vélez Málaga, which they considered him to have owed for seven years. On January 24, 1601, they are going to issue a new summons. This time, the document makes reference to previous instructions addressed to *Señor* Bernabé de Pedroso, telling him that Cervantes should be taken from the prison at Seville. Must one therefore deduce, as is sometimes done, a second incarceration of the ex-commissary officer? Since the facts reported are not dated, the affair seems likelier to be related to the jail episode of 1597, after which the Treasury redoubled its efforts in hopes of obtaining explanations from their former agent.

Besides, it is hard to imagine Fray Juan de Salazar's testamentary executor in custody again, at the very moment when he was devoting most of his time to *Don Quixote*. The letter from the Knight to his niece in the First Part is dated August 20, which date—if Cervantes is true to his habits—must be the one on which the novelist wrote it. But in what year? From the best evidence, 1602: chapters 28 to 30, which in the form of an interpolated tale narrate the unhappy love affair of Luscinda, unquestionably contain reminiscences of a late chivalric romance, *Policisne de Boecia,* published in Valladolid in the autumn of the same year. These two bits of evidence that point to writing activity suggest a more settled life, divided among Madrid, Toledo, and Esquivias, rather than new Andalusian wanderings, mixed with a second stay behind bars. Astrana Marín, in view of the friendship that Cervantes had formed in Seville with Don Fernando de Toledo, lord of Higares, asks whether Cervantes did not, on returning to Toledo, enter the service of this young aristocrat, in order to straighten out Don Fernando's accounts and help him administer his properties. Besides the fact that there is nothing to support such a hypothesis, it seems most unlikely that the ex-commissary officer had any desire to plunge into bookkeeping again. Thanks to the bequest from his brother-in-law, he was able to stop traveling the roads for a while and to give himself a little respite: everything leads us to believe that he used it in order to devote himself to his masterpiece.

When did his sisters decide to leave Madrid? Andrea was still there on February 8, 1603. On that date she acknowledged having received seven hundred *reales* in payment for sewing. Signed in Miguel's hand, the receipt attached to the document proves that the writer was living near her at the time. Andrea's departure probably took place in the spring. Her needlework was popular with high society, and she could not afford to lose her clientele; in order to survive, she had to fall into step. In the company of Magdalena, Constanza, and Isabel, she like so many other *madrileños* will swell the ranks of those who had followed the king and the court two years earlier. Had Cervantes thought of making the journey with them? He seems to have preferred to prolong his stay at Esquivias in order to put the finishing touches to his manuscript: from evidence we have through his niece Constanza, it appears in fact that he did not join his sisters until the beginning of summer 1604. If he decided to take the step at that time, it is because he had just found a publisher in the person of Francisco de Robles, the son and successor of Blas de Robles, who years before had published *Galatea*. While keeping his shop at the Guadalajara gate in Madrid, this important bookseller had settled in the new capital three years earlier. Under what circumstances did the two men meet each other? We do not know. What is certain, however, is that having undertaken to obtain the royal privilege necessary for the publication of his book in July, Miguel was ready to hand his manuscript over to the printer the following month. It required little else to persuade him to move to Valladolid in order to give to his re-entry into the literary world the necessary publicity. A few weeks later, after her mother's estate had been settled, to the benefit of her brothers and the creditors, Catalina took her leave of Esquivias. Thanks to the Knight of the Woeful Countenance, the long-separated couple begin living together again, late in the day, and will continue so until Miguel's death.

AT VALLADOLID

WHEN he moved the government of the realm away from Madrid, Lerma, as we have seen, was obeying motives not all of which were admissible. Nevertheless, Valladolid had certain attractions in its favor: a fertile region, improved by reforestation in the preceding century; a strategic position at the center of a network of communications; a dense population that exceeded sixty thousand inhabitants even before the court took up residence there, and in which, contrary to so many other Castilian urban populations, the working classes were preponderant. The city, which had been the seat of the chancery since the days of the Catholic Rulers, as well as the capital intermittently during the reign of Charles V, could aspire to a brilliant future. Ravaged in 1561 by a fire that destroyed her wooden houses, she had rebuilt according to the rules of modern urban development; and the reconstruction, while permitting easier circulation of traffic, had renewed the city's appearance: the Plaza Mayor, with its five hundred arches and two thousand windows, had no equal in all the Peninsula; Silversmiths' Street—the celebrated Platería—lined with expensive shops, where four carriages could pass abreast, was the very symbol of her prosperity; her palaces and churches outdid in number and luxury those of Madrid; shady promenades along the banks of the Pisuerga were easily the equivalent of the Prado and Retiro, which sweltered in torrid summer weather because they lacked running water.

With the arrival of the king and the installation of government agencies, the influx of courtiers, functionaries, and their families and servants was going to make the city burst its walls. Lerma, wanting to spare Valladolid the plague of illegally constructed houses—*casas del malicia*—common in Madrid, ordered that all the new houses should have three stories and that their facades should be painted blue and gold. The chroniclers of the day never cease praising the effect produced. What they fail to add is that the demand had so outstripped the supply that only the privileged had any hope of finding decent lodgings. Those who lacked contacts or ready cash saw themselves deprived of access to the better quarters of the city and had to accept housing in suburbs where unscrupulous promoters were rapidly erecting improvised constructions.

In one of these makeshift buildings, where masons were still at work, Cervantes is going to settle with his family: a three-story house that its owner, Juan de las Navas, rented as apartments to newcomers. Located in the neighborhood of the Rastro de los Carneros—the municipal slaughterhouse—it was twenty paces from the banks of the Esgueva and next to the Hospital of the Resurrection, where the action of *The Dialogue of the Dogs* opens and closes. Was the area a slum, as someone has claimed? "Slum" is probably too strong a word. Nevertheless, the nearby hospital and abattoir, the street-level tavern frequented by butchers, the filth that soiled the approach to the wooden bridge that crossed the stream, suggest a rather humble residence, proportionate to the modest resources of the writer. Curiously, this structure built in haste is going to shelter, around the Cervantes family, a whole colony of relatives and friends from Madrid, Toledo, and Esquivias who had come to sniff the air of the young capital and profit by its recent expansion. On the second floor, above the tavern, Miguel, Catalina, Andrea, Constanza, Magdalena, and Isabel install themselves; a serving-woman, María de Ceballos, will join them several months later. On the same floor, a cousin, Luisa de Montoya, the widow of the illustrious chronicler Luis de Garibay, is going to lodge, accompanied by her daughter and two sons. On the top floor, across from an apartment occupied by a friend, Mariana Ramírez, and her mother and two small children, lives Juana Gaitán; she has also left Esquivias, bringing her husband, her sister, and a niece. Finally, a certain Isabel de Ayala, an old gossip-monger, will occupy an attic room at the very top of the house. A total of twenty persons for thirteen rooms, many of which were tiny: this speaks volumes about the constraints that life in Valladolid imposed.

How did Cervantes tolerate this crowding? With a playful resignation that shines through in one of Master Glass's witticisms. Comparing the two capitals, the old and the new, Tomás Rodaja considers them equally balanced; but, he quickly adds, they have not received equal favors: Madrid has the advantage in sky and soil (*cielo y suelo*), Valladolid has it in cramped quarters (*entresuelos*—literally, "half stories"). History does not tell us whether the writer had in mind the noble dwellings of the Plaza Mayor or, more prosaically, the modest building on the Rastro de los Carneros. If he accommodated himself without too much bitterness to his miserable lodgings, it is because from week to week, the day when *Don Quixote* would come out of the shadows was approaching, and because, entirely preoccupied by that event, he paid no heed to the discomfort in which he was forced to live. We do not know what his daily occupations were during the six months that the printing of his manuscript took; but the odds are good that he avoided Treasury accountants, who were probably more concerned with the embezzlement of thirty thousand ducats that one of the secretaries of the Council of Finances had just committed. Did he spend much time in the waiting rooms of the palace? At the age of fifty-seven, he was no longer a man to play at petitioner; after being turned down by the Council of the Indies, after the worries that his Andalusian commissions had brought him, the king's service no longer had the least attraction for him. The weight of age, the first attacks of the illness that will carry him off eleven years later, the very modest comforts that the Salazar inheritance provided—at least temporarily— are all inducements for him to lead a more sedentary life, more propitious for his work as writer.

In all likelihood he renews acquaintance with his fellow writers, who have been flocking to the city for four years in quest of sponsors and patrons. Some were his contemporaries, like Gracián Dantisco, who had been a friend for years. Others, still young, like Luis de Góngora, were acquiring favorable reputations with their poetry; and their presence in the city contributed to its brilliance. Among these making their literary debuts, Francisco de Quevedo, although he was still at the university, was already carrying on polemics with Góngora; and Justus Lipsius, the illustrious Flemish humanist, had admitted him to the number of his correspondents. Thanks to these writers, Valladolid makes an undisputed claim to be the cultural capital of the realm, in the opinion of a public dazzled by the brilliance of the city's festivities and the variety of its amusements. The dramatic poets and their interpreters certainly play their part in this concert: the *comedia nueva,* whose formula Lope de Vega has perfected, arouses extraordinary enthusiasm, a passion that nobles and commoners share. This "new comedy," let us hasten to say, did not spring fully armed from the brain of its inventor. It is a collective creation whose vogue will last beyond the seventeenth century; it will remain to the end a product of mass culture, where the best will inevitably rub elbows with the worst; and, by means of the diversity of its themes and subjects, it will manage to produce theater from everything that can be transformed into theater.

In order for that metamorphosis to take place, there had to be an audience in a position to express its wishes, or at the very least its expectations. This audience, fragmented among different communities for a long time, is going to coalesce on a Peninsula-wide scale during the very years when Miguel is crisscrossing Andalusia and when, under the impulse of local religious brotherhoods, a network of permanent playhouses covers the whole kingdom. When the reign of Philip II ends, this audience is strong enough to hold its own against the enemies of the theater, who, taking advantage of the period of mourning that followed the Prudent King's death, succeeded in prolonging the closure of the *corrales.* After several months, the decree is revoked because of public pressure. As a countermeasure, opponents use their influence to control the entertainment industry and, in particular, to strengthen the laws concerning actors. A decree issued by the sovereign on April 26, 1603, specifies that no *comedia* may be performed during Lent and that plays must be banished from monasteries and nunneries. Wandering troupes that go from village to village are still tolerated. Eight companies of actors (the *compañías de título,* whose members are recruited each year by contract) receive a royal privilege and are the only troupes authorized to play in the large cities. Their managers—the all-powerful *autores*—benefit, conse-

quently, from the regime's favor; in exchange, they promise to cooperate closely with the municipalities. This collaboration is what is
going to assure the *comedia*'s exceptional diffusion.

The leading *autores,* who were at the same time directors, stage-
managers, adapters, and producers, are thus going to enjoy a veritable
monopoly. It is to them as well as to the spectators in the *corrales* that
Lope de Vega owes the recognition he so quickly received. But his
pre-eminence is not only a result of his skills as the perfect interpreter
of his nation's taste; it is also a testimony to the prodigious fecundity
of this Phoenix of Wits and, above all, to his ability to transfer onto
the stage, and to express in all keys, a society's feelings about its
innermost contradictions. This most popular poet of his day knew how
to hold up before a Spain recovering from the hazards of war, and quite
ready to abandon herself to the seductions of imaginary adventures,
the mirror in which she longed to contemplate herself.

Lope completed his apprenticeship at the time when Cervantes was
wearing himself out on commissions and official rounds. He acquired
his training mostly in contact with Valencian playwrights in the orbit
of Guillén de Castro who were also trying to invent a new art; he
studied their example and made their branch of the tree bear fruit. By
the time Philip III, because of general demand, decides to reopen the
theaters, Lope has fully mastered his craft. His supremacy is henceforth absolute; but it begins to arouse envy. Was Miguel among the
number of the envious? A day will come when he will celebrate Lope
as "Nature's prodigy," who, "seizing control of the kingdom of *comedia,* reduced all actors to vassals and brought them under his jurisdic-
tion." But for the present, relations between the two men have cooled
noticeably. In 1602, the temperature was still pleasant, if one can
trust the preliminary sonnet that graced the Phoenix's *Rhymes,* published that year in a volume with *Angelica's Beauty.* Punning on the
poet's name (*vega* means "fertile plain"), the author of *Don Quixote*
sings of the

> . . . pleasant and ever-verdant plain
> From which Apollo withholds his favor not;
> For he bathes it with the waters of Helicon.

But there is certainly irony in the two verses on the "holy throng of
cupids" (*amores,* which means both "cupids" and "love affairs") that
"chaste Venus augments and fosters" on that *vega.* For in *Angelica's*

Beauty Lope exalts in scarcely veiled terms the charms of Micaela de Luján, his mistress, for whom he had left his legal spouse and who will give him three children in quick succession.

What happened after that? Some believe that an incident occurred around 1603 in Madrid: Cervantes may have written a satire against Lope that stung him to the quick. Others suppose that Cervantes had become annoyed by the Phoenix's dictatorship of the Spanish stage and had reproached him publicly for his infractions of the "rules of art." In any case, that is the gist of the sweet-and-sour remarks that the Priest in *Don Quixote* will soon make on the subject of "a most fertile wit of these kingdoms" whose plays, "because of his desire to suit the taste of the actors, . . . have not all—as some of them have— come as near perfection as they ought." The allusion is all the more pointed because the Priest first attacks, without being specific, "modern plays," which he describes as "mirrors of nonsense," "models of folly," and "images of lewdness."

It is not certain that Lope had a preview of this discourse; but a letter in his hand, dated August 4, 1604, testifies to his irritation. In it he protests his horror of slander, "a thing more odious to me than my plays are to Cervantes." He also mentions "next year's budding poets" and ends with this barb: "There is none so bad as Cervantes or so stupid as to praise *Don Quixote*." An attack on a book known to a few initiates even before it is put on sale? No: merely an acerbic reference to the preliminary poems that Cervantes will admit he composed himself instead of calling on his fellow writers or the clever wits of the court. For the moment, Miguel is still only a disciple of the Muses, a malicious rhymester with whom the Phoenix intended to get even.

If the date of Lope's letter is correct—Astrana Marín has questioned it—at least one thing seems certain: in the summer of 1604 Lope had heard about the Manchegan Knight and alluded to him five months before the story of his adventures appeared. Nor is he the only one: in *Justina the Female Picaro,* by López de Ubeda, written between 1602 and 1604, the heroine is said to be more famous

> Than Don Quixote or Lazarillo,
> Than Alfarache or Celestina.

In addition, a Spanish Morisco named Juan Pérez, who became Ibrahim Tabilí after his expulsion from the Peninsula, reports (after a lapse

of thirty years) an incident he claims to have witnessed: in late August
1604, one of the customers of a bookstore at Alcalá, a passionate reader
of romances of chivalry, amused everyone with his vehement admiration. A student who was present made fun of him by exclaiming,
"Here's a new Don Quixote." This anecdote sounds a little too con-
trived to be perfectly credible. But the comparison of the different
pieces of evidence nevertheless reveals an anxiously waiting public. At
the dawn of the year 1605, in the early days of January, this waiting
is going to end: *Don Quixote* finally comes off the press; the masterpiece
is born.

THE BIRTH OF DON QUIXOTE

SEVEN years have passed since the day when Miguel first had the idea
for his novel, amid the discomforts of the prison at Seville. How many
hours did he steal from his tedious rounds between the Guadalquivir
and the banks of the Pisuerga in order to meet his creation in private?
How many pages did he have to begin anew so that his characters
might assert themselves, so that this new kind of epic might fall into
place? Cervantes is readily talkative when he is conjuring up the fictitious authors behind whom he hides and who are supposed to have
recorded the exploits of his hero; but he is much more reticent about
his own work as writer. The image that he has left us of himself is
that of a literary craftsman who has come to the end of his work and
who at the moment of writing his preface suddenly finds himself inde-
cisive:

> Many times I took up my pen to write it, and many I laid it down again,
> not knowing what to write. One of these times, as I was pondering with
> the paper before me, a pen behind my ear, my elbow on the desk, and my
> cheek in my hand, thinking of what I should say . . .

This self-portrait is not entirely candid; but we can easily believe that
doubt often assailed Miguel along the way, made more difficult by the
unforeseen turns of his eventful life. His moves from one place of
residence to another, his squabbles with his creditors, his problems
with his in-laws over inheritance, all constantly interrupt him at his
task, forcing him to drop and then take up the threads of his narrative

again. As he clearly explains, everything he needed in order to give free reign to his invention was implacably refused him:

> Tranquility, a cheerful retreat, pleasant fields, bright skies, murmuring brooks, peace of mind, these are the things that go far to make even the most barren Muses fertile and cause them to bring into the world off-spring that fill it with wonder and delight.

By what process was the masterpiece produced? Ingenious critics, by virtue of internal analysis alone, have attempted to clarify it. They believe that they have been able to reveal several strata, corresponding to the principal stages of its genesis. The minute examination of certain minor contradictions (about which we have already said a few words) does indeed allow us to perceive a sinuous progression, punctuated by hesitations, false starts, changes of mind. But Cervantes, by means of a revision of the work in its entirety, managed to smooth most of the rough places and, except for a few details, to fit the parts to the whole. This revision doubtless took place during the summer of 1604, when Francisco de Robles became the owner of the manuscript, for what was probably a modest sum—fifteen hundred *reales* at most. At the same time, the steps taken by the novelist and his publisher to obtain the necessary authorizations met with success. On September 26, they received the royal privilege. In the interval, the Madrid printer Juan de la Cuesta had started setting the book in type. In December, the last sheets were coming off the presses. And although the licentiate Murcia de la Llana was officially in charge of discovering errata, he had returned without qualms a text riddled with misprints. In the same month the *tasa*—a permit to sell—was signed; it fixed the price of the volume, paperbound, at 290.5 *maravedís*. For the eighty-three octavo sheets of which it was composed (664 pages), it was a reasonable price, provided that at least five hundred copies of this edition, printed on cheap paper, sold.

A few weeks earlier, Miguel had dedicated the fruits of his labor to a twenty-seven-year-old aristocrat, Alonso Diego López de Zúñiga y Sotomayor, duke of Béjar. It appears that this young man, a mighty hunter before the Lord, was not a generous Maecenas. Cervantes, who will soon drop the duke in favor of the count of Lemos, will have Don Quixote point out that there are few lords and grandees in Spain to whom one can pay homage with a book:

And not because they do not deserve it, but because they refuse to accept it, in order not to be forced to repay what it appears is due to the effort and courtesy of their authors.

What Cervantes himself does *not* point out is that the dedication addressed to the duke is nothing but a plagiarism of one offered twenty-five years earlier by the poet Herrera to the marquess of Ayamonte. As for Béjar, his name will again be associated with that of a writer of genius: in early 1614, Góngora will dedicate to him his immortal *Solitudes*.

Cervantes, in fact, was feeling sufficiently sure of himself to keep patrons and sponsors at a distance, as is obvious from his preface, a masterpiece of mischievousness and humor. If he pokes fun at his timorous fellow writers, whose works begin with flattering sonnets from obliging poets, and who interlard their prose with *sententiae* taken from the best authors, it is in order to emphasize his own audacity:

> I, however—for though I pass for the father, I am the stepfather of Don Quixote—have no desire to go with the current of custom or to implore you, dearest reader, almost with tears in my eyes, as others do, to pardon or excuse the defects you may perceive in this child of mine.

So he will not load himself down with epigrams and maxims. Who is going to compose the garland of sonnets with which his book is embellished? Amadís de Gaula, Belianís de Grecia, Orlando furioso— *alias* the author himself, hidden behind the masks he puts on one after the other. Who is going to furnish him with quotations and adages? Nobody; for, in the words of the "lively, clever friend" whom he introduces and to whom he pretends to confide his difficulty,

> . . . since this piece of yours aims at nothing more than to destroy the authority and influence which books of chivalry have in the world and with the public, there is no need for you to go begging for aphorisms from philosophers . . . but merely to take care that your sentences flow musically, pleasantly, and plainly, with clear, proper, and well-placed words . . . Strive, too, that in reading your story the melancholy may be moved to laughter, and the merry made merrier still; that the simple shall not be wearied, that the judicious shall admire the invention, that the grave shall not despise it, or the wise fail to praise it.

By the time his *alter ego* outlines this fine program for him, Miguel has put the final touches to the first series of his hero's exploits, which corresponds to Don Quixote's first two sallies. What Cervantes tells us he wants to do is to destroy "that ill-founded edifice of the books of chivalry." But what are we to think of this stated purpose? Must we accept without hesitation that our novelist has no other aim but the one he will assert again ten years later, when he is at death's door: "to cause mankind to abhor the false and foolish tales of the books of chivalry"? Scholars have often argued about how much credit to give to these declarations. There is, without doubt, something of a paradox in the insistence with which Cervantes advertises his iconoclastic ardor. In the year of grace 1605, the *Amadíses* and *Palmeríns* are books that people still read; but they are no longer fashionable works: far from it. What we know of their diffusion, what the men of the Renaissance tell of their popularity, proves that the romance of chivalry's vogue attains its peak during the reign of Charles V and declines slowly in the second half of the sixteenth century. Those who admit, sometimes unwillingly, how much enjoyment they get from reading such books are, clearly, witnesses from an earlier period: St. Ignatius of Loyola, St. Teresa of Avila as a very young adolescent, not to mention the emperor himself, a great lover of these tales.

After the middle of the century, there appear the first signs of an ebbing that is going to grow more apparent after the disaster of the Armada. The day is past when the conquistadores would baptize the territories they explored beyond the oceans with the names of imaginary countries—California or Patagonia—visited by their favorite heroes. Instead, it is a time for amusing stories that report the follies committed by stubborn readers of these fables: the story of the father who returns home and finds his household in tears because Amadís is dead; or the one about the student at Salamanca who, to rush to the aid of a damsel in distress, draws his sword while he is absorbed in his reading and terrifies the neighbors. As these sample anecdotes prove, the decline of the romances of chivalry is not due simply to the reproaches of moralists who, already under Charles V, were denouncing their indecency and silliness; nor is it explained by the hostility of civil and religious authorities; it corresponds above all to a change of taste. The deeds of paladins, the challenges offered to them by dwarfs, giants, or enchanters, rides that take them through mountains and forests, the love—more or less chaste—that they vow to the lady of their thoughts, are all things that formerly won the approval of connoisseurs but have now ceased to please those who set the tone.

The disaffection (someone has called it) of an aristocratic public that henceforth refuses to go along: having come of age, it no longer takes pleasure in narratives that, to repeat Bakhtin's formula, reduce the whole world to the categories of the "unforeseen," of chance, the marvelous, the unexpected. But we still need to untangle the reasons for this change of attitude. After all, even today we find an undeniable charm in these ingenuous fantasies that joyfully extol the delights of free adventure. If therefore the subjects of the Prudent King gradually turn away from romances, it is because, in that *fin de siècle,* when bureaucrats and financiers make the law, such books can no longer offer them the idealized picture of a world where they would have liked to live. Other forms of escape attract them, subtler perhaps, certainly more in line with the habits of a citified and sedentary elite, and consequently better suited to the new order of values. This is what the success of the pastoral demonstrates. It reflects the readers' own image transposed into a bucolic framework that fosters introspection. In spite of Berganza's raillery, this success, which *Don Quixote* echoes, will maintain itself during the entire reign of Philip III.

In his youth, Cervantes read and reread *Amadís,* "the best of all the books of this kind," which the Priest and the Barber, who undertake to examine the works that have unhinged the Ingenious *Hidalgo*'s mind, spare from the purifying bonfire. On the other hand, they send to the fire the most illustrious of Amadís's descendants. Do they share the opinion of the censors of former times, who discovered in these romances the hand of the Devil? Certainly not. The Priest, a perceptive reader of Aristotle, judges them in the light of the *Poetics* in order to separate the wheat from the tares, and incidentally to establish with his brother-ecclesiastic the Canon under what conditions these "lying fables" can be "suited to the understanding of the reader." At first sight, this subject would appear to interest no one but pedants and to be of no concern to the Knight. But Miguel's brilliant stroke was, in fact, to put the debate at the very center of his hero's project, thus uniting the theory with the practice of the novel.

THE FIRST MODERN NOVEL

WHEN he decides to "make a knight-errant of himself, roaming the world over in full armor and on horseback in quest of adventures . . . [putting] into practice all that he had read of as being the usual practices of knights-errant . . .," Don Quixote actually raises a dangerous question, one that Marthe Robert (following Leo Spitzer) formulates in a remarkable essay, and one that has remained a continual source of confusion for literature: "What is the place of books in reality? In what way does their existence matter to life? Are they absolutely true or true in an entirely relative way; and if they are true, how do they prove that they are?" The Ingenious *Hidalgo,* an exemplary reader, is going to put this truth to the test, only to discover—to his cost—the ambiguity of the relationships between literature and life.

One can say about the poor *hidalgo* who appears before us at the beginning of the novel that nothing suggests he is destined for immortality. Where was he born? "In a village of La Mancha" that the narrator prefers not to name. When did he live? "Not long ago." What was he?

> One of those gentlemen that keep a lance in the lance-rack, an old shield, a lean hack, and a greyhound for hunting. . . . Some say that his surname was Quixada or Quesada (for there is no unanimity among those who write on the subject), although reasonable conjectures tend to show that he was called Quexana.

But this insignificant being, of uncertain civil status, is suddenly going to be transformed: when he refurbishes the rusty armor of his ancestors, when he elevates his nag to the dignity of war-horse, when he baptizes himself with a pompous name that no one has ever borne before, he achieves a new existence that henceforth belongs to him in his own right, an existence that no one will be able to challenge. At the same time, however great his desire to put off the old man and to abolish his prehistory, he cannot break the ties that attach him to everyday living; whether he likes it or not, he belongs to his world. It is the *tuertos,* the wrongs, of the present that it is Don Quixote's self-imposed mission to redress; but his error is in wanting to make use of the weapons of the past.

Thus the program formulated by Cervantes in his preface becomes clear: properly interpreted, it announces the parodic movement that informs the novel from start to finish and controls, to a certain extent, its dynamics, from the instant Don Quixote, following Amadís's example, puts on his armor until the moment when the enchanters seize him to bring him back to his house. The burlesque epic of which he is the hero is in a constantly shifting relationship with the models to which it refers and from which it seeks to take its inspiration: the giants that Don Quixote attacks are only windmills; Mambrino's helmet, which he wins in battle, a barber's basin of reddish copper; the phantoms that the Knight attacks, peaceful penitents in white. Each time, reality gives the lie to the Knight's illusion; each time, Don Quixote clings obstinately to his fantasies. When Sancho begs him to be careful of the windmills, which have vanes, not arms, he replies with a scornful refusal:

> It is easy to see . . . that you are not used to this business of adventures. Those are giants, and if you are afraid, away with you out of here and betake yourself to prayer, while I engage them in fierce and unequal combat.

The reply is intended to be humorous; but when our *hidalgo* characterizes his adversaries as he does, he is only following a kind of logic, the logic of unreason. His madness is not dementia; it is the monomania of too subtle a wit; he is "ingenious" and a victim of a disordered imagination as well as a man who stubbornly rejects any code for deciphering the world but the one he has found in his romances.

Yet however stinging—or funny—his defeat may be, it never exhausts the meaning of his enterprise. Don Quixote's truth is not that of some disjointed puppet whom the vane of the windmill sends rolling in the dust. Nor is it mistaken, even in its parodic mode, for the truth of the incredible tales of which he proclaims himself the ardent defender— as in the conversation with the Canon, where in answer to pointed criticisms made by the Canon, who is a partisan of strict respect for literal verisimilitude, Don Quixote becomes (and not without talent) the singer of the adventures of the Knight of the Lake. Don Quixote's truth is summed up in the fundamental act in which he decides to roam the world, asserting with vehemence the identity that he has forged for himself: "I know who I am," he proclaims when he returns, all battered, from his first escapade, brought home to his village by a peasant neighbor. By unfailingly persevering in being Don Quixote, he miraculously transcends the limitations that weighed him down at the outset. Whereas Guzmán de Alfarache, until his final conversion, remains a victim of his shameful birth and exerts himself to convince us of his inability to free himself from it, Don Quixote, against winds and seas, holds his course as a free man, whose drama is that he stands between the prosaic world in which he is rooted and the ideal world toward which he tirelessly sets his face.

To revive knight-errantry is, in fact, to bring it back to life in a world that is not the same as the world of books, whether one likes it or not. Hence Cervantine "realism": the monotonous plains of La Mancha, the highways on which our *hidalgo* meets peasants, muleteers, and merchants, the inn where he stops—these are not simply the elements of a picturesque setting; they are the familiar signs of a present from which he is unable to abstract himself and which at the height of his rapture brings him inexorably back to earth. In order to renew his impetus and so preserve his autonomy, Don Quixote has no recourse but to reduce this present to its proper proportion by integrating it into his system of thought. So he explains his setbacks as the action of enchanters bent on his destruction: it is they who make his library disappear—walled up, actually, by the efforts of a diligent mason— and transform the giants into windmills in order to deprive him of the pleasure of defeating them. While remaining in the domain of illusion, he gives himself, with obvious satisfaction, the means of interpreting reality's refusal to cooperate; by this means he gradually builds up the ambiguous world of which he is the hero out of the ruins of the legendary world to which he ceaselessly refers.

Forced in spite of himself to make what is relative absolute, Don Quixote, as he meets those who appear on his route, acquires a presence that he would have lacked if his extravagant actions had led him to some asylum and doomed him to isolation. The pungent conversations that he has in the course of chance encounters, those words that give things a palpable solidity, are the very source of the illusion of life that flows from him. This explains the decisive importance of the servant who joins him for his second sally. Don Quixote and Sancho? Two inseparable persons whose respective temperaments pit them against each other, like the medieval figures of Lent and Carnival, and whose dialogue, someone has said, confronts the real with the ideal, prose

with poetry. Let us be careful not to force the opposition. The Ingenious *Hidalgo,* when necessary, can be chary of anything that threatens
to interfere with his fantasies. Because he wanted to test the sturdiness
of the helmet that he had made from pasteboard, he destroyed a week's
work with one swipe of his sword. The lesson is sufficient: he repairs
the damage, and he also refrains from any new trials, in order not to
spoil "a helmet of the most perfect construction." With regard to the
squire, he is not "a man with very little gray matter in his skull"; far
from it, even if appearances are against him. This naive character is
also endowed with cunning, though his prudence does not always save
him from sharing his master's defeats; he is likewise, in his own way,
a man who knows how to dream; lured by the promise of an island,
he will to the end have hopes of becoming its governor.

The picturesque pair formed by master and servant is not, therefore,
the association of two symbols; it is the fraternal union of two flesh-
and-blood beings, each endowed with a language that is uniquely his
own. They reveal their essence to us even before we ask ourselves what
they embody. In the course of the freewheeling conversations, wise or
funny, that accompany the narrative (as the counterpart of the reac-
tions and feelings they express in the face of adventure), their apparent
antagonism changes progressively into a subtle harmony. There even
comes a moment when, as if in spite of themselves, they begin to
"contaminate" each other. To Don Quixote, who presses him with
questions when he returns from his mission to Dulcinea, asking him
whether he did not smell, as he approached the lady of Don Quixote's
thoughts, "a Sabean odor, an aromatic fragrance . . .," Sancho retorts
without the slightest hesitation,

> All that I can say is . . . that I did notice a little odor, somewhat man-
> nish. She must have been all in a sweat from the hard work, which has
> toughened her up.

A common-sense reply? No: a cock-and-bull story. Sancho, whatever
he pretends, has never seen Dulcinea, even with the peasant girl's
traits that he describes in these terms. To calm the impatience of his
master, he has had to improvise a story. So in this case it is Sancho,
constrained and forced, who invents fantasies, while the Knight's
denial—"You must have been suffering from cold in the head or must
have smelled yourself"—is, paradoxically, a flash of lucidity.

Thus Don Quixote and Sancho appear—to anyone who would like to draw a line of separation between their two points of view—caught in the seesaw motion that, in the course of the story, makes us oscillate between the grotesque and the sublime, between reality and illusion. Furthermore, this pendulum movement that sets the rhythm of the narration connects not only the two protagonists in their respective perceptions of beings and things; it involves all the characters that the immortal pair encounter on their way. And these characters also have their portion of truth: the shepherdess Marcela, as rebellious against marriage as she is attracted by the free life of the country; the unfortunate Cardenio, whose amorous disappointments have brought him to the remotest parts of the Sierra Morena and whose madness engages in the strangest of dialogues with the Knight's madness; the beautiful Dorotea, by turns a tearful lover, betrayed by her seducer, then a quick-witted young woman who disguises herself as the *infanta* Micomicona in order to mystify the Ingenious *Hidalgo;* the Captive Captain, whose novelistic love affair with Zoraida the Moorish beauty is depicted against a backdrop of detailed memories of Lepanto and Algiers. In proportion as these characters successively intervene to enrich the action with episodic intrigues, Don Quixote and Sancho, who have become mere spectators, seem fated to disappear into the wings. Each time, however, the vicissitudes recounted by characters who have experienced them affect the Knight and Squire's own story; and the course of events promptly brings them back to the foreground, often by unexpected ways. So, when the principal action seems suspended by the reading of the story of "The Man Who Was Too Curious for His Own Good" (the manuscript of which the Priest has discovered at the inn), the frightful uproar created by Don Quixote when he attacks the wineskins reminds us just in time that he is still the epic hero par excellence. And he will remain the hero until the end of the First Part, because it ends with his return to the fold: put in a cage by enchanters (who are none other than the Priest and the Barber), he will be brought home, drawn by oxen, to his village.

The more the reader familiarizes himself with this multiple universe, the more he discovers overlapping planes, stories within stories, mirrors that reflect each other to infinity. This "Chinese-box" effect certainly owes much to all the deserted lovers who narrate their misadventures, and whom a providential set of circumstances finally reunites in the hostelry where Don Quixote not long since has been knighted

by a roguish innkeeper. Their stories—considered to be true—interlarded into the body of the novel itself, vary greatly in the ways they
are interpolated. But the Chinese-box effect is also a result of the skill
with which the novelist hides behind the pseudo-narrators to whom
he lends his voice and delegates his powers. The most fascinating of
these doubles is, without doubt, Cide Hamete Benengeli. An obvious
imitation of those Arab chroniclers who, by pure convention, are
responsible for books of chivalry, he is both the untruthful author from
whom Cervantes distances himself in order to judge the work that he
himself is in the process of writing, and at the same time the scrupulous historian who reveals to the reader his effort to capture his heroes
in all their fullness, thus making the reader enter into the very act of
literary creation.

It is often said that *Don Quixote* is the first novel of modern times
because in it, as Michel Foucault writes, similarities and signs "have
dissolved their former agreement": "similitude deceives, tending to
visions and delirium." But it owes its modernity also to a narrative
that has for the first time located the imaginary dimension in man's
interior. Instead of telling what happens to the hero from the outside,
it gives him the power to speak and the freedom to use that power as
he pleases, thus recreating the movement by which each character
invents himself, to the extent that he experiences the events. No one
before Cervantes was able to accomplish this Copernican revolution:
neither Montemayor, with his shepherds frozen in plaintive introspection, nor Mateo Alemán, with his *pícaro* in contorted soliloquy. Did
Miguel suspect the extent of his revolution at the moment when he
declares in his preface that he has "no desire to go with the current of
custom"? Surely neither he nor his readers understood its full implications. But the instant success of the book, its rapid and ceaselessly
extended diffusion, soon revealed to him that he had fulfilled expectations and that his instincts had not deceived him.

AN IMMEDIATE SUCCESS

AT the beginning of the Second Part of the novel, Don Quixote expresses
his amazement when he learns that someone has written the story of
his exploits. Sansón Carrasco, Bachelor of Arts, one of the characters

who will take part in his new adventures, retorts in a peremptory, somewhat facetious tone:

> So true is it, señor, . . . that in my estimation there are more than twelve thousand volumes of this history in print this very day. Only ask Portugal, Barcelona, and Valencia, where they have been printed, and moreover there is a report that it is being printed at Antwerp, and I am persuaded there will not be a country or language in which there will not be a translation of it.

We should not expect from Sansón the precise information that one would demand from an accountant. Besides the fact that he omits the Madrid editions by Cuesta, he refers to a Catalan edition that will not actually appear until 1617; and he mentions Antwerp where we must undoubtedly substitute Brussels. As for the "twelve thousand copies," the estimate is pure fantasy. The bachelor is a fictitious being, and his evidence is a stratagem of writing, by means of which The Novel is made part of the core of *this* novel. But one fact is certain: by the time that Sansón utters these exaggerated words, *Don Quixote* has really and truly conquered the Iberian public; and while it is also true that Sansón's final prediction smacks of irony, posterity will take upon itself the task of making it come true.

This success is not long in coming, as several converging indicators prove. In March of 1605, after the book's appearance, Francisco de Robles and Juan de la Cuesta must start work on a second Madrid edition, which will come out before summer. Several weeks earlier, in the first days of February, Cervantes had obtained a new privilege that extended his original grant—for Castile only—to Portugal and the realms of the old kingdom of Aragon. In April, Robles will receive Cervantes' exclusive authorization to print and sell the book throughout the Peninsula: an indispensable precaution, since two pirated editions had just been published in Lisbon; and a few months later, two more will appear clandestinely at Valencia and Zaragoza. This unfair competition may appear flattering; it nevertheless damaged the interests of the writer and his publisher. A document signed by Cervantes and dated April 12, 1605, mentions legal actions that Robles is preparing to institute against his dishonest colleagues. If the bookseller had had the nerve to bet on the enthusiasm of readers and had immediately negotiated a privilege that was less restrictive than the one

Miguel received, he would not have been forced to hunt down coun-
terfeiters.

Three months must have been enough time for *Don Quixote* to break
all sales records. Moreover, its reputation will not take long to cross
the ocean: in February, the first lot of the original edition is registered
at Seville and shipped to Peru. In April, a second load is sent across
the Atlantic. This makes it easier to see why Robles finds it necessary,
in the month of June, to put Cuesta's reprint on sale. From now on,
everybody knows the name of the Ingenious *Hidalgo;* his thin silhouette has become famous in association with the full-blown contours of
his faithful squire. Many people, of course, get wind of their exploits
only by hearsay, at a time when only a minority can read or has direct
access to the written word. But there are other ways of making Don
Quixote and Sancho familiar to illiterates: processions, ballets, and
masquerades present them at festivities and entertainments that use
current events as themes. They parade, for example, at Valladolid on
June 10, 1605, during a celebration (the reason for which we will
soon explain); and they will likewise reappear two years later in analogous circumstances, but this time in remotest Peru: in the interval,
their fame has soared.

From these pieces of evidence, we can guess the principal reason for
this success, without precedent since *Celestina.* Philip III's contemporaries hailed the appearance of a burlesque tale, a comic romance; and
it is because this novel made them laugh that they so quickly gave it
their approval. This essential dimension has often been lost sight of:
Romantic criticism in particular imposed its view of the masterpiece,
transfiguring it into a symbolic version of the conflict between the
Ideal and the Real, a view that has left an indelible impression. Such
an interpretation is, as we shall see, legitimate and coherent; but the
seventeenth century did not have the slightest premonition of it. Cervantes, one remembers, hoped that when reading his story the melancholy would be moved to laughter and the merry made merrier still.
He will later recall this challenge, uttered in his preface to *Don Quixote,* in the *Journey to Parnassus,* believing—correctly—that he had
achieved his goal. Furthermore, all those writers who in Cervantes'
wake make the Knight the hero of some literary fantasy—Guillén de
Castro, Quevedo, Calderón—present him to us in the guise of a ridiculous, even grotesque hero: a *triste figura* in the sense in which classical
Spanish understands that expression. Likewise, all the entertainments

in which he appears outdo each other in emphasizing his extravagant actions, which perfectly match witticisms attributed to Sancho. It is said that the king, when he saw a student laughing boisterously, declared to his retinue, "That student is either out of his mind or he is reading the story of Don Quixote." Even if the anecdote is of doubtful authenticity, it nevertheless sums up the opinion of a whole epoch.

If we underestimate this aspect of the book, it is because we no longer attribute to comedy the therapeutic and esthetic value it once had: it is for children and for them alone to laugh at the adventures of the master and his man, as if we had to deny the child in each of us. It is also because, lacking the necessary keys, we do not grasp all the subtleties of humor based on parody: the chivalric tales that are often its implicit point of reference have certainly become unfamiliar to us. And finally, it is because madness—as Michel Foucault has brilliantly demonstrated—is now a source of uneasiness for us: it is incongruous, even indecent, to make fun of a madman, as our ancestors loved to do; and we perceive as tragic the loneliness of the hero that Cervantes shows us misunderstood by everyone. In a word, the distance that separates our view of *Don Quixote* from the one that classical Europe formed of him reflects, beyond any doubt, a profound evolution of customs and sensibilities.

It is also necessary to understand the quality of this laughter for which we have lost the taste. Had Cervantes managed to create nothing but two buffoons (analogous to those that Avellaneda, the author of the apocryphal second part, would invent), the success of his great book would have been merely a flash in the pan. If his heroes' exploits have had this special power of suggestion from the very beginning, it is because their adventure assumed metaphoric value, beyond its stated purpose. By putting the truth of chivalric tales to the test, Don Quixote reveals—with typical lack of restraint—a characteristic phenomenon of modern times: the infectious power of literature over all those for whom it opens the gates of the imagination. And literature is free to use the indirect route of poetry or theater, or other ways and other modes of diffusion besides reading. All the characters of the novel are, in different degrees, infected: some in the comic mode, like the Priest and the Barber, whose disguises we have recalled; others in the tragic mode, like Grisóstomo, whose taste for the pastoral finally leads him to suicide.

At the same time, *Don Quixote* is not only, as has often been said,

the crossroads where the literary modes of the day converge. It is also
the synthesis of all the kinds of fiction favored by the men of the
Renaissance: each character's fate embodies a particular reference to
literature. In addition, the novel regenerates these "lying" fables by
putting the question of their validity at the very center of the lives
that unfold before our eyes. Just as the Knight revives in his own way
the deeds of Amadís, and as Grisóstomo gives a new impetus to the
pastoral through his death, so Cardenio, in the expression of the despair
that occupies him, rediscovers the love poetry of the *cancioneros,* while
Ginés de Pasamonte, promising the true history of his actions, unexpectedly lays bare the ambiguities of the picaresque. These partial
truths, constantly set in opposition by the play of points of view and
the Chinese-box arrangement of the different accounts, are finally reconciled in the bosom of a higher truth. Even Sancho adds his voice to
this concert. His sallies, retorts, proverbs, and jokes are additional
veins of the rich lode to which Cervantine fantasy owes part of its
flavor: folklore, in full vitality, widespread by oral tradition, and which
turns out to be another contributory factor. It is in the crucible of
folklore, let us remember, that the contradictory characters of the sim-
pleton and the wily peasant are forged, both assumed by Sancho with
equal success: Cervantes' art lies in decanting the elements from it in
order to fuse them into a creation that belongs to him alone.

A pre-eminently polyphonic work, *Don Quixote* thus manages to
fulfill a demand that none of the formulas tested up to that time had
been able fully to satisfy. Yet even though the poetic world that it
offers us found immediate favor with readers, its relationship to the
real world is as problematical as that which the Spain of the Golden
Age maintained with its own times. The odyssey of Don Quixote,
who dons medieval armor in order to play at righting wrongs, is an
eminently symbolic venture at the dawn of the seventeenth century: it
epitomizes to perfection the choices of a society faced with a reality
quite different from the one it had formerly known, a society forced
by the contradictions of this reality to take refuge in a dreamworld. In
1600, exactly five years before Cervantes published his masterpiece,
the *arbitrista*—amateur political theorist—Martín de Cellorigo made
a singularly lucid diagnosis of that society: "It appears that they want
to turn our country into a nation of enchanted people who live outside
the natural order." Spain's delusions have pulled her, in the throes of
a crisis—of power and of conscience, as Pierre Vilar correctly observes—

out of "the natural order." And behold, here she is, incarnated in the guise of an enchanted hero who obstinately looks for anachronistic solutions to the problems of his day: a ridiculous hero, but a hero whose extravagant actions nevertheless have value as an example, as if the better to permit Philip III's subjects to keep their distance, while subconsciously recognizing themselves in him.

SPAIN AT PEACE

IN the spring of 1605, which sees *Don Quixote* win such popularity, the duke of Lerma's star is burning with the greatest brilliance. Having firmly secured the king's favor, he can also count on the gratitude of the city fathers of Valladolid: with their blessing, he carries out profitable real-estate schemes, disguised as urban beautification. His prosperity naturally makes people envious; but no one challenges his power, even if the way he uses it displeases critical observers. Five years earlier, one of these critics, putting his hopes in the virtues of the sovereign, had predicted that the nation was assured of its recovery, "however low it may have fallen." Today, however, when the favorite is asserting his role as the real master, this prediction would sound strange. But who remembers it? Despite not having managed to pull the country out of stagnation, Lerma can at least boast of the support of Providence, which has just shown its concern for Spain in two ways: by favoring the successful outcome of negotiations with England, and in bestowing on Philip III the longed-for heir.

On April 8, 1605, Queen Margarita gave birth to a son. Because he came into the world on Good Friday, he was supposed by popular belief to enjoy the gifts attributed to sorcerers and soothsayers. Since these powers were inconsistent with royal majesty, it was thought more politic to predict an exceptional destiny for the future Philip IV: he would undoubtedly be a great king, having been born under such a sign. One can understand why the court and the city celebrated the occasion as it deserved and why, less than two months later, the baptism of the young prince should be an excuse for new rejoicing. In our time we are astounded, even scandalized, by these ostentatious and costly displays. Let us not forget, however, that the baptism of a prince, his marriage, his coronation, his funeral, were also public events of interest to the entire society, since the continuity of the body politic was considered to be bound up with the person of the monarch and with the transmission of life to his successors. Cervantes will allude to these festivities in one of his novellas in the Gypsy girl Preciosa's ballad, dedicated to the queen on the day after her churching, and which Preciosa sings to the accompaniment of a tambourine:

> Long may you live, O whitest dove,
> For you must give us twice-crowned fledgling eagles
> To frighten from the sky the furious birds of prey,
> To shelter defenseless virtues with their wings.
> .   .   .   .
> This pearl that you have given us,
> Oh Austria's mother-of-pearl, unique and singular—
> What machinations he destroys,
> What schemes he cuts short, what hopes he inspires!

Unfortunately, the future would give the lie to these prophecies: for under Philip IV, Rocroi and the Peace of the Pyrenees would mark the end of Spanish hegemony.

Among the representatives of foreign powers who had come to attend the ceremonies, the ambassador from England, Lord Howard, was to play the leading role. His visit, in fact, was not a simple courtesy but had a special objective: to ratify the treaty signed a year earlier in London with the new English king, James I. The failure of a landing on the coast of Ireland in 1601 had convinced Lerma that diplomats should henceforth have the prevailing voice. Elizabeth's successor, more conciliatory than the Virgin Queen, was in a similar state of mind. The Constable of Castile, Juan Fernández de Velasco, sent by Spain to London, had found, without too much effort, common ground for understanding with his counterparts: on August 28, 1604, the two powers put an end to a conflict that had lasted sixteen years. Consequently, Lord Howard's mission took on a broadly diplomatic character: his arrival became an excuse for celebrating with one grand gesture both the baptism of the heir to the throne and the return of a unanimously desired peace.

What piques one's interest in this affair is that the ambassador chosen by James I was none other than the admiral who, together with Essex, had occupied and devastated Cádiz with impunity, nine years earlier. Cervantes, whose ironic verses one may remember, could not have failed to make the connection. Others will express their surprise without beating around the bush, like the anonymous author of this sonnet long attributed to Góngora:

> The queen gave birth: the Lutheran came with heretics
> Six-hundred strong and heresies; we spent a million
> In fifteen days on gifts and wine and hospitality.
>
> We made a brave show—oh, foolish mistake—and offered
> Entertainments, which were feats of legerdemain,
> To the angelic legate and the spies of the man who swore
> To the treaty on Calvin's works.
> .   .   .   .
>
> We stayed poor; Luther went away rich.
> They commanded Don Quixote, Sancho, and his ass
> To write an account of these accomplishments.

This sarcastic poem expresses with a certain asperity an indignation that our hero, taught by experience about the inanity of warlike enterprises, did not share. It also confirms the popularity that the Ingenious *Hidalgo* and his faithful servant had acquired in less than six months. Perhaps the final allusion refers to a burlesque interlude presented as a curtain-raiser for the spectators at a bullfight organized in the Plaza Mayor on the day after Corpus Christi. According to the chronicler Pinheiro da Veiga,

> . . . Don Quixote appeared in the foreground dressed as a soldier of fortune, alone and without company, with a large hat on his head and a baize cloak, with sleeves of the same material, velvet breeches, and good boots with swallow's-beak spurs, pounding the flanks of a wretched gray nag with a sore on its lower back made by the coach-harness and coachman's saddle; and Sancho Panza his squire was in front. [Don Quixote] was wearing carefully placed spectacles to give him greater dignity, and his chin was held high . . .

Furthermore, the historiographer of the important events of which the sonnet gives us a vivid picture may well have been Cervantes himself. According to a document dated fifteen years later, he was supposed to have been commanded to write a *relación* of the festivities given at

Valladolid on that occasion. It is certainly unfortunate that this occasional text has been lost.

Scholars would especially like to know, by means of this *relación*, the exact makeup of Lord Howard's retinue. William Shakespeare was among the gentlemen of the bedchamber placed at the service of the Constable of Castile during his mission to London in August of 1604. Did the author of *Hamlet* accompany the British ambassador to Valladolid the following year, as Astrana Marín supposes? If so, it would be tempting to imagine, as certain scholars have done, a summit meeting of the two giants of literature. But let us stop dreaming. Only one thing is certain: Howard and his compatriots, when they return to the banks of the Thames at the end of June, are going to spread the word about Don Quixote's exploits. In 1607, even before the first translation of the novel is in the works, the dramatist George Wilkins will have one of his characters say, in a comedy played on the stage of the Globe, "Boy, hold this torch for me, for I am armed and ready to fight a windmill."

The bullfight on June 19 was marred by a heroic-comic incident, it is said. One of the gentlemen who had made bold to enter the arena was knocked off his horse by a particularly combative bull. The fall might have had fatal consequences; the victim escaped, however, with nothing but bruises. Góngora dedicated to him a satirical poem that has a certain charm:

> Let us celebrate with stirrups short
> And bewail with stirrups long
> The humiliating fall of Don
> Gaspar de Ezpeleta.
> Oh, if only I were a poet, how
> Much paper would I use
> To say some things about this man:
> I'd say the fool fell off
> To let everyone catch on—to him;
> I'd say the gentleman,
> Considering his looks and budget,
> Has had little experience in the arena,
> And his valet even less . . .

It would be helpful to have Miguel's testimony on this affair, and not merely to satisfy idle curiosity. The person whose embarrassment the poet of the *Solitudes* describes for us was in fact going to die a few days later under tragic circumstances. On June 27, 1605, while Valladolid was painfully recovering from the English ambassador's visit, Gaspar de Ezpeleta was fatally wounded near the Rastro de los Carneros, in front of the place where Cervantes had chosen to live with his family. This apparently chance coincidence is going to upset the writer's existence profoundly. The ordeal that will result from it will be of short duration, certainly; but it will nevertheless be one of the bitterest that he will have to experience.

THE EZPELETA AFFAIR

WHO was Don Gaspar de Ezpeleta? A young man of good family who, as they say, had gone bad. Of Navarrian ancestry (he was born in Pamplona in 1567), he first served in Aragon in the king's army. Made a Knight of St. James after the death of Philip II, then sent on a mission to Flanders, he was involved in dubious intrigues at Paris that landed him in prison and could have led him to the scaffold. Extracted from this difficult situation by the Constable of Castile, he joined the army again and fought courageously at Ostend before returning to Spain at the end of 1604. His appeals to the Council of Castile for pensions and subsidies met with mixed success; surviving documents on the subject give us a glimpse of a hothead and a debauchee always short of cash: "He deserves little consideration because of his behavior and actions," says one of them. So it is easier to understand why Góngora chose to make a laughingstock out of this disreputable personage, who, having left wife and child in Pamplona, was leading a gay life in Valladolid. A boon companion of the marquess of Falces, the captain of the King's Archers, he was openly and notoriously the lover of Inés Hernández, the legitimate (and illiterate) wife of a royal clerk named Melchor Galván.

Such is the person who is going to break unexpectedly in upon the life of *Don Quixote*'s author. On the evening of June 27, around eleven o'clock, shouts for help coming from the street disturb the silence of the night. Attracted by the cries, the two sons of Luisa de Garibay, a neighbor who shared Miguel's landing, find a man at the door of their house bleeding copiously. Carried by them to their mother's apartment—with the assistance of Cervantes, who came to lend a hand—

the wounded man receives first aid from Magdalena. A surgeon, brought to the bedside in haste, immediately discovers two deep wounds: one in the right thigh, the other in the lower stomach. A priest who has come with the surgeon will hear the man's confession without delay.

What had happened in the lonely surroundings of the Rastro de los Carneros? To clarify this question was the task of the justice of the peace (alcalde) Villarroel, who appeared shortly afterwards, accompanied by two officers. Interrogated by Villarroel, the victim—who was none other than Ezpeleta—is going to stick to a version of the events that could not be more succinct: after having taken leave of the marquess of Falces, with whom he had shared supper, Don Gaspar was supposedly accosted by a stranger dressed in black as he passed the Hospital of the Resurrection; a duel followed, in the course of which his adversary had stabbed him twice with a sword before disappearing into the night. This account, excessively brief, called for more investigation: it failed to mention, in particular, that Ezpeleta had dismissed his servants when he left Falces; it also said nothing about the small shield he was carrying at the time. But Villarroel is going to conduct his interrogation in a very odd way. When the wounded man's valet, Francisco de Camporredondo, implicates Melchor Galván—whose house was quite near—by name, the alcalde (who because of his functions was in constant contact with the clerk) will carefully keep the adulterous wife and jealous husband out of his investigations. This omission is all the more suspect since the magistrate, taking advantage of an instant when he believes no one is looking, is going to remove and hide a note, folded twice, that the victim had in one of his pockets. Even worse, one of Juana Gaitán's boarders, Isabel de Islallana, will state that she saw the assailant and that she would be able to identify him; yet her testimony will not be used.

Unexpectedly, it is going to be the occupants of the building, and they alone, who interest the investigating magistrate. Juana Gaitán, whose second husband, Diego de Hondaro, had departed this life not long before, had on numerous occasions received visits from the dukes of Pastrana and Maqueda, two aristocrats who had had difficulties with the police. Her friend Mariana Ramírez, who had recently begun to share the same apartment, had been convicted of concubinage with a certain Diego de Miranda, the homonym of the Knight of the Green Overcoat, whom Don Quixote will later meet on his travels. All this set the neighborhood talking, especially Isabel de Ayala, the sanctimonious gossip from the garret, who was outraged by the immoral acts committed on the lower floors. Miguel and his family were not going to escape her slanders. In order to supply the needs of his relations, our hero had gone into business with various partners, including a Genoese merchant named Agustín Raggio and a Portuguese financier, Simón Méndez, who, it appears, was planning to send Cervantes to Toledo to collect some government bonds. So a whole world of shady figures with whom he had dealt during his Andalusian years resurfaces, a world that had continued to exert a strange influence over him. In her deposition before Villarroel, Cervantes' sister Andrea will say of him, "He is a man who writes and is in business": a man, she will explain, "who has friends, because of his competence." No one has managed to capture the mystery that emanated from his personality and his occupations better than Andrea, with these simple words.

Unfortunately, Simón Méndez had just been put in prison for debts, while Cervantes, if we are to believe an allusion in Pinheiro da Veiga, was continuing to visit gambling dens. This was more than enough to provide tattle for the old gossip, intrigued by the spectacle of an idle man surrounded by four women with no visible means of support. The deposition that she has left is going to call into question the respectability of her neighbors: she states that the Cervantes family received scandalous visits day and night and that Isabel de Saavedra flaunted her relationship with Simón Méndez.

Thus Cervantes found himself involved in an affair in which he was nevertheless an outsider. The testimony of the victim, the one important witness, could have proved his innocence; but unfortunately Gaspar de Ezpeleta was going to give up the ghost at dawn on June 29, before he could corroborate his first statement. His only gesture before dying was to give Magdalena a silk dress in gratitude for the care he had received from her, a gesture which would only compromise her in the eyes of the malevolent. The next day, Villarroel had the author of Don Quixote incarcerated, along with ten other persons, among them Andrea, Isabel, Constanza, Juana Gaitán, Mariana Ramírez, and Diego de Miranda. Magdalena, paradoxically, did not appear in the lot. As for Catalina, she was at that time absent from Valladolid, having gone to Esquivias with one of her brothers to set family affairs in order. An irony of fate: Miguel found himself stranded in the same prison where his grandfather and his father had been shut up before him. Once again, he found himself in the clutches of adversity. The bitterness

left over from this incident will show through in an episode from
Persiles that presents us with Auristela and Periandro unjustly accused
of a murder that they have not committed. They struggle to plead
their case before some magistrates, in vain, "because when these pen-
pushing tyrants began to suspect that the pilgrims had wool, they
wanted to shear them to the bone, as usual." Was Villarroel also corrupt? What is certain is that he did everything in his power, whether
on his own initiative or that of some highly placed personage, to muddy
the waters and allow the real delinquent to escape punishment.

The injustice committed was, however, too flagrant for the alleged
suspects to remain behind bars for long. The new depositions collected
by Villarroel, beginning with Ezpeleta's landlady's, will suffice to
exonerate them. With regard to Cervantes and his family, they will
have no difficulty refuting Isabel de Ayala and disproving her inane
accusations. Their respective declarations are found among the pieces
in the dossier. They reveal to us, among other details, the existence of
the mysterious Santi Ambrosio, whom Andrea de Cervantes had married when she was still living in Madrid and whose widow she now
was. They tell us likewise that Isabel de Saavedra, the daughter of the
greatest writer of his day, was illiterate. Freed conditionally after forty-
eight hours, the accused will however be confined to their domiciles.
On July 5, they request an end to this house-arrest. Miguel will demand,
in addition, that Ezpeleta's effects be removed, because "they are rot-
ting from the blood on them." Not until July 18 will their request be
granted and the affair considered closed; but Villarroel will accompany
his decision with two vexing decrees: Diego de Miranda will be invited
to leave the city, and Simón Méndez is prohibited from entering the
building on the Rastro. In spite of the suspicion that hangs over him,
Melchor Galván will not be interviewed a single time: an outraged
husband, a royal clerk to boot, had the right to cleanse his honor, and
he was not accountable to the police. As for Cervantes, his reputation
was all the more tarnished as the success of his novel had pushed him
to the front of the stage: seen as a dubious speculator, habitué of
gambling dens, a father who turned a blind eye to his wayward daughter's love affairs, he found himself exposed to public malice and had
no desire to tread the pavements of Valladolid any longer. On this
occasion, circumstances will be favorable to him: the fat years that
Lerma's caprice had brought to Philip III's ephemeral capital will soon
come to an end.

A NEW DEPARTURE

CERVANTES seems to have prolonged his stay on the banks of the Pisuerga until autumn. What did he do for the whole summer? We can imagine him attending to his daily occupations in the house on the Rastro, going to mass at San Lorenzo, cautiously approaching the *mentidero*— "gossip mill"—of the Corrillo, where men exchanged the latest news. We would also like to believe that he had enough energy to take up his pen again and to write some of his future exemplary novellas. *The Fraudulent Marriage* has Valladolid as a setting; *The Dialogue of the Dogs,* as we have already pointed out, opens and closes in the Hospital of the Resurrection. Did he start work on these two stories, one inside the other, during the hottest part of summer? The fact that the author of *Don Quixote* sets the action of one of his stories a few steps from the house he inhabited for two years does not mean that he sketched from life the places to which he refers: what the glance merely skims in a distracted way can stand out in startling relief in the eyes of the memory. Perhaps Valladolid owes her literary transfiguration to the distancing that Cervantes achieves when he leaves the city, while before that she was nothing to him but the daily setting for a prosaic existence.

What clearly did take up a considerable part of his time is the prosecution of all the swindlers who were trying to profit from the success of his novel. A document of July 25, 1605, reports on a court action instituted by Robles against the Valencian book publisher Juan Ferrer, who was at that moment preparing a new pirated edition. Robles, who had himself just brought out Cuesta's reprint, which appeared in Madrid in June, seems finally to have compromised with his fellow publisher Ferrer, making a deal to the benefit of their respective interests. At least that is what the extraordinary similarity of the two editions, the authentic and the apocryphal, leads one to suspect. Perhaps we should see an allusion to that compromise—reached to the detriment of the novelist—in Master Glass's disillusioned remarks on the way certain publishers delude their authors when they print a work at his expense, "for instead of fifteen hundred, they print three thousand books, and when the author thinks that *his* copies are being sold, it is someone else's."

In compensation for not seeing himself treated as he should have been by those who were getting rich from his creations, Miguel could at least draw some comfort from the renown that his heroes had acquired, a renown of which Pinheiro da Veiga has left us a significant indicator. When he tries to describe a ridiculous suitor (who in order to declare his passion had thrown himself at the feet of three beauties who were enjoying the cool shade during the afternoon promenade), an image comes spontaneously to his mind that depicts the personage: "A Don Quixote dressed in green, very emaciated and tall." This scene, which made all the passers-by roar with laughter, appears to have taken place only a few days before the Ezpeleta affair: the way that Pinheiro reports it to us shows that by that date the Ingenious *Hidalgo* had become a proverbial figure, and that the borderline between literature and life had thus been abolished.

That the hero of a novel should enjoy such a privilege could not fail to make certain people in the literary world envious. The most vindictive appears to have been Lope de Vega, whose acerbic words we may recall. Perhaps the Phoenix believed that Cervantes had written a certain sonnet *de cabo roto* (with truncated words at the end of the verses) aimed at him, in which the works of which he was said to be proudest were excoriated. The response was not long in coming, whether Lope himself took up his pen or whether he charged one of his disciples with the task—a sonnet of the same cut, but of unprecedented violence and crudeness:

> I, who know nothing about la- or li- or le-
> Or whether you, Cervantes, are co- or cu-,
> Say only that Lope is Apollo and that you
> Are a Frisian drawing his chariot and a two-footed swine.

> It was Heaven's decree that you should lose your hand
> In Corfu so that you should cease to write.
> You have spoken, you ox, but said moo. May you suffer a painful
> *Quixotada* [pain in the rump]!

>   Honor to Lope, woe to you,
> You coltish old fool; for he is like the sun,
> And if he becomes irate, he will rain on you.

> That trivial *Don Quixote* of yours now goes
> Through the world from arse to arse, or serves
> As wrapping paper for spices and cheap saffron,
> And finally will end up in dumps and privies.

Not only does the poem attack Miguel's work, as one can see; it also defames his person: his suspicious origins—the swine was an unclean animal for Judaizers (lapsed converts)—his wound at Lepanto, his physical ailments. It spares nothing.

Nine years later, in the "Postscript" to the *Journey to Parnassus,* he will recall this painful incident obliquely:

> While I was in Valladolid, they brought a letter to my house for me, with one *real* of postage due; a niece of mine accepted it and paid—she should never have paid!—the postage; but she gave me as her excuse that she had often heard me say that money was well spent on three things, charity, a good doctor, and postage for letters, whether from friends or from enemies; because friends' letters give advice, and from enemies' letters you can get some idea of what they are thinking. They gave it to me; and inside it was a sonnet—poorly written, dull, with no grace or wit whatever, saying bad things about *Don Quixote.* But what bothered me was the *real,* and I resolved from then on not to accept a letter with postage due . . .

This account has a certain dignity; but we do not know what the victim's immediate reaction was: it may have been as violent as the attack of which he had been the object. Once in a while, Cervantes bared his teeth; and he could wield treacherous allusions very effectively. He will show this on other occasions.

Other cares are going to distract him from this tedious quarrel. At the beginning of autumn, an insistent rumor begins to circulate and swell little by little: the court is preparing to return to Madrid. In fact, Lerma and the city fathers of Madrid have already begun negotiating. On January 24, 1606, the news is announced officially. Two months later, the first convoys leave Valladolid. By the end of April, the transfer will be finished. This about-face, after an interval of five years, will astonish everyone. To justify it, it was said that the fogs that prevail during winter on the banks of the Pisuerga were harming the sovereign's health: these deleterious vapors were responsible for impetigo, from which the royal family had been suffering, and they had started the epidemics of measles, smallpox, and plague that had struck the city the previous year and were threatening it again. It was also rumored that Madrid had paid very dearly for a decision so favorable to her interests: 250,000 ducats were to be paid to the king each year for ten years, to which was to be added a sixth of the total sum of rents received by the city. Finally, she had promised to take charge of moving the court. It is more than likely that Lerma had his share of this pact. But in any case, wisdom dictated the return to the capital of Philip II. With the surge of Atlantic commerce and the growing importance of Portugal in the peninsular ensemble, the country's center of gravity was shifting toward the south. Handicapped by the shortage of cloth (both industrial and artisan-produced), by failing productivity, and by the limits of local capitalism, Valladolid was too far to the north to become the driving force that people had anticipated. Let us add as a minor detail of history that the dowager empress María had been dead for three years and consequently no longer threatened to countermand the favorite's plans.

That Cervantes left Valladolid in autumn, two months before the announcement of the court's departure, may be gathered from a piece of evidence traditionally adduced by his biographers: his signature is missing on the petition presented by Magdalena and Andrea to obtain their brother Rodrigo's unpaid salary. Had he gone to Salamanca (where the action of *Master Glass* takes place) on business? Had he not instead returned to Esquivias, where his wife was expecting him and where he seems to have spent most of the year 1606? Whatever the case, his sisters will not wait long before packing their bags to return to Madrid on the heels of their clientele. It is there that Catalina and Miguel will find them, eighteen months later, for a last stay that will end with Cervantes' death.

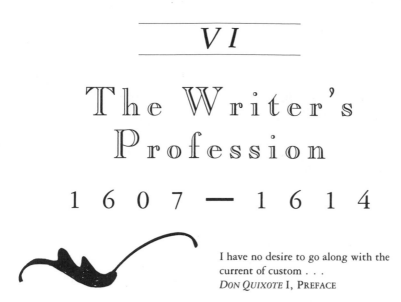

VI

The Writer's Profession

1 6 0 7 — 1 6 1 4

I have no desire to go along with the
current of custom . . .
DON QUIXOTE I, PREFACE

ISABEL'S LOVE AFFAIRS

CERVANTES is beginning his sixtieth year. The time has come for him to put an end to his wanderings. Madrid, where he arrives accompanied by Catalina, shows him the smiling face of a city that has recovered her prerogatives. Still joyful because of the court's return, she is preparing herself to experience an unprecedented expansion. Her population has already reached one hundred thousand souls and is surpassed by Seville alone. Only pessimists are surprised by a prosperity tightly bound up with the presence of the king and his entourage, a prosperity that would not survive another royal departure. *Solo Madrid es corte,* all of Spain repeats incessantly. The adage has a double meaning: Madrid is the only possible capital, and Madrid is nothing more than the capital. *Madrileños* retain only the flattering sense of this ambiguous saying; the reverse of the coin is for the envious.

As the object of Philip III and Lerma's attentions, the Spanish Babylon is going to receive new embellishments; but it is only after Miguel's death that the urban landscape will show tangible signs of improvement. In spite of the munificence of her aristocrat builders, the palaces, hospitals, and monasteries retain their modest proportions. As for the restoration of the Alcázar, undertaken before the king's return, it will take fifteen years for the castle to grow a new skin. The sight that greets foreigners is still that of a tangle of ill-paved, stinking lanes, bordered by houses of brick and mud. Only a few important arteries—Main Street, Atocha Street, Toledo Street—can bear comparison with those of the great European capitals. But it is there that the real heart of the city beats, where the luxurious shops are concentrated, where at every moment courtiers and beggars rub elbows, where gawkers and idlers meet to exchange the latest news: the paved courtyard of the palace, the steps of San Felipe, the actors' *mentidero* are all "factories of lies" where information—true or false—circulates, where public opinion is forged, where reputations are made and unmade.

Where did Cervantes find lodgings when he arrived? We have no idea. He seems for a while to have chosen a residence on Duke of Alba Street, near the Estudio de la Villa at which he had once been a student. But we must wait until February 1608 to know from a reliable source that he is lodged in the Atocha quarter, directly behind Antón Martín Hospital, "in Don Juan de Borbón's buildings." A year later he moves, without changing neighborhoods, to Magdalena Street, behind the palace of the duke of Pastrana, a few steps from Robles's bookstores and Cuesta's print shop, his favorite observation posts. He will make the best of this modest residence, which he will eventually leave at the end of two years.

As at Valladolid, Miguel and his wife once again bring together the four women who make up the rest of the tribe. But the writer's daughter, Isabel de Saavedra—unlike her cousin Constanza, who remains in the bosom of the family—will fly away from the nest before long. Toward December 1606, she marries a certain Diego Sanz del Aguila, a personage as mysterious for us as Santi Ambrosio, the late husband of Andrea de Cervantes. In spring of the following year, Isabel brings into the world a daughter, who will bear the name Isabel Sanz del Aguila y Cervantes; a year later, in June 1608, she becomes a widow. This sad experience would have been hard on her without the consolation, moral and material, of a protector by the name of Juan de Urbina (whom we mentioned at the time of the business with Ana Franca), who is going to be closely associated with the writer's affairs from now on. This kindly fifty-year-old man, the secretary of the duke of Savoy, whom he had met in Valladolid, enjoys an enviable position, thanks to his business sense: his landed property, his stocks, his real estate, his ready cash make him an ideal catch for an unscrupulous *arriviste,* as Isabel de Cervantes seems to have been. Though he had a wife and several children—a married daughter had just made him a grandfather—Urbina had been living alone in Madrid since the court's return: at the beginning of summer of 1606, his wife and daughter had in fact left for Italy with the duke's children. From all evidence, Isabel set about to supplant them, either out of daughterly affection— some scholars insist that Urbina was her real father—or because she was his mistress, as seems most probable.

We know nothing of the way in which this illicit love affair, of which little Isabel may well have been the fruit, began. In any case, Diego Sanz can hardly have had time to do more than lend his name to the child. As for his loving wife, she will endure her widowhood somewhat more easily because on June 24 Urbina sets her up with her daughter on Montera Street, in a house quite close to the one he himself occupies on Jardín Street. A significant detail: the dwelling is rented in the name of his servant, Francisco Molar.

Isabel will not remain without a husband for long: on September 8, 1608, she marries Luis de Molina, who appears to have owed this piece of good luck to his association with Miguel. Like his father-in-law, Molina had been a prisoner in Algiers, from which he had returned in 1598; like him, he was associated with the world of finance and business in his capacity as an agent for the Stratta, a powerful Genoese banking family; like him, he had married around the age of forty, richer in debts than in revenues, but endowed with a sinecure—he was a clerk of the crown—which protected him from poverty. Did the two men know each other well enough for Cervantes to be able to force Molina upon Isabel and Urbina? The records that have come down to us concerning this affair do not permit us to make such conclusions. But everything suggests that the marriage contract, signed two days before the ceremony, was preceded by hard bargaining. In the terms of that document, Isabel brought 10,000 ducats as a dowry, paid by her father—officially. Cervantes was, of course, incapable of giving such a sum: six months earlier, on November 23, 1607, he had been forced to request of Robles an advance of 450 *reales*. The real donor was none other than his daughter's lover, whose funds were put up as security—at Molina's insistence—until the payment of the dowry was complete. In exchange, the clerk promised to marry Isabel within the month, in default of which he was required to pay the young woman an indemnity of 1000 ducats. Isabel herself signed an identical contract. The house on Montera Street became the property of the child Isabel Sanz, her mother and stepfather to have the use of it. In case of the death of the little girl, Miguel was supposed to inherit the dwelling; but in fact a secret clause provided that it should revert to Urbina, its legitimate owner.

The auspices were unfavorable for a union contracted under such conditions. Nevertheless, it will last for twenty-three years. Isabel is anything but pleased by the match found for her: a man who, among other precautions, had refused to consummate the marriage until half the dowry had been paid. And it is to her aunt Magdalena, not to her husband, that Cervantes' daughter will turn for help in recovering her mother, Ana Franca's, inheritance. But she will manage to cooperate with her husband for the defense of their common interests. Indeed, before long Molina will clash with Urbina on money questions in which both seem to have been in the wrong. Certainly the presents, the clothing, and the furniture bestowed on Isabel by her protector were enough to excite Molina's greed as well as to wound his pride. In his will, dictated on December 25, 1631, he will humbly admit having "consumed and wasted" a large part of his wife's dowry, and he names her his only heir. But Isabel will not relent toward him to the end of her life. Refusing to leave part of her domestic property to her spouse, she will grant him only a pittance of 200 ducats, "because the Lord God was pleased to give him to me for a companion."

Cervantes' attitude in all of this affair may seem shocking. But it can be explained both by his desire to keep up appearances and by his haste to extricate himself from a difficult situation: once Isabel remarried, it was thenceforth incumbent upon the husband and not the father to guard her honor or, failing that, to suffer the effects of her misconduct. Had the author of *Don Quixote* dreamed of a different fate for her? Accustomed as he was to the wayward behavior of the women in his family, the misfortunes of his only daughter should not have surprised him, and we can understand why his wife, co-signer of the famous contract, gave him her help and support. Indeed Catalina was all the more interested in having done with Urbina's protégée because Constanza, who had remained under the family roof, had just met with new mishaps. A notarial document of December 18, 1608, gives an account of a court action instituted by the young woman against a certain Francisco Leal. The nature of the complaint is not specified, but it is easy to guess. Like her mother and her aunt, Constanza will obtain the modest sum of 1000 *reales* as reparations: a small amount in exchange for her tarnished reputation, but enough to keep her in Catalina's esteem. When the time comes, Cervantes' wife will name Constanza in her will. Isabel, on the other hand, will be conspicuous by her absence, while, as a supreme insult, Molina will appear among the number of heirs.

> O disobedient daughters,
> Who outstripping the course of years
> Take pleasure before the proper time:
> May God confound, may Heaven curse you!

Cervantes put these imprecations in the mouth of a comic graybeard; it is doubtful that he himself ever uttered them. With no illusions regarding his offspring, he armed himself with resignation and had no other ambition than to live in peace. But it was still necessary for him to get free of those who continued to pick quarrels with him, beginning with his former associates, who were still snapping at his heels. On November 6, 1606, the agents of the Treasury renew the charge: they demand sixty ducats in unpaid debts and invite him to appear before them within ten days. Did Miguel ask his son-in-law to intervene? We have lost the response that he will address to his persecutors a fortnight later, but it appears that this time his explanations were judged satisfactory. The question of the Vélez Málaga accounts will not arise again.

Having settled accounts with his king, Cervantes also wants to settle his accounts with God. The weight of years, the increasing burden of infirmities, the attacks of the illness that will carry him off eight years later, all are signs of a decline whose end he does not hide from himself: "My age," he will soon write in the prologue to the *Exemplary Novellas,* "does not permit me to make light of the next life." Catalina and Andrea are going to show him the way he should go: on June 8, 1609, after a year of novitiate, they take the habit of the Third Order of St. Francis, following Magdalena, who had preceded them by several months. This solemn contract is a farewell to the world and its false appearances—though even on this occasion, Andrea will claim, oddly enough, to be the widow of General Alvaro Mendaño, a military nobleman who seems never to have existed.

Miguel was no less concerned for his salvation, although he does not go so far along the path of renunciation. Two months earlier, on April 17, he had affiliated himself with the Confraternity of the Slaves of the Most Holy Sacrament (also sometimes called simply the "Confraternity of the Most Holy Sacrament"). This religious brotherhood, recently founded, recruited members among literary men: a good number of them will join with the author of *Don Quixote*. What history does not tell us is whether all of them will manage to obey the strict rules that membership in this order imposed on its followers: wearing a scapular, fasting and abstinence on prescribed days, absolute continence, daily attendance at the offices, spiritual exercises, visiting hospitals, simplicity of life and habits. Cervantes is considered to have followed this program to the letter; but one may rest assured that Lope—twenty years younger than he, of course—did not display such constancy and ardor.

Cervantes' delayed fervor has not failed to intrigue scholars. How does it square with the ironic jabs, the impertinent allusions to the affairs of the Church, that run through Cervantine texts? Cervantes, thoroughly familiar with the Gospel, is a master at the art of hinting, whether he is making irreverent fun of the clergy or calling into question certain superstitious practices current among his contemporaries. The strict observance of rites, the profitable devotion to souls in Purgatory, the bead-telling of Tartuffes of all sorts: these are some of the themes that he touches on playfully, without acrimony, but not without humor. To speak (as has been done) of *fabliau*-like anticlericalism is to misunderstand this ironical criticism, which bears the authentic stamp of its time. But it is by no means certain that this comes from reading Erasmus. In our opinion, Cervantes' disaccord with the general tone of his period in matters of religion does not reveal the influence of a particular current of thought but rather expresses the choices of an open mind that is inimical to prejudice but nevertheless respectful of dogma and formal worship. He is a humanist in the widest sense of the term, not trained in musty libraries but in the school of life and adversity.

If this is so, how are we to interpret this fervor, so insistently flaunted? How are we to understand the unexpected forms that it takes? As a necessary precaution for the benefit of the guardians of orthodoxy? As a concession to three women who, in their old age, spend far too much time in church? Or as the maturely thought-out decision of a man who, in the evening of his life, has rediscovered the profound meaning of *ecclesia* and intends to bind faith and works together more tightly? Scholars have often related this piety, of Tridentine cast, to the insistence with which our author will soon protest the purity of his intentions in the preface to the *Exemplary Novellas*. They have also detected its influence in the expurgation, carried out under his supervision, of a passage in *Don Quixote* where the Knight, in order to recite "a million Ave Marias," provides himself with a rosary made from his shirttail. That is one explanation, perhaps, among others for a revision about whose genesis we know nothing; the reasons that may have motivated Cervantes elude us. For those of us who judge him on his actions alone, let us at least concede that his reasons were surely neither unimportant nor petty, because the "rare inventor" never renounced his vocation.

THE SHADOW OF DEATH

MIGUEL remains true to his convictions: he is going to prove it at the time of the expulsion of the Moriscos. The dispersion of the Andalusian Morisco community decreed by Philip II after the failure of the Alpujarras uprising had been only a half-measure. Other hotbeds continued to exist in Castile, Aragon, Valencia: other communities just as attached to their language, to their customs and their traditions. In Castile, where they were shopkeepers and craftsmen, the Moriscos most often formed small nuclei. In Aragon, on the other hand, where they were generally shepherds, in Valencia and Murcia, where they tended the *huertas* (irrigated market gardens), their position was infinitely more ticklish. Though protected by the local nobility anxious to keep its workforce, and representing in certain zones more than a third of the population, they were the butt of Old Christian hostility. All the more mistrusted because they were prolific, resistant to all assimilation imposed by force, accused of being the accomplices of Barbary pirates, they were the favorite target of zealots, in whose opinion Spain would not find herself until she closed in upon herself, until she rid herself of all those who were determined to remain different.

The idea of a general expulsion, first proposed by a few hotheads, will not be put into effect for a long time. The indecision of Philip II, aware that the Moriscos were officially Christian; the resistance of Val-

encian barons, who were unwilling to see their *fellahin* depart; the
technical difficulties raised by their banishment, all discouraged even
the most willing. At the death of the Prudent King, those in favor of
using force will go on the offensive again. Led by Ribera, the archbishop of Valencia, supported by the queen, who had been won to
their point of view, they are going to lay siege to the new sovereign
and his favorite. Lerma, hesitant at first, ends by deciding to take the
step: assured of compensation, the barons give in at the very moment
when peace with the Low Countries frees the fleet from its military
missions and allows the government to consider transporting Moriscos
to North Africa. On April 9, 1609, the day when the Twelve-Year
Truce with the United Provinces is concluded, Philip III signs the
fatal decree: virtually the entire population of Moriscos—250,000 to
300,000 persons, including women and children—is forced to leave
the Peninsula. It will take five years to complete the operation.

Spain will unanimously, or almost unanimously, applaud this measure: *le plus hardi et le plus barbare conseil dont l'histoire de tous les siècles
précédents fasse mention* ("the most daring and barbarous plan that the
history of all preceding centuries records"), as an expert in the matter—Cardinal Richelieu—will say. Only Cervantes, almost singly, will
introduce a discordant note into this concert, and it cannot have escaped
the readers of his day, however unskilled they may have been in reading between the lines. The anti-Morisco diatribe that Berganza pro-
nounces in *The Dialogue of the Dogs* is a masterpiece of irony *per se.*
Though it supposedly summarizes the grievances of Old Christians
against an active and prolific minority, it expresses a vision of things
that is much more complex than the official version, which was founded
on exclusively religious arguments. A priceless detail: the "pack of
Morisco dogs" that Berganza vituperates is embodied in the character
of the Andalusian gardener who has generously taken Berganza in. But
it is with the Ricote episode, one of the most moving in the Second
Part of *Don Quixote,* that we put our finger in the wound of the Morisco
community. Ricote, Sancho's fellow countryman, whom he unexpectedly meets on his way into exile, symbolizes the case of thousands of
innocent people who, though divided between two cultures, were loyal
subjects of their sovereign. With an eloquence that is odd (to say the
least), Ricote attributes the bold resolution taken by His Majesty to
divine inspiration; but his tone does not deceive us when he describes
the effects of banishment on himself and his co-religionists, a punish-

ment which he considers "the most terrible that could be inflicted on us":

> Wherever we are, we weep for Spain; for after all we were born there, and it is our native land. Nowhere do we find the reception our unhappy condition needs; and in Barbary and all the parts of Africa where we counted upon being received, assisted, and welcomed, it is there they insult and ill-treat us most. . . . And now I know by experience the meaning of the saying, "Sweet is the love of one's country."

This cry of despair says more about it than the most carefully argued defense against the inanity of the principle invoked to legitimize the expulsion: the Moriscos were never collectively responsible for the offenses or crimes imputed to a few of them, and nothing justified the fate imposed on them indiscriminately. It was not only a serious political error; the expulsion was a sin. But to point this out, even in veiled words, it was necessary to have the courage of the author of *Don Quixote*.

In autumn of the same year, on October 9, 1609, Andrea de Cervantes suddenly dies, a victim of a fever about which we know nothing: a brutally sudden death, as the absence of a will proves. The oldest of Miguel's sisters will have a quiet funeral, as befitted a woman of modest means and (what is more) a tertiary of St. Francis. The burial register of her parish, San Sebastián, describes her as the "widow of Santi Ambrosio, a Florentine, sixty-five years old." General Alvaro Mendaño, who appeared unexpectedly when she took the habit, had apparently returned to his non-existence.

Six months later, another death is going to cast a pall over the writer's life: that of his granddaughter, Isabel Sanz. It will be the pretext for a sordid legal battle arising from a clash between Urbina and the child's parents. When the death is announced, the duke of Savoy's former secretary makes a decision fraught with consequences: he declares himself absolved of the rest of the dowry promised to Isabel de Molina. Even worse, on March 27, 1610, he reclaims his rights to the house on the Red de San Luis where the young woman has been installed with her husband and of which—in principle—she retains use for life. Cervantes undeniably has a hand in this transaction: recognized *pro forma* as legal owner of the property, under the terms of the contract signed the previous year, he has renounced his fictitious rights in favor of Urbina, on the sole condition that revenue allegedly earned from the house shall be donated to charitable works. But Cervantes has seriously underestimated his daughter's reaction. Considering herself swindled, Isabel starts legal proceedings against her father, in order to nullify the agreement. The break between Miguel and his daughter is now complete. As for Urbina, embarked on an affair whose complications he has not foreseen, he is going to seek a compromise: first by bringing Molina into his business affairs, which will provoke new contentions; then, when the time for the payment of the dowry has expired, by paying the sum of 22,000 *reales* as compensation to the ménage. But this provisional settlement will not occur until after new vicissitudes that will go far to poison the existence of the unfortunate writer.

In this atmosphere of hostility and bitterness, Cervantes seems to have found comfort in his wife: more than the Soldier in *The Judge of Divorces* could expect from his wife Doña Guiomar. Yet, for us, Catalina's personality still remains cloaked in mystery. What little we know about her during these years concerns her entrance into the Third Order, of which she was already a novice, and in which it will be her turn to make her profession on June 27, 1610. Eleven days earlier she had made her will before a notary: it mentions explicitly the "great love and good company" that the two spouses have given to each other. This might be nothing but a simple formula, customary in this sort of document, if Catalina had not taken care to give Miguel the use of her property for life, while leaving most of it to her brother Francisco, as one would have expected. Since this property was pledged to pay debts contracted previously by the Salazar family, Cervantes could not complain of having been neglected. On the contrary, in case Catalina should die first, it was not Cervantes but his brother-in-law who would have to settle the estate. Besides the marriage bed, bedclothes, and household furniture, Catalina left her husband, symbolically, two parcels of land. Perhaps she felt uneasy about them, with regard to her brothers; that would explain why she asked to be buried beside her father in the choir of the church at Esquivias, "near the steps of the high altar." After she becomes a widow, she will change her mind and ask to lie near her husband.

Andrea's younger sister, now called Magdalena de Jesús, will not wait long to follow her elder sister to the grave. On October 11, 1610, it was her turn to make a will. According to her wishes, her funeral was to be as simple as possible, "with as little pomp as my heirs deem suitable." The heirs, to tell the truth, could hardly have had illusions about the imaginary property listed in an appendix to the document: the 300 ducats that Fernando de Lodeña had promised to pay the woman he had seduced, twenty-five years earlier, and the share that was coming to her from Rodrigo's unpaid salary, demanded from the state in vain. Miguel, on this occasion, will renounce his portion in favor of Constanza. Magdalena herself understood the true worth of the document perfectly: "I leave no heirs for my estate because I have no property and have nothing left of any value." Apparently she had been ill for several months, and she will die on January 28, 1611. She will be interred according to the custom of the order in which she had made her final vows one year earlier: in a Franciscan habit, without a veil over her face. The interment is in conformity with her wishes as well as with her resources, and its costs—twelve *reales*—will be paid by the monks. The son of the dead woman's seducer, a poet in his spare time, will compose one of the prefatory sonnets for the *Exemplary Novellas*. Having the same Christian name as his father, he will perpetuate the name of Fernando de Lodeña.

Judging by his sister's funeral, Miguel was in financial straits again, at the very moment when Juan de Urbina, the object of Isabel's attacks, could be of no help to him. Did he believe that his in-laws would agree to come to his aid? That is how some scholars explain his departure for Esquivias in the spring of 1611, and the prolonged stay that he seems to have made there, until the end of the year. But Francisco de Palacios was managing, without much room to maneuver, an estate loaded with debts, and he was in no condition to offer hospitality indefinitely. After Miguel returns to Madrid in January of 1612, Catalina will have to agree to a new endowment in favor of her brother, doubtless to reimburse him for sums spent or advanced by him on that occasion.

Miguel's return to the *Villa y Corte* is going to be accompanied by another change of dwelling. For almost two years, he had been living not on Magdalena Street but on a neighboring street, at number 3 León, which is where his sister gave up the ghost. During the first months of 1612, the Cervantes family, henceforth reduced to the married couple and Constanza, moves to a nearby dwelling situated behind the cemetery of San Sebastián, at number 18 Huertas Street, "facing the buildings where the Prince of Morocco used to live." (This prince was none other than the famous Don Felipe de Africa, whose conversion to Catholicism we have mentioned and whom the ex-commissary officer doubtless saw at Carmona in the course of his Andalusian tours.) This "humble cottage," this "ancient and dreary dwelling" that Cervantes mentions in the *Journey to Parnassus,* had as its only advantage being situated two steps from the principal *corrales,* in what was at the time called "the Muses' quarter." Like Lope, whose house and little garden are today a pilgrimage site, Quevedo and Vélez de Guevara will be among the numerous writers who set up their household gods there. By an irony of fate, the street where the Phoenix chose to live is today called Cervantes Street.

Don Quixote's author is not going to venture outside the capital again except for brief comings and goings. On July 2, 1613, he returns for the last time to his home town. This journey to Alcalá marks a new stage in his spiritual evolution: after the example of his wife and his sisters, he becomes in turn a novice of the Third Order. That this ceremony should have taken place on the banks of the Henares is no doubt because Miguel wished to take his vows in the presence of Luisa, his elder sister by one year, who will soon be elected prioress of the nunnery she had entered almost half a century earlier. Is he going to take leave of the world and say adieu to literature? Quite the contrary: twelve days later, on July 14, he dedicates his *Exemplary Novellas* to Lemos. Through the periods of mourning and the disappointments of a difficult life, the seven years in Madrid are paradoxically the most fecund of his career as a writer.

THE WORLD OF LITERATURE

CERVANTES rejoins the court at Madrid at the very moment when his reputation is crossing the Pyrenees. In May 1607, duly authorized by Robles, the Brussels bookseller Roger Velpius publishes a new edition of *Don Quixote.* It is unusually accurate, and it will serve as the basis for the pungent English version that Thomas Shelton boasts of having finished in that same year, "in the space of forty days," but which will not appear until 1612. In July 1608, a third Madrid edition comes off Juan de la Cuesta's presses. At the same time, Nicolas Baudoin publishes at Paris the *Nouvelle du Curieux malavisé* (Novella of the Man Who Was Too Curious for His Own Good), a French translation of one of the interpolated stories. The following year, Jean Richer offers his French compatriots a selection of extracts from *Don Quixote:* Grisóstomo's funeral and the famous speech on arms and letters appear in a prominent place in this anthology. Simultaneously, César Oudin starts work on a translation of *Galatea,* which he will dedicate to *les dames françaises.* For the time being, Miguel appears to be unaware of this universal enthusiasm. On the other hand, he had surely heard tell of the festivities at Salamanca in 1610 that marked the beatification of St. Ignatius, during which a *Triunfo de Don Quixote* paraded through the streets of the city. And he discovered that a new edition of his book had just appeared in Milan.

Surrounded by this aura of recent fame, our aging writer intends to take his place in the world of literature once more. A regular visitor to Robles's shop—where sources assure us that Robles also maintained a gambling establishment—Cervantes does not limit himself to frequent visits to the *mentideros;* he also shows his face in the salons of a city that has once again become the intellectual capital of Spain. While there is no reason for us to doubt his religious fervor for an instant, his entrance into the Confraternity of the Most Holy Sacrament is also the gesture of a professional who wishes to make his presence known. This congregation, founded with the double patronage of Cardinal Sandoval and Lerma, was also an academy where writers courted the Muses with the Lord's blessing. One can understand why Lope de Vega participated actively in its creation, even if he soon limited himself to pontificating at plenary sessions only. Vicente Espinel, Quevedo, Salas Barbadillo, Vélez de Guevara will all seek admission. On Corpus Christi of 1609, Cervantes appears to have distinguished himself by contributing to a garland of poems composed in honor of the Almighty; but we have lost the verses, which, it is said, won him first prize. His participation is attested to again in 1612. This same year, Fray Diego de Haedo's *Topography and General History of Algiers,* in which the heroic conduct of an *hidalgo* from Alcalá is praised, finally comes off the press; so Miguel sees himself taken back forty years into the world of captivity, at the moment when he is preparing, after six years of silence, to face the readers' verdict for the third time. During this period, the strict discipline instituted by the statutes of the confraternity begins to be relaxed. Three years later, in February of 1615, the Trinitarians whose monastery housed the Congregation will ask it to return to more austere customs. This request will be rejected by the majority of the members, who will move their headquarters to the monastery of the Friars Minor of the Holy Spirit. Only six voters will oppose this decision. It is possible that Cervantes was among their number: out of fidelity to the original rule but also out of sympathy for the order that had once snatched him from the hell of Algiers.

His participation in literary competitions doubtless gave him the opportunity to make the acquaintance of the most celebrated of his patrons, Don Pedro Fernández de Castro y Andrade, seventh count of Lemos. A refined mind and enlightened protector of *belles-lettres,* this grandee will manage to win the gratitude of the best writers of his time: Lope, Góngora, Quevedo, among others, will benefit from his generosity. The nephew of the duke of Lerma, whose daughter he had also married, he is destined for the highest posts. Scarcely out of adolescence, he had become president of the Council of the Indies; in the spring of 1610, at the age of thirty-four, he is named viceroy of Naples. Anxious to set up a literary court, he asks his secretary, Lupercio Leonardo de Argensola, to choose those who will accompany him to Italy. Góngora aspires to be in the retinue; so does Cervantes: to revisit the places of his youth, to remove himself from Isabel's chicaneries, to cease living from hand to mouth. Argensola is a friend of long standing. Had he not once bestowed the most eloquent praise on *Galatea?* Had Cervantes not repaid it through the mouth of the Priest in *Don Quixote?* A distinguished humanist, an estimable poet, the viceroy's secretary is nevertheless, unfortunately, a mediocre talent afraid of being eclipsed by those more gifted than he. With the help of his brother Bartolomé, he is going to engage only those hack writers who he is sure will not put him in the shade. Posterity has forgotten their names.

Góngora had experienced the same disappointment, a short time earlier, with the duke of Feria, sent to Paris to carry the king of Spain's condolences when Henri IV died. He will not tolerate this double rebuff easily, as is evidenced by a sonnet in which spitefulness rivals wit:

> My lord the Count went off to Naples;
> My lord the Duke went off to France;
> Dear princess, *bon voyage;* today
> I'll give some *escargots* penance.

Cervantes is also going to resent this snub, all the more deeply since, as Martin de Riquer has recently shown, he seems to have made his

way to Barcelona in an effort to obtain an audience with Lemos, while
the new viceroy was preparing to leave for Naples. Without success.
Instead of blaming his protector for it, however, he will save his barbs
for the two brothers. In the *Journey to Parnassus,* he will say, in effect,
that the pair, known for their poor eyesight, disregarded him because
they were "short-sighted":

> I hoped for much because they promised much;
> But it may be that newer cares have forced
> Them to forget the words they spoke.

His age, his infirmities, the sad state in which Magdalena found herself, were all serious handicaps for him, it is true. Could he have
tolerated a gilded exile? Would he have gotten on well with his colleagues? It is hard to imagine this full-fledged sexagenarian suddenly
taking leave of his country and his family, then laying his projects
aside in order to fulfill his obligations as courtier. All things considered, it was better for him—and for us—that he did not leave for
Naples. His relations with Lemos, who remained aloof from these
intrigues, will not be compromised by them in the least: on the contrary, they are going to intensify and deepen.

Since he cannot have the court of Naples, Miguel falls back on the
literary academies that are then flourishing in Madrid, such as the
Academia del Parnaso, otherwise known as the Academia Selvaje, whose
meetings will take place, beginning in 1612, on Atocha Street at the
palace of its founder, Don Francisco de Silva y Mendoza. These assem-
blies of clever minds are also the field of combat where those who take
part face each other: a small world rent by harsh rivalries but amused
by these quarrels before it puts them into verse. Philip III's Spain is
mad about poetry; from the grandee to the student, from the craftsman to the canon, everyone tries to compose rhymes, "because poetry
is not in the hands but in the mind, and a tailor is as capable of being
a poet as a field marshal." Among these dilettanti, only the idle who
are sheltered from want can spend their time in the salons. There they
rub shoulders with professional writers, to whose criticism they submit the fruits of their labor, or they dispatch an improvised poem,
with uneven results. Cervantes took part in these poetic tournaments.
On a day in March of 1612, Lope will borrow Cervantes' glasses in
order to read some of his own verses: "[His spectacles] looked like

badly fried eggs," the Phoenix tells us. The author of *Don Quixote*
discovered that the best writer among those present did not necessarily
carry off the prize: "Try to win the second prize, for favoritism or the
author's standing determine the first, while justice alone accounts for
the second award," Don Quixote advises his younger fellow poets.
This judicious warning appears to have gone unheeded. Lope de Vega
writes to his protector, the duke of Sessa:

> People talk of nothing but the Academies that all the lords and many of
> the poets attend. [At the Academia del Parnaso] a Licentiate Soto and the
> famous Luis Vélez chewed each other out poetically; the affair went as far
> as get-your-shield-and-meet-me-outside; there were princes on both sides;
> Mars was never so contrary to the lady Muses.

While his reputation is spreading across Europe, Cervantes too is
amusing himself with these comical confrontations. After Italy, after
the Low Countries, where a second Brussels edition of *Don Quixote*
appeared in 1611, it is Germany's turn to welcome the Ingenious
Hidalgo: in 1613 his presence is reported at Heidelburg during a mas-
querade offered to the Elector Palatine. But it is in England that his
success shines brightest. First Wilkins, then Middleton, Ben Jonson,
and Philip Massinger echo his renown. In 1611, Fletcher takes his
play *The Coxcomb* from the story of the man who was too curious for
his own good. Nathaniel Field adapts it, in turn, in his *Pardon for the
Ladies.* The same year, Beaumont joins with Fletcher to write a farce
entitled *The Knight of the Burning Pestle.* This "knight" is only a young
grocer who dreams of cleaving giants in twain; he is a character that
people may think comes from the race of Don Quixote, say the two
authors. But they claim right of primogeniture so shamelessly that in
spite of themselves they reveal their hero's ancestry and their own debt
to Cervantes. The following year Thomas Shelton publishes the translation that has been slumbering in his desk drawer for four years, *The
Delightful Historie of the Most Ingenious Knight Don Quixote de la Mancha.*
It will be a genuine bestseller. One year later, Fletcher—again—col-
laborates with Shakespeare on a play inspired by Cardenio's madness.
It was still being performed in 1653, but it has unfortunately been
lost since then.

And France does not lag far behind. In 1611, a particularly auspi-
cious year, a new Spanish-language edition of *Galatea* appears in Paris,

intended probably for use in teaching Spanish. At the same time, César Oudin, a great fan of Cervantine prose, takes up the gauntlet thrown down by Shelton and begins to translate *Don Quixote* into French. It will take him four years to get to the end of his task: about the same time it took Cervantes to bring out the collection that he had been writing over the years and that will confirm his reputation, the *Exemplary Novellas*.

THE STORY OF A MANUSCRIPT

THE story of the Cervantine *Novellas* is rather a long one, a story that we know only in part but which undoubtedly begins during the last years of Philip II's reign: at least that is what one can deduce from the examination of an essential document from the dossier, the Porras Manuscript.

At about the same time that Miguel was putting the finishing touches to the First Part of *Don Quixote,* a prebendary of the Cathedral of Seville, Francisco Porras de la Cámara, was busy providing entertainment for the leisure hours of his employer, Cardinal Niño de Guevara. Porras assembled a whole assortment of tales and anecdotes copied by his own hand or his secretary's, among them two anonymous tales that probably came to him without their author's name but whose titles are familiar to us: *Rinconete and Cortadillo* and *The Jealous Extremaduran.* Rediscovered at the end of the eighteenth century, this miscellany must have suffered numerous vicissitudes for forty years before being thrown into the waters of the Guadalquivir during a riot in 1823. The Liberal book collector who owned it, a victim of the fury of a mob manipulated by Fernando VII's henchmen, will never be consoled for the loss of the precious manuscript. But at least he had had time to make several copies of it and to compare the text of the two novellas with the version published by Cervantes in 1613. The examination of the variants is of the greatest interest: it allows us, in fact, to evaluate the revision carried out by the author with a view to publication. In particular, it reveals the changes undergone by the story of the jealous Extremaduran: originally, old Carrizales' naive wife gives in to the efforts of her seducer; but in the definitive version, she puts up such stubborn resistance that she exhausts the suitor, and the two supposed lovers fall asleep, chastely, in each other's arms. The shock the gray-

beard suffers when he discovers them embracing is no less severe than
if they had in fact consummated their adultery; but the reader is invited
to draw quite a different lesson from the experience. We will return
to it at the proper time.

The transcription made by Porras proves, then, that there was an
earlier version of these two novellas in circulation, notably *Rinconete*,
which is also mentioned in the First Part of *Don Quixote*. Recently, a
scholar has suggested that the stories were actually written by an anonymous author and that Cervantes, after making the corrections that
we have described, claimed authorship. The "trial balloon"—the reference in *Don Quixote*—supposedly convinced him that nobody would
dispute the authorship of *Rinconete* with him. He carried out this hoax
in 1613, presumably; hence the peremptory tone of his preface, where
he claims that the works are his own, "neither imitated nor pur-
loined."

However ingenious this hypothesis may be, it boils down to
attributing remarkable hypocrisy to an author who in 1614 will himself be the victim of Avellaneda's imposture, and he will deeply resent
the publication of the apocryphal *Don Quixote*. In addition, the differences between the two versions are insufficient to show that a second
pen, the plagiarist's, took over from the first; besides which, we do
not have Porras' original or the final manuscript version at our disposal. If then Miguel is the author of the two novellas, he benefitted
from their reception in the circle of which the licentiate Porras was a
member. Since this salon was almost certainly Sevillian, the writing
of the two works surely dates from Cervantes' stay in Andalusia during
those obscure but fertile years that he spent in the shadow of the
Giralda, between his leaving prison and his final return to Castile. But
what about the ten other novellas in the 1613 collection? Without
precise criteria for dating, their chronology, as we have already said,
has given rise to the most contradictory hypotheses. *The English Spanish Lady,* whose heroine is a survivor of the Sack of Cádiz, has for a
long time been considered one of the earliest. As in the case of *The
Generous Suitor,* today scholars prefer to see it as a late work, written
after the author's return to Madrid, in any case. *The Gypsy Girl, Master
Glass, The Noble Scullery Maid, The Fraudulent Marriage,* and *The Dialogue of the Dogs,* as a group, contain references to outstanding events
from the first ten years of the seventeenth century: the unprecedented
success of *Guzmán de Alfarache,* the return of the court to the banks of

the Mazanares, the birth of the future Philip IV, the increasing hostility of public opinion with regard to the Moriscos. But some of these allusions are perhaps contemporary with a final revision, later than the composition itself. As for *The Call of Blood, Two Young Ladies,* and *Signora Cornelia,* nothing allows us to fix the time of their composition.

To complicate the facts of the matter even more, the Porras collection included a third anonymous novel, *The Pretended Aunt* (La tía fingida), whose authorship has caused oceans of ink to flow. Some have inferred from its indecency that Miguel, out of scruples, left it out of the 1613 edition. In our day, there is rather a tendency to deny Cervantes' paternity. The "aunt" in question, an experienced procuress, renews her "niece's" virginity three times in order to raise her price and assure the prosperity of her commerce. This smutty detail is not in the manner of our author. Cervantes does not detest either bawdy allusions or ribald jokes; he does not recoil before a risqué situation, provided it is artistically justified. But unlike Quevedo, he never takes pleasure in obscenity for its own sake.

In the spring of 1612, in all likelihood, he finished his last revisions, on his return from Esquivias, in the gloomy lodgings on Huertas Street. The official *aprobación* on the first page of the edition of the *Exemplary Novellas* is in fact dated July 9, 1612. Issued by a Trinitarian monk, Fray Juan Bautista Capataz, it was drafted in the very monastery where, up to that time, the Confraternity of the Most Holy Sacrament had been holding its meetings. In the *Journey to Parnassus,* Miguel will recall the sallow complexion of this poet-monk:

> Barefoot and poor, but fairly clothed
> With the trappings that Fame provides.

Confirmed on the same day by Dr. Gutierre de Cetina, this favorable opinion will be corroborated on August 8 by Fray Diego de Hortigosa, a co-religionist of the first censor. Did Miguel wish thereby to proclaim his total submission to Holy Church? Did he intend to use this opportunity to recall the bonds that united him to the Redemptorists? As best we can follow it, his spiritual itinerary would incline us to respond in the affirmative. He will not hesitate, however, to baptize with the name Hortigosa the go-between that he brings on stage in the interlude *The Jealous Old Husband* (El viejo celoso): with Cervantes, creativity never loses its rights.

It will take him three months to obtain the *privilegio* (copyright) destined to protect him from pirate publishers, the very same who seven years earlier had profited shamelessly from *Don Quixote*'s success. After new negotiations that will require more than a year, the copyright will be extended beyond Castile to the territories of the crown of Aragon. On July 31, 1613, the book receives one final *aprobación*, signed this time by a young fellow writer, Alonso Jerónimo de Salas Barbadillo. This *aprobación* is in fact an eloquent panegyric: Salas, a fervent admirer of Miguel, takes delight in underlining the "well-deserved esteem enjoyed within and without Spain by his brilliant wit, which is unique in its inventiveness and richness of language." The censor becomes a literary critic, and a highly favorable critic at that.

All that was left was to find a publisher willing to buy the manuscript. This time, again, it will be Robles. The late date of the bill of sale, signed on September 9, 1613, has caused scholars to suppose that Cervantes first made a tour of other publishers and that he did not approach Robles until he had given up on the others. In view of Miguel's fame, did he regard the sum offered to him as insufficient? "There is not one [publisher in Madrid] who does not want to acquire publishing rights for nothing," declares one of the heroes of *Persiles,* "or at least for such a low price that it doesn't benefit the author of the book." Let us beware of believing all the words that a writer gives to his characters and that critics have too often made him endorse without further ado. The 1600 *reales* agreed to by Robles are a sum that was by no means scandalously small for the period; but it had long since been paid out in the form of advances: hence a contract drafted in such a way that it merely validates a tacit agreement, entered into many months earlier, no doubt.

This explains why in late spring Juan de la Cuesta has the manuscript of the *Novellas* in hand. He will finish printing it at the beginning of the month of August. A few days earlier, on July 14, 1613, the author dedicates his book to the prince he had once hoped to accompany to Italy. Tradition required that a dedicatory epistle be at the same time a panegyric of a generous Maecenas and a request asking him to take the work offered to him under his wing. Miguel, as we have seen, liked to affirm his independence. He is going to restate it with brilliance:

So, to avoid these two irrelevant matters, I here omit the grandeeships and titles of Your Excellency's ancient and royal house, together with your innumerable virtues, natural as well as acquired . . . Nor do I beg Your Excellency to accept this book as its guardian, for I know that if it is not good, though I put it under the wings of Astolfo's hippogryph and under the shadow of Hercules' club, the Zoiluses, Cynics, Aretinos, and Bernias will not refrain from sharpening their criticism, vituperating it without respect for anyone. I beg Your Excellency simply to note that I am sending to you a little something: twelve stories that, had they not been fashioned in the workshop of my mind, might aspire to stand next to the finest. I send them off [to you there in Italy] such as they are, and I remain here, extremely satisfied, because it seems to me that I am beginning to show in a small way my desire to serve Your Excellency as my true lord and benefactor.

This page, as anyone can see, is a testimony of respect and gratitude. But above all, it radiates the legitimate self-assurance of a writer who knows what he is worth, for whom, in the last analysis, the only thing that counts is the verdict of the reader.

We can understand why he reserves the best part of these preliminaries for the reader: a preface up to the standard of the one that he wrote eight years earlier for *Don Quixote.* Its elegance makes it a true anthology piece; but its humor has occasionally given rise to amusing misunderstandings. So we are told, by way of preamble, that the illustrious Jáuregui, as good a painter as he was a refined poet, would have willingly executed a portrait of the author, had anyone asked him to do so. An obscure artist of the beginning of this century, José Albiol, will take it upon himself to flesh out this fantasy when he exhibits the famous painting one fine day. A memorable discovery, but suspicious at the very least, as two incongruous details of this artificially crackled canvas prove: the indication of the name of the subject (*Don* Miguel de Cervantes: Cervantes himself, careful not to overstep his rank as *hidalgo,* never calls himself *don*); and the date assigned to the masterpiece (1600), which would mean that Jáuregui, a precocious genius, acquitted himself of his commission at the age of seventeen. The picture in question will nevertheless amaze eminent Cervantists; and the Real Academia Española, to which Albiol made a gift of it, has never permitted an expert examination, in order not to have to acknowledge the hoax.

The only authentic portrait we have is the one that the author has slipped into this preface in stead and in place of Jáuregui's, and that he desires to offer his well-beloved reader:

> This face that you see here, with aquiline profile, chestnut hair, smooth, bald forehead, cheerful eyes and curved (though well-proportioned) nose, silver beard which not twenty years since was golden, large moustache, small mouth, teeth neither undersized nor oversized (because he has only six) . . . his body between the two extremes, neither large nor small, lively color, fair rather than dark, somewhat stoop-shouldered, and not very light on his feet; this, I repeat, is the face of the author of *Galatea* and *Don Quixote de la Mancha.* . . . He is usually called Miguel de Cervantes Saavedra.

Such is the image that Miguel wants to leave to posterity. However strong his pride at having fought at Lepanto and endured the horrors of captivity with head held high, from now on his works take precedence over his service record. Here is a writer who speaks to us about himself, ceaselessly varying the ceremonies of introduction addressed to the reader, whom he makes his witness, his confidant, his mediator, and his accomplice by turns. Here he is, submitting his new masterpiece to a public that has already adopted him.

A SPANISH BOCCACCIO

> And furthermore, it is my opinion—and it is true—that I am the first to have written novellas in the Castilian language; for the many novellas that are circulating in print in Spanish are all translated from foreign languages; but these stories are my own, neither imitated nor plagiarized: my wit engendered them, my pen gave birth to them, and they are growing up in the arms of the printing-press.

CERVANTES' insistence on claiming that he is the first may seem suspect. But there is no doubt about it. Previously, Spain had practiced the *cuento* (brief tale) and the apologue, in strict observance of the canonical forms that the Middle Ages had bequeathed to the Renaissance: a mere shadow play, a succession of incidents schematized by an omniscient narrator who, for his imaginary audience, pulls the strings of his marionettes and then reveals the moral of the story. Juan de Timoneda, the Valencian bookseller whom Miguel undoubtedly visited upon his return from Algiers, had set the pattern of these fictions impregnated with folklore; he called them, symptomatically, *patrañas* (tall tales), thereby giving us to understand that they are addressed to a reader previously won over and ready to accept the most naive conventions.

It will be necessary to wait until the twilight of the sixteenth century to see Spanish literature acclimatize the novella, in the sense that we give to that term today: instead of a spate of events sketched in a short narrative, it describes a crisis whose effects are revealed through the feelings and choices of those who face it. In 1559, the admirable *Story of the Abencerraje* (Historia del Abencerraje) had anticipated this change, recounting the moving idyll of a Moorish beauty and her chivalrous suitor against the backdrop of the last days of the Reconquest. At the end of Philip II's reign, Mateo Alemán seizes the torch with the four stories included in his *Guzmán de Alfarache.* But in fact they are only interpolated tales, and by that date Cervantes had already produced the first fruits of his talent.

Was he, consequently, venturing into virgin territory? Certainly not. Before him, Boccaccio and his followers had perfected the *novella,* where the narration, concentrated around a central element, highlights what is unique in a character and his destiny. Spain did not wait for the author of *Don Quixote* before importing the term *novella* from Italy or offering her warmest welcome to a previously unknown genre. The *Decameron,* translated into Castilian in the early years of the fifteenth century, went into five successive editions, and it appears in a prominent place in Isabel the Catholic's library. The vigilance of the Inquisitors, who list the work among the number of books prohibited by the *Index* of 1559, will put an end to this brilliant career; but the vogue of the *novellieri* will not be compromised thereby. Miguel, during his years in Italy, read Boccaccio in the original, the Roman Inquisition having authorized the republication of the expurgated works. He also familiarized himself with Boccaccio's imitators, whose chastened tales had acquired the rights of citizenship in Spain: Matteo Bandello's *Tragic and Exemplary Stories* had been published in Castilian at Salamanca in 1589, and Cervantes seems to have bought the French translation some years later, during a stay in Seville; Giraldi Cinzio's *Hecatommithi* had been published at Toledo in 1590 and would enjoy an extraordinary diffusion throughout Spain. But as Miguel underlines in his preface, these are all novellas imported from abroad and more often adapted than really translated. In all respects, therefore, he did pioneer work.

Cervantes did, in fact, take up the challenge of the Italians; but he did it while keeping his distance. The man whom Tirso de Molina will soon call "our Spanish Boccaccio" undoubtedly studied the example of the *novellieri;* he even borrowed the formal characteristics of the genre that they had raised to a position of honor; but he refrained from any servile copying. The resemblances pointed out from time to time are vague references that do not authorize one to speak of imitation. Salas Barbadillo is one of the first to take note of them, while rendering homage to the inventiveness of the *Exemplary Novellas,* an inventiveness in which our poet was, by his own admission, without rival.

But we must look for signs of originality where it truly appears. With regard to plot alone, the Cervantine novellas often limit themselves to reviving traditional motifs, conventional situations whose origin goes back to remotest antiquity. Long-thwarted love finds a way and ends with a happy union: *The Gypsy Girl, The Generous Suitor, The Noble Scullery Maid, The English Spanish Lady* offer us four variations on this classic theme. Marriage is reparation for an offense born of the impulsive desire of a daring seducer: *The Call of Blood, Two Young Ladies, Signora Cornelia* illustrate this scheme. Or as happens in *The Fraudulent Marriage* and *The Jealous Extremaduran,* the outcome frustrates, sometimes tragically, the sinful designs of those who break the laws of nature. Kidnappings, duels, recognitions are frequent milestones on the characters' ways. But the charm of these stories is in their manner rather than their matter. What they give us is, in fact, not simply a sum of fragmentary experiences; it is the way the heroes live and feel their experiences in the course of a quest that leads them to the discovery of themselves, a quest that draws us irresistibly in their train. This self-discovery may provide a reward: shared happiness that, far from being guaranteed in advance, is not achieved until the end of a long period of self-denial. Inversely, the self-discovery may provide the shock through which the guilty character internalizes his punishment and agrees to pay the price of his error.

From this shift of accent, which is compatible with the genius of the novella and which subordinates the *what* to the *how,* derives the economy of the Cervantine story, above and beyond the array of plots in operation. It is, consequently, possible to appreciate the suppleness of his formula, which is not reducible to a pre-formed model. Anxious to exploit all its resources, the author of *Don Quixote* adapts it to his purpose each time, without hesitating to leave the beaten path, should the occasion arise. Hence the odyssey of Rinconete and Cortadillo through the Sevillian underworld ends on a sort of *fermata:* a wise decision—to leave this place of perdition as quickly as possible; then we are immediately told, with a little stab of irony, that it will be several months before it is put into effect. Likewise the Italian peregrinations of Master Glass seem to foreshadow a series of repercussions; but they are in fact only a curtain-raiser: Tomás Rodaja, the licentiate, does not become himself until the moment when he is struck by madness. In constant fear of breaking into a thousand pieces, he thenceforth takes refuge in paradox and aphorism. As for the autobiography of Berganza, a *pícaro* on four legs who receives the gift of speech one fine evening, it is inserted into the weft of a dialogue carried on with his companion Cipión, a dialogue transcribed by Captain Campuzano, the hero of *The Fraudulent Marriage,* for the edification of his friend Peralta. The result is a box-within-a-box that is a genuine challenge to the conventions of writing.

Cervantes (as will be obvious) also challenges the canons that habitually govern the relationship between reality and fiction. Critics have often gone into ecstasies over the realism of the *Exemplary Novellas;* some have even declared that realism is their predominant factor. But as we have already said, it is important not to misunderstand the way the narrator and characters see the world's stage: they do not record the show of people and things; if they try to render concrete details, it is in order to reconstruct a unique experience as it unfolds and to make us share it, while raising it to a universal plane. Hence, whatever the setting, their indifference to ready-made picturesque elements. Hence, inversely, the high value put on meaningful details: describing the banks of the Guadalquivir, where Rinconete and Cortadillo linger to sightsee, the narrator keeps only

> . . . the great throng of river-people, because it was during the time for loading the fleet, and there were six galleys in port, the sight of which made [the boys] groan and even dread the day when their crimes would bring them to dwell on shipboard for life.

Whether these fears are well-founded or not, it is the hero's point of view that gives meaning to this setting; *that* is what metamorphoses descriptions and narratives, incorporating them in the characters' dialogues; that is what transmutes a sudden vision into a *mise-en-scène*. Sometimes one gesture is enough for the being who appears before our eyes to reveal his essence without realizing it. Take, for example, the starving soldier who makes his entrance at the door of the Hospital of the Resurrection (from the beginning of *The Fraudulent Marriage*):

> . . . It was quite clear, because he was using his sword as a cane and because of the weakness of his legs and the yellowish cast of his face, that (although the weather was not very warm) he had probably spent twenty days sweating out all the infection that he had contracted in perhaps an hour. He was taking small steps and walking unsteadily, like a convalescent.

This is enough to make us pay attention to this syphilitic who bears the stigmata of his misfortune and whose condition and fate we will discover little by little.

Cervantine realism, in the final analysis, is the art of capturing each being in his situation, struggling with himself, with another, with all of society. It follows that, according to the circumstances, the world in which these beings evolve and reveal themselves can be the outskirts of Toledo, where the action of *The Call of Blood* takes place, as well as the Sevillian house that has become the prison of Leonora, the wife of the jealous Extremaduran. It can also be the watery expanses over which the hero of *The Generous Suitor* sails in pursuit of his beloved, captured by pirates. It can be, finally, a *trompe-l'oeil* universe: the apparent scenery of our daily life, refracted by the madness of a glass licentiate or by the speech of an eloquent dog. Is this stupendous dialogue between Cipión and Berganza, recorded by a feverish charity patient on his hospital cot, unbelievable? This is what the licentiate Peralta retorts to his friend Campuzano, who believes that he has heard and almost seen with his eyes the two four-footed comrades. But it is enough for Peralta to read their conversation for him—and for us with him—to enjoy its "inventiveness and skill" without "arguing further . . . whether the dogs talked or not." Did the conversation really take place? That is beside the point. The dialogue *takes* place in perfect coherence: that is all we need in order to believe in it.

In the *Journey to Parnassus,* Cervantes will say in three lines what his objectives were:

> With my *Novellas* I opened the way whereby
> The Castilian tongue can reproduce a piece
> Of fantasy with perfect naturalness.

This paradoxical fiction, in which truth escapes the norms of what is verifiable, is an example of audacity that Aristotle would not have found objectionable. The author of *Don Quixote,* an assiduous reader of Aristotle's commentators, managed to see beyond the letter of their interpretations in such a way as to rediscover the spirit of the *Poetics.* In this light, the twelve novellas that he has left us deserve to be called "exemplary": they are in fact twelve experimental fictions that systematically explore the ways of novelistic creation. This particular meaning of *ejemplar,* a highly ambiguous epithet, is certainly the most compatible with the spirit of our times. But how did the seventeenth century itself understand Cervantine "exemplariness"? Miguel, it appears, had his own ideas on the subject. What little he said about it does not dissipate all the mist; but it can save us from errors that are too often committed.

SOME EXEMPLARY NOVELLAS

I have given them the name *exemplary,* and if you consider it carefully, there is not one from which you cannot derive some profitable example; and did I not wish to avoid discussing this subject at too great length, perhaps I might show you the tasty and morally beneficial fruit that could be derived from all together as well as from each by itself.

THERE is something troublesome about this foreword. Is the author addressing his Dear Reader? Or does he want to disarm a censor, whom he offers to guide, only to disappear at the decisive moment? People have read his statement in many ways: for some, it is the expression of heroic hypocrisy; for others, the evidence of delayed repentance. But that is to see only a minor aspect of the matter; we must look further.

Cervantes is not the first to have developed this theme. The Middle Ages, in order to legitimize "lying" fables, preferred to present them as *exempla:* by fixing attention on an episode of human existence, they became a mirror created to help the reader correct himself. In the spiritual climate of the Counter-Reformation, which was attentive—

in the extreme!—to literature's power of persuasion, the exemplariness of fictional narrative is going to become the criterion of its truthfulness. The Counter-Reformation will demand that fictions offer the reader an array of *casus*—instances—that are lessons for life, from which he may derive "tasty and morally beneficial fruit," unlike the licentious stories of the *Decameron,* whose message is independent of any explicit reference to a standard. Thus Giraldi Cinzio, going along with this moralizing aim, will assign to his *novelle* an explicit intentionality, a deliberately edifying objective, that undoubtedly favored their diffusion in Spain. In the same line of thought, Suárez de Figueroa will, somewhat later, define the *novela* as "a most ingenious composition which obliges one to imitate or avoid an example," thereby delineating the two faces of exemplarity.

Did Miguel share their views? Let us say, rather, that he was sensitive to some of their concerns. The corrections made on the version preserved by Porras attest to an urge for decency which in the 1613 preface occasionally looks like a veritable obsession:

> One thing I will venture to say to you: that if I should somehow discover that reading these novellas might induce a person who reads them to have some evil desire or thought, I would cut off the hand with which I wrote them rather than publish them.

One might think that the four censors from whom he requested the explicit *aprobaciones* were intent on calming his scruples, after he decided to give his manuscript to the printer. But did they suggest amending and expurgating it? Anyone who can answer that is clever indeed. From a careful study of the texts, of which we have two stages, it appears that though Cervantes attenuated some unsuitable phrases or suppressed a few naughty allusions, he generally made corrections of details that do not bring his original design into question. We can judge this by the epilogue of *Rinconete and Cortadillo:* aware of the depravity of Sevillian customs, Rincón is ready to "advise his companion that they should not continue to live much longer in a way of life which was so idle and wicked, so insecure, so licentious and dissolute." This resolution certainly does honor to Rincón; but he fails to put it into practice; for, as the narrator immediately adds,

> . . . Led astray, however, by his youth and lack of experience, he continued to live in this manner for several more months, during which things

happened to him that require a longer story; and so we will leave telling about his life and miracles for some other occasion . . .

An open ending, but also an ironical moral message that cannot be measured by standards of narrow conformity.

We also need to look twice at *The Jealous Extremaduran* before attributing the *rifacimento* to prudence or prudery. In the Porras version, the heroine commits adultery with Loaysa; in the definitive version, we are told that

> . . . at the most opportune moment, she showed [her courage] against the base efforts of her sly deceiver, because his strength was insufficient to overcome her, and he exhausted himself in vain; she remained the victor; and both fell asleep.

This chaste sleep would be astounding did it not confirm what we suspected about the suitor: this feckless young man, who out of bravado has sworn to storm the fortress, has only the appearance of a seducer. As a perfect representative of such "idle, foppish, honey-tongued people," he is in reality impotent, disqualified by his scheme and unworthy of Leonora's favors because of his conduct. The adultery is consequently only a simulacrum; the innocent girl whom Carrizales has shut up in a gilded cage is saved from its taint. The old man, a victim of appearances, dies of sorrow, as in the original story; but he now takes responsibility for his mistake. Hence the value of the death-bed pardon that he grants to his tearful wife, whom his swoon prevents from "telling the whole truth of the case." Once she becomes a widow, Leonora will chose to end her days in a nunnery.

So the exemplariness of the *Novellas* does not pre-exist before the narrative; it is consubstantial with it. And it falls to the reader—and to him alone—to extract the moral from a story whose power of suggestion derives from its being both fiction and truth, capable of surprising as well as convincing. The narrator is unwilling and unable to provide the key to this ambiguous story. The dénouement that he contrives, whether it be a reward or, on the contrary, punishment, is not the sanction of some *deus ex machina* or the verdict expected from a cooperative Destiny; it is the terminus of the symbolic journey, studded with obstacles, that the hero has accomplished from beginning to end, the exit from the labyrinth into which his star has led him and where he has wandered for so long. For Ricardo, the generous suitor, to win Leonisa's heart means not only to deserve her gratitude because he helps her escape from the Turks; it also means that he has been generous enough to leave her free to choose the person she loves. For Andrés Caballero or Tomás de Avendaño, to marry a Gypsy girl or a noble scullery maid is not to play at Prince Charming with a Castilian Cinderella; it is first of all to learn to love her for herself, while respecting her desires and her plans, ready to lead a servant's life in the inns or to share the Gypsies' existence. But (someone may ask) is it not a stylized Gypsy life, embellished with the charm of the novelistic? It is also, let us say, a transfiguration of a world of outcasts, more coherent and more convincing than the negative stereotypes that Gypsies inspire in the literature of the period. It matters little, of course, that Preciosa and Constanza, the heroines, both turn out to be from the cream of the nobility. The providential recognition *in extremis* that permits them to resume their rank is not merely a literary convention; it is a way for society to accept the decrees of Nature and so to put the seal of approval on the union of two hearts.

Certain critics have observed that the *Exemplary Novellas* show us that reality cannot be other than the way it is. It reveals itself in these stories with its compromises and falsehoods, with its share of chance and necessity. But chance is not enough to put things in order or necessity enough to prevent things from being put in order; the choices that we make on a road sown with ambushes, where good and evil sometimes exchange their masks, also interfere: in other words, the exercise of our free will in our struggle with the disorder of a world whose secret harmony we are striving to discover. To achieve this, it is necessary, on occasion, to ponder the example of those who seem highly unlikely to have been called upon to show us the way: pseudo-innocents like Rinconete, whose look of astonishment sees through appearances; madmen of the type of Master Glass, who, because they see the world upside down, set it on its feet; pedigreed dogs like Berganza, able to share man's fate while separating themselves from the human universe. This, when all is said and done, is the "hidden mystery" alluded to by the author in his preface, the secret that the stories are supposed, according to him, to conceal.

Barely off the presses, the *Novellas* are going to experience a rapid success: four editions in ten months, among which is a pirated edition that appeared in Pamplona and a counterfeit edition published at Lisbon. Twenty-three editions will confirm this enthusiasm in the course of the century. The novellas are going to inspire numerous emulators and so give a patent of nobility to a genre that Spain will cultivate with remarkable steadfastness. Tirso de Molina will be the most brilliant disciple of "the Spanish Boccaccio." Castillo Solórzano, Salas Barbadillo, Liñán y Verdugo, María de Zayas will follow in his footsteps in turn. Even Lope de Vega will attempt to take up the challenge in his *Novellas for Marcia Leonarda,* hailing in passing, with faint praise, those fictions "in which Miguel de Cervantes did not lack a certain grace and style." England, so fond of *Don Quixote,* will offer them an equally warm welcome: even before procuring a complete translation of them, Englishmen will stage in free adaptations *The Gypsy Girl, The Noble Scullery Maid, Two Young Ladies, Signora Cornelia, The Call of Blood, The Generous Suitor,* and *The Fraudulent Marriage.* As for France, she is going to worship them: translated in 1615 by Rosset and d'Audiguier, reprinted eight times in the course of the seventeenth century, the *Exemplary Novellas* in their original version will be the favorite reading of all those who pride themselves on knowing Spanish. For the successors of Rotrou and Corneille, they are going to provide a whole repertory of situations that will be the delight of the *comédie romanesque.* For the prose writers of the Grand Siècle—Urfé, Voiture, Scarron, Sorel, Segrais—they will constitute models that these authors will unfailingly imitate. This admiration of *gens de goût*—men of taste—will cause the Cervantine *Novellas* to be preferred over *Don Quixote;* it is not until the eighteenth century that the latter will take its revenge, recovering a supremacy that has not been disputed since then.

JOURNEY TO PARNASSUS

"THE author of *Galatea* and *Don Quixote de la Mancha*" is the caption with which Cervantes embellishes his self-portrait; and he adds by way of clarification, "the man who wrote the *Journey to Parnassus,* in imitation of Cesare Caporali of Perugia." This last piece of information always surprises readers today; but it reveals the high esteem in which Miguel held a late product of his genius that posterity has relegated to obscurity.

Who was this Cesare Caporali? A minor writer, a native of Perugia,

Italy. Like Cervantes, he had served the Acquaviva family before disappearing toward the end of the century. His *Viaggio in Parnaso*, contemporary with *Galatea,* had enjoyed a modest success; it was reprinted
twice. The author of *Don Quixote* claims to have imitated it. To be
more accurate, he borrowed the basic idea of Caporali's poem. Like his
model, he tells us the story of a burlesque odyssey, his own ascent of
Mount Parnassus, and his appearance before Apollo, who is surrounded by the chorus of Muses. But the Cervantine expedition has a
profoundly original character, nevertheless. Caporali is perched on a
mule; Cervantes prefers to straddle his destiny, in order to "leave his
fatherland and rise above himself." After saying farewell to Madrid
and to its *corrales* and *mentideros,* he takes the road, with eight *maravedís'* worth of cheese and a loaf of bread in his saddlebags. At Cartagena he embarks on a galley made of strophes and verses. This ship,
guided by Mercury, must go to the aid of Parnassus, which is threatened by an army of twenty thousand rhymesters. It is soon joined by
a battalion of writers (the list of whose names, padded with allusive
references, rather disconcerts modern readers), puts out to sea, and
arrives in Greece after skirting the coast of Italy.

Mercury's companions, whom Apollo greets when they arrive, receive
a warm welcome. Only Miguel is forgotten during this affair, and he
has to recall his services before the god shows him a semblance of
interest. The assailants appear, and their attack provokes temporary
confusion; but they are finally repulsed by a hail of novels, satires, and
sonnets. Our hero, sprinkled by Morpheus with a soporific liquor, falls
asleep and awakens at Naples, where great festivities are being given
at the behest of the viceroy. Will the count of Lemos, Cervantes' protector, finally admit him into his service? Alas, this Neapolitan interlude is but a dream, and Miguel comes to in Madrid. Thoroughly
annoyed, he concludes,

> I sought my former dwelling, with its gloom,
> And threw myself exhausted on the bed;
> For a journey, when it's long, is very tiring.

To judge from an allusion in the *Exemplary Novellas,* the preface of
which dates from the summer of 1613, the poem was ready for the
printer at that time. But it will not be published until November
1614. Duly decked out with the usual *aprobaciones,* it will be dedicated

to the son of a dishonest magistrate of the Royal Council, a fifteen-year-old adolescent named Rodrigo de Tapia. Meanwhile, Cervantes has enriched his *Journey* with a "Postscript" (Adjunta) in prose. In this epilogue, he reports to us his encounter with Pancracio de Roncesvalles, one of his most fervent admirers. Pancracio, an imaginary person, delivers to him a series of humorous ordinances against bad poets, issued by Apollo in an effort to see that Parnassus shall no longer be exposed to their attacks.

Three thousand eleven-syllable lines, divided into eight cantos; a hundred and fifty fellow writers mentioned, hailed, and praised by the author: this anti-epic certainly has its dead parts. We no longer understand the cultural references of the seventeenth century, and we have become impervious to the charms of mythological satire. With regard to the parade of poets that Miguel encounters in the course of his journey, it is accompanied by allusions that are often not easy to decode. This parade, one critic has said, smacks of school exercises: an *aggiornamento,* in fact, of the "Song of Calliope," in which Cervantes had already enumerated his friends and rivals. But it is necessary to go beyond superficial analogies: by considering carefully the comings and goings of shameless rhymesters between the two camps that face each other, the betrayals and defections that they commit, and Apollo's refusal to tell us the names of the nine poets that he is crowning, one gradually discovers, behind the ready-made panegyrics, a disillusioned view of undeserved reputations and triumphant hypocrisy. Only the truly creative are valued at their just worth: the Argensola brothers, in spite of unkept promises; Quevedo, whose buffoonish muse receives well-deserved homage; Góngora, above all, admired for his *Polyphemus,* the ambitious masterpiece in which the Baroque ideal is realized for the first time.

What Miguel tells us about his own writings, what he allows us to glimpse of his ideas and his literary tastes, could hardly fail to hold our attention. But these revelations have for years been taken for what they are not: facts for use in literary handbooks. Today, students have a better grasp of what is truly interesting about them: they are the scattered fragments of a personal history. This mythical voyage without doubt is a sort of revenge, a way of joining Lemos without having to pass through his subordinates. But it is also a pilgrimage to the sources. Tearing himself away from the setting of his present life, from that *Villa y Corte* whose familiar places he recalls, the narrator carries us along on a tour charged with echoes of his previous wanderings: from the Gulf of Narbonne to the Gulf of Genoa, from the mouth of the Tiber to the Straits of Messina, from the shores of Corfu to the Bay of Naples, we watch the places that struck his imagination and his sensibility pass in review.

In this space remodeled by memory, the hero of the day gradually emerges: "Miguel de Cervantes, Huertas Street," as it says in the address on the letter from Apollo that Pancracio hands him. Cervantes, the singer of his own escapades as well as the interlocutor of gods and men, fills out the picture of himself bit by bit before our eyes. Each encounter adds a brushstroke to his portrait; but each one of these touches has its own value. Certain ones suggest his decrepitude:

> I, a sly one; I, a rhymester grown old.

Others recall a lack of education that the narrator admits with ironical detachment. Some describe his virtues, his merits, the fame that his writings have brought him:

> O thou the Adam of poets, O Cervantes!
> . . . .
>
> Thy works to all the corners of the earth
> [have traveled] upon the back of Rocinante.

Finally, others reveal his patience and resignation in adversity; when he appears before Apollo, for example:

> "Fold thy cape and seat thyself upon it."
> . . . .
>
> "It seems, My Lord," I answered, "that you fail
> To notice that I have no cape."

All this play of light and shadow appears against a backdrop of former exploits, of past troubles, of present disappointments, of future plans. Hounded by bad luck but aware of his gifts as a *raro inventor,* Miguel goes beyond this lucid appraisal of his fortunes and misfortunes to project himself toward the unsettled future that lies before him. He constructs his persona where lived experience and the imaginary come together, composing a heroic image of himself, not as the sum of judgments passed on him but through and beyond their very contradictions.

Cervantes undertakes this quest for a unique identity, one irreducible to a pre-established "essence," with the same ardor that Don Quixote displays. But, faced with the mystery of his fate, he does not tell us whether he has achieved his goal: as Ginés de Pasamonte says, his life is not over yet; it is not his business to anticipate the verdict of future ages. He will simply confirm, in the turn of a strophe, what his white hair leads us to suspect. He who aspires

> To sing with a voice so well attuned and strong
> That everyone will think I am a swan
> And that I'm dying . . .

knows that he is giving us his poetic testament. It is the farewell of a man who, afraid that he is deceived by his dreams, is protecting himself from them by smiling.

DRAMATIC ILLUSION

THE passion for theater, which Cervantes had harbored since adolescence, seized all of Spain after Philip III created the conditions for a new upsurge, when he authorized the re-opening of the *corrales*. And with the return of the court to Madrid, this passion infects the *Villa y Corte* with a virulence unknown until then.

Miguel had not broken his ties with actors during his stay in Andalusia. But his contract with Osorio remained a dead letter. His prison episodes in Seville, his departure for Valladolid on the eve of the publication of *Don Quixote,* his resettlement on the banks of the Manzanares after the Ezpeleta affair, were vicissitudes that had kept him away from the boards and relegated him to the uncongenial role of censor of fashionable *comedias.* A *madrileño* once more, he discovers a world of idlers avid for amusement, who every day hasten to applaud—or hoot— a repertory that must be constantly renewed. Staging remains extremely simple; what has been elaborated in the course of time, on the other hand, is the program of these performances. The *comedia,* with its three thousand verses and three acts, is the chief attraction, of course; but interludes, ballets, and masquerades fill up the intermissions, multiplying the forms of illusion. The *autores* are still, as before, the true masters of the game: producers as well as directors, they are the unavoidable intermediaries whom poets outdo each other to court. But the *autores* themselves must meet the demands of a turbulent public: to win the favor of the redoubtable *mosqueteros*—groundlings—is no easy affair.

Lope de Vega, backed by a cohort of disciples, is still the favorite playwright of these professionals. His astonishing fertility, his prodigious inventiveness, make him the idol of lovers of theater. But the Phoenix is no longer the same man. While remaining attentive to the *corrales,* he tends to guide their demands instead of limiting himself to responding to them day by day. He personally supervises the publication of his plays, thereby defending his property, which is threatened by plagiarists' swindling and actors' infringements. In this same period, he gives the Academy of Madrid the first reading of his *New Method for Writing Plays,* an occasional verse epistle composed, it appears, between 1605 and 1608 and aimed at winning over the educated, who, like the Priest in *Don Quixote,* reproach him for his willingness to compromise and bend the rules. Lope, a skillful tactician, begins by displaying his knowledge of the precepts, with a great backup of quotations drawn from the authorities. Then he pretends to plead guilty: he has chosen, he says, to speak the language of ignorance to the vulgar who provide him with a living. This ploy, however, is merely the easiest way for Lope to justify his artistic daring. Alternating theoretical reflections with practical advice, he lists and defends the innovations that he has introduced: the mixture of tragic and comic, the plurality of times and places, the primacy of action over character, the distribution of roles among traditional character types, polyphonic versification that adapts meters and strophes to the different tonalities. He also underlines the effectiveness of his formula: a plot quickly brought to a crisis, rich in possibilities, that keeps the intelligent spectator in suspense as well as amused by the impertinence of the valet-jester. Finally, he points out its contingent character: the poetics of the new *comedia* is not a catalogue of untouchable norms; it is a response to the taste of the period; it is the fruit of practical experience, constantly readjusted to the test of facts.

Perhaps Cervantes had not yet returned to Madrid before this verse epistle was read for the first time. But he assuredly obtained a manuscript copy of it before rereading it at leisure in the printed version that will be published in 1609. He will never come to accept his rival's views. He will have the grace to concede publicly the supremacy that was unanimously accorded to Lope at the time; but Cervantes will not follow his lead, even so. Not out of fidelity to some supposed classical tradition, invoked by pedants, of course, though never observed by the Spanish stage, but rather for complex reasons that are not entirely esthetic: Lope's preferential treatment by actors; the excesses to which his prodigal genius led him ("He is a splendid colt, but still unbridled," Góngora will say of him); and finally the compromises of his imitators, who in order to satisfy a massive demand too often produced "what sells," a theater of pure consumerism. So Cervantes pinpoints without the least indulgence the hackneyed conventions of plays *à la mode:* the impertinence of the buffoon, the keystone of the system, whose constant presence beside his master seems incongruous and jarring; or the string of marriages that caps every happy ending and whose arbitrary character he will often denounce. On the other hand, he learns to accommodate himself to the plurality of times and places. In *The Saintly Scoundrel* (El rufián dichoso), where Cervantes preaches by example, he shows us *Comedia* calming the scruples of *Curiosidad:*

> Time changes every thing and betters Art,
> Nor is it hard to increase Invention's store.
> I [Comedy] was good in ancient times
> And am not bad, if you consider it,
> Though I no longer hold all those grave precepts
> That Seneca, Terence, Plautus, and others well-known—
> The Greeks—gave me and left in their admirable works.
> Some of them I've dropped and some I keep;
> For Custom, no slave to Art, will have it so.

"To increase Invention's store" (in Spanish, "to add to what has been created") is certainly not the manifesto of an innovator. It is the simple statement of a situation in which Miguel chooses sides. The author of *Numancia* sounds more like a man who misses the days when his first plays achieved success, more like a survivor of a bygone age, than a dogmatist ever ready to legislate in the name of Aristotle. But if he is willing to make a few concessions to current fashion, he does not intend to renounce his convictions. At the very moment when his prose is giving him the chance to reclaim the audience he thought he had lost, we see him dreaming, if not of defying his younger colleague on his own ground, at least of occupying there the rank that he deserves. Let us hear him confide his hopes and disappointments in what will be the preface to his *Eight Plays* (Ocho comedias):

> Some years ago, I found myself once more at leisure, and, thinking that time had not yet dimmed my reputation, I took up writing plays again. But I found no birds in last year's nests; by which I mean that I found no producers who would take them off my hands, though they knew I had them; and so I put them in the bottom of a trunk and consigned and condemned them to perpetual silence.

Cervantes does not tell us the names of the *autores* on whom he had counted and who so disappointed his expectations. Perhaps Gaspar de Porres, who had once staged *The Mix-up* and for whom he apparently intended *The Bagnios of Algiers*—with a leading role for Catalina Hernández, Porres' wife. But Porres will end his career in 1609. Perhaps also Nicolás de los Ríos, more benevolent than his fellow *autor*. But he is going to die prematurely in 1610, and Cervantes will honor his memory in *Pedro de Urdemalas*. If he believed that he could improve his finances with the quickly earned ducats that successful poets were pocketing, this hope, too, vanished into thin air. To cap his misfortune, the death of Margarita of Austria, the wife of Philip III, which occurred on October 3, 1611, was going to bring about the closing of the *corrales* until summer 1613. Miguel's divorce from the world of the stage was complete.

What to do in these circumstances? Since the *autores* refused to help him, he had no other recourse but to do without them. On July 22, 1614, in the "Postscript" to the *Journey to Parnassus,* he confides his new plan to Pancracio de Roncesvalles: to have his plays printed,

> . . . so that [the reader] can see at leisure what goes by so quickly or is suppressed or misunderstood when plays are performed. And plays have their seasons and times, like songs.

A doubly revealing admission. Cervantes no longer feels the theatrical fever that makes the hearts of *madrileños* beat and that has possessed him for so long; he is henceforth a solitary person who enjoys the more private pleasures of reading in the silence of his modest home. But his desire for revenge is no less keen. Perhaps his *comedias* will achieve unexpected success outside the usual circles, if offered to a public of faithful readers: a fine opportunity to surprise shortsighted producers! To reverse the usual procedures was worth a gamble; but he still needed to find a publisher. Rejected by Robles, who is disinclined to plunge into this risky venture, Cervantes is going to approach one of his colleagues: but what he tells us about the reception he received is proof of his new partner's reluctance:

> At that time a bookseller told me that he would have bought them, if one of the licensed *autores* had not told him that you could expect a lot from my prose but nothing from my poetry; and to tell the truth, it grieved me to hear it. . . . I went back and looked over my plays and some interludes of mine that were packed away with them, and I saw that none of them were so bad as to not deserve to come out of the dimness of that *autor*'s wit and into the light of other *autores* who were less finicky and more understanding. I lost patience and sold them to the aforesaid bookseller, who has had them printed as he offers them to you here. He paid me reasonably well for them. I took my money meekly, without having to worry about arguing with actors.

This bookseller was named Juan de Villarroel. In July of 1615, he is going to receive the royal copyright, without which Miguel cannot send the manuscript to the printer. In mid-September, he puts the work, barely off the presses, on sale: *Eight Plays and Eight Interludes Never Performed* (Ocho comedias y ocho entremeses nunca representados). The book will once again be dedicated to Lemos. Cervantes, who had rendered homage to "the great Lope de Vega" in his preface, will let fly a Parthian arrow in the dedication in an acid allusion to actors who "from sheer cautiousness, have nothing to do with any but great works and important authors, although they make mistakes now and then." He will do it again in the interlude *The Vigilant Guard* (La guarda cuidadosa), which presents a shoemaker in ecstasy over some verses that "sound to me like Lope's, as do all things that are, or appear to be, good."

A year earlier, in the "Postscript" to the *Journey to Parnassus,* the author of *Don Quixote* claimed *six* plays and *six* interludes, whose immediate publication he announced. So he had made an effort to . expand the collection, unless he took a sheaf of unpublished works from his trunk and brought them up to date for the occasion. There are critics who believe that he resumed work on some of the plays from the period of *Numancia* and revised them: *The Forest of Love* (El bosque amoroso), *The Great Turkish Lady* (La gran turquesca), and *The Mix-up* would then be works incorrectly believed to have been lost. Re-baptized respectively *The House of Jealousy* (La casa de los celos), *The Great Sultana* (La gran sultana), and *The Labyrinth of Love* (El laberinto del amor), they would have been preserved for us at the cost of a more or less extensive revision. This hypothesis is not sufficiently well grounded to be convincing. We may assume, at least, that while Cervantes was at Seville or Valladolid, he had sketched out those plays that he decided to publish in 1615: *The Bagnios of Algiers,* for example, whose plot presents obvious coincidences with the Captive's story, interpolated in the First Part of *Don Quixote.* Others, however, were written shortly before their publication: this is probably the case with *An Entertaining Play* (La entretenida) and *Pedro de Urdemalas,* as well as the majority of the eight interludes.

Scholars wish that the author had clarified these thorny questions. But the admirable preface that he put at the beginning of the collection tells us only what he wanted to us to hear. Nevertheless, this piece of eminently subjective evidence is irreplaceable for Cervantes' views on the rise of one of the three great classical European theaters, as well as for the way in which he resigned himself to be nothing more than its precursor.

A THEATER ABOUT TO BE BORN?

WITHDRAWN from the *corrales* and unknown to the Madrid public, Cervantes' theater met with nothing but misunderstanding or indifference for years. Eclipsed by *Don Quixote* and the *Exemplary Novellas,* it became the prey of specialists who, at the beginning of this century, undertook to dissect it with their scalpels: respectable savants, but prisoners of esthetic notions imposed by the triumph of the Italian-style stage and all the more anxious, consequently, to judge rather than to comprehend works that did not meet familiar criteria.

Only the interludes escaped their condemnation, though the reputation of these farces turns out to be the result of a misunderstanding. The *entremés,* an unpretentious entertainment performed between two acts of a *comedia* (hence its name), aimed to relax the spectators; so it showed them ordinary mortals' ridiculous actions and failings, taken from everyday life. Lope de Rueda, whose repertory Miguel had applauded as an adolescent, had opened the way. Rueda's *pasos,* the direct ancestors of the interludes, felicitously exploit a whole gamut of comic behaviors, embodied in types fixed by tradition: the duplicity of the unfaithful wife, the misfortune of the overly trusting graybeard, the cleverness of the inventive student, the gaffes of the ignorant peasant (who is often more sly than he appears to be), the blustering of the braggart soldier. Taking up these tried-and-true situations, Cervantes put them in a setting drawn with sure strokes, whether the background is Madrid—the Guadalajara gate, Toledo Street—where the action of *The Judge of Divorces, The Vigilant Guard,* and *The Pretended Biscayan* (El vizcaíno fingido) takes place, or the highly stylized rustic setting of *The Aldermen of Daganzo* (Los alcaldes de Daganzo) and *The Miraculous Puppet Show* (El retablo de las maravillas).

This was enough for them to be considered *cuadros de costumbre,* quaint pictures of a bygone world. But even in the theater, the author of *Don Quixote* is not simply an observer of ephemera. The subject matter of his interludes is, above all, a kind of permanent folklore whose vitality we can appreciate even today in its proverbs, songs, and jokes. The grumbling wives in *The Judge of Divorces* are close relations of the *maumariées*—unhappily married women—of French *fabliaux;* the servant girl in *The Vigilant Guard,* courted by both a starving soldier and a prosperous sacristan, transposes in her own way the vacillations of the heroines in the Transalpine *bruscello;* the surreptitious entry of the suitor whom Hortigosa introduces into the house of *The Jealous Old Husband* (El viejo celoso) is already found in the same form in Aristophanes and Aesop; the invisible show that the charlatans of *The Miraculous Puppet Show* present derives from a polymorphous fable that will later inspire Andersen to write *The Emperor's New Clothes.*

Cervantes does not simply rejuvenate this folklore by adding allusions to the events and customs of his day. He renews its substance by grafting onto it the desires and fantasies of a Spain in crisis: first of all, the obsession with the *mancha,* the "taint" of Jewish blood or bastardy that forces the peasants of *The Miraculous Puppet Show* to proclaim that they see the wonders being described, since Jews and bastards are supposed not to be able to see them. Cervantes has also given his interludes force and vigor, thanks to the power of gesture and language. Sometimes the sequence of action or characters is enough to take the place of conventional explanations: for example, the successive appearances of the plaintiff in *The Judge of Divorces,* or the imaginary episodes that make up *The Miraculous Puppet Show.* Most frequently, the deception or trickery depicted on stage gives rise to a genuine plot, rich in repercussions and in unexpected situations: the inventiveness of the killjoy student in *The Cave of Salamanca* (La cueva de Salamanca), who, while duping a too-credulous husband, saves the adulterous wife from a difficult situation into which she has gotten herself; the effrontery of Lorenza, the heroine of *The Jealous Old Husband,* who, barricaded in her bedroom, describes in detail for the benefit of her aging husband the charms of the suitor who is making love to her. Codified situations, of course, but situations that retain their freshness thanks to the resources of expressive speech that has the power to imitate life; thanks also to the ballet of entrances and exits, to the counterpoint of gesture and mimicry, to the countermelody of dances and refrains.

Were they nothing but *genre* scenes, the interludes would deserve no more than a quick mention, a brief and condescending tribute. But Cervantes is not a moralist who depicts or denounces prejudices and false appearances. He invents a freewheeling theater, then sets it in motion; and it is the marionettes that he brings to life before our eyes who themselves, when the time comes, drop the masks that gave them human form and reduce the beings that they are supposed to represent to nothing but appearances. Thus in *The Jealous Old Husband* the adultery that takes place offstage can be described by the very woman who is committing it; the barber and the sacristan in *The Cave of Salamanca,* transformed by the student into peace-loving devils, can put the cuckolded husband's suspicions to rest; and *The Miraculous Puppet Show* opens our eyes by setting before us our own image, cast in the double reflection of an imaginary puppet show and in the characters who watch it.

In their own way, the interludes—minor works that reveal a major author—formulate the burning questions that had thrust Don Quixote out onto the roads of La Mancha: the debate between the real and the fictitious is brought to life on makeshift stages—without provoking, even for a moment, any resistance from the comic genre that contains it. On the other hand, the more ambitious *comedias* preserved by Villarroel have suffered from constant comparison with Lope's masterpieces. But they need to be appreciated for themselves, it seems to us. Some of them express an original view of Islam—different from what is customary in Turkish fantasies—in which lived experience shows through the novelistic fictionalizing. *The Bagnios of Algiers,* inspired by his captivity; *The Gallant Spaniard* (El gallardo español), which makes us relive the Turkish siege of Orán; *The Great Sultana,* which shows us Amurat at the feet of a captured Christian woman: all reveal in spite of their nationalistic fervor a carefully shaded picture of relationships between Christians and infidels.

Other plays, however, transport us into a universe of free fantasy. *The House of Jealousy* and *The Labyrinth of Love* borrow their subject matter from Ariostian tales. *An Entertaining Play* makes the very heart of Madrid the setting for a strange comedy whose confusions are the result of a supposed incest. *Pedro de Urdemalas* leads us, as we follow in the footsteps of its truculent hero, into a world saturated with rural folklore. Finally, *The Saintly Scoundrel* draws on history to present the true story of the conversion of a Sevillian libertine: Cristóbel de Lugo, touched by grace, tears himself away from the underworld and from criminals to die in the odor of sanctity in a Mexican monastery. The Cervantine *comedias,* combining the most divers motifs, woven from multiple references, fuse Poetry and History in the same crucible, where literature and life come together.

There is no doubt that the man who conceived them failed to master his craft fully. It was an arduous undertaking: how was he to transcribe the actions presented on stage without subjecting himself to current fashions? How to "re-present" them, in the fullest meaning of the word, while developing their meaning as an ensemble? Deprived of contact with the stage, cut off from a public with which he could have engaged in a fecund dialogue, Cervantes forged an experimental art that suffered from not being tested: hence the array of formulae that he tried out one by one, where episodic sequences, held together by a network of symbolic correspondences, are multiplied, often to the detriment of the action. Hence also the fluctuations of his experiments with compromise, which were influenced by the success of the *comedia nueva* but different from the pattern imposed by the Phoenix. *An Entertaining Play,* where serving men and women end by relegating their masters to the wings, and where a drunk lackey acts as confidant, can be read as a questioning of fashionable *comedias,* with their stereotypes and conventions. Nevertheless, it represents, in an oblique way, a late concession to the *arte nuevo.*

How could the *corrales* possibly have welcomed this problematical theater, which never reduces the complexity of experience to a simple, effective scheme, just when Lope was making his own formula prevail? Yet there is something very new in this quest for a different language, capable of creating by the magic of the word a world transfixed by ambiguity and doubt. It is this search that provides us with the mirror-tricks in *The Bagnios of Algiers, The Labyrinth of Love,* and *An Entertaining Play,* which by inserting theater into theater, ceaselessly plumb the changing relationships between Being and Seeming. *Pedro de Urdemalas* offers us the subtlest variation of this fascinating theme: having become an actor at the end of the play, Pedro exits from the real stage to go act on an imaginary stage; and the real play ends as the imaginary show is about to begin.

This quest, in one play after another, also expresses the movement by which characters ask themselves the meaning of their existence. Lope's heroes, swept away by opposing wills, defy established conventions; but they are in fact only trying to rediscover the values that sustain them, within a world order fixed for all eternity. Thus they identify themselves with a "Nature," taken for granted, that they vaguely aspire to unite with and to which they spontaneously adhere. The characters created by Cervantes also set out in search of themselves; but they invent themselves in proportion as they discover themselves, in order gradually to construct an identity that belongs exclusively to themselves.

Cristóbal de Lugo, the Saintly Scoundrel, gambles his destiny on a throw of the dice (like Goetz, in Sartre's *Le Diable et le Bon Dieu*): he swears, if he loses at cards, to become a highway man. When he wins, contrary to expectation, he decides to become a saint, thereby inverting the terms of his wager. Though he cooperates in the divine plan— the opposite of Goetz, who cheats—he nevertheless embodies a life-plan by virtue of a choice for which he alone is responsible. This sovereign freedom also belongs to Pedro de Urdemalas, a sort of Till Eulenspiegel who borrows his disguises and tricks from folklore. Pedro not only frees himself from his prehistory when he turns himself into a Protean actor, but, having become a "chimera," as he calls himself, he expresses himself henceforth only on the imaginary plane, thus evading any status that would cripple him by defining him. Thanks to this shape-shifting, he asserts himself fully as a being-in-process, finding his deepest truth there.

Will Cervantes' theater, which was misunderstood by his contemporaries, ever become a part of our present-day repertory? Now that the dictatorship of the "closed box" stage has come to an end, when a different theatrical apparatus has begun to alternate with the Italian-style stage, when modern techniques offer infinite possibilities to the director, this venture is no longer inconceivable. A few have already tried to carry it out: García Lorca, who, on the eve of the Spanish Civil War, as the inspirer of an itinerant troupe, brought the interludes "to the sunlight and pure air of country towns"; Jean-Louis Barrault, to whom we owe a memorable French adaptation of *Numancia* that would reveal Cervantes' theater to the Parisian public; Jacques Prévert, whose *Le Tableau des merveilles* marries the subversive audacity of *The Wonderful Puppet Show* with the ideals of the Front Populaire; closer to our own day, Francisco Nieva, the originator of a sumptuous production of *The Bagnios of Algiers.* These scattered attempts serve as valuable examples for us; one hopes that they may be continued by other experiments, so that this theater about to be born can finally come to life.

VII

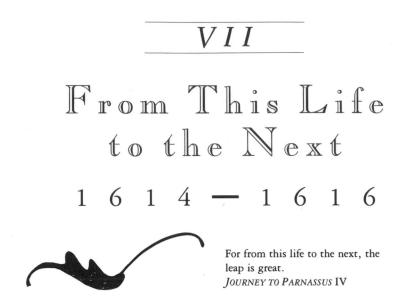

From This Life to the Next

1 6 1 4 — 1 6 1 6

For from this life to the next, the leap is great.
JOURNEY TO PARNASSUS IV

THE RETURN OF THE HEROES

Don Quixote, who left home one July evening accompanied by Sancho, is later brought back by force, thanks to the cleverness of his neighbors, the Priest and the Barber. But, convinced that he has been the victim of evil enchanters, he does not recover his sanity. The account of his return to the village shows him to us not only possessed by his monomania; it also allows us to foresee new adventures. Niece and Housekeeper, according to the narrator,

> . . . were kept in anxiety and dread lest their uncle and master should give them the slip the moment he found himself somewhat better, and, as they feared, so it happened.

Thus Cervantes seems to be promising a sequel to his novel. Unsure, however, of the reception that the First Part might get, he leaves room for doubt, prudently relying (as usual) on the discretion of Cide Hamete, his mouthpiece:

> The author of this history, though he has devoted research and industry to the discovery of the deeds achieved by Don Quixote on his third sally,

has been unable to obtain any information respecting them, at any rate none derived from authentic documents. Tradition has merely preserved in the memory of La Mancha the fact that Don Quixote, the third time he sallied forth from his home, betook himself to Zaragoza, where he was present at some famous jousts which took place in that city, and that he had adventures there worthy of his valor and his high intelligence.

These lines lift a corner of the veil on what the Second Part would be like, if it ever managed to see the light of day. The text also says specifically that the adventures of the Ingenious *Hidalgo* would end with his death. But in case the project should turn out badly, it also justifies—in advance—the possibility of giving it up, by hiding behind the silence of the archives: we would have to abandon hope of ever knowing how it ends, for want of eyewitness accounts on which the author could base this "true story." Cervantes thereby leaves himself a clear field, by playing skillfully on the device of the fictitious narrators.

Fortunately for us, he made up his mind to take up his pen again and finish his undertaking. The readers of 1605 are the first to deserve credit: full of enthusiasm for the Manchegan knight's exploits, they clamored for his return to the stage. If their wish was granted, it is probably because they had in the person of Robles a very eloquent advocate. The success of the First Part had been an excellent piece of business for the Madrid bookseller, and he had every interest in repeating his brilliant coup. But in order to do so, he first had to persuade the author. Robles must have applied friendly pressure on Miguel, after his return to the *Villa y Corte*. The appearance at Brussels of a new edition of the masterpiece and the preparation of a second Madrid reprint, through the efforts of Cuesta, must certainly have been weighty arguments. Cervantes was not indifferent to them. But how long did he wait before making up his mind? That all depends on the date assigned to Sansón Carrasco's allusion, at the beginning of the Second Part, to the popularity of the First Part and to the twelve thousand copies "in print this very day." If it dates from 1611—the most likely hypothesis—then Cervantes must have delayed four or five years: 1611 is the period of the author's last stay in Esquivias. By that date, seven reprintings, legal or clandestine, had expanded the audience of the first edition. Abroad, translators had set themselves to work: in England, Thomas Shelton had even finished his version and had gone in search of a publisher; in France, Baudoin and Richer had opened the way that César Oudin was to follow.

It will take Miguel four years to finish the job. Four years for seventy-two chapters: a faster rhythm than the one he had kept up while writing the fifty-two chapters of the First Part, spaced out over nearly six years. A remarkable performance. Even though he was rid of the Treasury agents, during all this period he experienced numerous domestic problems. And let us not forget either the *Exemplary Novellas,* to which he is going to devote most of his time up to 1612, or the other works in the mill—poems, novels, stories, plays, interludes—that he is writing in his spare time. The publication of the *Novellas* in the autumn of 1613 frees him from a heavy burden and makes him available once again. But before rejoining the Ingenious *Hidalgo,* he attempts to reassure a public that is without doubt growing impatient. He has, he tells them, finished the *Journey to Parnassus,* and he has not yet given up hope, "if life does not desert me," of offering to his admirers *The Travails of Persiles* (Los trabajos de Persiles): "But first you will see— and before long—the deeds of Don Quixote and the witticisms of Sancho continued."

Let us not take "before long" literally. The letter that Sancho, as governor of Barataria, addresses to his wife Teresa comes a year later than this declaration. It is dated July 20, 1614, and it appears in chapter 36 of the Second Part, that is to say, about halfway though the book. In anticipating himself this way, Cervantes wanted to pledge his word to Robles, who was doubtless growing irritated at seeing him scatter his efforts and dawdle over works that the publisher probably judged to be minor ones. A clever businessman, Robles knows in fact what the public prefers. In 1612, Thomas Shelton finally brings out his translation of *Don Quixote;* and in 1613, ten editions of the masterpiece, all in Castilian, are circulating around Europe; in 1614, it is César Oudin's turn to publish the first French translation. In the Old World, as in the New, ballets, parades, and masquerades provide dramatic evidence of the fame of the Knight and the popularity of his Squire. The time could not be riper to repeat the achievement.

Cervantes is now convinced. On July 22, 1614, two days before writing Sancho's letter, he composes the "Postscript" *(Adjunta)* to the *Journey to Parnassus.* The task is completed: the poem is ready to send to the printer. *Don Quixote* now becomes the immediate objective. The novelist works in great haste: in the course of the summer, in little more than two months, he writes no fewer than twenty-three chapters. Then the unforeseeable suddenly happens: at the end of September, there appears at Tarragona, thanks to the efforts of the bookseller Felipe Robert, *Book Two of the Ingenious Hidalgo Don Quixote de la Mancha,* "which contains his third sally, and is the Fifth Part of his adventures." Nine years earlier, Miguel had hinted at a sequel; one year earlier, he had announced its eminent publication; but a newcomer beats him to the draw, so to speak, a native of Tordesillas, whose name appears on the cover of the book as the licentiate Alonso Fernández de Avellaneda.

A MASKED IMPOSTER

WHILE pondering a new chapter, Cervantes sees a friend enter his house. This person, with a grave expression, hands him a volume that has just come off the press. Our writer, putting on his famous spectacles, immediately begins to "flip through it . . . without saying a word," as Don Quixote will do. Biographers have given free reign to their imaginations on this subject, needless to say. But in fact we know neither how Miguel found out about the apocryphal sequel nor what his first reaction was like. Was he really taken by surprise? In a day when ideas about literary property were different from ours and when, in addition, a very broad concept of creative imitation prevailed in literature and art, a famous poet or simply the lucky author of a successful book was almost certain to have emulators. Thus in Cinquecento Italy, Ariosto's *Orlando furioso* had taken up the gauntlet thrown down by Boiardo with his *Orlando innamorato.* In Renaissance Spain, the vogue of *Celestina* had caused a flood of continuations, more or less faithful to the spirit of the original, which authorizes literary historians to speak of a "Celestinesque genre." During the reign of Philip II, *Lazarillo de Tormes* had in its turn engendered a whole tribe of descendents, while Gaspar Gil Polo continued Montemayor's *Diana* with a *Diana in Love* that is not unworthy of its model. More recently, in 1602, a certain Mateo Luján de Sayavedra had brought out a *Part Two of Guzmán de Alfarache,* while Alemán was still working to finish his own. The practice, as one can see, was widespread.

How could *Don Quixote* escape this common fate? In his 1605 pre-

face, Cervantes had stated that he was not the father but the stepfather
of his hero; in the course of his tale, he had hidden behind the fictitious chroniclers of the supposedly true story; he had announced new
adventures without telling us who their narrator would be. A third
sally of the Knight? Let us not lose hope (he declares, in substance) of
learning more about it. But instead of committing himself further, he
prefers to reply with Ariosto, by adapting to his purpose the last verse
of *Orlando furioso*:

Forse altri canterà con miglior plectro

("Perhaps another will sing with better plectrum," that is, continue
this story with greater skill.) To end on this note—even if it is part of
the humor—was tantamount to an invitation; and an unknown person
hastened to accept it.

A masked person rather than an unknown one. For more than four
centuries, scholars have been asking questions about the personality of
the mysterious Avellaneda—in vain. Up to now, all the efforts expended
to identify him have been, admittedly, useless. Biographers believe
they have found, one after another, at least ten persons of all sorts and
conditions hiding behind the pseudonym: literary men, among them
Mateo Alemán, Bartolomé de Argensola, and, of course, Lope de Vega
(who in fact might well have written the preface); a great lord, the
duke of Sessa, the friend and protector of Lope; a Dominican friar,
Juan Blanco de Paz, whose slanders Miguel had endured in Algiers;
another Dominican, Fray Luis de Aliaga, the very confessor of the
king. Some have even asked themselves, in desperation, whether the
author of the apocryphal *Don Quixote* was not really and truly named
Avellaneda. But this has not provided a way out of the labyrinth.
Cervantes, through the mouth of his hero, suggested a path of investigation when he observed that the forger's language was Aragonese,
because (he tells us) Avellaneda "sometimes writes without articles."
It is, however, necessary to understand the meaning of this remark: it
is not the peculiarities of a style larded with regionalisms that are held
up to criticism but rather the errors and clumsy expressions that the
style contains. More significant are the writer's tics uncovered by modern criticism: quotations in Church Latin, exaggerated praise of monastic
life, repeated allusions to the cult of the rosary. They seem to point
the finger, not at some cleric or scholastic, but at the soldier-writer

Jerónimo de Pasamonte, who (one may recall) inspired Cervantes with the idea for the galley slave Ginés. Pasamonte, of Aragonese origin, may have put his pen at the service of Lope, thus helping to complicate even more the already tangled history of the squabble between the two great writers. Ginés de Pasamonte, let us note in passing, will reappear in the authentic Second Part, in the guise of Maese Pedro, the puppeteer whose little figures are cut to bits by the Knight. The hypothesis is interesting; but it is only a hypothesis, lacking truly provable arguments. Until we know more, Avellaneda will remain a mystery to us.

This pseudonym, had it been adopted for a purpose that its bearer could openly acknowledge, would have been a harmless deception, the customary spice of one of the hoaxes regularly practiced in the literary world. We find all of their characteristic traits at the beginning of the volume: the *aprobación* and the licence to print that grace it are of course false, for the simple reason that the two signers did not have the power to authorize the edition; also false is the mention of Felipe Robert, a printer who had closed his shop a year earlier; equally false is the place of publication, because in all likelihood Avellaneda had his book printed at Barcelona. Everything considered, Miguel might have been amused, without paying the matter much attention, by this unlooked-for disciple's indirect homage: a sort of student's joke, obvious from the start in the dedication addressed "to the mayor, aldermen, and gentlemen of the noble city of Argamasilla, fortunate homeland of the gentle knight Don Quixote."

But there is the scandalous abuse in the preface, with its string of calumnies and insults. We may grant that Avellaneda—with Lope's intervention, perhaps—was trying to set himself apart from his predecessor and will even concede that he was bound to compare his prologue with those that Cervantes has left us: he wanted his to be "less boastful and hostile to its readers" than *Don Quixote*'s preface, while being "humbler" than the preface of the *Exemplary Novellas*. With the virulence that is usual in such writing, this prologue was supposed to take the wind out of the sails of the *raro inventor* in order to persuade him to show more modesty. But what is unacceptable is that the Aragonese writer should have taken unfair advantage by stringing together a series of attacks *ad hominem*. He makes fun, openly, of the infirmities of his victim, "who himself admits that he has only one [hand]." Then he shamelessly attacks Cervantes' age, before taunting him with having "more tongue than hands," more ability to slander than courage, adding,

> And since Miguel de Cervantes is already like San Cervantes Castle * from sheer age, and so crotchety because of his years that everything and everybody annoys him, and is so friendless because of it that when he wanted to adorn his books with high-sounding sonnets, he had to foist them off (as he says) on Prester John of the Indies or on the Emperor of Trebizond, because there was not a titled nobleman in Spain, perhaps, who would not consider himself offended to hear Cervantes speak his name . . .

One may recall that this is what the Phoenix had already implied in his letter of 1604. Meanwhile, Miguel had renewed his friendship with his readers: hence the acerbic conclusion by the apocryphal novel's preface-writer:

> Let him be satisfied with his *Galatea* and his plays in prose—which is what most of his novellas are—and stop boring us.

Avellaneda, not content with assuming the paternity of these insulting remarks, will return to them in the course of his story by attributing to his own hero defamatory statements about Catalina de Salazar, called *conversa* by the Knight and suspected of unfaithfulness to her husband. Cervantes a cuckold? The author of the anonymous sonnet from Valladolid had already said it crudely enough, though he actually did little more than gloss a proverb that plays on Miguel's surname and jeers at the antlers that grace the brow of *ciervos*—deer—and people named Cervantes. A *cervantes,* in the Golden Age, was (in plain language) a deceived husband; and our Cervantes must have had to endure this joke innumerable times during his life. What personal grievances could the Aragonese have harbored against Cervantes to insult him so grossly? Perhaps he (Pasamonte?) was resentful that Cervantes had presented his homonym Ginés as a lawless, faithless galley slave. Perhaps, whether his name was Pasamonte or not, he also simply envied Cervantes' genius. To put Don Quixote and Sancho back in the saddle for the length of one episode was doubtless within the grasp of any hack writer. But it was quite another matter to bring them to life and keep

---

* A medieval fort at the gates of Toledo, also called San Servando.

them alive from the beginning to the end of their new adventures. And between the original masterpiece and the apocryphal sequel, there is not a shadow of a comparison possible. They are not simply separated by a chasm: they are two different worlds. The plot constructed by Avellaneda is not, in itself, very interesting: Don Quixote and Sancho set out for Zaragoza, in accord with what had been announced; once there, they take part in the jousts and cover themselves at every turn with ridicule or opprobrium; city-dwellers at heart, they go from town to town, stop at Alcalá, then at Madrid, each of their stages punctuated by grotesque or repulsive incidents; on the road they acquire a female companion named Bárbara, a former prostitute whose filthiness is equaled only by her stupidity. Their peregrinations end at Toledo, where Don Quixote will live out his days in an insane asylum.

A puppet accompanied by a buffoon: that is how the Knight and his Squire appear to us throughout the story. This portrayal derives from the way the two heroes react to situations that confront them: incapable of understanding them, strangers in the world in which they move, they tirelessly reproduce, with mechanical regularity, the same stereotyped behaviors, the same incongruities, the same slapstick. The spectacle of their extravagant actions is thus an index of the indifference, or rather the antipathy, that the author feels toward his characters, as if Avellaneda wanted to cover them with the aversion that he claims to feel for books of chivalry. Each of their adventures concludes with a setback that brings them the worst humiliations and drags them toward an inexorable downfall. Never, consequently, do we feel we see Don Quixote and Sancho act before our eyes. Cervantes' heroes embodied a project that they pursued obstinately in spite of their disappointments. Avellaneda's creatures are not alive; they are simply marionettes that gradually fall apart, drifting along at the mercy of events. Their apparent relationship is merely a dialogue between two deaf men, a perpetual alternation between two redundant and verbose soliloquies.

The only merit of this mediocre book is that it is a perfect foil, a gauge against which we take the measure of a masterpiece by simply observing the counterfeit that it inspired. But in order to assume this uncongenial role, it was not enough for the apocryphal *Don Quixote* to have made use of the services of a pirate publisher. It had to survive bestsellerdom, to pass into posterity somehow or other. The only person who could save it from its ephemeral nature and snatch it from oblivion was, of course, Cervantes; and he will succeed in doing so.

THE RESPONSE TO THE CHALLENGE

TEN years earlier, Mateo Alemán, the victim of a similar mishap, had avenged himself properly. His plagiarizer, a Valencian named Juan Martí, had also hidden behind a pseudonym, calling himself Mateo Luján de Sayavedra. Alemán then had the idea of involving Martí in his hero's new adventures. He makes him Guzmán's companion, in the person of a beggar named Sayavedra, a poor excuse for a companion (we hasten to add), who, after making friends with our *pícaro* in Rome, steals his baggage and runs away. He meets Guzmán again at Bologna and becomes his accomplice and shadow; finally, he embarks for Barcelona with the *pícaro*. Sayavedra goes mad, believes that he is Guzmán de Alfarache, and in his delirium throws himself overboard. This cruel ending to a symbolic story speaks volumes about the resentment that Martí's dirty trick had roused in the Father of the Picaresque Novel.

Cervantes is going to proceed in a different way, though his response will be no less vigorous. Mateo Alemán takes out his spite exclusively on the author of the hoax, pursuing him with his fury and saving a shameful fate for him at the end. Cervantes, on the contrary, is going to respond to his adversary's remarks with disdain; on the threshold of the Second Part, he settles the score in one of those prefaces at which he was so successful and for which Avellaneda provides an introductory subject. Miguel knows with what feverish eagerness people are awaiting his reply. Unfortunately, this expectation is going to be disappointed:

> God bless me, gentle or even plebeian reader, how eagerly must you be looking forward to this preface, expecting to find there retaliation, scolding, and abuse against the father of the second Don Quixote—I mean him who was, they say, begotten at Tordesillas and born at Tarragona. Well, the truth is, I am not going to give you that satisfaction, for though injuries stir up anger in humbler breasts, in mine the rule must grant an exception. You would have me call him ass, fool, and insolent intruder, but I have no such intention. Let his offence be his punishment: "with his bread let him eat it"; let him worry about it.

Did Miguel ever learn who was hiding behind the name Avellaneda? He appears never to have concerned himself with this unknown person, whom he will reproach expressly for only one thing, the personal insults:

> What I cannot help resenting is that he charges me with being old and one-handed, as if it had been in my power to hinder time's passage, or as if the loss of my hand had occurred in some tavern and not on the grandest occasion the past or present has seen or the future can hope to see. If my wounds have no beauty in the beholder's eye, they are, at least, honorable in the estimation of those who know where they were received. The soldier shows to greater advantage dead in battle than alive in flight.

The reply has a certain elegance; but it also exudes the melancholy of a survivor of a bygone era. In Philip III's Spain, people have short memories. How many are left to silence Avellaneda and his like when they scoff, "Lepanto: never heard of it"?

There is only one way to have done with the counterfeiter: send him into oblivion before the very eyes of the scoffers. Just like the madman in the apologue, who inflated the first dog he met, as if it were a wineskin, accosting passers-by to be witnesses of his exploit, so Avellaneda thought that writing a book was child's play. But here he is, caught in his own trap. The implicit conclusion: let him go to the madhouse himself, and let us hear no more about him.

There remains the *corpus delicti,* the apocryphal second part. Miguel is going to save his best arrows for it; but he is going to do so as an artist of genius, by incorporating it indirectly into the very substance of his own fiction. First, Don Quixote meets two readers of Avellaneda's novel in his travels. Disappointed by the foolishness of what they have just read, they submit the work to Don Quixote's verdict. He contents himself with leafing through it, but he still discovers "two or three things in this author that deserve to be censured," in particular the fact that Teresa, his squire's wife, has been renamed María Gutiérrez. An insignificant example, but chosen on purpose to catch the pretended historian *in flagrante delicto*—and to provoke the astonishment of Sancho, who is nonplussed by this registry-office error. "Don't be surprised," the two gentlemen reply to Sancho:

> ". . . He makes you a glutton and a fool, and not in the least witty, and very different from the Sancho described in the First Part of your master's history."

"God forgive him," said Sancho. "He should have left me in my corner without troubling his head about me."

Confronted with a caricature of himself, Sancho vehemently claims his true essence—thereby gaining additional reality. And Don Quixote is also quite anxious to set himself apart from his double. He does not confine himself merely to damning the apocryphal work every time he uncovers a new copy of it. Since the impostor went to Zaragoza, he himself will refrain from setting foot there:

> ". . . And by that means I shall expose to the world the lie of this new history writer, and people will see that I am not the Don Quixote he speaks of."

Having thus recovered his full autonomy, the Ingenious *Hidalgo* will be ready for the most extraordinary of his encounters: the meeting with one of the characters invented by the plagiarizer. Avellaneda's Quixote, imprisoned at Zaragoza for having obstructed justice, is freed thanks to the intervention of a Morisco gentleman named Don Alvaro Tarfe. Cervantes is going to introduce this newcomer, Tarfe, into his own story. Don Alvaro, who in all good faith claims to be a friend of the Knight of the Woeful Countenance, is approached courteously by the real Don Quixote. Naturally, Tarfe does not recognize him. How could it have been otherwise? The man who stands before him has nothing in common with the person he saved from the hands of the executioner. Sancho, also a victim of the same misunderstanding, loses his temper and heaps abuse on the swindler who is passing himself off as Sancho:

> "That Sancho your worship speaks of, gentle sir, must be some great scoundrel, bore, and thief, all in one; for I am the real Sancho Panza, and I have tons of clever remarks. . . . And the real Don Quixote de la Mancha . . . is this gentleman before you, my master; all other Don Quixotes and all other Sancho Panzas are deceptions and illusions."

This is more than enough to convince Don Alvaro:

> ". . . In the few words that you have spoken, you have uttered more witticisms . . . than the other Sancho Panza in all I ever heard from him."

Persuaded that he has been the plaything of enchanters, the Morisco gentleman thanks Sancho for having opened his eyes; he will agree willingly to confirm the tenor of his statement before a notary.

While perpetuating the memory of Avellaneda's novel, Cervantes has also given it the *coup de grâce*. He underlines the examples of lack of verisimilitude, as necessary; but he entrusts to his own characters the task of showing that this abortive history is also a false history. Caught in the crossfire between the narrator and his heroes, the apocryphal *Don Quixote* never recovers from this counterattack that brings together, in one impulse, both criticism and creation. Miguel, master of the game for which he has made the rules, remains without difficulty master of the terrain.

The encounter with Alvaro Tarfe comes just before the end of the "real" adventures of Don Quixote and Sancho. In January of 1615, Cervantes brings the work to a close. It must have taken him barely six months to compose the last fifteen chapters of his novel. There remain the preliminary negotiations for its publication: they will be accomplished in two months. Robles, in possession of two *aprobaciones* in correct legal form, signed by Márquez Torres and Valdivieso respectively, and armed with a twenty-year copyright good for the entire Spanish Empire, hastened to turn the manuscript over to Juan de la Cuesta. At the end of October, Miguel writes the preface in which he gives the impudent licentiate a piece of his mind. On the last day of the same month, he dedicates the work to his acknowledged Maecenas, "whose Christian charity and well-known generosity support me against all the strokes of my parsimonious fortune." Once again, Lemos maintains his reputation. But another protector is also encouraging the writer's projects: Cardinal Sandoval y Rojas, the duke of Lerma's uncle. Cervantes was doubtless presented to him during one of the meetings of the Confraternity of the Most Holy Sacrament. He will put him together with Lemos in the stirring tributes that he pays the two princes who, he says, have come to his aid "unsought by any adulation or flattery of mine." We find the same tune repeated by all the writers who benefited from their generosity; so Miguel is expressing himself without hypocrisy, as a man who has only to boast of the belated attention of which he has been the object, in the evening of his life.

A few weeks later, at the end of November, the Madrid public was holding in its hands the long-awaited book, the *Part Two of the Inge-*

nious Knight Don Quixote de la Mancha. By Miguel de Cervantes Saavedra, Author of Its First Part. With the object of reclaiming his property—who can blame him?—Miguel was offering his readers a sequel "cut by the same craftsman and from the same cloth as the *First {Part}.*" Having become a Knight *(caballero)*, the Ingenious Gentleman *(hidalgo)* sees his promotion duly recognized by being inscribed on the title page of the account of his new adventures—an extended *(dilatado)* account, according to the author, brought to its conclusion, but also amplified and broadened: fidelity to the design conceived fifteen years earlier, from which the masterpiece had sprung, but also evidence that it has surpassed and overflowed that first sketch, a daring challenge that is going to be met.

DON QUIXOTE, CONTINUATION AND CONCLUSION

THE readers of 1615, however impatient they may have been, see their expectations fulfilled. The authentic Second Part not only confirmed the qualities of the First, it raised the novel to the peak of perfection, guaranteeing an immediate success that posterity will merely corroborate.

As Cervantes had himself announced, this volume deals with Don Quixote's third and final sally, in which Sancho is, of course, involved, and which takes the two companions far from their village. Having set out for Zaragoza, they revise their plans en route and eventually go as far as Barcelona—in the steps of their creator—before taking the road home. This expedition has three phases. The first is the adventures at the beginning (among which the arrival at El Toboso, the enchantment of Dulcinea, the single combat with the Knight of the Woods, the descent into Montesino's Cave, and Master Peter's puppet show stand out). Next, the stay with the duke and duchess, who, in order to amuse themselves at the expense of their guests, start the pair on a series of carefully staged adventures that include the disenchantment of Dulcinea, the ride on Clavileño, Sancho's governorship in Barataria. Finally, coinciding with the discovery of the apocryphal sequel, the visit to Barcelona, where Don Quixote is defeated by the Knight of the White Moon. Having promised at the insistence of his adversary not to bear arms for a year, our dejected hero returns to his village, where he will die after having recovered his reason.

This third sally looks to new horizons, in comparison with the preceding escapades. Let us recall the First Part: master and man, having arrived in the Sierra Morena, had gone directly to Maritornes' inn and had not left it until the final intervention of the false enchanters. From now on, they extend the field of their explorations: the pastoral setting of Camacho's wedding, the majestic banks of the Ebro, the manorial forests that surround the duke's palace, the village where Sancho will carry out his duties as governor. The urban setting of Barcelona, from which the Mediterranean stretches as far as the eye can see, extends the space of the fiction even more. At the same time, the beings who appear through chance encounters, either as full-fledged actors (as is more often the case) or as mere extras, offer us a whole range of sorts and conditions: peasants and shepherds, actors on tour, clandestine Moriscos, highwaymen, country squires, Catalan gentlemen, grandees surrounded by their households—an entire *comédie humaine* parades before our eyes as if to anchor the action more firmly in daily reality and to accentuate further the impression of lived experience; likewise, after Ricote (the living embodiment of the Morisco problem), Roque Guinart (an authentic Catalan bandit, with whom Don Quixote has a memorable interview) ensures the intersecting of adventure with present-day reality.

Far from becoming lost in this expanded world, Don Quixote and Sancho, on the contrary, become the pivot around which it turns. From the outset, they impose their presence by the very way in which they animate the plot. Instead of allowing themselves to be carried along by events or wandering as their fancy dictates, they set themselves a precise goal—Zaragoza and its jousts—and stick to it, not allowing themselves to be sidetracked from their route, even if they happen to prolong their stops beyond what they may have foreseen. Their stay with the duke certainly suspends their journey and even forces them to be separated briefly; but they continue to occupy the foreground, at the pleasure of their host. And while it is true that Don Quixote decides not to attend the Aragonese jousts and changes his itinerary *in extremis,* he thereby confirms his free determination.

The result is an architecture different from what the author had conceived ten years earlier. In the First Part, the principal action often gave way to secondary actions that ended up by complicating the story:

the two protagonists then became observers of adventitious events; at times, even, they were simply listeners to interpolated narratives. Cervantes, in a sort of retrospective examination, will insist on defending this technique, for which he apparently received criticism. However, he will renounce this ambitious construction, which at times threatened to dissipate the reader's attention. This time, he will say, I have decided not "to insert stories, either separate or interwoven, but only episodes, something like them, arising out of the circumstances the facts present, and even these sparingly, and with no more words than suffice to make them plain." So he justifies the inclusion of six episodic stories that, thanks to the direct and sometimes decisive participation of our two heroes, are organically bound to the principal action. Doña Rodríguez, the duchess's duenna, appeals to Don Quixote, defender of widows and orphans, to force her daughter's lover to keep his promise and marry the young lady. At the initiative of the duke, who seizes the opportunity to enrich the repertory of his masquerades, the Knight challenges the man he believes to be a vile seducer to judicial combat in the lists. But Don Quixote faces a mere straw man, set up for the requirements of the spectacle, since his real adversary is absent, having fled in haste: hence the flood of misunderstandings and cross-purposes. Another example of this subordination: the nocturnal escapade of Diego de la Llana's daughter, who, "in order to see the whole town," leaves her house in men's clothing. This novelistic enterprise, which might form the basis of some Italianate novella, has Barataria as its setting. It is suddenly cut short by the appearance of Governor Sancho, whose officers have caught the beautiful girl and who sends her home to her father after a strongly worded sermon.

So Don Quixote's plan not only determines the itinerary that he and his servant undertake; it also controls the movement of the story and its economy. Such a design, obviously, does not simply express the curiosity of a country gentleman who suddenly feels the urge to see the world. For the Ingenious *Hidalgo,* taking part in the Zaragoza jousts means manifesting, in the fullest sense of the word, his existence: to show himself in the flesh to all those who know him only through the story of his exploits. He learns of this story even before setting out again on the highroads. Illiterate Sancho is the first to find out about it, and he hastens to inform his master:

> "Last night the son of Bartolomé Carrasco, who has been studying at Salamanca, came home after having been made a bachelor, and when I

went to welcome him, he told me that Your Worship's history is already in books, with the title of *The Ingenious Gentleman Don Quixote of La Mancha.* And he says they mention me in it by my own name, Sancho Panza, and the lady Dulcinea del Toboso too, and various things that happened to us when we were alone, so that I crossed myself in amazement at how the historian who wrote them down could have known them."

Don Quixote is no less excited; but he is not astonished by the tour de force that amazes his servant, which he himself considers well within the capability of any enchanter. His anxiety is different: "If . . . such a history did indeed exist, as the story of a knight-errant, it was bound to be grandiloquent, lofty, imposing, splendid, and true." But does it fulfill all of these conditions? In other words, does it conform to the canon of the epic, which is not poetically true unless it transfigures the hero whose exploits it extols?

What Sancho tells us about it—Sancho being thrilled to learn that his acts overlap with his masters'—suggests that it does not; and that is precisely what is going to come out in the explanations offered by Sansón Carrasco. To judge by what the bachelor tells us, the ideal epic the Knight dreamed of is in reality a funny chronicle composed by a Moor and translated from Arabic into Castilian for the universal amusement of everyone: a chronicle that, consequently, depends on the particular truthfulness of the story; a chronicle true to the point of including the most humble details:

"The sage left nothing in the inkwell . . . He tells all and sets down everything, even to the capers that worthy Sancho cut in the blanket."

Even the beatings received by the Ingenious *Hidalgo* are described with great precision.

An astounding debate then begins on this delicate question. On the one hand, Don Quixote censures Cide Hamete for having contravened the precepts of the *Poetics*. He might fairly have passed over in silence these beatings that he records with such exactitude:

"There is no need to record events which do not change or affect the truth of a history, if they tend to bring the hero of it into contempt. Aeneas was not in truth and earnest so pious as Virgil represents him, nor Ulysses so wise as Homer describes him."

To which Sansón, inverting the argument, replies: because Cide Hamete wanted to write as a historian and not as a poet. It is Sansón's turn to quote Aristotle, slyly, in support of his opinions:

> ". . . It is one thing to write as a poet, another to write as a historian. The poet may describe or sing things, not as they were, but as they ought to have been, while the historian has to write them down, not as they ought to have been, but as they were, without adding to or subtracting from the truth."

In this way, from the initial discovery of the First Part to the final revelation of the authentic sequel, criticism and creation keep up an uninterrupted dialogue, on which the very substance of the novel feeds.

What is actually in play is not the literary tastes of Don Quixote or the esthetic choices of the pseudo-narrator; it goes beyond the controversy that sets the *hidalgo* against the bachelor. It is the demand that others recognize the image of himself that the Knight wants to leave behind; it is also—through all his wavering between the profile he dreams of and the one forced on him—his obstinate demand for an independence that he asserts with stubborn persistence. Hence he refuses to read Cide Hamete's story; hence he vigorously denounces Avellaneda's sequel, in his anxiety to set himself apart from his double, from the impostor who has stolen his name. He draws renewed strength from his demand; but, at the same time, he finds himself divided between his historical character and his poetic character: amending the one, then exalting the other, he lives to the end in what Marthe Robert, in a happy phrase, calls his perpetual vagabondage between his real-life existence and his paper existence.

THE NEW ODYSSEY

IF Cervantes delayed in deferring to Robles's wishes, it was because reviving his heroes presented him with a double risk: if Don Quixote and Sancho remained the same, they would inevitably ossify; changed, they would find their consistency affected. In order to surmount these alternatives, their creator decided to gamble (successfully, as it turned out): to bring the pair face-to-face at once with the image that readers had formed of them. Master and servant, as Thomas Mann correctly observed, live on the reputation of their own reputations. Such a thing had never before occurred in literature. The two heroes, anxious to dissociate themselves from books and legends that spread suspect truths about them, renew themselves in the course of situations to which they adapt their conduct; but to preserve their essence still remains their sole ambition.

Hence the outlines that their odyssey now assumes. In the First Part, Don Quixote was, as certain critics have observed, the "jack-of-all-trades of his own epic": while he was forging his identity, he invented, in the same impulse, his own world; as a result of his madness, the inn became a castle and the windmills giants. Now, though he takes to the highways again, he no longer transforms things; it is circumstances or, quite simply, men who fabricate a world to suit his exploits or his wishes. On occasion, adventure comes of its own accord. Trusting in his star, the hero goes resolutely to meet his fate: thus he will defy a lion in its cage, only to have the wild beast turn its back on him; or he will descend to the depths of Montesinos' Cave, where he will have, as he says later, the most extraordinary adventures.

More often, the adventure is born of some individual's will, even if we do not discover that person's involvement until later. The enchantment of Dulcinea is clearly the invention of Sancho, who, in order to conceal from his master that he has not carried out the mission with which he has been charged, identifies the first peasant girl who comes into view as the Lady of Don Quixote's thoughts; he brazenly insists that Don Quixote, who naturally claims not to recognize her, is the plaything of enchanters once more. The love of Gaiferos and the fair Melisendra is enclosed in the space of a marionette theater; Don Quixote, a victim of dramatic illusion, bursts onto the scene, to the great harm of the puppeteer and his puppets. The vicissitudes that punctuate the stay at the duke's palace are essentially the result of a gigantic practical joke, in which servants and vassals collaborate, each playing the role that is assigned to him: Clavileño is a wooden courser on which our two heroes, blindfolded, believe they are taking a celestial ride; Dulcinea, who suddenly reappears in a phantasmagorical setting, is only a page in women's clothing; the Isle of Barataria, of which Sancho becomes governor, is peopled with supernumeraries who until the final upheaval execute their instructions to the letter. Finally, Don Quixote's two combats with his fellow knights-errant (the one against the Knight of the Wood, victorious; the other against the Knight of the White Moon, unfortunate) are both hoaxes: in both, the adversary is none other than Sansón Carrasco, who is metamorphosed into a paladin to suit the occasion.

In this *trompe-l'oeil* universe, the borderline between the hero's illusions and the reality that surrounds him is not fixed, as it was formerly. Don Quixote now operates in a world of appearances, an unsettled world that reflects his own inner world while distorting it. At one moment it is created out of nothing by a demiurge who may be Sancho, Maese Pedro, the duke, or Sansón; at other times, it is arranged like a dream that we relive through the narrative of which it is the object. The resultant play of mirrors is multiplied to infinity, without our being able to draw with a steady hand the border between Being and Seeming: even Teresa Panza, in spite of her robust good sense, eventually gives up trying when a page bringing a necklace from the duchess and a letter from Sancho the governor appears before her. One of those present at this scene summarizes the general feeling perfectly: persuaded that it is "the doings of our fellow townsman Don Quixote, who thinks that everything is done by enchantment," he asks to touch and feel the page "to see whether [he is] an ambassador of the imagination or a man of flesh and blood."

The reader-accomplice, of course, smiles at this confusion, because he knows what he is supposed to believe about this affair. But he begins to feel less assured as he follows the developments of the adventure of Dulcinea: the disenchantment under certain conditions promised by the wizard Merlin is a conclusion one might expect in third-rate fiction. But Merlin is one of the duke's bit-part actors; Dulcinea has never been under a spell; and neither Don Quixote nor Sancho has ever met her in his life. Does the reader now want to ask the narrator for help? Then he is in trouble. The "admirable things" that the Knight claims to have seen in the Cave of Montesinos are such that Cide Hamete, forced to rely on the hero's word alone, is close to believing that he is dealing with an apocryphal adventure, though he judges it impossible that Don Quixote could be lying. Even Don Quixote asks himself whether he has dreamed up what happened to him during his descent. As for Cide Hamete, he is himself a fictitious narrator, whose efforts, always suspect, constantly sow doubt in our minds. "A genuine adventure?" asks Cide Hamete. "A credible adventure?" asks the reader. So many questions unanswered by an episode that is nevertheless an essential stage in the spiritual itinerary of the character.

Illusion is constantly being married to artifice in the course of this odyssey that, paradoxically, is intended to take revenge for the "real" Don Quixote on the phantoms that have usurped his identity. This revenge of Truth over Falsehood is also intended to protect us from the vertigo that, as Borges observes, makes us wonder whether we ourselves are not also fictional beings. Nevertheless, it contributes to the multiplication of planes and perspectives, because this truth remains a truth of books, and because the struggle of a hero preceded by his reputation brings the over-and-done-with novel into the heart of the ongoing novel. Don Quixote, determined to stand for Life, remains, to the end, a creature of Fiction. What makes him fascinating is due largely to this ambiguity. It shows through even in his conversation. He prudently answers the duchess, who asks him whether Dulcinea is imaginary or real, that "there are things the proof of which must not be pushed to extreme lengths." As for knowing whether he "begot and gave birth to [her] in his brain," that is a pointless question, in his opinion:

> "I have not begotten nor given birth to my lady, though I behold her as she necessarily must be, a lady who contains in herself all the qualities to make her famous throughout the world . . ."

This is enough to cause the duchess to renounce further inquiry: Dulcinea's essence is independent of her existence; it resides in her perfection.

Don Quixote's caution is not without a touch of slyness, to the point of making us occasionally suspect the apparent ease with which the Knight seems to allow himself to be duped. A phrase that he whispers into Sancho's ear, when his squire gives a mind-boggling account of his flight on Clavileño's back, speaks volumes about Don Quixote's lucidity:

> "Sancho, as you would have us believe what you saw in Heaven, I require you to believe me as to what I saw in the Cave of Montesinos. I say no more."

Critics have concluded that Don Quixote has become somewhat "Sanchified," while at the same time his squire, convinced that he is really the governor of Barataria, is becoming "Quixotized" after his fashion.

We certainly see the confirmation of a reciprocal contamination between master and servant, of which we had a foretaste in the First Part. But the experience of power opens Sancho's eyes. He bids farewell to his vassals, leaving them "filled with admiration not only at his remarks but at his firm and sensible resolution." Don Quixote, on the other hand, remains convinced that he has revived knight-errantry, and his conviction is all the stronger because everyone makes an effort to maintain it: some in order to make fun of him, others because he is famous, thanks to the account of his previous adventures. His stay in Barcelona, where he makes a triumphal entry and sees himself received with all honors, marks the apogee of his career while taking his derangement to its limit. Under these conditions, his defeat by the Knight of the White Moon is not simply one more practical joke, it is the fall from the Tarpeian Rock following the exaltation of the Capitol. Forced to lay down his arms and take the road home, the Ingenious *Hidalgo* finally starts on the way that will lead him to sanity. When he recovers his reason on his deathbed, he becomes Alonso Quijano again; he lays aside his immoderate ambition and pride. But he insists in vain— however deep his repentance—that he is no longer Don Quixote: it is not in his power to renounce his identity. Alonso Quijano gives up the ghost after having denounced the books of chivalry; but in the death certificate that the notary prepares, it will say that Quijano is commonly called Don Quixote de la Mancha; and in fact it is with this name that he has passed into eternity.

DEATH AND TRANSFIGURATION

COULD Don Quixote have ended his days in some other way? Thomas Mann asked himself this same question. To strike him down with a violent death while he was still mad would have meant giving him an absurd fate; but contriving a peaceful old age would have amounted to condemning him to an end unworthy of him. Alonso Quijano recovers his wits only to go from life to death. But it is neither to expiate his error nor to prevent some new Avellaneda from sending him forth on the highways again; it is because this outcome is the logical conclusion of a plan—one that dooms our hero to be contradicted at the very moment when he believes that he has achieved his purpose. All during his odyssey, the Ingenious *Hidalgo* exerts himself in his determination to surpass himself; both the truth and the mystery of his character reside in this split between his vocation and his destiny, and (depending on how one perceives this mystery) in its capacity to produce new meanings. Cervantes' contemporaries gave the Second Part a reception similar to that which the First Part had received. Because they were sensitive to the parodic flavor of this pseudo-epic, they took delight in the exploits of a madman. Quevedo will compose a farcical poem on the touching subject of Don Quixote's will, while Lope de Vega, in a retort in one of his *comedias,* will go so far as to dream of

> . . . a female Don Quixote
> Who will make the whole world laugh.

This is the only way classical Europe understood the Knight of the Woeful Countenance. Saint-Amant, in *La Chambre du débauché,* recalls Don Quixote's "most grotesque adventures" and shows him to us "in pitiful estate . . . in a great ditch full of mud, ground to bits, like grain":

> *Dans un grand fossé plein de boue,*
> *Aussi moulu comme le grain.*

A little later, Charles Sorel will mine the same vein with his *Berger extravagant,* which transposes quixotic follies into the pastoral mode. In Restoration England, Samuel Butler will imagine his Hudibras, the preposterous champion of the Presbyterian cause, in the guise of a potbellied knight, flanked by a squire who is equally ridiculous. It is a time when the burlesque is triumphant, an epoch still faithful to the spirit of Carnival, even though the arrival of the modern state is accompanied by the emergence of new values. One wonders whether, with the evolution of taste and habits, some happy few did not have a different opinion: Molière, for example, who in 1660 will play—if "quite badly"—the role of Sancho in *Don Quichot ou les Enchantements de Merlin,* "a play revised by Mademoiselle Béjart" which we have unfortunately lost; or La Fontaine, who admits to us that Cervantes delights him; or Saint-Evremont, who, we are told, "constantly read *Don Quixote* and finished it only to begin it again." These overly restrained allusions tantalize without satisfying our curiosity.

In the eighteenth century there appear the first signs of a change that will become more evident in the course of years, proving the rule that every great work escapes from its creator. Though the Knight's misadventures continue to make people laugh, Spain's decay confers a new significance on them. This insane man, who obstinately defends the heroic ideals of a bygone age, who encounters misunderstanding in everyone he meets on his way, and who does not give up his illusions until his deathbed, prefigures for the men of the Enlightenment the decline of his nation. It is German Romanticism that takes the decisive step: as the expression par excellence of human duality, the synthesis of drama and epic, the symbol of the encounter of Being and Non-being, the quixotic adventure is going to become a mythic odyssey whose protagonist will be the hero of modern times. This transfiguration of the masterpiece has occasionally been censured as a misinterpretation. It certainly neglects the author's avowed purpose; it considers the values which had such great meaning for the first readers as merely accessory; and it is bound, as are other phenomena, to the exaltation of the individual, which in the nineteenth century became the supreme recommendation. But if these readers saw Don Quixote with different eyes, if he revealed a profile that no one suspected earlier, it is not only because they wanted to see him that way; it is also because his relationship to the world predisposed him to show himself in that light. Let us take a single example: Don Quixote acts incongruously when he frees the chained galley slaves, who furthermore thrash him instead of obeying his commands and presenting themselves before Dulcinea loaded down with their chains; nevertheless, he objectively accomplishes an act of justice by delivering the condemned men, who are victims of an iniquitous sentence that decreed a punishment not fitted to their crimes. According to the perspective that one adopts, the episode can be read in two different ways, and these readings complement each other without annulling each other.

An additional word: the Romantics, even if they kept their distance from parody, were not insensible to the comic strain in Cervantes. But in the inexhaustible abundance of the work, they prefer not the burlesque or the humorous but the third dimension of the comic element, sympathetic laughter, which recreates in us the clarity with which master and man regard their own exploits. At the end of a night of wakefulness and anguish, the two companions discover that the din which had terrified them was coming from six fulling mills, alternatively pounding the millrace:

> Don Quixote glanced at Sancho and saw him with cheeks puffed out and his mouth full of laughter, obviously on the point of exploding. In spite of his vexation, the knight could not help laughing at the sight of his squire, and when Sancho saw his master begin, he let go so heartily that he had to hold his sides with both hands to keep himself from bursting with laughter.

By doing so, they bring to light the tension of opposites that this masterly book contains, a tension that is symbolized by a hero divided between wisdom and madness, an *hidalgo* doubly *ingenioso* in the sense in which the seventeenth century understood it: "overly imaginative" and "keen-witted."

Grandiose in his project, which snatches him from time and space, yet laughable in his failure, which reintegrates him in spite of himself, Don Quixote, by obstinately denying history, certainly contributes to the expression of its contradictions. His enterprise, far from exhausting itself in one immediate meaning, translates a secret aspiration that slumbers in each of us and is independent of the values to which the original project refers; consequently, it means infinitely more than all the successive possible meanings that have been attributed to it. For Turgenev, the Knight incarnated faith in an eternal truth superior to the individual. For Unamuno, he was identified with his thirst for immortality. What strikes us today is less the message that it delivers than the movement that epitomizes that message: not an ideal that is necessarily contingent, but rather the double movement whereby the world resists or hides itself from the hero, the more he tries to confront it, thus deepening the split—tragic or comic—between reality and its representation. From Dickens to Melville, from Flaubert to Dostoevsky, from Kafka to Joyce and García Márquez, the modern novel has tirelessly returned to this epic parable. That Cervantes unknowingly opened the way for these writers brings him singularly close to us; even more, perhaps, the fact that he is the first to have led us into the very heart of novelistic illusion by revealing—the better to preserve it—the lie on which all fiction bases its truth.

PRELUDE TO THE PERSILES

DECEMBER 1615: the Second Part of *Don Quixote* has just come off the presses. In a few days, Cervantes will live through his last Christmas.

A year is coming to an end, a year filled with dealings with patrons, booksellers, censors: twelve months of a life that for us is virtually identified with the task of writing. What about the hours that Miguel steals from his pen? Is he still a habitué of the *mentideros?* Does he continue to attend the salons? We imagine him concerned with religious activities, assiduous at his Order's services, careful to fulfill the duties required by his vows: pious occupations that his declining health doubtless forces him to restrict but that he is determined to fulfill to the extent his strength permits.

Around him, the circle of his relatives continues to shrink. It has already been four years since Magdalena joined Andrea in the tomb. Constanza is about to set up her own household on Baño Street— without severing connections with her family, however. Isabel, on the other hand, has cut off all contacts with her father. And she is more than ever at daggers drawn with Urbina, who (it will be remembered) had agreed to pay her 2,000 ducats, according to the terms of the settlement agreed upon with the Molinas. Did he hope to discourage the young woman by dragging out the negotiations? In that case, he misjudged her. Isabel, with the assistance of her notary husband, will not hesitate to direct the fulminations of the law against him and to have him jailed from January to August 1614, until he settles his debt. Because of his position, the ex-secretary of the duke of Savoy will enjoy preferential treatment: instead of being sent to the common jail, he will be lodged, at his own expense, in the house of the police lieutenant; but he will not leave it until he pays up.

We presume that this arrest took Cervantes by surprise. Even had he been warned in time, he was in no position to change the course of events. The affair was of such a nature that he could not ask any of his patrons to interfere. As for paying the sum in litigation, it was obviously out of the question: even more than his dignity as the offended father, the state of his resources absolutely prohibited it. We owe to the licentiate Márquez Torres, one of the censors of the Second Part of *Don Quixote,* an anecdote that tells us much on the subject, and we must thank this excellent personage for having inserted it in the text of his *aprobación:*

I truly certify that on the twenty-fifth of February of this year of 1615, when His Eminence Don Bernardo de Sandoval y Rojas, the cardinal archbishop of Toledo, my lord, went to repay a visit from the ambassador of France, who had come to discuss matters dealing with the marriages of the French and Spanish princes, many of the French gentlemen who came in the ambassador's retinue, as courteous as they were cultivated and fond of literature, came up to me and my lord the cardinal's other chaplains, anxious to learn what clever books were most highly regarded, and when I mentioned by chance this one, which I was [at the time] censoring, they had scarcely heard the name of Miguel de Cervantes when they began to sing his praises, extolling the esteem in which his works were held in France as well as in the neighboring kingdoms: *Galatea,* the First Part of which some of them almost knew by heart, and the *Novellas.* Their praises were such that I offered to take them to see the author of these works, which they gratefully received with a thousand demonstrations of their genuine desire to do so. They questioned me closely about his age, his profession, his quality and quantity. I found myself forced to tell them that he was old, a soldier, a gentleman, and poor. To which one responded in these very words: "Then Spain does not make such a man rich and support him from the public treasury?" Another Frenchman retorted with this witty remark: "If poverty will force him to write, then may it please God that he never have wealth, so that, though he is poor, he may make the whole world rich with his works."

Márquez Torres does not record the ambassador's name. (It was not the duke of Mayenne, who had come to Madrid three years earlier, but Noël Brûlart de Sillery, sent to Spain to negotiate the union of Louis XIII and Ana of Austria.) Nor does he tell us whether the visit so greatly desired by the French gentlemen actually took place: even so, modern Frenchmen should be grateful to their compatriots for having done honor to their nation. But fame had not freed Cervantes from worries about money: he himself in his dedication to Lemos will mention his financial straits. The emperor of China, he will tell his Maecenas, has tried to interest him in becoming rector of a college where his subjects may learn Castilian, with *Don Quixote* as their textbook:

I asked the bearer if His Majesty had provided a sum for my travel expenses. He answered that the thought had not even crossed his mind.

"Then, brother," I replied, "you can go back to your China posthaste or at whatever haste you are bound to go, as I am not fit for so long a journey and, besides being ill, I am very much without money, while emperor for emperor and monarch for monarch, I have at Naples the great count of Lemos, who, without so many petty titles of colleges and rectorships, supports me, protects me, and does me more favor than I can wish for."

An ambiguous testimonial, which mixes gratitude and flattery with pride, but even so suggests real destitution.

Perhaps Miguel is going to ameliorate his financial situation a little when, in the fall of the same year, he sells the manuscript of *Don Quixote* to Robles. In any case, it is around this date that he moves for the last time. Together with Catalina and María de Ugena, their servant, he leaves Huertas Street for a nearby house located at the corner of Francos and León streets. Recently rebuilt, it undoubtedly had a better appearance than their previous lodgings. Cervantes is going to occupy its ground floor, since the royal notary Gabriel Martínez, the owner of the property, kept the second floor for himself. Three of the windows of the apartment were level with the gathering place for actors, the *mentidero de los comediantes:* this gave our poet an impregnable lookout post over all those thespians who had made a sour face when offered his plays and had forced him to give them to the printer.

However severe his disappointment had been in this matter, Miguel has turned over a new leaf. A new project occupies him, or rather an undertaking begun long since, then suspended for years, but which now mobilizes what is left of his energy: *The Travails of Persiles and Sigismunda.* The idea for this "northern tale," as the author will call it, belongs (some have said) to the program outlined ten years earlier in *Don Quixote* by the Canon, who is the champion of expurgated romances of chivalry:

> [For] though he had said so much in condemnation of these books, still he found one good thing in them, and that was the opportunity they afforded to a gifted intellect for displaying itself. They presented a wide and spacious field over which the pen might range freely . . . For the unrestricted range of these books enables the author to show his powers, epic, lyric, tragic, or comic, and all the moods the sweet and winning arts of poetry and oratory are capable of, for the epic may be written in prose just as well as in verse.

The worthy ecclesiastic does not limit himself to these declarations: he admits to his fellow churchman the Priest that he has written a hundred pages of a story in accordance with these rules and claims that, when he submitted it to laymen and scholars, it met with "an agreeable approval" from all of them. We seem to hear Cervantes speaking. Was he in fact referring to the *Persiles,* or rather (as Daniel

Eisenberg has recently suggested) to a different romance entitled *Bernardo,* which shortly before his death he will claim to have begun? One thing is virtually certain, in any case: the first chapters of the *Persiles* are contemporary with the first adventures of the Ingenious *Hidalgo.* They appear to go back to those mysterious years between the imprisonments at Seville and the move to Valladolid. They contain, in fact, reminiscences of Greek and Latin authors who by means of recent translations were then enjoying renewed popularity. How did the author of *Don Quixote* come to take up the thread of his tale again? In point of fact, however happy he was to know that he was being read all over Europe, he doubtless experienced some secret annoyance at owing his renown to the comical exploits of a madman. His rivals could hardly fail to point out that he had turned away from the noble genres and had even refrained from cultivating the verse epic, the most prestigious among them. Did not even his admirers— those whose opinions he valued, like the French gentlemen encountered by Márquez Torres—give preference to *Galatea* and the *Novellas,* without mentioning, apparently, the Knight of the Woeful Countenance? He intended to show these people of taste what he was capable of. While the Canon, according to his own account, had decided not to continue his romance, Cervantes himself, in the evening of his life, takes up the task again. As if to keep his readers in suspense, he constantly tells them about this project. In 1613, in the preface to the *Novellas,* he enjoys piquing the readers' curiosity: "If life does not desert me, I will offer you the *Travails of Persiles,*" he declares at the moment of leavetaking. A year later, in the *Journey to Parnassus,* he becomes a little more explicit:

> I am now upon the point—to use the phrase—
> Of giving to the press the great *Persiles,*
> Whereby my works and my renown I'll multiply.

A year later, he publishes one after the other his theater and the Second Part of the *Quixote:* two new opportunities for promising his great book, while he simultaneously tries his hand at all the genres, extending the scope of his creativity with an ardor that the presentiment of his approaching end makes more and more feverish.

There are two reasons for this insistence: the fear of dying too soon, and Miguel's uncertainty about the reception that the educated public will give the book. This is how he addresses Lemos in the dedication of *Don Quixote* (October 31, 1615):

> I beg [to take my leave] from you, offering Your Excellency *The Travails of Persiles and Sigismunda,* a book I shall finish within four months, God willing, and which will be either the worst or the best that has been composed in our language, I mean those intended for entertainment. Yet I repent of having called it the worst, for, in the opinion of friends, it is bound to attain the summit of possible excellence.

On the first point, Cervantes is going to keep his word, except that he will take eight months instead of four to reach the end of the road: exactly the time that he has left to live. He will dedicate the romance to Lemos four days before giving up the ghost. Villarroel, to whom Catalina will entrust the manuscript, will publish it in January 1617.

A NORTHERN TALE

IF he had died four months earlier, Cervantes would have left this world at the same time as Don Quixote. Posterity would have been happy with such a picture. But with the help of destiny, our author decided differently. As if he wanted to close the way that he had opened, he preferred to leave us, as a sort of literary testament, the expression of an ideal that is no longer to our taste.

The fact is that, until recently, the *Persiles* has been the object of a misunderstanding. Readers have seen these northern adventures as a sort of romantic dream to which Cervantes surrendered on the eve of his death. While he had formerly condemned the lack of verisimilitude in chivalric fables, in a senile lapse he must have renounced his earlier convictions in order to draw us into a boreal world peopled by fantastic creatures and woven of incredible episodes. But nothing could be further from the truth. On the contrary, the author of *Don Quixote,* faithful to his esthetic ideals, wanted to take up the challenge of the believable unbelievable. The romances of chivalry were fond of showing us a paladin splitting with one blow of his sword a giant the size of a tower, or scattering in a trice an army of a million men. The *Persiles* hopes to substitute a controlled fantasy for these unacceptable extravagances: in it, in conformity with the canons of the *Poetics,* the extraordinary continues to be possible from start to finish. It remains to be seen what this requires.

"It is a book that dares to compete with Heliodorus, though it may get a beating for its audacity." Miguel identifies, in the preface of the *Exemplary Novellas,* the model he has chosen to follow quite freely, the Greek romance of the third century of our era. Renaissance humanists had exhumed and translated its principal masterpieces, *Theagenes and Chariclea* by Heliodorus and *Leucippe and Clitophon* by Achilles Tatius, which are now familiar only to scholars. But in the Europe of the sixteenth and seventeenth centuries, these works enjoyed considerable vogue. In fact, since antiquity they have provided the pattern for what was going to become the romance of adventures. Not in the sum of elements that they borrow from previous genres (the heroes' thwarted love affair, escapes studded with obstacles and unpleasant surprises, a geographical setting as vast as it is varied), but in the arrangement that they set before us: an accumulation of fortuitous events that break into the life of the characters and constantly change the course of their adventures, without ever affecting their being or their feelings.

In a sense, the romance of chivalry is an unfaithful heir, a tainted offspring of the Greek romance; so one can understand why the Canon, while pruning its naive elements and excesses, makes an effort to preserve its mold:

[Now the author may picture] ". . . some sad, tragic incident, now some joyful and unexpected event; here a beauteous lady, virtuous, wise, and modest; there a Christian knight, brave and gentle; here a lawless, barbarous braggart; there a courteous prince, gallant and gracious; setting forth the devotion and loyalty of vassals, the greatness and generosity of nobles. Or again . . . the author may show himself to be an astronomer, or a skilled cosmographer, or musician, or one versed in affairs of state, and sometimes he will have a chance of coming forward as a magician if he likes . . ."

And our Canon concludes,

"If this is done with charm of style and ingenious invention, aiming at the truth as much as possible, he will assuredly display such perfection and beauty that it will attain the worthiest object any writing can seek, which, as I said before, is to give instruction and pleasure combined."

Now, at the cost of supreme effort, Cervantes intends to carry out this program, which he attributes to his spokesman and which he had already begun to work on while on the banks of the Guadalquivir. And indeed the outline of *Persiles* corresponds point by point to that which the worthy ecclesiastic sketches; its expressed objective is no less in conformity with the stated ideal: to unite profit and pleasure, as Horace had already recommended. So the outline of Persiles and Sigismunda's wanderings becomes clear. As in Heliodorus, shipwrecks, captures, imprisonments, separations, recognitions punctuate the progress of the narrative. But the desperate flight of the lovers in the *Ethiopica* is metamorphosed into a pilgrimage that takes the heroes from the ice of the Far North to Rome. This pilgrimage responds to a mysterious vow that Sigismunda has resolved to fulfill before marrying Persiles. To the end of her journey, she will travel under the name of Auristela, while Persiles, who passes himself off as her brother, disguises himself with the name Periandro. Condemned by their vow to a chastity so perfect it becomes somewhat disturbing, the two young people reject any move that would lead them astray from the narrow path. They exist only in relation to the obstacles that arise in their way and that bring them into contact with cruel savages, greedy corsairs, or libidinous suitors.

As a tale of wonders, *The Travails of Persiles and Sigismunda* opens up for the imagination the two approaches to what Aristotle calls the extraordinary but possible. The first is the way of travel, which produces numerous scenes from a disconcerting world that is based on the cosmographies of the time and which take place on the boundless seas that bathe the Nordic isles. There, ships are trapped in ice floes, hunters streak across the snow on skis, and the sorcerers rampant there assume the wolf's-face of lycanthropy. The second is the way of chance and surprise, where in the course of dramatic incidents that spring from jealousy and vengeance, hypocrisy or desire, Periandro and Auristela are alternately victims and observers. The incidents that punctuate their pilgrimage in barbarous lands redouble from the moment the heroes, having arrived in Christian lands, reach Italy by way of Portugal, Spain, and France. These incidents show us that men's malice is equally present where the light of the True Faith shines; but they constitute at the same time the ordeals that face the lovers until the happy ending. These ordeals, which mark the stages of their itinerary, confer a transcendent meaning on their pilgrimage by identifying it with a sort of mystical quest for an Absolute which, *in fine,* their imminent union symbolizes, a union sealed with the sign of a bliss that fuses with their salvation.

If the Canon dreamed of an expurgated narrative, *Persiles* surpasses his hopes by offering to its readers an updated Greek romance, adapted to the ideals and values of Spain after the Council of Trent: a romance that one can call Baroque in its objective, its general economy, and its movement. One must do justice to the beauties it contains, which have caused it to attract interest once more: the contrast between the boreal setting of the first adventures and the sun-bathed landscape where the lovers' pilgrimage terminates; the expanded number of characters from the realm of the extraordinary and weird, consistent with the witchcraft of the Far North as well as with the unpredictable events that occur on the shores of the Mediterranean; the intertwining of the principal narrative with episodic stories that complicate its course; the comings and goings of different narrators who, by means of incessant flashbacks, mix themes characteristic of an "untamed" kind of marvel with the controlled wonders of the principal narrative: these narrators, by enclosing—at will, it would seem—the fictions they produce one inside another, play upon the dissonances thus obtained in order to erase the border between the real and the fabulous.

Our novelist never pushed his ambitions so far, never combined to this extreme the theory and practice of prose fiction in his writing. To repeat Avalle-Arce's apt description, *Persiles* is at the same time a romance, the idea of a romance, and, for the period in which it was born, the summation of all possible points of view on the novelistic genre. This is, furthermore, the way that readers of the time seem to have understood it. Reprinted five times in the year it appeared, immediately translated all over Europe, it is going to enjoy, especially in France, a success that will last until the middle of the seventeenth century. Today, we have difficulty understanding this success. However fond we may be of the Baroque and literary experimentation, this book, which attracts us, charms us in certain places, even fascinates us occasionally, leaves us—in spite of everything—unsatisfied as soon as we have closed it. Some episodes certainly hold our attention and bring us back; but they often have only a tenuous connection with the central plot: for example, the story of Feliciana de la Voz, the seduced girl whom Periandro and Auristela discover in the hollow of a tree with her child, and who finally manages to mollify a father and brother quite ready to sacrifice her on the altar of family honor; or, in an entirely different key, the misadventure of the two students from Salamanca, who, in order to excite the compassion of naive villagers, pass themselves off as Christian slaves who have escaped from the galleys— until the moment when the *alcalde,* a genuine captive, unmasks the two impostors, to their great embarrassment. These *bravura* passages are some of Cervantes' best; they show us a writer in full control of his art, master of his pen until his last breath; but they are the scattered fragments of a splendid edifice through whose empty rooms we wander endlessly. Among those who out of curiosity have read *Persiles* from start to finish, how many can claim to have reread it through for pleasure?

There is, it seems to us, an accessory reason for what we must call our disappointment or frustration: the author never managed to finish his work. For fifteen years, Cervantes gave the book only the time taken here and there from other works or other occupations. It was only in the last year of his life that he truly worked on it steadily, with a haste made even more feverish by the presentiment of his end. *Persiles* suffers from this disconnected progress, the signs of which can be discovered in an attentive reading. It also suffers from the inevitable: death took Miguel before he could revise his manuscript.

But the deepest origin of our disaffection is no doubt the fact that *Persiles* represents the antipodes of our own concept of the novel. One can of course find it in the narrative procedures, the tricks of writing with which other Cervantine fictions have made us familiar. But it lacks what is in our eyes the essential element: the way a hero interiorizes the events in which he finds himself involved, in order to turn them into the thread of his existence, the material of an imaginary life. The obstacles that he encounters, the conflicts that he feels, change him little by little, indeed they transform him by the end of his journey. Don Quixote at Barcelona is Don Quixote more than ever; but he is by no means the same being he was when he appeared. There is nothing of this in Persiles and Sigismunda: whether they are observers or actors in the vicissitudes that make up the stages of their adventure, they are beings that do not evolve. From the subterranean prisons of Isla Bárbara to the glorious stay in the Eternal City, the ordeals that they face confirm them in their identity, their determination and constancy; but the trials do not change them at all. They remain immutable and incomplete. Their strategic position at the heart of the book verifies a constant of the Greek romance, as revised and corrected by Tridentine ideology: in accord with the biblical *omnes sumus peregrini super terram* (we are all wanderers upon the earth), this ideology makes their pilgrimage an allegory of human life elevating itself little by little to perfection. But their destiny is alien to us: in the sidereal space of *Persiles,* we contemplate in silence the majestic course of two abstractions.

ON THE THRESHOLD OF ETERNITY

APRIL 1616: Persiles and Sigismunda are coming to the end of their pilgrimage. So is Cervantes. The Holy City to which he has managed to bring his heroes prefigures the Heavenly City whose gates Divine Mercy will soon open for him. Did he hope to delay the fatal moment for a while? Six months earlier he was still brimming with projects reported in his prefaces and dedications: a play—*Fooled with Open Eyes* (El engaño a los ojos)—whose title suggests one of his favorite artifices; a romance—*Bernardo the Famous* (El famoso Bernardo)—doubtless inspired by the exploits of the mythical hero of the Reconquest; a collection of novellas—*Weeks in the Garden* (Las semanas del jardín)— and finally the constantly promised, inevitable Second Part of *Galatea.* All are forms of defiance aimed at death by a man who has so much to say and who does not want to leave until he has said it all. What has become of all this literary production? For two centuries people have rummaged in vain through archives in the fond hope of finding a trace of it. Exhausted by the effort, they have concluded that the author, in the fever of his last months, promised more than he could deliver and that his drafts, at best, were no more than sketches. But now an American Cervantist, Daniel Eisenberg, believes that he has discovered a fragment of *Weeks in the Garden,* or at least that is what he claims in a recently published study, after a careful examination of *The Dialogue of Selanio and Cilenia,* preserved in the holdings of the Colombine Library at Seville. The dialogue was attributed to Cervantes more than a century ago, but Eisenberg defends the attribution with new arguments. Recalling the heated debates over the authorship of *The Pretended Aunt,* one foresees busy days ahead for scholars.

Cervantes apparently has too little time left to dispel our doubts by giving to the printer the works that he has started. For six months

Persiles has taken all his strength. Now he knows that his end is near; he also knows that "from this life to the next, the leap is great" and "that the appearance of death, in whatever guise it may come, is frightening." As Madrid's winter is giving way to the first warmth of a spring that has just arrived, he begins to prepare himself for the great journey. A letter in his handwriting, addressed to Cardinal Sandoval, dated March 26, at one time persuaded scholars that Cervantes tried to take leave of his Maecenas. This letter is now known to be a forgery. On the other hand, it is proven beyond question that Cervantes withdrew from the Confraternity of the Most Holy Sacrament: the massive influx of the elite of the aristocracy, following Lerma, had turned it into a worldly club where he no longer felt at home. He preferred, following the example of his sisters and Catalina, the Third Order of St. Francis, of which he had been a novice for nearly three years. On Easter Even, April 2, 1616, he takes his final vows. The ceremony is recorded in the Book of the Order, which says that it took place at the writer's house: a revealing bit of evidence of the extent of his frailness.

In this condition, how could he have traveled, two days later, the twelve leagues (about eighteen miles) that separate Esquivias from Madrid? How could he have had the strength, eight days later, to mount his nag again and return to his house? This journey, described in the preface to *Persiles,* seems to be literary fantasy, a pretext that Cervantes uses to tell us the story of his encounter, on the way back, with one of his admirers. An unlikely encounter, if one pays close attention to the circumstances under which it is supposed to have taken place; nevertheless an encounter in which the essential elements have the ring of truth. What rings true is the enthusiasm of the unnamed person, a student "dressed in gray," who, when he realizes whom he is addressing, leaps from his horse and grabs the poet's hand, saying,

"Yes, yes; this is the cripple who is sound, the great man, the jolly writer, and, in short, the joy of the Muses!"

True also the polite denials of the author of *Don Quixote,* who even so cannot conceal his pride at having been recognized, at having—at last—earned by means of his writing an identity that, because of his success, from now on forms part of a story. True also the comments about Miguel's illness; the interlocutor dashes his feeble hopes by saying,

> "This illness comes from hydropsy, which all the water in the Ocean Sea, were it sweet enough to drink, will not cure. Señor Cervantes, Your Worship should set limits to drinking and not neglect eating; that way you will get well without any other medicine whatsoever."

True also the answer of Señor Cervantes, who shows himself to us without illusions about the effects of this treatment:

> "That is what many people have told me," I replied; "but I cannot stop drinking all I want, as if I were born for that alone."

Brushstrokes copied from experience: they permit this imaginary story to "satisfy the understanding" of a reader of whom Miguel, alone once more, takes leave with one last promise:

> Perhaps a time will come when I can take up this broken thread and say what is left to say, and what needs to be said.

An extraordinary farewell from a writer who until his last breath refuses to call it quits!

Nevertheless, at the time when he is writing these lines, April 20, 1616, our novelist knows that he is doomed. The "hydropsy" diagnosed by the student, the unquenchable thirst that he himself reports, are the symptoms of illness from which he has suffered for several years: diabetes, some have affirmed, unless it is a question of cirrhosis of the liver, two diseases without cure in those days and before which doctors were helpless. Two days earlier, on Monday, April 18, the licentiate Francisco Pérez, almoner of the Trinitarian monastery, had come to administer the Last Sacraments. The day after the ceremony, Cervantes took advantage of a short respite to address the admirable dedication of *Persiles* to Lemos:

> I wish that those old verses, famous in their day, that begin "With my foot now in the stirrup . . ." did not suit my letter so perfectly, because I could begin it with the same words, saying,

> With my foot now in the stirrup,
> And the hour of death at hand,
> Great Lord, I write this letter . . .

Yesterday they gave me Extreme Unction, and today I am writing this.
Time is short, my pains increase, my hopes wane; and yet I cling to life
in my desire to live on, and I would like to delay it until I have kissed
Your Excellency's feet; for it might be that the contentment in seeing
Your Excellency safely in Spain would be such that it would restore my
life. But if it is decreed that I must lose it, then may the will of Heaven
be done, and may Your Excellency at least know of this my wish . . .

"I cling to life in my desire to live on," with the sole object, the dying
man adds, of offering to his illustrious patron the works he has promised, especially "the conclusion of *Galatea,* of which I know Your
Excellency is fond." (It is truer than ever that in the author of *Don
Quixote* the man and the writer are a single entity.) But indeed, he
adds with melancholy, if by some piece of good luck Heaven should
allow him to live longer, "it would not be luck but a miracle." There
will be no miracle. On Wednesday, April 20, Cervantes dictates the
preface to *Persiles* at a single stroke. "My life is ending," he concludes,
addressing the reader. And—if the chart of his pulse rate is any indication—

. . . it will finish its course this Sunday at the latest; and I shall finish the
race of life. . . . Farewell, witticisms; farewell, jests; farewell, cheerful
friends: for I am dying, and anxious to see you again soon, happy in the
next life.

These are the last words of his that have come down to us. On Friday,
April 22, a little more than a week after William Shakespeare, Miguel
de Cervantes breathes his last. His death is recorded in the registry of
San Sebastián, his parish. It is noted that he named his wife executrix
of his estate, that he had ten masses said for the repose of his soul, and
that he was buried in the Trinitarian monastery. He was buried on
Saturday, according to the rule of the Third Order, with his face
uncovered and wearing the Franciscan's rough habit. In the course of
time, his relatives will pass away one by one. Constanza, his niece,
will be the first to die, in 1622; Catalina, his wife, will follow her,

four years later; Isabel, his daughter, will survive him until 1652, without leaving any children.

Today there are no descendents of Cervantes. His will has been lost. As for his remains, they were scattered at the end of the seventeenth century, during the rebuilding of the monastery that housed them. There remain only the works of the *raro inventor,* who thanks to *Don Quixote* has become a legend. Each generation has contributed a stone to the edifice since then, constructing an image of the author that seems to it to be the only "true" one. In the nineteenth century, some extolled him as a secretly subversive humanist, the ancestor of modern liberalism; others, in reaction, made him the praiser of the values of Hapsburg Spain: two versions of the same kind of hero-worship that will lead well-intentioned persons to transform the soldier of Lepanto into a receptacle of all knowledge or a paragon of all virtues.

Annoyed by this naive adulation, Unamuno, in his *Life of Don Quixote and Sancho,* scandalized his readers by exalting the immortal pair to the detriment of their creator, who is surpassed by heroes whose destiny he did not foresee. We ought to keep this deliberate paradox (which we should take as such) in mind. After the studies of Américo Castro, following the First World War, we have in fact discovered if not a thinker, at least a writer in the fullest sense of the term: the father of the modern novel. Even if we no longer consider this writer an unwitting genius, the meaning of his work today (as Unamuno reminds us, in his fashion) is no longer reducible to the purpose for which it was intended. Behind the artist, whose technique we scrutinize and whom we make an effort to comprehend, the man of flesh and desires (who one day late in life decided to take up the pen again) obstinately eludes the diagrams in which we would like to capture him. Impenetrable, his mystery fascinates us because it is the key to an experience attainable only through the writings—an experience that our own, as readers, constantly encounters. So Cide Hamete understood it, and he preferred to let his own pen have the last word:

> For me alone was Don Quixote born, and I for him; it was for him to act, for me to write; we two together make but one.

A Note on the Spanish Monetary System in the Golden Age

CREATED in 1497 by the Ordinance of Media del Campo, this system remained stable throughout the sixteenth and part of the seventeenth centuries. It defined coins of gold, silver, and a copper-silver alloy called billon that were measured in units of account called *maravedís*. In the period of Philip II, the standard coins were the gold *escudo* ("shield"), worth four hundred *maravedís,* and the silver *real* ("royal") worth thirty-four *maravedís*. Older coins, the gold ducat and the double ducat, called the doubloon, still circulated.

It is impossible to give simple, accurate equivalents of these coins for the period included in this book. Not only did the values and even the names of the coins vary according to period and region, but in the sixteenth and seventeenth centuries, cash was scarce and its buying power much greater in relation to its intrinsic worth. Nevertheless, for the purpose of comparison, using the price of a gram of 22-carat gold at 1989 prices (about $10), we can assign values as follows:

gold *escudo*	$34.00
silver *real*	$1.00
gold ducat	$36.50
gold doubloon	$73.00
(*maravedí*	$.085)

Using this scheme, we can calculate that Cervantes' 500-*escudo* ransom was the equivalent of $17,000 in gold. His annual salary while he worked for the government as a traveling commissary officer, paying his own expenses, was in the neighborhood of $10,000. Cervantes received about $1,500 for the First Part of *Don Quixote,* which cost $20 for the 664-page volume.

Family Trees
and
Maps

The Salazar Family

Francisco
de Salazar
(† 1584)
marries
Catalina
de Palacios
(† 1588) ——————————— Juan de Palacios
(† 1595)

Catalina
de Salazar
(1565–1626)
marries
Miguel
de Cervantes
(1547–1616)

Francisco
de Salazar Palacios
(1577–1652)

Fernando
de Salazar Palacios
(1581–?)

The Cervantes Family

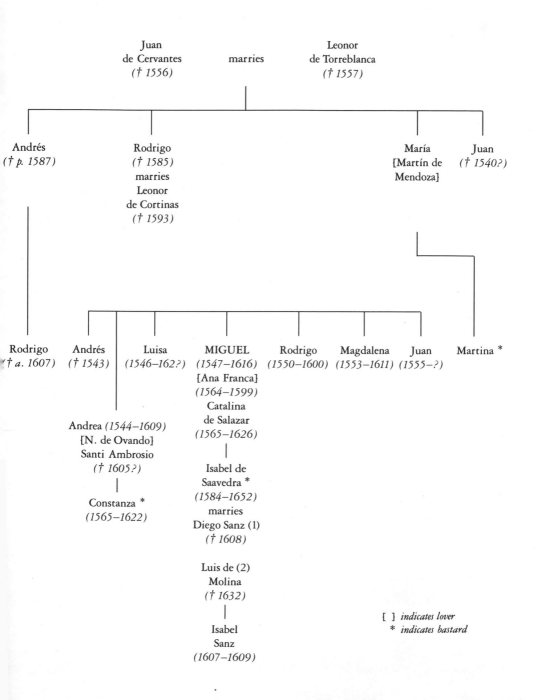

Juan
de Cervantes
(† 1556)

marries

Leonor
de Torreblanca
(† 1557)

Andrés
(† p. 1587)

Rodrigo
(† 1585)
marries
Leonor
de Cortinas
(† 1593)

María
[Martín de
Mendoza]

Juan
(† 1540?)

Rodrigo
(† a. 1607)

Andrés
(† 1543)

Luisa
(1546–162?)

MIGUEL
(1547–1616)
[Ana Franca]
(1564–1599)
Catalina
de Salazar
(1565–1626)

Rodrigo
(1550–1600)

Magdalena
(1553–1611)

Juan
(1555–?)

Martina *

Andrea (1544–1609)
[N. de Ovando]
Santi Ambrosio
(† 1605?)

Isabel de
Saavedra *
(1584–1652)
marries
Diego Sanz (1)
(† 1608)

Constanza *
(1565–1622)

Luis de (2)
Molina
(† 1632)

Isabel
Sanz
(1607–1609)

[ ] *indicates lover*
* *indicates bastard*

The Hapsburgs

(Spanish Versions of Names)

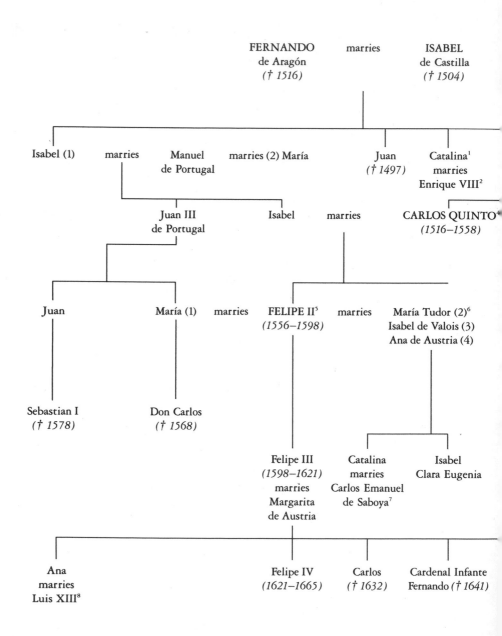

FERNANDO de Aragón *(† 1516)* marries ISABEL de Castilla *(† 1504)*

Isabel (1) marries Manuel de Portugal — marries (2) María — Juan *(† 1497)* — Catalina[1] marries Enrique VIII[2]

Juan III de Portugal — Isabel marries CARLOS QUINTO[4] *(1516–1558)*

Juan — María (1) marries FELIPE II[5] *(1556–1598)* marries María Tudor (2)[6] / Isabel de Valois (3) / Ana de Austria (4)

Sebastian I *(† 1578)* — Don Carlos *(† 1568)*

Felipe III *(1598–1621)* marries Margarita de Austria — Catalina marries Carlos Emanuel de Saboya[7] — Isabel Clara Eugenia

Ana marries Luis XIII[8] — Felipe IV *(1621–1665)* — Carlos *(† 1632)* — Cardenal Infante Fernando *(† 1641)*

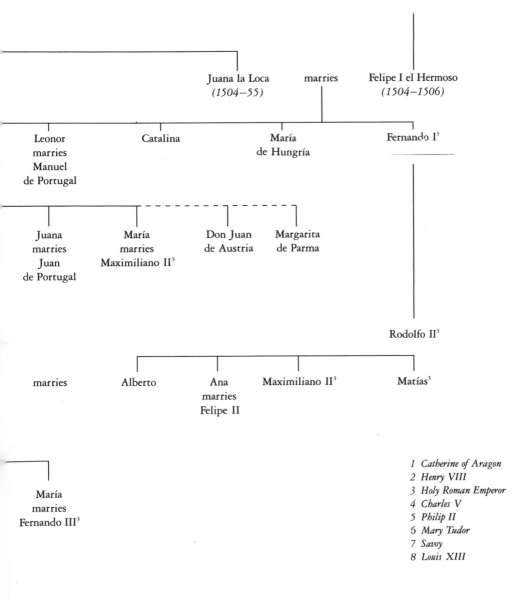

Maximiliano[3]

Juana la Loca   marries   Felipe I el Hermoso
(1504–55)   (1504–1506)

Leonor   Catalina   María   Fernando I[3]
marries   de Hungría
Manuel
de Portugal

Juana   María   Don Juan   Margarita
marries   marries   de Austria   de Parma
Juan   Maximiliano II[3]
de Portugal

Rodolfo II[3]

marries   Alberto   Ana   Maximiliano II[3]   Matías[3]
                       marries
                       Felipe II

María
marries
Fernando III[3]

1   Catherine of Aragon
2   Henry VIII
3   Holy Roman Emperor
4   Charles V
5   Philip II
6   Mary Tudor
7   Savoy
8   Louis XIII

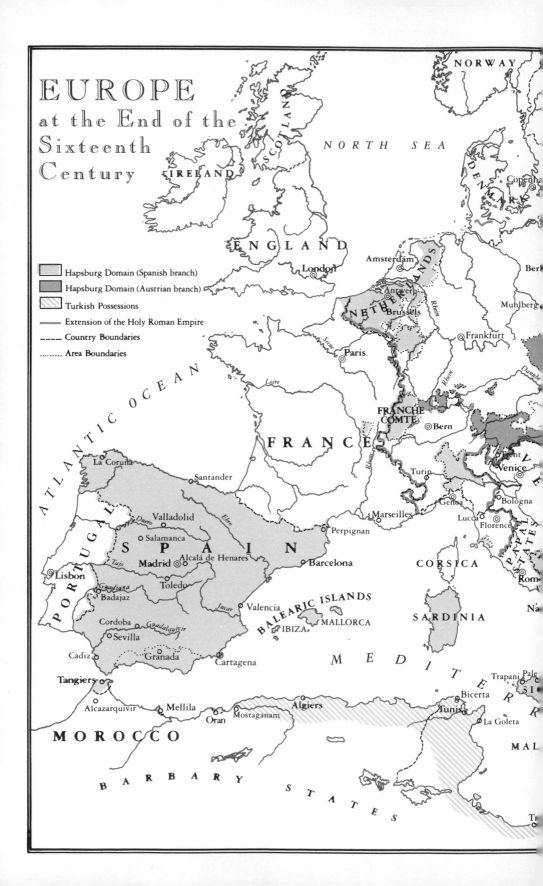

EUROPE
at the End of the
Sixteenth
Century

NORWAY

NORTH SEA

SCOTLAND

IRELAND

DENMARK

Copen

ENGLAND

London

Amsterdam

NETHERLANDS

Antwerp

Brussels

Rhein

Ber

Muhlberg

Frankfurt

Muhlberg

◻ Hapsburg Domain (Spanish branch)
◼ Hapsburg Domain (Austrian branch)
▨ Turkish Possessions
── Extension of the Holy Roman Empire
---- Country Boundaries
.... Area Boundaries

Seine

Paris

FRANCHE
COMTE

Rhein

Danube

ATLANTIC OCEAN

Loire

FRANCE

Bern

La Coruña

Santander

Turin

Trent

Venice

VE

PORTUGAL

Valladolid

Duero

Ebro

Perpignan

Marseilles

Genoa

Bologna

Lucca

Florence

PAPAL STATES

Rom

CORSICA

Salamanca

SPAIN

Madrid

Alcalá de Henares

Barcelona

Tajo

Lisbon

Toledo

Guadiana

Badajaz

Jucar

Valencia

BALEARIC ISLANDS

IBIZA

MALLORCA

SARDINIA

Na

Cordoba

Guadalquivir

Sevilla

Cadiz

Granada

Cartagena

MEDITERR

Trapani

Pale

SI

Tangiers

Bicerta

Alcazarquivir

Mellila

Oran

Mostaganam

Algiers

Tunis

La Goleta

MOROCCO

MAL

BARBARY   STATES

T

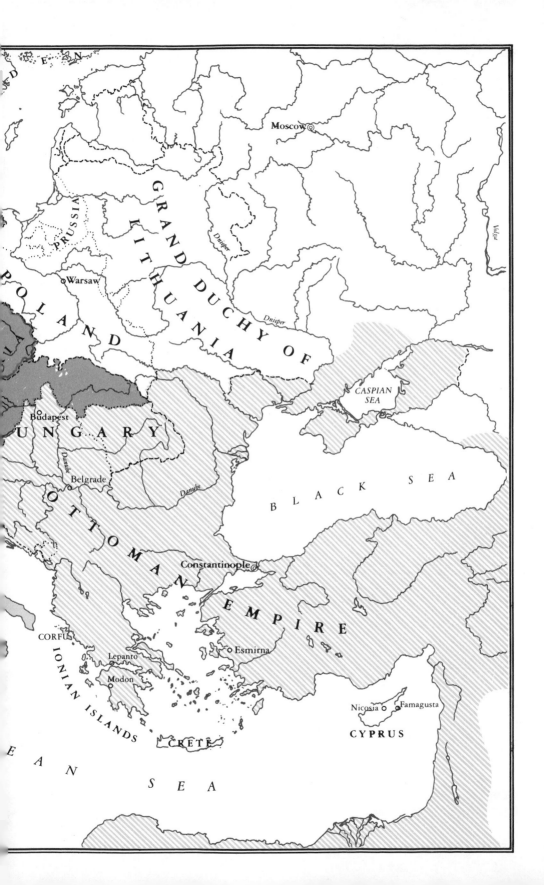

La Coruña
GALICIA
ASTURIAS
Santander
FRANCE
Saintes-Maries de la Mer
Marseilles

León
Pamplona
Rosellón
Cadaqués

LEÓN
CASTILLA LA VIEJA
Burgos
ARAGÓN
CATALUÑA

Valladolid
Numancia
Zaragoza
Barcelona

Duero
Ebro
Tarragona

Salamanca
Segovia
Guadalajara
ISLAS BALEARES
MENORCA

Ávila
El Escorial
Henares
MALLORCA

Madrid
Alcalá de Henares

Tomar
Illescas
Arganda
Cuenca

Santarem
Esquivias
Valencia
IBIZA

Lisbon
Toledo
Tajo
CASTILLA LA NUEVA

Guadiana
La
Mancha
Júcar
Denia

Badajoz
Argamasilla

EXTREMADURA
Ciudad Real

Córdoba
Baeza
Murcia

Guadalquivir
Úbeda

Sevilla
Ecija
Castro del Río
Cartagena

PORTUGAL
Cabra
Granada

ANDALUCÍA
Las Alpujarras

Cádiz
Ronda
Málaga

Tangiers

MEDITERRANEAN SEA

Main Province Boundaries _ _ _ _ _

SPAIN
at the End of the
Sixteenth Century

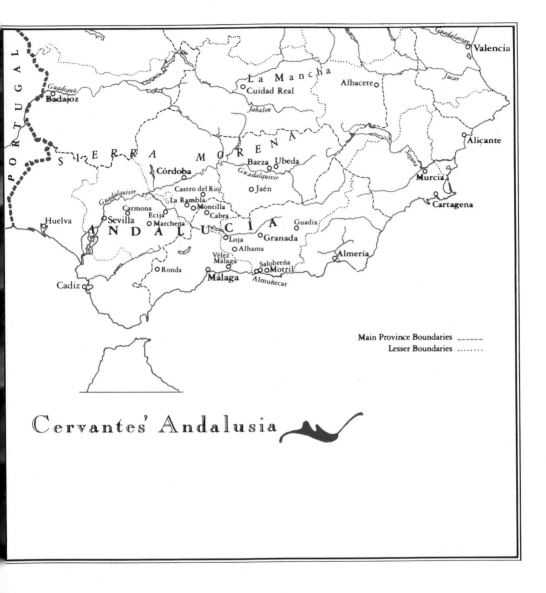

PORTUGAL

Guadiana
Badajoz

S I E R R A   M O R E N A

La Mancha
○ Cuidad Real
Jabalon

Albacete○

Guadalaviar
Valencia

Jucar

Alicante○

Córdoba ○
Baeza ○ ○ Ubeda
Guadalquivir
○ Jaén

Segura

Murcia ○

○ Cartagena

Guadalquivir
Castro del Rio ○
La Rambla ○ Montilla
Carmona ○ ○ Cabra
Huelva ○ Ecija ○
○ Sevilla ○ Marchena
A N D A L U C I A
○ Loja ○ Granada
Guadix ○

Vélez ○ Alhama
Málaga ○
Ronda ○ Salobreña
Cadiz ○ **Málaga** ○ Motril
Almuñecar

Almería ○

Main Province Boundaries _____
Lesser Boundaries ....

Cervantes' Andalusia

Chronology

1547   Sept. 29 (?) Miguel de Cervantes is born in Alcalá de Henares.
        Death of Francis I of France and Henry VIII of England.
        Victory of Muehlberg over the German Protestant princes.
        First *Index* of prohibited books. First purity-of-blood statutes.

1551   Rodrigo de Cervantes leaves for Valladolid.

1553   Rodrigo joins his father at Córdoba.

1554   Philip (Felipe), son of Charles V, marries Mary Tudor.
        Lazarillo de Tormes.

1556   Juan de Cervantes, Miguel's grandfather, dies.
        Charles V's abdication. Accession of Philip II.

1557   Leonor de Torreblanca, Miguel's paternal grandmother, dies.
        Philip II's first bankruptcy.

1558   Charles V and Mary Tudor die. Accession of Elizabeth I of England.

1559   Treaty of Cateau-Cambrésis. Death of Henri II. Philip II marries Isabel of Valois.
        Montemayor, *La Diana*.

1561   Madrid becomes the capital.
        Birth of Góngora.

1562   Birth of Lope de Vega.

1563   Cornerstone of El Escorial laid. End of Council of Trent.

1564   Rodrigo de Cervantes moves to Seville.

Failure of Turkish attack on Orán.

Birth of Shakespeare.

1565   Luisa de Cervantes enters nunnery at Alcalá.

Failure of Turkish attack on Malta. Revolt of the Low Countries.

Lope de Rueda dies.

1566   Rodrigo de Cervantes takes a house in Madrid.

1567   Miguel's first poems.

1568   Miguel studies under Juan López de Hoyos. First writings.

Imprisonment and death of Don Carlos. Death of Isabel of Valois.

Revolt of Moriscos at Granada.

1569   The Sigura affair. Miguel in Rome.

Ercilla, *La araucana*.

1570   Miguel serves Cardinal Acquaviva in Rome.

Occupation of Cyprus by the Turks.

1571   Miguel wounded at Lepanto. Convalescence in Messina.

Formation of the Holy League. Battle of Lepanto.

1572   *Soldado aventajado*. Takes part in naval campaign under Don Juan de Austria. Winter quarters in Sicily.

Pius V dies. Corfu and Modon campaigns.

1573   Takes part in Don Juan de Austria's new expedition.

Separate treaty between Venice and the Turk. Don Juan takes Tunisia.

Mateo Vázquez made secretary to Philip II.

1574   Winter quarters in Sardinia (?), Naples, and Sicily.

Euldj Alí recaptures Tunisia.

1575   Stay in Naples. On the way to Spain, Miguel is captured by Barbary pirates near the coast of Catalonia. Captivity in Algiers.

Philip II's second bankruptcy.

1576   First attempt at escape.

Sack of Antwerp by Spanish troops. Don Juan regent of the Low Countries.

1577   Rodrigo, Miguel's brother, ransomed. Second attempt at escape. Hassan Pasha becomes king of Algiers.

El Greco arrives in Toledo.

1578   Third attempt at escape.

Assassination of Juan de Escobedo. Don Juan de Austria dies.

King Sebastian of Portugal killed in the battle of Alcazarquivir.

1579   Fourth attempt at escape.

Fall of Antonio Pérez.

Opening of the first theaters in Madrid.

1580   Miguel ransomed by Trinitarian monks. Return to Madrid, via Valencia.

Philip II becomes king of Portugal.

1581   Mission to Orán. Stay in Lisbon.

St. Teresa of Avila dies.

1582   In Madrid. Letter to Eraso. *El trato de Argel* (?).

Herrera, *Poesías*. Gálvez de Montalvo, *El pastor de Fílida*.

1583   *Numancia* (?).

Juan de la Cueva, *Comedias y tragedias*.

1584   Affair with Ana Franca de Rojas. Birth of Isabel de Saavedra.

Marries Catalina de Salazar in Esquivias.

Philip II moves into El Escorial.

1585   First Part of *La Galatea*. Contract with Gaspar de Porres. Miguel's father, Rodrigo, dies.

St. John of the Cross, *Cántico espiritual*.

1586   Periodic stays in Seville.

1587   Departure for Seville. Commissions at Ecija.

Preparation for the Armada.

Lope de Vega is exiled from Madrid.

1588   New commissions. Catalina de Palacios, Miguel's mother-in-law, dies.

Failure of the Armada.

El Greco, *Burial of the Count of Orgaz*.

1589   New commissions. Stays in Esquivias and Madrid (?).

St. Teresa, *Works*.

1590   Miguel writes petition to Council of the Indies. Writing of "The Captive's Tale."

Revolt of Aragon.

1591   Commissions in the region of Granada.

Flight of Antonio Pérez. Death of Mateo Vázquez.

1592   Incidents at Ecija and Teba. Jailed at Castro del Río. Contract with Rodrigo Osorio.

1593   Commissions in environs of Seville. Miguel's mother, Doña Leonor, dies.

"La casa de los celos" (ballad).

1594   End of Anadalusian commissions.

1595   Tax collector. Tour through the kingdom of Granada.

Accession of Henri IV of France.

1596   Sack of Cádiz by Howard and Essex.

        López Pinciano, *Philosophía antigua poética*.

1597   Miguel jailed at Seville.

        Philip II's third bankruptcy.

1598   In Seville. "Soneto al túmulo de Felipe II." Death of Ana Franca.

        Magdalena de Cervantes takes in Isabel de Saavedra.

        Treaty of Vervins with France. Isabel and Alberto become regents of the Low Countries. Philip II dies. Accession of Philip III. Government of the duke of Lerma.

        Birth of Zurbarán. Lope de Vega, *La Arcadia*. Closing of theaters.

1599   At Seville. Stays in Castile (?).

        Outbreak of plague.

        Mateo Alemán, First Part of *Guzmán de Alfarache*. Birth of Velázquez.

1600   Departure for Seville (?). Stay in Toledo. Miguel's brother Rodrigo dies in the Battle of the Dunes.

        Reopening of theaters. Birth of Calderón.

1601   Court moves to Valladolid.

1602   At Esquivias. Differences with Treasury officials. Writes *Don Quixote*.

        Lope de Vega, *La hermosura de Angélica*.

1603   Death of Elizabeth I of England.

1604   At Valladolid. Confrontation with Lope de Vega.

        Treaty with England.

        Mateo Alemán, Second Part of *Guzmán de Alfarache*. Lope de Vega, *Primera parte de las Comedias*.

1605   First Part of *Don Quixote*. Ezpeleta affair.

        Birth of Philip IV. Lord Howard's embassy.

        López de Ubeda, *La pícara Justina*.

1606   Isabel de Saavedra marries Diego Sanz. Cervantes in Esquivias (?).

        Court returns to Madrid.

1607   At Madrid. Birth of Isabel Sanz.

1608   Diego Sanz dies. Isabel de Saavedra marries Luis de Molina. The Urbina affair begins.

1609   Magdalena, Catalina, and Andrea de Cervantes become novices in the Third Order of St. Francis. Miguel joins the Confraternity of the Slaves of the Most Holy Sacrament. Andrea and Isabel Sanz die.

        The Twelve-Year Truce with the United Provinces. Beginning of the expulsion of the Moriscos.

        Lope de Vega, *Arte nuevo de hacer comedias*.

1610   Urbina affair continues. Count of Lemos named viceroy of Naples. Miguel gives up hope of joining Lemos.

Henri IV of France assassinated.

1611   Magdalena dies. Stay at Esquivias. European dissemination of *Don Quixote*.

Margarita de Austria dies.

Temporary closing of Madrid theaters.

1612   Miguel attends literary salons in Madrid.

Haedo, *Topographía e historia general de Argel*.

1613   At Alcalá. Novice in the Third Order. *Novelas ejemplares*. Góngora, *Primera Soledad*.

1614   *Viaje del Parnaso*. Avellaneda affair.

Avellaneda, second part of *Don Quixote*. El Greco dies.

1615   *Ocho comedias y ocho entremeses*. Second Part of *Don Quixote*.

Louis XIII of France marries Ana of Austria, Philip III's daughter.

1616   Miguel takes final vows as tertiary of St. Francis. Dedication of *Persiles* to Lemos. Miguel dies in Madrid on April 22.

Shakespeare dies.

1617   Posthumous publication of *Persiles*.

Bibliography

THOUSANDS of books and articles—of varying quality, needless to say—have been written about Cervantes, his life, and his works. José Simón Díaz's twenty-year-old *Bibliografía de la literatura hispánica* (Madrid, vol. 8 [1970], 4–442) lists 3,700 *selected* titles. In the limited space available here, it is difficult to choose or even offer guidance for further readings. The following observations and suggestions are provided for the non-specialist.

What we know about the life of Cervantes is the result of research carried out since the first third of the eighteenth century by the earliest biographers of the author of *Don Quixote* (Mayáns, Pellicer, Navarrete) and by generations of scholars, among whom C. Pérez Pastor and F. Rodríguez Marín are outstanding. Documents uncovered through their efforts come from public archives (Simancas, Seville, Madrid) as well as from parochial and notarial archives. We lack a *Corpus Cervantinum*, that is, a methodical presentation of these documents with commentary. James Fitzmaurice-Kelly years ago made an expanded outline of such a work (*Miguel de Cervantes Saavedra: A Memoir*, Oxford, 1913; Spanish translation, with additions, Oxford, 1917). This study is still useful, but it needs to be updated. The notarized statements made by Cervantes after his return from captivity, transcribed at the beginning of this century by P. Torres Lanza, have recently been republished (*Información de Miguel de Cervantes de lo que had servido a S. M. . . . ,* Madrid, 1981).

We also lack a critical biography worthy of the name. Most of the lives of Cervantes are actually novelized accounts. The monumental work of Luis Astrana Marín, *Vida ejemplar y heroica de Miguel de Cervantes Saavedra* (Madrid, 1948–58), 7 vols., is questionable in its methods and biases, but it contains a considerable amount of data, some of it previously unpublished, and it is consequently an essential reference work.

The most reliable edition of the complete works of Cervantes—at least of those which are extant—was prepared by R. Schevill and A. Bonilla y San Martín (Madrid, 1914–31), 19 vols. The *Clásicos castellanos* series has republished *La Galatea*, ed. J.-B. Avalle-Arce (Madrid, 1968), 2 vols. The *Clásicos Castalia* series offers *Don Quijote de la Mancha*, ed. L. A. Murillo (Madrid, 1978), 3 vols.; the *Novelas ejemplares*, ed. J.-B. Avalle-Arce (Madrid, 1983); the *Entremeses*, ed. E. Asensio (Madrid, 1970); the *Poesías completas*, including the *Viaje del Parnaso*, ed. V. Gaos (Madrid, 1974–81), 2 vols.; and the *Persiles*, ed. J.-B. Avalle-Arce (Madrid, 1969).

Among numerous English translations of *Don Quixote* available, the Norton Critical Edition, edited by Joseph R. Jones and Kenneth Douglas (New York, 1981), contains background materials, including samples of texts parodied by Cervantes (e.g., *Amadís*) and selections from important critical works.

The work of Américo Castro, whatever one's reservations regarding its value, inaugurated the modern age of Cervantine studies. His *El pensamiento de Cervantes* (Madrid, 1925; reprinted with additions, Barcelona, 1972) presents the author of *Don Quixote* as a humanist with Erasmian leanings, out of tune with official Spanish attitudes. Subsequently, Castro rejected this point of view and profoundly altered his thinking. *Cervantes y los casticismos españoles* (Barcelona, 1966) and *Hacia Cervantes* (Madrid, 1967) develop a different hypothesis, that of Cervantes the *converso,* vindicating by means of his works the values rejected by the majority. Castro's Erasmian Cervantes comes through in the works of M. Bataillon, "Cervantes, penseur, d'après le livre d'Américo Castro" (*Revue de Littérature comparée* 8 [1928], 318–338) and *Erasme et l'Espagne* (Paris, 1937), where Cervantes' Christianity as a whole is examined.

CERVANTES AS WRITER HAS BEEN APPROACHED FROM DIFFERENT ANGLES:

J.-B. Avalle-Arce, *Nuevos deslindes cervantinos* (Barcelona, 1975)
J.-B. Avalle-Arce and E. C. Riley, *Suma cervantina* (London, 1973), a status report on Cervantine studies, in collaboration with well-known specialists.
F. Ayala, *Cervantes y Quevedo* (Barcelona, 1974)
Louis Combet, *Cervantes ou les incertitudes du désir* (Lyon, 1980), a "psycho-structural approach" to Cervantine works.
F. Márquez Villanueva, *Fuentes literarias cervantinas* (Madrid, 1973)
M. Molho, *Cervantes: raíces folklóricas* (Madrid, 1976)
E. C. Riley, *Cervantes' Theory of the Novel* (Oxford, 1962)

On *Don Quixote:*

John J. Allen, *Don Quixote: Hero or Fool?* Part I (Gainesville, 1971), Part II (Gainesville, 1979)
J. Casalduero, *Sentido y forma del "Quixote"* (Madrid, 1966)
Maxime Chevalier, *L'Arioste en Espagne (1530–1650): Recherches sur l'influence du "Roland furieux"* (Bordeaux, 1966)
D. Eisenberg, *A Study of Don Quixote* (Newark, 1987)
Ruth El Saffar, *Distance and Control in "Don Quixote": A Study in Narrative Technique* (Chapel Hill, 1975)
Mia I. Gerhardt, *"Don Quichotte": La vie et les livres* (Amsterdam, 1955)
George Haley, ed., *El "Quijote" de Cervantes* (Madrid, 1984)
P. Hazard, *"Don Quichotte" de Cervantès: étude et analyse* (Paris, 1931)
J. A. Maravall, *Utopía y contrautopía en el "Quijote"* (Santiago de Compostella, 1976)
F. Márquez Villanueva, *Personajes y temas del "Quijote"* (Madrid, 1975)
R. Menéndez Pidal, *De Cervantes a Lope de Vega* (Madrid, 1940)
J. Ortega y Gasset, *Meditaciones del "Quijote"* (Madrid, 1957)
H. Percas de Ponseti, *Cervantes y su concepto del arte: Estudio crítico de algunos aspectos y episodios del "Quijote"* (Madrid, 1975), 2 vols.
R. L. Predmore, *El mundo del "Quixote"* (Madrid, 1958)
M. de Riquer, *Aproximación al "Quijote"* (Barcelona, 1970)
A. Rosenblat, *La lengua del "Quijote"* (Madrid, 1971)
Knud Togeby, *La Composition du roman "Don Quichotte"* (Copenhagen, 1957)
P. Vilar, "Le temps du *Quichotte,*" *Europe* 34 (1956), 3–16
Maurice Bardon, *"Don Quichotte" en France au XVIIe et au XVIIIe siècle* (Paris, 1931)

J. J. A. Bertrand, *Cervantes et le romantisme allemand* (Paris, 1914)

A. J. Close, *The Romantic Approach to "Don Quixote"* (Oxford, 1978)

René Girard, *Mensonge romantique et vérité romanesque* (Paris, 1961)

Marthe Robert, *L'Ancien et le Nouveau: De "Don Quichotte" à Franz Kafka* (Paris, 1963)

A. Welsh, *Reflections on the Hero as Quixote* (Princeton, 1981)

On *La Galatea:*

J. B. Avalle-Arce, *La novela pastoril española* (Madrid, 1974)

F. López Estrada, *La "Galatea" de Cervantes: Estudio crítico* (La Laguna, 1948)

On the *Novelas ejemplares:*

A. G. de Amezúa, *Cervantes creador de la novela corta española* (Madrid, 1956–58), 2 vols.

J. Casalduero, *Sentido y forma de las "Novelas ejemplares"* (Madrid, 1962)

A. Forcione, *Cervantes and the Humanist Vision: A Study of Four Exemplary Novels* (Princeton, 1982)

————, *Cervantes and the Mystery of Lawlessness: A Study of El casamiento engañoso y El coloquio de los perros* (Princeton, 1984)

R. El Saffar, *Novel to Romance: A Study of Cervantes' "Novelas ejemplares"* (Baltimore, 1974)

G. Hainsworth, *Les "Novelas exemplares" de Cervantès en France au XVIIe siècle* (Paris, 1933)

M. Molho, "Remarques préliminaires," in Cervantes, *El casamiento engañoso y Coloquio de los perros: Le Marriage trompeur et Le Colloque des chiens* (Paris, 1970)

On Cervantes' plays:

J. Canavaggio, *Cervantès dramaturge: un théâtre à naitre* (Paris, 1977)

J. Casalduero, *Sentido y forma del teatro de Cervantes* (Madrid, 1967)

A. Cotarelo y Valledor, *El teatro de Cervantes* (Madrid, 1915)

R. Marrast, *Miguel de Cervantès dramaturge* (Paris, 1957)

On *Persiles:*

J. Casalduero, *Sentido y forma de "Los trabajos de Persiles y Sigismunda"* (Buenos Aires, 1947)

A. K. Forcione, *Cervantes, Aristotle, and the "Persiles"* (Princeton, 1970)

————, *Cervantes' Christian Romance: A Study of "Persiles y Sigismunda"* (Princeton, 1972)

T. D. Stegmann, *Cervantes' Musterroman "Persiles": Epentheorie und Romanpraxis um 1600* (Hamburg, 1971)

Several apocryphal works have been attributed to Cervantes. Some of them are patchworks made from bits and pieces, like the famous "Epístola a Mateo Vázquez," supposedly rediscovered in the last century, which borrows part of its verses from a speech in *El trato de Argel*. Others are anonymous works, and it remains to be proven that they were in fact written by the author of *Don Quixote:* the novella *La tía fingida*, the religious drama *La soberana Virgen de Guadalupe y sus milagros y grandezas de España*, various pieces of poetry, and a number of interludes (*De los habladores, De los curiosos, De los romances, De la cárcel de Sevilla, El hospital de los podridos*. The texts of these works will be found in the Aguilar edition of Cervantes' *Obras completas*, ed. A. Valbuena Prat (Madrid, 1954).

Concerning the supposed portraits of the writer, none, as we have said, is trustworthy. The one attributed to Jáuregui is clearly inspired by the self-portrait included in the preface of the *Novelas ejemplares*. It was probably concocted at the beginning of this century by a forger named José Albiol. The rediscovered portrait in the collection of the marquess of Casa Torres, which is certainly by Jáuregui, is not a picture of Cervantes but of Don Diego Mesía de Ovando, the count of Uceda. See E. Lafuente Ferrari, *La novela ejemplar de los retratos de Cervantes* (Madrid, 1948).

Avellaneda's *Don Quixote* has been republished in the *Clásicos castellanos* series by Martín de Riquer, preceded by a substantial introduction (Madrid, 1972), 3 vols. The best general study is still Stephen Gilman's *Cervantes y Avellaneda: estudio de una imitación* (Madrid, 1948). There is a recent English translation of the apocryphal sequel: A. W. Server and J. E. Keller, *Don Quixote de la Mancha (Part II): Being a spurious continuation of Miguel de Cervantes' Part I* (Newark, Del., 1980).

Several works give us a clearer idea of the period in which Cervantes lived. The great reference work is still F. Braudel's *The Mediterranean and the Mediterranean World in the Age of Philip II*, tr. Sian Reynolds (New York, 1972), 2 vols. Michel Lesure, in *Lépante: La crise de l'Empire ottoman* (Paris, 1972), gives us a remarkable analysis of the conflict in which the author of *Don Quixote* took part.

ON SIXTEENTH- AND SEVENTEENTH-CENTURY SPAIN IN GENERAL, ONE MAY CONSULT THE FOLLOWING:

P. Chanu, *L'Espagne de Charles Quint* (Paris, 1973), 2 vols.

M. Defourneaux, *La Vie quotidienne en Espagne au Siècle d'Or* (Paris, 1964)

A. Domínguez Ortiz, *The Golden Age of Spain 1516–1659*, tr. James Casey (New York, 1971)

J. H. Elliott, *Imperial Spain 1469–1716* (1963; Penguin ed., 1970)

J. Pérez, *L'Espagne au XVIe siècle* (Paris, 1973)

P. Vilar *et al.*, *L'Espagne au temps de Philippe II* (Paris, 1965)

On political and military questions:

I. A. A. Thompson, *War and Government in Hapsburg Spain, 1500–1640* (London, 1976)

G. Parker, *Felipe II* (Madrid, 1984)

F. Tomás y Valiente, *Los validos en la monarquía española de Siglo XVII* (Madrid, 1963)

On economic, social, and cultural aspects:

A. Molinié-Bertrand, *Au Siècle d'Or: L'Espagne et ses hommes (La Population du Royaume de Castille au XVIe siècle)* (Paris, 1985)

B. Bernassar, *Valladolid et ses campagnes au XVIe siècle* (Paris, 1967)

Ruth Pike, *Aristocrats and Traders: Sevillian Society in the Sixteenth Century* (Ithaca and London, 1972)

N. Salomon, *La campagne de Nouvelle-Castille à la fin du XVIe siècle* (Paris, 1964)

A. Domínguez Ortiz and B. Vincent, *Historia de los moriscos: vida y tragedia de una minoría* (Madrid, 1978)

H. Kamen, *Inquisition and Society in Spain in the Sixteenth and Seventeenth Centuries* (Bloomington, 1985)

Spanish literature has been and continues to be the subject of innumerable scholarly studies, and it would be impossible to offer even a brief overview. For those who read only English and want a handy survey, the standard work is still G. Brenan's *The Literature of the Spanish People* (Cambridge, 1951).

Index